AF564698

CREATIVE ACTIVITIES AND THE LAW

Human Rights Approach

CREATIVE ACTIVITIES AND THE LAW

Human Rights Approach

Edited by

S.D. SHARMA
Dean, Faculty of Law,
Kumaon University,
S.S.J. Campus, Almora

Foreword by

HON'BLE JUSTICE S.B. SINHA
Judge, Supreme Court of India

DEEP & DEEP PUBLICATIONS PVT. LTD.
F-159, Rajouri Garden, New Delhi-110027

CREATIVE ACTIVITIES AND THE LAW
Human Rights Approach

ISBN 978-81-8450-017-2

Typeset by THE LASER PRINTERS, 8/15, 3rd Floor, Subhash Nagar, New Delhi-110027.

Printed in India at NEW ELEGANT PRINTERS, A-49/1, Phase I, Mayapuri, New Delhi-110064.

Published by DEEP & DEEP PUBLICATIONS PVT. LTD., F-159, Rajouri Garden, New Delhi-110027. Phones: 25435369, 25440916. E-mail: deep98@del3.vsnl.net.in
Sales Showroom: 2/13, Ansari Road, Daryaganj, New Delhi-110002
Phone/Fax: 23245122

Contents

S. B. Sinha
Judge
Supreme Court of India

January 16, 2007

Foreword

In this era of globalization, liberalization and rapid economic development, there is a threat to creative property due to abuse of advances in information technology sector. Having realized the existence of such a menace, the international community has taken several steps in trying to curb it, and save this property. Such intellectual creations are given much importance due to the commercial value of these creations as well as recognition of the efforts of the creator in making it. Although there are several international instruments and local laws that provide for the protection of such creative activities, there are a large number of issues that need to be addressed.

It is the duty of the state to protect the life and property of its citizens. The intellectual property of human beings is also one such property that requires this protection and encouragement, since it evolves in the minds of individuals who expend a lot of time, energy and resources in creating it. This is a basic human right that is to be guaranteed to all, simply by virtue of its nature, i.e. the fact that the creation of intellectual property is an activity involving significant amounts of effort. As the eminent jurist Kant has stated, 'property is part of human personality', and every kind of property must be sheltered. Intellectual property can be of numerous kinds, but one type that is most common is the copyright. The Copyright vests in the author the right to prevent any action being taken on the copyrighted material, such as the right of broadcasting, right of first publication and the right to make, sell and distribute copies.

Human rights, as recognized by the Universal Declaration of Human Rights, the International Covenant on Economic Social and Cultural Rights, and the Indian Constitution, are inclusive of the right to culture and to property. But the first international recognition of the right to intellectual property came in the TRIPs, wherein the right to protection of creative works is clearly mentioned. The Agreement also imposes the important duty of providing for a mechanism of protection on the State. The prevailing law would ensure that the state safeguards the interests of the creators, thereby making available a human right of the protection of copyrights. Apart from the Copyright Act, which has been passed by the Indian Legislature, there is a need to go beyond and ensure that there is a deeper level of protection for such creative works. Thus, the connection between copyright and human rights is one of ensuring the protection of inventiveness of individuals through a deeper and stronger law.

This book entitled "Creative Activities and the Law: Human Rights Approach" traces and analyses the International and Indian law on this subject, while also bringing out the relation between copyright and human rights. The chapters of this book also directly reflect the research papers of the participants of the National Seminar organized by the Faculty of Law, Kumaon University, S.S.J. Campus, Almora, on the 10th and 11th of September, 2005. Having been a part of this Seminar, as the Chief Guest, I have had the opportunity to go through the various papers presented by the participants at this Seminar. This Seminar was unique, interesting and successful. I believe that the material in this book will be useful to lawyers, judges and legislators.

Dr. S.D. Sharma, Dean, Faculty of Law of Kumaon University, and his colleagues and all the organizers, deserve to be commended for this successful, extremely useful and distinctive Seminar.

New Delhi

S.B. SINHA
Judge, Supreme Court of India

Preface

Human beings have capacity, desire and different ideas to create new things for the society. Due to these unique and special qualities, they have always created new things for all kinds of development of the society. These things are the property of the creators. Created things of human being are called intellectual properties. In present era, under the system of legal specialization, these properties are protected by the different laws—like Copyrights, Trademarks, Patents, Designs, Bio-Diversity, Protection of Farmers' Rights, and other such intangible property laws. Today, people are realizing the importance of intellectual property and its augmentation, because it is playing vital role in the development of society universally, such as in the field of music, pictures, photos, computer software, designs, training modules, etc.

The subject-matter of this book is related to the creative activities of human beings and its protection under the law with reference to human rights. The present concept of human rights was developed after the Second World War in the middle of 20th century. Presently, every right of human being is being recognized as a human right. Thus right related to intellectual property is also a human right. Although the concept of human right is ancient one, however the present source of it is Universal Declaration of Human Rights, 1948. According to the Articles 17 and 27 of Declaration, human activities are the human rights of human being. Same is the provision under Article 15 of the International Covenant on Social, Economics and Cultural Rights, 1966. In this context new dimension was started after the TRIPS 1994. By the TRIPS a special body, the Council for TRIPS (commonly known as TRIPS Council) on which each WTO member is represented, has been established to administer the operation of the TRIPS. The meeting of TRIPS Council was held in Cancun in September 2003 and the latest meeting was held on 17th December 2005 at Hong Kong.

Creative activities of human beings are protected by law. In Napster case (2001), U.S. Court held that user of hard of drive without need will be vicariously liable for the copyright infringement. Contrary view was adopted by the US Supreme Court on 12th October, 2004 in Grokster case.

I am indebted to many well-wishers including my colleagues of Law Faculty. Faculty was inspired by Prof. R.C. Pant, Hon'ble Former Vice-Chancellor, Kumaun University to publish this book. The faculty is grateful to him for inspiration and kind co-operation. This work would not have been completed without the blessing and help of Prof. K.C. Joshi, former Vice-Chancellor of Kumaun University and retired Dean and Head of the Faculty of Law, S.S.J. Campus, Almora. The editor express his deep sense of gratitude to Sri Brij Kishore Sharma, Chairman Copyright Board, New Delhi, for his guidance. The Faculty of Law is also thankful to the Ministry of H.R.D., New Delhi for financial assistance. I am grateful to Prof. C.P. Barthwal, Vice-Chancellor, Kumaun University for his kind co-operation in the publication of this work. Dr. Priti Saxena, Head, Department of Human Rights, B.B.A. University, Lucknow also deserves appreciation for her co-operation in the publication of this Book.

I am highly indebted to Hon'ble Justice S.B. Sinha, Judge, Supreme Court of India for finding time to become Chief Guest of the Seminar on this project. I also express my gratitude to Shri G.S. Bhatia of Deep & Deep Publications Pvt. Ltd. for his interest and co-operation in bringing out this publication.

S.D. SHARMA

List of Contributors

1. **Shri Brij Kishore Sharma**, Chairman Copyright Board, New Delhi.
2. **Prof. S.K. Verma**, Former Director of Indian Law Institute, New Delhi.
3. **Prof. K.C. Joshi**, Former Vice-Chancellor, Kumaun University and Ex-Head & Dean, Faculty of Law, S.S.J. Campus, Almora.
4. **Prof. Basant Ram**, Director Experiment Station, G.B. Pant University of Agriculture and Technology, Pant Nagar.
5. **Prof. Saleem Akhtar**, Professor in Law, Aligarh Muslim University, Aligarh, U.P.
6. **Dr. Priti Saxena**, Head, Department of Legal Sciences, B.B.A. University, Lucknow.
7. **Dr. D.K. Bhatt**, Reader in Law, Kumaun University, Faculty of Law, Kumaun University, S.S.J. Campus, Almora.
8. **Prof. Ram Naresh Chaudhari**, Former Dean, D.D.U., University of Gorakhpur, U.P.
9. **Shri J.S. Bisht**, Lecturer in Law, Faculty of Law, S.S.J. Campus, Almora.
10. **Prof. Kailash Chandra Sodani,** Dean Faculty of Law, College of Law, Mohanlal Sukhadia, University of Udaipur, Rajasthan.
11. **Sunil Asopa,** Assistant Professor, University College of Law, Mohan Lal Sukhadia University, Udaipur, Rajasthan.

12. **Mrs. Nidhi Deepak,** Lecturer, I.P.S. Law College, Ghaziabad, C.C.S. University, Meerut.
13. **Dr. Satish Chandra,** Lecturer in Law, Government Law College, Gopeshwar.
14. **Dr. Shekhar Chandra Joshi,** Faculty Member, Department of Drawing and Painting, S.S.J. Campus, Almora.
15. **Dr. Meena Pathani,** Reader and Head, Department of Political Science, S.S.J. Campus, Almora.
16. **Shri Brishketu Sharan Pandey,** Student, National Law University, Jodhpur.
17. **Dr. Devesh Darshan Pant,** Superintending Engineer (Rtd.), 16A, Kalidas Road, Dehradun, Uttaranchal.
18. **Dr. Bhawani Prasad Panda,** Reader, P.G. Department of Law, Berhampur University, Orissa.
19. **Dr. R.K. Pathak,** Reader, Department of Law, D.D.U. University, Gorakhpur.
20. **Dr. Kala Munet,** Assistant Professor, College of Law, M.L.S. University, Udaipur, Rajasthan.
21. **Dr. S.P. Meena,** Assistant Professor, College of Law, M.L.S. University, Udaipur, Rajasthan.
22. **Deepak K. Pandey,** Associate Member, Computer Society of India, Mumbai.
23. **Dr. S.R. Sharma,** Lecturer in Law, Government M.S.J. College, Bharatpur, Rajasthan.
24. **Dr. S.K. Pandey,** Reader in Law, J.N.P.G. College, Lucknow, U.P.
25. **Dr. P.C. Joshi,** Reader and Head, Department of Law, S.S.J. Campus, Almora.
26. **A.K. Pandey**, Reader in Law, H.N.B. Garwal University, Campus Badshahithaul, Tehari Garhwal, Uttaranchal.
27. **Ms Pallavi Gupta,** Lecturer, BJJR Institute of Law, Bundelkhand University, Jhansi, U.P.
28. **O.N. Mishra,** Reader, Department of Law, University of Lucknow, Lucknow.

29. **Mr. Syed Sadiq H. Abidi,** Lecturer, University of Law College, Lucknow University.
30. **Dr. S.C. Roy,** Principal, Bihar Institute of Law, Raja Bazar, Patna.
31. **Dr. (Miss) Kiran Saksena,** Principal, T.N.B. Law College, T.M. Bhagalpur University (Bihar).
32. **Dr. S.M. Shukla,** Lecturer, T.N.B. Law College, T.M. Bhagalpur University (Bihar).
33. **Dr. V.K. Singh,** Head, Department of Law, T.M. Bhagalpur University, Bihar.
34. **Syed Naseer H. Rizvi,** Lecturer, University of Law College, Lucknow University, Lucknow.
35. **Dr. R.K. Chaubey,** Reader in Law, Faculty of Law, Allahabad University, Allahabad.
36. **Dr. Subhash Chandra Gupta,** Reader and Head, HNB Garhwal University, Pauri (U.A.).
37. **Mr. Rakesh Chandra,** Student, National Law University, Bangalore (Karnataka).
38. **Tapan Chandola,** Student, L.L.M. from M.J.P. Rohilkhand University, Bareilly, U.P.
39. **Mr. Jay Prakash Yadav,** Lecturer, L.L.M. from M.J.P. Rohilkhand University, Bareilly, U.P.
40. **Dr. Subhash Chandra Singh,** Head and Dean, Faculty of Law, Kashi Vidhaya Peeth, Varanasi, U.P.
41. **Mrs. Jyoti Priyadarshini, Shrivastav,** PGDPM, Reader, Department of Management Studies, Amrapali, Institute Haldwani.
42. **Samarika Singh,** National Law Institute University, Bhopal.
43. **Apoorva Bhumesh,** National Law Institute University, Bhopal.
44. **Dr. S.D. Sharma,** Dean, Faculty of Law, Kumaun University, S.S.J. Campus, Almora.

Law Relating to Creative Activities*

BRIJ KISHORE SHARMA

I feel honoured in coming to the great city of Almora. Since ancient times The Himalaya has been treated as the abode of Bhagwan Shiva. Our great Rishis performed penance in the Himalaya. Kalidasa while describing Bharat says:

Asya Uttarasyam dishi devatma Himalayo nam nagadhirajah

Himalaya is Devatma. From my childhood I have known it as the place where Swami Vivekananda established Advait Ashram from where such books were published that transformed India. It is the place associated with the poet Sumitranandan Pant and novelist Ilachandra Joshi. It is a jewel in the crown of mother India.

We have gathered here to think collectively in regard to certain aspects of *intellectual property*. The objects of intellectual property are the creations of the human intellect. This is the reason

*For the National Seminar organized by the Faculty of Law, Kumaun University, Almora, on 10th September, 2005.

why this property is called the *intellectual property*. The property consists of pieces of information which can be incorporated in tangible objects at the same time in an unlimited number of copies at different locations all over the world. The property is not in those copies but in the knowledge or information presented in those copies.

A special characteristic of intellectual property is that it is limited in point of duration. After the death of the author the property subsists for 60 years. After that it passes to public domain. It becomes free. Copyright is a tribute to creativity. In India we treat the creator as God. The author has the right to receive credit as the author and to receive remuneration for his creative work.

Our Ministry for Human Resource Development is being guided and goaded by WIPO to make people conscious of the existence of IP rights. This WIPO (World Intellectual Property Organisation) was established by a convention on July 14, 1967. Its object is to work to protect various I.P. rights. These rights may be grouped as IP rights, neighbouring rights and the industry-related rights. Its headquarters are in Geneva. It is one of the 16 specialised agencies of the UNO.

In the Dunkel Drafts in Uruguay Round of multilateral trade negotiations, an important agreement was related to TRIPS (Trade Related Intellectual Property Rights). In 1994, as part of the WTO package TRIPS agreement was adopted. In 1996, two more treaties were adopted, the WIPO Copyright Treaty (WCT) and WIPO Performances and Phonographs Treaty (WPPT). These were specially designed to deal with the new digital technology and the network environment.

The Copyright Act, 1957 was amended in 1994 and 1999 to incorporate some of these changes.

The WIPO should only recommend inclusion of certain provisions in the national law. It must leave room for adaptation and changes according to the local necessities. Our Copyright Act considers playing music in functions connected with marriage ceremonies a *fair dealing* for which no licence is needed. We must make exceptions for small shops selling sugarcane juice, or pan or tea in small towns or roadside villages which are manned by a single person and where the investment is minimal. In the USA they are called *mom and pop* establishments.

The USA, it is well known had different copyright laws when it was a net importer of copyright material. When it became net exporter of such material it has changed the laws. National interest is supreme. At the same time, law must take into account the national peculiarities. The US has made a law called Fairness in Music Licensing Act, 1998. Under the Act musical works may be played or performed without licence by retail establishments that are smaller than 2000 sq. ft. and food service establishments that are smaller than 3500 sq. feet. The European Community contended that the provisions of the US Act were inconsistent with the TRIPS agreement. A panel was appointed in 2000. It recommended that US be requested to bring its Act in conformity with TRIPS. The US did not accept the recommendation. The matter went for arbitration. The award was adopted in 2001. It determined that the US must pay about 1 million US $ to the European community as damages every year. The US has chosen to pay.

Similarly the US which accounts for one-third of the total Green House Gases (GHG) emission in the world has not yet signed the Kyoto Protocol which is a voluntary treaty signed by 141 countries for reducing GHG emissions. India should also consider its interests and refrain from signing a treaty under pressure.

Every Copyright Act is an attempt to balance the economic interests of the author as also of the investor who ventures to exploit it (the publisher in case of books, the producer in case of films and sound recordings) and the society at large. But there is one aspect which I consider is very important, which is not seen and noticed in the glitter of money. I invite your attention to this dimension of copyright.

I believe that an author, an artist, a dramatist or a performer is not entirely motivated by economic gains. The Marxist doctrine that considered man as motivated by economic gain alone has been demonstrated to be wrong. Changes in Russia, Eastern Europe and China, etc. support this statement. The philosophy of Marx like that of Freud is no more regarded as scientific or even logical.

An author writes a book, a poet composes a poem and a dramatist creates a drama to present something new. It may be an idea, a thought or a doctrine. It may be knowledge or information. It can be conclusions based on available data derived by applying a new methodology.

The author desires that what he has to say reaches a large number of people. A thought or an idea is a vehicle for bringing change in the society. A powerful idea moulds a whole civilization. The propagation of good ideas can make this world a better place to dwell. An evil thought can make human existence nasty, brutish and short.

Till now Copyright Law has endeavoured to break national barriers and given protection to authors, poets, musicians, performers, etc. across whole continents. National boundaries have been made inoperative. It has almost become a part of Human Rights and gained universal acceptance.

But now the time has come to look at the other aspect. The non-economic aspect. Dissemination of knowledge of the contents of a book is what is desired by every author. It is the ambition of every author to put his thought in the agenda or curriculum of the universities and academies. He wants it to become the subject of discussion in the marketplace, the pub and the coffee-house. He wants to influence the course of human thought and civilization. The question is how far has the world community helped him in achieving it.

There are nations in the present day world where books are being declared contraband, where books are considered as worse than narcotics drugs. There are states whose foundation is ignorance. They subscribe to the principle that he who controls the thought controls the man. Such governments do not allow books to enter their boundaries. The result is indoctrination. The people are brainwashed. In their ignorance the people do not know what is right. In such a situation their conduct is in conformity with what they are made to think is right.

A closed society poses a danger to the world. We know what the Nazis did to the German people. The indoctrination led to extermination of 3 million of innocent people and a World War. The closed society represented by Stalin killed its own 40 million nationals. A state impervious to competing thoughts headed by Pol Pot liquidated 20 million human beings. It is again a closed society in which the people are led to believe that they have come to know the ultimate truth. All other humans who do not subscribe to it have no right to live. People under the influence of such closed doctrine are the ones who think they are obeying the commands of God by destroying World Trade Towers, taking school children as hostages, attacking temples and killing thousands of human beings.

God has endowed man with intelligence so that he may distinguish between good and evil, the noble and the ignoble, the beautiful and the ugly, welfare and destruction. By keeping man confined to a closed society we make him a denizen of Orwell's 1984 or Huxley's *Brave New World* where thought is controlled, where ignorance is strength, to obey the commands of a dictator is the only purpose of life.

The Universal Declaration of Human Rights adopted by the United Nations holds freedom of speech as a vital right. At the height of the Second World War, President Roosevelt said:

> In the future days, which we seek to make secure, we look forward to a world founded upon four essential human freedoms. The first is freedom of speech and expression—everywhere in the world. The second is freedom of every person to worship God in his own way—everywhere in the world. . .

He spoke in 1941. The year 2006 is coming to an end but the above two freedoms are still not available everywhere in the world. We find that Taslima Nasreen is driven out of her country. Her crime is writing a book. Author Salman Rushdie is put on a hit list because he wrote a book. Where is the right of the author to express himself?

In the 21st century there exist societies which have not known political thought. They are not aware of the existence of different philosophical systems. They do not know that there is a discipline called social thought.

There must be competition of ideas, doctrines and thoughts. The consumer has a choice in the market. The thinking man must have choice to read. This would be possible if the world recognizes that the author has an unrestricted right to enter all countries. Books are not a merchandise which may be banned.

Every author craves readers. A wide and discerning readership is the dream of every author. A great author is revered more than a rich author. A great author reaches those places also where the rays of the sun do not penetrate *Jahan Na Jaye Ravi Wahan Jaye Kavi.*

In India the Hindu tradition of allowing different thoughts is at least 6000 years old. The Vedas proclaim *Aa No Bhardra Kratavo Yantu Vishwataha.* Let noble thoughts come to us from all directions. Truth is not the monopoly of one individual. God is not an arbitrary being. God does not bind itself inextricably with one Book or one Messiah. Eternity is illimitable. Infinity knows no boundaries. The Hindu does not relate himself to one book or one seer. With this heritage I beseech all of you to look beyond the economic rights of the author. The right of the author to be read, heard and discussed everywhere in the world.

Injustice anywhere is threat to justice everywhere. A closed society anywhere in the world puts the whole world in peril. If there was any doubt about it earlier even after the misdeeds of Libya, Pakistan, Sudan, Iraq, etc. the doubts have vanished after the happenings of September 2001 in USA, 2002 in Beslan, Russia, February 2005 in Madrid and July 2005 in London.

In a closed society lies sound truthful and murder becomes respectful. The only way to change it is to recognise that the author, the film-maker, the musician and the poet has a right to sell or exhibit his work in all parts of the world.

Free exchange of ideas and thoughts will widen the horizons. Thoughts are the fastest vehicles of change. Martin Luther's thoughts introduced reformation. Even after the death of Socrates and Christ their thought permeated and changed the world. Buddha's teaching affected and influenced the whole of the civilized part of Asia. A closed society is an uncivilised burden on the world. Intolerance and bigotry cannot survive in the pure air generated by thoughts.

Give this freedom to the authors and the books and you will lay the foundation of brotherhood of mankind. You will usher peace and prosperity.

We Hindus believe that every sentient being is a part of the divine being. Keeping that in mind I bow to God who is enshrined in each of you. *Namaskar.*

New Vistas of Human Creative Activities and their Protection under Copyright Law— A Human Approach*

S.K. VERMA

CONCEPTUALIZING INTELLECTUAL PROPERTY

The term "Intellectual Property" sounds very technical, and most of the people have no idea what it comprises. It is, however, amazing that it touches almost all our daily activities. If one talks about computer, it probably works using patented technology, has a brand name as a trademark, and has a form protected as an industrial design. The software used to access a site could be covered by copyright as could be text and images on this site. Similarly, a simple cup of tea may be holding a cupful of Intellectual Property Rights (IPRs). The shape of the cup, the brand

*Lecture delivered at the National Seminar organized by the Faculty of Law, Kumaun University, Almora on September 10-11, 2005.

name of the tea, the geographical provenance of the tea leaves, all could qualify as intellectual property.

Intellectual property rights broadly means the legal rights which result from intellectual creativity in the industrial, scientific, artistic and literacy fields. The objects of intellectual property are the creations of the human mind, the human intellect, and that is why this kind of property is called "intellectual property." IPRs refer to a bundle of legal doctrines, which regulate the use of information, in the form of ideas, expressions, etc. They are statutory rights, territorial in operation and negative in their ambit, excluding others thereby from exploiting or encroaching upon those rights. They are granted under the national laws of each country. Intellectual property is nothing but legal concept of ownership applied to intangibles. It is not a property right (as is understood for tangibles) but monopoly right limited in time and space. They allow the creator of a work or an inventor the exclusive right to commercially exploit his creation or invention for a limited period of time. After the end of the statutory period, they come into the public domain and accessible by all. The IP right can also be sold, licensed or otherwise disposed of by the right-holder.

The various branches of IP law—patents, trademarks, designs, copyright, trade secrets, etc. confer legal exclusivity to the holder in the market place. The TRIPS Agreement covers within its ambit: (i) copyright and related rights; (ii) trademarks (including service marks); (iii) geographical indications; (iv) industrial designs; (v) patents; (vi) layout designs (Topographies) of integrated circuits; and (vii) trade secrets. It has also introduced the IP protection for plant varieties.

IPRs—Significance

Like all monopolies, intellectual property is also liable to be abused, if not safeguarded against. As IPRs are private economic rights, they need to be managed properly by their owners. Main reasons for their protection are two-fold: (i) to give statutory expression to the moral and economic rights of creators in their creations and such rights of the public in access to those creations, and (ii) to promote, as a deliberate act of government policy, creativity and the dissemination and application of its results and to encourage fair trading which would contribute to economic and social development. Implicitly, the very premise of IPRs aims at creating a balance between the interests of the holder of the right by rewarding him for his creation for a limited period of time and contributes to the scientific, cultural and economic enrichment of the society.

IPRs are assuming increasing importance world-wide due to their economic significance as well as its role in enhancing and cultivating the creative potential of the society. IPRs make it possible for the creators and innovators to establish themselves more readily, to penetrate new markets with a minimum of risk, and to amortize the investments made in the research that led to the innovations in the first place. For example, the right to obtain a patent for an invention stimulate the investment of money and effort in research and development; the grant of a patent encourages investment in the industrial application of the invention. It also encourages R&D activities in a country, which ultimately help in its growth. On the flip side, these rights block competitors and are used to improve one's bargaining position in the market.

Human Rights Interface of IPRs

Intellectual property rights are considered to be diametrically opposite to human rights, concerned only with the economic returns without any social perspective. It is because the character of intellectual property rights as human rights is perhaps not fully appreciated so far. Intellectual property regimes are created with a social perspective, seeking to balance the moral and economic rights of creators and inventors in the form of copyright and patents, with the wider interests and needs of the society. A main justification for copyrights and patents stated to be that incentives and rewards to inventors and creators result in benefits for the society.[1] A human rights approach to intellectual property takes what is often an implicit balance between the rights of the inventors and creators, and the interests of the wider society within intellectual paradigms and makes it far more explicit and exacting. While holders of intellectual property, the creators and inventors, must receive an appropriate reward from the society for their efforts (by having exclusivity/monopoly over their creation for a limited period of time), the IPRs should, at the same time, contribute to the scientific, cultural and economic enrichment of society.

Patents are granted for inventions, comprising technological innovations, which are considered to bring social benefits to society by stimulating and sustaining economic growth of the society.[2] The patent question is ultimately one of social welfare. The patent system imposes certain costs and provides certain benefits to society. Ideally, the system should be designed to maximise net benefits to society. In case of copyright, to encourage the production of creative works, society must secure the economic rights of their creators. Copyrights, like patents, establish a form of monopoly control that solves the problem of appropriability and thereby establishes economic incentives to create and make public artistic works. Society stands to gain from copyrighted works only if the ideas and information they embody are widely disseminated (copyright exists in expression and not in ideas), rather than restricting those ideas. Anglo-American copyright law explicitly reaffirms the fundamental social interest in the spread of ideas and information embodied in copyrighted works by providing for "fair use", which permits limited production of copyrighted works without the author's permission for purposes of criticism, scholarship, teaching and news reporting.[3]

The underlying approach of IPRs is not entirely economic but to create a balance between human rights and the IP rights. The Preamble to the Convention establishing the World Intellectual Property Organization (WIPO) provides that the mandate of WIPO is "to encourage creativity, to promote the protection of intellectual property throughout the world", including all sections of human society. The recognition and protection of intellectual property is premised on the twin objectives of recognizing the rights of the creators, including inventors, over their creations by rewarding them with monopoly rights for a limited statutory period and helping in the development and growth of the society from these creations by obligating the right-holder to disclose his creation. Just as human rights law recognizes the need for protecting and mutually balancing human rights through non-discriminatory democratic legislation, intellectual property law emphasises on the balancing of rights of the creators of IP and the society at large. Thus while the creators/inventors of IPRs should be rewarded for their efforts (by having exclusivity/monopoly over, their creation for a limited period of time), the intellectual property rights should, at the same time, contribute to the scientific, cultural and economic enrichment of society.

The International Covenant on Economic, Social and Cultural Rights (ICESCR) is the major human rights instrument addressing these objectives. There are other important international human rights instruments also, which recognize these goals and in fact complement intellectual property law. Article 27 of the Universal Declaration of Human Rights (UDHR) is the basis, which recognizes a series of claims or rights of individuals in this regard. Nevertheless, the most significant provision, recognizing the human rights character of intellectual property is Article 15 of the ICESCR. It specifies that State Parties recognize the right of everyone both to "enjoy the benefits of scientific progress and its applications" [Art. 15(1)(b)] and "to benefit from the protection of the moral and material interests resulting from any scientific, literary or artistic production of which he is the author." [Art. 15(1)(c)].

To be consistent with human rights norms, the subject matter considered to be appropriate for copyright and patent protection and the paradigm to be adopted have to meet the following considerations:

- Intellectual property rights must be consistent with the understanding of human dignity in the various international human rights instruments and the norms defined therein;
- Intellectual property rights related to science must promote scientific progress and access to its benefits;
- Intellectual property regimes must respect the freedom indispensable for scientific research and creative activity; and
- Intellectual property regimes must encourage the development of international contacts and cooperation in the scientific and cultural fields.[4]

Article 2 of the ICESCR directs each State Party to undertake "steps, individually and through international assistance and cooperation, especially economic and technical, to the maximum of its available resources, with a view to achieving progressively the full realization of the rights recognized."

These interests/rights must also be safeguarded in the context of Millennium Development Goals, adopted by the UN General Assembly, which recognize the crucial importance of reducing poverty and hunger, improving health and education, and ensuring environmental sustainability. The international community has set itself the target of reducing the proportion of people below poverty line to half by 2015, along with associated specific targets for improving health and education and environmental sustainability.

Whether and how Intellectual Property Rights (IPRs) could play a role in helping the world meet these targets—in particular, by reducing poverty, helping to combat diseases, enhancing access to education and contributing to sustainable development, protecting our cultural heritage, safeguarding the food security for the country, is a matter of serious consideration. It is also necessary to know how IPRs can create obstacles to meet these targets and, if so, how those obstacles can be removed.

A human rights approach establishes a requirement for the State to undertake a very rigorous and desegregated analysis of the likely impact of specific innovations, as well as an evaluation of proposed changes in intellectual property paradigms, and to utilize this data to assure non-discrimination in the end result and to see the fruits of these innovations reach to all sections of the society. The most appropriate means to fulfil these goals has been a matter of considerable controversy and conflict between countries in the North and the South, particularly with regard to the role of IPRs, Scholars and policy-makers on the protection and enforcement of IPRs hold strong views though there is no reliable data to check these views objectively.

Some argue strongly that IPRs are necessary to stimulate economic growth, which, in turn, helps in poverty reduction. By stimulating invention and new technologies, IPRs help to increase agricultural or industrial production, promote domestic and foreign investment, facilitate technology transfer and improve the availability of medicines necessary to combat diseases. They are also of the view that there is no reason why a system that has worked for developed countries would not work for developing countries. Others argue equally vehemently the opposite. In their view, IPRs do little to stimulate invention in developing countries, because the necessary human and technical capacity may be absent there. These countries believe that it is not in their economic interest to implement stronger patent laws at their present development stage and accuse develop countries for seeking to impose "technological colonialism" through strong IP regime.[5] Intellectual property regime, as defined in TRIPS Agreement has created an intellectual feudalism and kept marginalized sections of the society out of its preview, except for exploitation.

In assessing these opposing arguments, it is important to remember the technological disparity between developed and developing countries as a group. What role the intellectual property can play to plug this gap is a serious subject for every developing nation. Law is a regulating force in which lawyers, judges and academicians, as social scientists have great role in giving the direction to the law in the growth of the society. In the case of developing countries, several recent reports by international agencies, and particularly from the UK Commission on IPR (Sept. 2002), have reflected on the likely impact of the globalization of IP protection on developing countries which may result into heavy costs, but with less perceivable benefits for them. In this context, the following pertinent issues are for consideration:

- Is the intellectual property system is fair for both producers and users of intellectual property?
- Can economic development be stimulated and sustained by intellectual property protection?
- Can the IPRs benefit the indigenous and traditional communities from the use of their biological resources and their traditional knowledge?
- Will the healthcare needs of these societies be met under the new IPR regime?
- Will the IPRs help in meeting the needs of education and research of these countries?
- What role the new technological advancements, particularly Internet, has in the protection of IPRs?

Ambit of IPRs

Intellectual property is traditionally divided into two branches: "industrial property" and "copyright". Industrial property covers within its breadth all the IPRs, except copyright.[6] At the international level, they are regulated through treaties and agreements, which lay down the substantive standards and procedures for enforcement of these rights. These treaties aim to harmonize law and procedure on intellectual property to be registered in several countries. Prior to the Agreement on Trade-Related Intellectual Property Rights (TRIPS), 1994, two international conventions—the Paris Convention for the Protection of Industrial Property, 1883 and the Berne Convention for the Protection of Literacy and Artistic Works, 1886, were concluded to administer these rights. Whereas the Paris Convention was concerned with the protection of industrial property, covering patents, trademarks, industrial designs, utility models and confidential information, the Berne Convention was related to literary and artistic works. The WIPO, which was constituted in 1967, administers all the principal treaties on different IPRs (totaling 23). The TRIPS Agreement is outside the purview of the WIPO.

The Paris and Berne Conventions laid down the broad framework for the protection of IPRs, leaving it to the members to lay down the standards thereto. They were permissive in nature, the TRIPS Agreement is prescriptive in approach. The TRIPS Agreement has aimed on harmonization of IP laws, by requiring all WTO Members to provide minimum standards of protection for a wide range of IPRs, though they are free to exceed them. These standards have to be given effect through national legislation. A special body, the Council for TRIPS (commonly known as the TRIPS Council), on which each WTO Member is represented, has been established to administer the operation of the TRIPS. The TRIPS Council is responsible for reviewing various aspects of TRIPS as mandated in the Agreement itself and also as requested by the biennial WTO Ministerial Conference, the last of which was held in Cancun in September 2003 and the next was also held in December 2005 at Hong Kong.

The TRIPS has, however, provoked a lot of discussion in developing countries, particularly in India. Among the most debatable issues raised by the TRIPS are:

- Whether the objective set out in Article 7 that IPRs should contribute to the transfer of technology is achievable, particularly in respect of developing country members of the WTO.[7]

- The perceived tensions between Article 8, which allows countries to adopt measures necessary to protect public health,[8] and to prevent abuses of IP rights, provided they are TRIPS consistent, and with other requirements in the Agreement. These include the requirements to provide patent protection for pharmaceutical products, limitations on the conditions for issuing of compulsory licenses (Article 31) and on the scope of provisions providing exceptions to patent rights (Article 30). The Doha Declaration on TRIPS and Public Health adopted at the WTO Ministerial Meeting on 14 November 2001 and the Decision of TRIPS Council of 30 August 2003 are attempts to address the issue. The Declaration and Decision together cover within its ambit the public health problems of developing countries resulting from HIV/AIDS, TB, malaria, and other epidemic, and allow them to take necessary treasures.
- The requirement to protect test data against "unfair commercial use" in Article 39 which deals with undisclosed information (trade secrets).
- The justification for providing additional protection for geographical indications for wines and spirits, (Article 23) and whether this additional protection should also be extended to cover other or all geographical indications, viz., Basmati, Darjeeling Tea, etc.
- The extent to which patents should be allowed on inventions relating to living forms, for example microorganisms [Article 27.3(b)], and the requirement to provide IP protection for plants. In that context, the compatibility of TRIPS with agreements such as the Convention on Biological Diversity (CBD) has been raised and the protection of traditional knowledge has become a matter of great urgency in the light of cases such as *Neem* and *Turmeric*.
- The cost of meeting the requirements of TRIPS for many developing and least developed WTO Members in relation to the administration of IP rights and their effective enforcement (Art. 67: Technical Cooperation).

TRIPS became effective from 1 January, 1995. Developed

countries of WTO were given one year to comply whilst developing countries and countries with transition economies were given until 1 January, 2000. Developing countries, which were required to extend product patent protection to new areas such as Pharmaceuticals, a further five year period was provided before such protection had to be introduced. Least Developed Countries (LDCs) are expected to enact TRIPS by 2006 although the Doha Ministerial Declaration on Public Health has now allowed them a further 10 years in respect of pharmaceutical products, till 2016 (Art. 65).

After becoming party to the TRIPS, India has enacted/ amended its IP laws, viz., (i) The Copyright Act, 1957 as amended in 1999; (ii) The Trade Marks Act, 1999; (iii) The Patents (Amendment) Act, 2002 and 2005; (iv) The Semi-Conductor Integrated Circuits Layout-Design Act, 2002; (v) The Geographical Indications of Goods (Registration and Protection) Act, 1999; (vi) Designs Act, 2000; (vii) The Protection of Plant Varieties and Farmers' Rights Act, 2001; and (viii) The Biological Diversity Act, 2002. Other Act of relevance is Customs Act, 1962 and a new Act on Data Protection is underway.

Copyright and Neighbouring Rights

Copyright protection covers all "literacy and artistic works" such as writings, including scientific and technical texts and computer programs; databases that are original due to the selection or arrangement of their contents; musical works, audio-visual works, works of fine arts, including drawings and paintings, movies, photographs and computer programs. It protects authors' original forms of expression and does not protect ideas (which are protected by patents). *Related or neighbouring rights* protect the contributions of others who add value in the presentation of literacy and artistic works to the public, viz., performing artists, such as actors, dancers, singers and musicians; the producers of phonograms, including CDs and broadcasting organizations. The subject-matter of copyright and related rights include every production in the literary, scientific and artistic domain, whatever the mode or form of expression, provided the work is original intellectual creation. But it is not necessary that the work should pass the test of imaginativeness or inventiveness. The protection is independent of the quality or the value attached to the work, as well as even the purpose for which it is intended and even when it has little in common with literature, art or science, such as purely technical guides or engineering drawings, or even maps.

In addition to granting economic rights, copyright also bestows "moral" rights that allow the creator to claim authorship of the work and prevent its mutilation or deformation that could harm the creator's reputation or integrity (Sec. 57, Copyright Act). By giving creators incentives in the form of recognition and fair economic rewards by way of *royalties* and protecting their *moral rights*, copyright and related rights help in human creativity and thus in the growth of the society.

Any serious enquiry into the subject of IP and development, however, has to consider the crucially important role of copyright and the copyright-based industries (including publishing, film, television, radio, music and now computer software as well) in the production and dissemination of knowledge and knowledge-based products. These industries supply the intellectual "raw material" for science and innovation, as well as for education and instruction in general, and they have helped to bring about dramatic increases in productivity through aiding the creation of information-based products like desktop publishing software, electronic mail or sophisticated scientific computer databases. Moreover, the copyright-based industries have developed into a huge source of wealth and employment creation in the knowledge-based global economy. In the US, for example, their overall combined value has increased at such a rapid rate in the last thirty years, that together they currently contribute more than $ 500 billion to US gross domestic product and sold almost $ 80 billion in exports in 1999.

India is counted among the top seven publishing nations of the world with a sizeable portion of her publications being in English and is known all over the world for its excellence in software technology, though developed countries, viz., US, UK, Germany, France and Italy between themselves produce nearly two-thirds of global exports of books. We also have a thriving music and film industry, which look towards its protection from onslaught of piracy. It is one of the largest markets for audio and video-cassettes. India has a huge potential in the field of computer software. The software industry has been growing at an amazing rate of over 50% on an average, since the last decade. Between 1994-95 and 2001-02, the industry's gross earnings expanded from $ 787 million to $ 10.2 billion and has become the second largest exporter of computer software in the world. The growth of the Indian software industry has been projected from US $ 16 billion in 2002 to US $ 87 billion in 2008.[9]

Besides protecting creative potential of the society, copyright contributes to a nation on economic-front as well. The copyright-based industries and industries based on neighbouring rights, together are huge generators of employment world-over. The national exchequer benefits from the contribution made by these industries in the form of excise duty, sales tax, income tax, etc. from the production and sale of right-related products.

Like other IPRs, copyright is a limited monopoly. It is limited in the 'scope' of the rights granted and in terms of 'time'. In India, the copyright subsists in any work of art for 60 years, including computer programme, as against the TRIPS' 50 year period (Sec. 38 of the Copyright Act, 1957). The most worthy criticism of IPRs in general and copyright in particular is that they tend to create monopolies which are loathed in a socialistic set-up like that of ours. In order to strike a balance between the society's need for access to knowledge and the need to rewarding creators, limited uses of copyright protected works are permitted without author's consent. These *limitations and exceptions* (made a part of the Berne Convention and evolved over-time) are not only to give the author sufficient incentive to produce new works to satisfy the public interest, but also to ensure that parts of existing creative works are available freely to build upon in the creation of new works by the society. The Berne Convention provides limitations or exceptions to exclusive rights in accordance with "three-step test", i.e.,

(1) they must be confined to certain special cases;
(2) these cases do not conflict with the normal exploitation of a work; and
(3) they must not unreasonably prejudice the legitimate interests of the right owner.

The doctrine of 'fair use' of copyright has been given legal recognition in many jurisdictions. Reproduction of a work exclusively for the personal and private use, including research study, teaching or amusement; making quotations from a protected work, after duly acknowledging it; fair dealing with the protected work for the purposes of reporting current events in print or electronic media, criticism and comment, etc. come under "fair use". Section 52 of Indian Copyright Act permits certain activities which do not amount to infringement of copyright. Important in this 'exception list' are reproduction of literary, dramatic, musical or artistic works for educational purposes, e.g., research, review, reporting in newspapers, magazines and periodicals, etc. But for determining "fair use", it must take into account that whether or not it has a commercial nature or is for non-profit-making educational purposes, the nature of the copyrighted work as a whole and the effect of this use on the potential market for or value of the copyrighted work. This is perfectly in accordance with the societal needs to educate the vast masses and to give a fillip to research activities.

Technological Challenges

The growth of copyright is inter-twined with the growth of technology, which could be traced to the advent of printing press by Gutenberg in 1436. Whereas printing technology gave a fillip to learning and advancement of knowledge at the advent of modern era, it in turn led to adoption of unfair practices such as unauthorized printing by competing printers. This led to the Royal Charter in 1556 granting copyright to the Stationers' Company. With the advent of computers, computer programs were also brought under the copyright protection. However, right from the invention of the printing press every technology has challenged or threatened the copyright regime. Latest challenge is the digital technology whereby the works like music, sound recording, computer programs, writings, photographs, etc. could easily be transported across the networks in a matter of seconds. In feet, the same technology, which could be used for the enormous benefit to the creators, has sounded death knell of copyright. With a click of the mouse, a perfect replica of a copyright work can be produced.

Internet, by opening up the electronic frontier, has dissolved the national boundaries and has broken the barriers of distance. It has also given birth to other umpteen problems, viz., cyber crimes such as fraud, pornography, to name the few. At a bare minimum, Internet is an information, marketing and advertising device capable of reaching an ever-widening number of citizens, consumers and buyers. Along with the digitization, networking and World Wide Web have changed the copyright regime fundamentally:

- Digitization of information and communication has made reproduction easy;
- Networking of computers has rendered distribution of copyrighted work easy; and
- World Wide Web has made publication of copyrighted material very easy.

Together, the new Information and Communication Technologies (ICTs), and in particular the Internet, have enabled unauthorized creation of unlimited, perfect and costless copies of protected works, as well as their almost instantaneous and worldwide distribution, which poses an unprecedented challenge to copyright law. Digitization (through DVD, CD-Rom and broad base) has also enabled the rapid development of the multi-media product, combining written text with sounds and images, still and moving. The digital work would always copy perfectly.

In the digital environment, the *most fundamental issue* that has emerged in the field of copyright is the scope of protection, i.e., how these rights are defined, and what exceptions and limitations are permitted. Other important issues include:

- How these rights are enforced and administered in this environment;
- Who in the chain of dissemination of infringing material can be held legally responsible for the infringement; and
- Questions of jurisdiction and applicable law.

Few other pertinent questions are: when multiple copies are made as works traverse the networks, does the reproduction right implicated by each copy? Is there a communication to the public when a work is not broadcasted, but simply made available to individual members of the public if and when they wish to see or hear it? Does a public performance take place when different individuals on the monitors of their personal computers or other digital devices view a work at different times?

Similar questions are raised about exceptions and limitations to rights. Are existing exemptions and limitations, written in a language conceived for other circumstances, too broad or too narrow? Some exceptions, for example, for research and education, if applied literally in the digital environment, could eliminate large sectors of existing markets. Whether they can be considered as the "fair use" of the copyrighted work? Others may implement valid public policy goals, but be written too restrictively to apply to network transmissions. Thus, new circumstances may call for new exceptions. These questions must be examined in the light of the general standard of "three-step test" established in copyright treaties for the permissibility of exceptions and limitations. This standard needs to be examined afresh to determine how would this standard apply in the digital environment, while safeguarding the owner's legitimate interest.

Issues of enforcement and licensing of copyright are not new, but take an added dimension and urgency when works are exploited on digital networks. In order for legal protection to remain meaningful, right holders must be able to detect and stop the dissemination of unauthorized digital copies. It is necessary to protect the economic interests of the right-holder and moral interests of the author of the work. And, in the context of e-commerce, workable systems of online licensing must evolve, in which consumers can have confidence. The answer to these challenges to a great extent will lie in the technology itself.

Digital revolution has led to peer to peer (P2P) file-sharing on the Internet, allowing users to copy MP3 files (files that store audio recordings in a digital format) directly from the hard drive of another user without the need, as in the well-known *Napster* case (2001) in the U.S., to rely on a central index which facilitates the transmission of these files amongst the users. The *Napster* was held vicariously liable for copyright infringement. But in a more recent *Grokster* case before the Federal Appeals Court in California, USA, it was held that absence of any central control over how users used the P2P systems in question meant that unlike *Napster*, there was no liability on the suppliers for vicarious or contributory infringement of copyright. On appeal to the US Supreme Court, *certiorari* was granted on 12th October, 2004 by framing a question that contrary to long established principles of secondary liability in copyright law, the Internet-based file sharing services be immunized from copyright liability for the millions of daily acts of copyright infringements that occur on their services as in *Grokster.*

There is evidence that the phenomenon of P2P now takes in films as well as music and computer programs and games, following the development of compression and broadband technologies. On the question of the impact of this activity on entertainment industry, it is difficult to imagine. Other factors, such as the state of the economy, the easy availability of CDs and DVDs, in the form and containing the tracks that users want, will also have a bearing on the sales of pre-recorded music, films and software. Cases like *Napster* have demonstrated the inadequacies of the copyright laws *vis-a-vis* the digital technology. It has been verily stated that the value of any digital product without protecting its intellectual property is ZERO.

WAY AHEAD

Developments world over on copyright front so far have very much focused on entertainment industry—to develop, use and enforce means to control digital content due to enormous amount of money involved. But the question may be asked, should those means be applied to other sectors of copyright industry (such as publishing) whose activities more generally be considered to contribute to education, research and the advancement of knowledge. How will the new measures be impacting libraries and archives—which enjoy "fair use" exception and support the publishing sector? The answers have to be sought for these issues for the society's growth.

Though these developments have threatened the rights of authors and copyright holders, at the same time, there is a growing trend within the publishing and software industries towards distribution of content on-line, together with access restrictions enforced by digital rights management systems, such as encryption technologies and anti-circumvention measures, supplemented by contract law and *sui generis* forms of databases protection. This sophisticated form of technological protection has given copyright holders the capacity to limit non-public performances and rescinds traditional "fair use" rights to browse, share, or make private copies of copyrighted works in digital formats, since works may not be accessible without payment, even for legitimate uses. This has the potential to affect adversely the research.

In order to address these issues, in 1996, the WIPO adopted two treaties: the WIPO Copyright Treaty (WCT) and WIPO Performers and Phonograms Treaty (WPPT), known as Internet Treaties, to deal with the challenges of internet to the copyright and to prevent unauthorized access to and use of creative works on the Internet or other digital networks. But they do not address the access to copyright work for "fair use" purposes. Both these treaties are in force since 2002. India is not yet a party to these treaties. Certain other countries have adopted specific legislation, viz., the US Digital Millennium Copyright Act, 1998 and the Singapore Copyright Act, 1987 as amended in 1999 deal with some of the issues arising out of the use of Internet. But the territorial jurisdiction in respect of the breach of copyright through Internet has not been adequately addressed in any of these instruments. Since Internet is a global phenomenon there is a need of harmony in the laws of all countries, which is not so easy to come by. India needs to put in place a viable mechanism to address these issues and undue delay could be confused with "legal impotency".

Copyright problem posed by the Internet is only one aspect of the matter. Other areas like broadcasting, satellite transmission, cable transmission, data bases, distribution rights, fixation rights, reproduction rights have also raised serious copyright problems. IP protection of databases is a very important issue for science, research, innovation and creativity, given the global proliferation of computerized information services. Advances in information and communication technologies have made digital databases of factual information an essential resource for accelerating the growth of knowledge and for producing new discoveries. The expansion of Internet facilitates their wide dissemination and easy use. At the same time, the same technologies make unauthorized uses and wholesale misappropriation of these valuable databases relatively simple. The central issue here is, the balance between addressing concerns of database creators regarding the provision of incentives and protecting investment in new database products and services and, on the other, safeguarding customary access to the data they contain by users from the scientific, education and library communities. In the famous 1991 case *of Feist Publications Inc.* Vs. *Rural Telephone Service Co.*, the US Supreme Court denied protection to a telephone directory on the grounds that collecting of names, address and telephone numbers was not an original creative work. In India, databases are protected as "literary work" under section 2(o) of the Copyright Act. Computer databases are also protectable as literary work[10] even when they only involve "sweat-of-the-brow" and may not involve any creativity or selection skills.[11]

In the case of databases, Berne Convention [Art. 2(5)] accords protection but that protection is generally been considered to apply only to *selection and arrangement of the contents, and not to the contents* themselves. Granting protection to the contents of a database is not far from controversy. The WIPO in 1996, failed to evolve any consensus for a treaty. At present different practices exist. In some countries they qualify protection under trademark, in others under copyright.

The WIPO is also currently discussing the issues related to protecting broadcasting and other digital products as well as the rights of the broadcasting organizations. The liability of Intermediate Service Providers (ISPs) and on-line service providers also need serious consideration, who at present in most of the jurisdictions are liable for their intentional acts only.

The Information Technology Act, 2000 (IT Act) of India gives immunity to ISPs (Sec. 79), if the offence is committed without his knowledge or that he had exercised all due diligence to prevent the commission of the offence. The case in point is the infamous case of MMS sex clip involving a Delhi school children and the subsequent arrest of the officials of baazi.com, an Internet portal. The IT Act does not deal with cases of pornography or ISPs liability adequately, nor does it deal with the IPRs. This requires an amendment of the IT Act, which is now on the anvil. In talking about the amendments to the Copyright Act, it may perhaps be advantageous to have the benefit of legislations abroad. Even in the limited area of protection to service providers, the practice in other jurisdiction is of some relevance, such as the US Online Copyright Infringement Liability Limitation Act. This Act inserts a new section in the US Copyright Act, 1976. There is also the European Parliament and Council Directive, 1997, the Singapore

Electronics Transactions Act, 1998, the German Multimedia Law, 1998, the Australian Broadcasting Services Amendment (Online Services) Act, 1999, Schedule 5, and so on.

As is evident, information technology revolution has the potential to increase the access to information and knowledge in developing countries like ours, but there are also threats to access and diffusion of knowledge and technology from these technological changes. India should adopt pro-competitive measures to achieve the goals of education and knowledge transfer. There should be broad exemptions for educational, research and library uses under the copyright laws. In fact, while framing a legislation on any IPR aspect, viz., software, biotechnological inventions, plant variety, etc. a human approach must be kept in sight, taking into account the national interests, public policy, morality and protection of environment.

The copyright laws of India are as good as those of many advanced countries, but, like many other developing countries, piracy is rampant because of poor enforcement of laws and lack of awareness. Though piracy can never really be eliminated, it could *albeit* be controlled and minimized by effective legislation and enforcement coupled with public education and awareness. While buying a copyrighted product, majority of consumers do not look at copyright notification. As long as price is low (as generally is the case with pirated products) users do not mind buying pirated products even knowingly. This raises the related issue of pricing of copyrighted products, which should be affordable.

The Copyright Act prescribes criminal and civil remedies against any infringement. Punishments prescribed for violators are stringent and comparable to those of many countries in the world. Criminal remedies include imprisonment and/or monetary fines depending upon the gravity of the crime, seizure, forfeiture and destruction of infringing copies and the tools used for making such copies. Civil remedies are also available against violators. The legal machinery to enforce the rights of the owner is possible through: (1) the Copyright Board, and (2) the courts. The 1984 amendment has made copyright infringement a cognizable, non-bailable offence. However, enforcement mechanism is weak.

Beside the end-users, the awareness level is very low even among the law enforcement agencies. In the case of law enforcement agencies, beside lack of knowledge of law on copyright, their inadequate number to combat piracy is a contributing factor. For an effective IP regime, a good infra-structural support is a *sine qua none,* which requires not only good legislation, but also workable administrative machinery and physical facilities, which are presently not of an appropriate level.

CONCLUSION

We are living in an era of knowledge economy. Knowledge economy is one in which, in addition to capital and labour, technology and knowledge upon which such technology is based is the third factor of production. Earlier knowledge was to be shared with the increasing use of IPRs, now it is to be capitalized and monopolized. Societal concerns are taking a back seat. But good IPR system has to draw a balance between these conflicting interests. Knowledge is intangible and non-rivalrous. It does not lessen by sharing with others. Thomas Jefferson aptly said it:

> He who receives an idea from me, receives instruction himself without lessening mine; as he who lights his toper at mine, receives light without darkening me.

The time, however, has come to think of a new paradigm on intellectual property, of which the copyright law is but one part, to make it an engine of innovation and inventiveness to cater the needs of vast humanity around us. Assessment of our strength, weaknesses, opportunities and threat (SWOT) analysis indicate that in the emerging knowledge economy we have a vital stake. We have a vast pool of trained skilled manpower. Our computational skills are well acknowledged. Our indigenous and traditional knowledge is very rich. Our entertainment industry is very vibrant. We have a vast pool of content creators in the entertainment and information sectors. Entertainment and media law is the emerging field which holds enormous opportunities for creation of wealth for the stakeholders, including the young lawyers. These are the areas where law has to keep pace with the market expectations by protecting the genuine interests of the right-holders.

The challenges posed by Internet and digital medium are

fascinating, which have dazzled the law and policy-makers and put many questions, which still elude answers. These challenges must be met by putting in place a workable IP regime in our national interest. This is true also in the case of software patents, biotechnological inventions, plant variety, etc. The issues of public policy, morality and protection of environment should be kept in view. For this, a human approach is necessary where everybody thrives with the new knowledge, the creator getting due return for his creation and the common man being benefited with the new ideas. Law's approach must be to draw a balance for all the stakeholders for the societal growth. It is also important to note that though we have entered the digital age, our thinking and outlook continues to remain in the analog mode. We are accustomed to deal with the problems posed by new technology (whether telecommunications, bio-technology, or computer software), by adopting a sector-wise approach. We need to take a comprehensive and holistic approach.

At the end, I wish to thank the Faculty of Law, Kumaun University for giving me this opportunity to share my thoughts on intellectual property in general and copyright in particular. I hope that the deliberations in this two-day seminar will achieve the objectives of dissemination of information on IPRs and provide valuable guidance to policy-makers.

NOTES AND REFERENCES

1. Audrey R. Chapman, "A Human Rights Perspective on Intellectual Property, Scientific Progress and Access to the Benefits of Science" in WIPO/United Nations High Commissioner for Human Rights, *Intellectual Property and Human Rights* (WIPO, 1999), 127.
2. It is generally being argued that society-benefits greatly from technological innovation and should therefore encourage it. See, Robert P. Benko, *Protecting Intellectual Property Rights: Issues and Controversies*, (1987, American Enterprise Institute for Public Policy Research, Washington, D.C.), 22.
3. Art. 52(1) of the [Indian] Copyright Act, 1957 as amended, provides the instances of "fair dealing."
4. Chapman, *op. cit.* at p. 138.
5. A.E. Carroll, "Biotechnology and the Global Impact of U.S. Patent Law: Not Always the Best Medicine", *The American University Law Review* (1995), 2464-66.
6. According to Art. 2(viii) of the WIPO Treaty, 1967, Intellectual Property

includes: (i) literary and scientific works, (ii) performance of performing artists, phonograms and broadcast, (iii) inventions in all fields of human endeavour, (iv) scientific discoveries, (v) industrial designs, (vi) trademarks, service marks and commercial names and designations, and (vii) protection against unfair competition.

7. Art. 7 of TRIPS reads: "The protection and enforcement of intellectual property rights should contribute to the promotion of technological innovation and to the transfer and dissemination of technology, to the mutual advantage of producers and users of technological knowledge and in a manner conducive to social and economic welfare, and to a balance of rights and obligations."
8. Art. 8 provides: "Members may, in formulating or amending their national laws and regulations, adopt measures necessary to protect public health and nutrition, and to promote the public interest in sectors of vital importance to their socio-economic and technological development, provided that such measures are consistent with the provisions of this Agreement."
9. The National Task force has Set a target of US $ 50 billion annual export of software and services by the year 2008.
10. *Sham Lal Paharia* Vs. *Gaya Prasad*, AIR 1971 All 182.
11. *Govindan* Vs. *Gopalakrishna*, AIR 1955 Mad. 391; *Burlington Home Shopping* Vs. *Rajnish Chibber*, 61 (1996) *Delhi Law Times* 6.

Plant Variety Protection and Farmers' Rights

Basant Ram

The demand for extending intellectual property protection to agriculture in developing countries has met with counterclaims for granting farmers' rights. Developing countries are currently attempting to fulfil these demands by evolving new IPR regimes that simultaneously protect the rights of breeders and farmers.

HISTORY OF GATT AND WTO

The General Agreement on Tariffs and Trade (GATT) came into existence in 1947 as a temporary arrangement to settle disputes amicably regarding world trade. It sought substantial reduction in tariffs and other barriers to trade and to eliminate discriminatory treatment in international commerce. India is signatory to GATT since 1947 along with 22 other countries signing the first post-war multilateral agreement on trade liberalization. In GATT negotiations on various issues were being held regularly. Eighth round of such multilateral trade negotiations on trade started in September 1986 at Uruguay. In this round some bold decisions were taken. One such decision was agriculture to be treated as a tradable commodity. Another decision was to form a World Trade Organization (WTO) to succeed GATT as an inter-governmental organization. WTO was established on January 1, 1995. The headquarter of WTO is at Geneva, Switzerland. At present 148 nations are members of the WTO including India. The WTO is a permanent organization and it has got an equal status as of I.M.F. and the World Bank though it is not a funding agency. With its creation, multilateral trade entered a new phase. New issues such as Intellectual Property Rights (IPRs), investment measures, trade in services, agricultural policies, etc. appeared on the agenda of international trade. The important WTO Agreements having a serious impact on agriculture were: Agreement on the application of Sanitary and Phytosanitary Measures (SPS), Agreement on Technical Barriers to Trade (TBT), Anti-dumping Agreement on subsidies and countervailing measures, agreement on Safeguards and Trade Related aspects of Intellectual Property Rights (TRIPS). There is a General Council for all kinds of policy decisions in WTO. Each member-country is a permanent representative of the General Council. Policy decisions in WTO are taken in Ministerial Conference and decisions are taken by consensus of all the member-countries of WTO. So far five Ministerial Conferences have been organized, the first was in Singapore (1996), the second in Geneva (1998), the third in Seattle (1999), the fourth in Doha (2001) and the fifth conference was organized in Cancun in 2003.

TRIPS AND UPOV

Agriculture has been brought at par with other industrial trade sectors in terms of common institutional framework for conducting trade relations among members, protection of IPR and services. The application of IPRs to living things is of recent origin. Vegetatively propagated plants were first made patentable in the United States in the 1930s. Protection of plant varieties in the form of plant breeders' rights became widespread in the second half of the 20th century. The Article 27.3(b) of TRIPS requires that plant varieties need to be protected either by patenting or by a *sui generis* method or by a combination of both. Patents on plants are granted in certain countries such as the USA, Japan and Australia under certain conditions. The patent laws in Europe exclude plant varieties from patenting; these are protected by the *sui generis* methods. In Europe, the plant variety protection has been given a separate legal system, commonly known as Plant Variety Rights or Plant Breeders' Rights. Such rights originated from and through the enactment of the International Union for the Protection of New Varieties of Plant (UPOV) which was signed in Paris on December 2, 1961, and subsequently revised three times. Mainly the countries are bound by either UPOV (1978) or UPOV (1991) Conventions. It had 53 States as on October 15, 2003. UPOV is an inter-governmental organization and not a 'treaty' as such. Countries are not obliged to join UPOV as a result of their affiliation with any other organization or the ratification of any specific treaty. Membership to UPOV is purely voluntary. The Convention requires member-countries to provide IPRs specifically for plant varieties. This form of IP protection is often referred to as Plant Breeders' Rights (PBRs). As a result of the PBR, the plant breeder is granted a legal monopoly over the commercialization of their plant varieties. Protection allows the breeder to try to recover the costs associated with the development of the variety. By conferring protection on plant varieties, UPOV also aims to provide an incentive to individuals or companies to invest in plant breeding, thereby providing a positive stimulus in the plant breeding industry. The rights granted are for a specific time only (depending on the plant variety), and upon expiration of the time period, the protected variety passes into the public domain. It is meant to encourage agricultural growth, investment and trade by ensuring an amicable agreement with those who have developed the new plant varieties. The TRIPS does not mention or refer to the provisions of UPOV, nor does it indicate the precise steps to be taken for protecting plant varieties, except that it promulgates that plant varieties are to be protected. Developing countries are therefore, free to enact their own Plant Variety Protection (PVP) law that would be consistent with the TRIPS. In the new law the farmers' rights as well as the researchers' rights could be upheld in accordance with the traditional practices of the country.

PROTECTION OF PLANT VARIETIES AND FARMERS' RIGHTS ACT, 2001

Many developing countries have an agricultural economy that is geared towards the domestic as opposed to the export market. Such an economy is dependent upon farmer-produced seed of varieties that are both maintained and further adapted to their local growing conditions by small-scale farmers. As a result, some developing countries have chosen a *sui generis* system of plant protection that is not compliant with UPOV in that it allows farmers to improve and adapt the seed in order to make it more successful in the local conditions.

India is one of the first countries in the world to have evolved a *sui generis* system of IPR legislation for protection of plant varieties simultaneously granting rights to both breeders and farmers. India has enacted two legislations—Protection of Plant Varieties and Farmers' Rights Act, 2001 and the Biological Diversity Act, 2002 which are significant in terms of both in the domestic and international context.

Under the Indian, 'Protection of Plant Varieties and Farmers' Rights Act, 2001' plant varieties are divided into four main classes: new variety/breeders' variety, extant variety, farmers' varieties and essentially derived varieties. The regime for plant protection is similar to that set out by UPOV and the requirements for protection are novelty (N), distinctness (D), uniformity (U) and stability (S). A New Variety/Breeders' Variety means a plant grouping except micro-organism defined by certain characteristics under the Act. It is new if it meets specified criteria which are Novelty, Distinctness, Uniformity and Stability (NDUS). It is an exclusive right for the breeder to produce, sell, market, distribute, import or export the variety. The duration of protection is initially for nine years renewable up to total period of 18 years for trees and vines while for other crops it is initially for six years' renewable up to total of 15 years. An Extant Variety is a variety available in India, which is notified under Section 5 of the Seeds Act, 1966; or a variety about which there is common knowledge; or any other variety which is in the public domain. An extant variety should meet the criteria of Distinctness, Uniformity and Stability (DUS) or as specified under the regulations. Novelty feature is not required for registration of such extant varieties. It provides an exclusive right to produce, sell, market, distribute, import or export the variety if claimed by the breeder and in cases where not claimed by breeder, the Central Government or State Government shall have the right. The period of protection is for 15 years from the date of notification of that variety by the Central Government under Section 5 of the Seeds Act, 1966. A Farmers' Variety is a variety which has been traditionally cultivated and evolved by the farmers in their fields; or is a wild relative or land race of a variety about which the farmers possess the common knowledge. An Essentially Derived Variety is a variety that itself is predominantly derived from such initial variety, while retaining the expression of the essential characteristics that result from the genotype or combination of genotypes of such initial variety but is clearly distinguishable from such initial variety. The criteria of such varieties are genera or species specified by the Central Government and tests to determine if it is an EDV or not. The rights provided are same as that for a breeder of a new variety provided that the authorization by the breeder of the initial variety to the breeder of essentially derived variety may be subject to terms mutually agreed upon by both the parties. The protection cover provided is initially for nine years and is renewable up to total of 18 years for trees and vines and for other crops it is initially for six years renewable up to total of 15 years.

Application Procedure

Before making an application for registration of a plant variety the following points should be kept in mind such as denomination assigned to such variety accompanied by an affidavit that variety does not contain any gene or gene sequence involving terminator technology, complete passport data of parental lines, geographical location in India and all such information relating to the contribution, if any, of any farmer, village, community, institution or organization in breeding, evolving or developing the variety, characteristics of variety with brief description on novelty, distinctiveness, uniformity and stability, a declaration that the genetic material for breeding has been lawfully acquired and a disclosure by the breeder or other persons making application for registration if the genetic material is conserved by any tribal or rural families in the breeding or development of such variety.

Who can Register?

A plant variety can be registered by any person claiming to be the breeder of the variety or successor of the breeder of the variety or any person being the assignee of the breeder of the variety in respect of the right to make such application or any farmer or group of farmers or community of farmers claiming to be breeder of the variety or any person authorized to make application on behalf of farmers or any University or publicly funded agricultural institution claiming to be breeder of the variety.

Farmers' Rights

Farmers' rights are based mainly on the idea that farmers also contribute to agricultural innovations and deserve recognition and rewards just as breeders do. Over 85% of the seeds amounting to roughly 52 lakh tons that are planted in Indian fields every year are supplied by the farming community. In most developing countries, farmers are the main source of seed supply and a large amount of the seed requirements are met through farmer-to-farmer exchange. The importance of farmer-to-farmer exchange of seeds has been stated as one of the reasons for upholding farmers' rights under any breeders' legislation in India. The new PPV&FR legislation ensures that farmers have the right to exchange seed and would not be prevented from sharing seeds with other farmers provided he/she does not sell the seed as a brand name (the breeders' registered name). 'Branded seeds' means any seed put in a package or any other container and labelled in a manner indicating that such seed is of a variety protected under this Act. However, the incentive to share seeds would also be influenced by the ability to claim ownership rights over farmers' varieties provided under the Act. If it becomes possible for farmers to register their varieties under the act, they would have a greater incentive to charge for use of the variety rather than giving it away freely to other farmers. The direct exchange between farmers to farmers may also be mediated by a relatively new actor NGOs in the system.

Several provisions have been made in this Act to strengthen the farmers' rights such as farmers' privilege which allows farmers to save, use and exchange seed but not sell seed without penalty under plant breeders' right systems. Farmers' rights as ownership, which refers to the rights of farmers to claim ownership over their varieties equivalent to breeders. There is a provision that if a farmer who is engaged in the conservation of genetic resources of land races and wild relatives of economic plants shall be entitled for recognition and reward from the gene fund provided that material so selected and preserved has been used as donors of genes in varieties registrable under this Act. It essentially refers to the rights and rewards that farmers deserve for contributing to agricultural innovation and growth (benefit sharing). It has also been provided under this Act that a farmer can claim compensation if the variety is not performing as reported. Such claim may be made to the Protection of Plant Varieties and Farmers' Rights Authority and it will decide the amount of compensation.

Copyright Act in Digital Environment: Management, Law and Policy

SALEEM AKHTAR

INTRODUCTION

The Recent Internet revolution has introduced new dimensions in the field of Intellectual Property. Internet is often called as "Global Copy Machine," which is decentralized, unregulated and anarchic. Its world-wide user have a belief that the work/contents placed on the Internet should be available with out charge for use; copying, unlimited copies and alteration except in cases where the content placed on Commercial on line service. On the other hand, Threat from cybersquatters on unfair use of reputed Trade Marks, Domain Names, indiscriminate copying of information from diverse web-sites, unauthorized distribution of copyrighted material such as recorded Music, Vedio Games, Software, etc., through the cyber space by digital pirates are challenges to be met by creators, owners, traders and enforces of Intellectual property rights. Internet also provides information about various subjects such as educational, entertainment, Commercial, Governmental activities and services.

Today very high stakes bottle is raging in Cyberspace over copyright protection. The owner's of copyright work want a extensive copyright safeguards on the Internet. The Internet has been considered as the greatest threat to copyright holders in present Digital Environment.

The scope of this research paper is limited to a critical assessment of the Copyright Act in Digital Environment with respect to management, Law and Policy. The objective is to critically evaluate the legislative measures and response of Indian judiciary to the stiff challenges faced by it by way of protection of the copyright holders exclusive right in present scenario.

AN HISTORICAL OVERVIEW

The Copyright Act, 1957

The Copyright Act, 1914 has been in operation till 1957 and was replaced by the Copyright Act of 1957 with minor adaptation and modifications. It was a remarkable accomplishment of Independent India's legislature that it accorded so much of importance to the intellectual property rights. In fact, there were number of reasons which paved the way for the early revision of the copyright law such as changed constitutional status of India and non-compliance of the Brussels Act, 1948, Bern Convention and the Universal Copyright Convention of 1952 by the Copyright Act of 1914. Moreover, advanced methods of communication and technology rendered modernization for the existing law inevitable.

The Act is divided into 15 chapters and contains 79 sections. Apart from this, the government has been empowered to frame copyright rules under section 78 of the Act. The government has thus framed copyright rules which deal with matters of procedure for application of licences for translations, performing rights societies, relinquishment and registration of copyrights and ancillary matters.

The chapters I, III, IV and V contains law of copyright and its ownership; Chapter XI deals with infringement; Chapter IX devoted to International copyright law, Chapter X stipulates registration of copyright and prescribes remedies. Chapters II, V, VII and X deal with powers and functions of the Registrar of

Copyrights and Copyrights Board. Chapter VIII deals with the rights of Broadcasting authorities.

Despite all this, the Act was not sufficiently farsighted. For instance, it does not protect the right of the performers adequately. But the fact remains that the country had its own law of copyright for the first time in contemporary history; and for weal or woe, it represented the law-policy choices made by its independent legislature.[1]

The 1983 and 1984 Amendments

The new sections 32A and 32B were inserted by these amendments which envisaged "compulsory licences" for publication of copyrighted foreign works in any Indian language for the purposes of systematic and organized instructural activities at a low price with the permission of the Copyright Board on certain conditions. Another significant change was the insertion of Section 19A which empowered the Copyright Board to order revocation of the assigned copyright upon a complaint where either the terms are "harsh" or where the publication is unduly delayed. The 1984 amendment also prescribed stringent punishments for piracy and effective procedures to inhibit it.[2]

The 1994 and 1999 Amendments

The 1994 Amendment brings Indian Law in conformity with the Uruguary Round Agreement on Trade-Related Intellectual Property Rights (TRIPS). These amendments have also enlarged the scope of the protection of computer programs and restricted the rights of foreign broadcasting organizations and performers and confers power on central government to apply chapter VIII to broadcasting organizations and performers in certain other countries under new Sections 40A and 42A respectively.

WHAT IS COPYRIGHT: MEANING

The copyright has comprehensively been defined under Section 14 of the Act of 1957 as exclusive right to do or authorize other(s) to do certain acts in relation to:

- Literary, dramatic or musical works;
- Artistic work;

- Cinematograph film; and
- Sound recording.

On the other hand, Black's Law Dictionary defines copyright as the right in literary property as recognized and sanctioned by the positive law.

Copyright is only in expression of an idea. There is no copyright in an idea. There is no copyright in idea or a concept, theme or plot. What is protected is not the original thought or information, but the original expression of thought or information is some concrete form.[3]

There is no copyright in idea, subject matter, theme, plots or historical or legendary facts. Violation of copyright is confined to the form, manner, arrangement and expression of the idea by the author.[4] Copyright is a beneficial interest in movable property. It can be transferred as per any beneficial interest in movable property.[5]

INFRINGEMENT

A. What is Infringement of Copyright?

Section 51 of the Copyright Act, 1957 defines "infringement" in general terms which may be sum up as:

(a) Doing anything without licence for which the owner of the copyright has exclusive rights;
(b) Permitting for profit without licence any place to be used for the communication of the work to the public where such communication constitutes an infringement of the copyright in the work; and
(c) Making for sale or hire, selling or offering for sale or hire, distributing, exhibiting in public or importing into India any "infringement copy of the work."

However, bringing one copy in India for private and domestic use of the importer is permitted.

Section 2(m) of the Act defines "Infringing copy" means reproduction of copy or import in contravention of provisions of the Copyright Act of any of the following:

(a) reproduction of literary, dramatic, musical or artistic work otherwise than in form of cinematographic film;
(b) copy of cinematographic film by any means;
(c) recording embodying "sound recording" by any means; and
(d) sound recording or visual recording of a programme or performance where "broadcast reproduction rights" or "performer's rights" subsists.

Further, for the purposes of Section 51, even reproduction of a literary, dramatic, musical or artistic work in the form of or cinematograph film is also deemed to be an "infringement."

B. Nature of Infringement

The essence of the law of copyright is that it will not permit one man to make profit and appropriate to himself the labour, skill and capital of another. The law is strong enough to restrain what otherwise would be an injustice. At every stage in the law of copyright, and of performing rights, the author of a work has certain exclusive rights with regard to certain "restricted acts". If these acts performed by another person without the consent of the owner of the copyright, than the person infringes the copyright in that work. [Section 1(2) of the U.K. Copyright Act, 1956] Sections 2(5)(a) and 3(5)(a) of the U.K. Copyright Act, 1956 laid down the restriction in only general terms, such as, in the case of literary, dramatic and musical works and again in artistic works, reproducing the work in any material form.

C. Acts which do not Constitute Infringement

The use of a copyright work by any person other than the owner of copyright is an infringement. However, the Copyright Act recognizes certain acts which are done by a person other than owner do not amount to infringement such as—

1. Fair scholarly uses;
2. Educational uses;
3. Media reporting uses;
4. Uses of state produced materials;
5. Making of records of literary, dramatic or musical works;
6. Performance of such works;
7. Use by public libraries;

8. Use of engraving, etc.;
9. Cinematograph film—Use by makers and exhibitors; and
10. Uses relating to artistic works.

D. Test for Determination of Infringement

The definition clause of the 1957 does not define infringement as such but the definition of an infringing copy in Section 2(m) provides some standards and criteria for the determination that an infringement has occurred. Following two elements are required to determine the test[6] of infringement, namely;

1. There must be sufficient objective similarity between the infringing work and the copyright work or a substantial part thereof.
2. The copyright work must be the source from which the infringement work is derived.

In the case of *Willian Hill (Football)* Vs. *Ladbroke (Football)*[7] (name of the journal) it was held that the test of infringement is not how much is taken but it depends on the worth of the work taken.

In the case of *Jarrold* Vs. *Housto,*[8] a third element was identified. It was held that whether there has been an "animus furandi," i.e. intent to commit fraud on the part of the defendant for the purpose of saving labour, was an important consideration in arriving at the conclusion of occurrence of any infringement.

The general principle is that no infringement of the plaintiffs rights takes place where a defendant has bestowed such mental labour upon what he has borrowed and has subjected it to such revision and alteration as to produce an original result. The ultimate test is "has there been a reproduction of the plaintiffs work in a substantial form."[9]

E. Infringement of Literary, Dramatic, Musical, Artistic, Cinematograph Film and Sound Recording Works

As regards book and literary work, "a literal imitation of copyrighted work with some variations here and there" would undoubtedly constitute infringement.[10] But most cases involved situations and contests where criterion of "substantial reproduction" requires to be explicated. Ever since the landmark Deb and Cooper cases, Indian courts have held that quantitative criteria should not be held decisive. In other words, the number of words, paragraphs or pages copied is not decisive; even a small amount of copying may infringe copyright.[11]

The asymmetry between film producers and authors of other protected works becomes accentuated when the author of a dramatic or literary work has established infringement.[12] This is so, because of the fact that "a film has a much broader perspective, wider field and bigger background" and it is always possible for the film-maker to give "a colour and complexion" which distinguished in many ways the strong or dramatic theme from the film. The Supreme Court of India, whose above-quoted words[13] testify to the considerable difficulties in this area, however, adopted in *R.G. Anand* Vs. *Delux Films*, the "doctrine of dominant impact" even as regards this question. The test was formulated thus: "If the viewer after seeing the film gets a total impression that the film is by and large a copy of the original play, violation of copyright may be said to have been proved.[14]

The Apex Court, while dealing with the law relating to the copyright and its infringement in *R.G. Anand Case* after careful consideration and elucidation of the various authorities laid down the following important propositions:[15]

1. "There can be no copyright in an idea, subject-matter, themes, plots or historical or legendary facts and violation of the copyright in success is confined to the form, manner and arrangement and expression of the idea by the author of the copyrighted work.
2. The Court should determine whether or not the similarities are on fundamental or substantial aspects of the mode of expression adopted in the copyrighted work. If the defendant's work is nothing but a literal imitation of the copyrighted work with some variations here and there it would amount to violation of the copyright. In other words in order to be actionable the copy must be a substantial and material one which at once leads to the conclusion that the defendant is guilty of an act of piracy.
3. One of the surest and the safest test to determine

whether or not there has been a violation of copyright is to see if the reader, spectator or the viewer after having read or seen both the works is clearly of the opinion and gets an unmistakable impression that the subsequent work appears to be a copy of the original.

Justice Murtaza Fazal Ali, had relied on American cases[16] with reference to the term 'infringement and copyright'. In this context, it would be relevant to refer to those passages relied upon by the Apex Court.

> "Infringement of a copyright is a trespass on a private domain owned and occupied by the owner of the copyright, and, therefore, protected by law, and infringement of copyright, or piracy which is a synonymous term in this connection, consists in the doing by any person without the consent of the owner of the copyright, of anything the sole right to do which is conferred by the statute in the owner of the copyright."

This is observed by the U.S. Supreme Court in the case of *Bobbs-Merrill Company* Vs. *Isidor Straus and Nathan Straus*.[17]

Similarly, the U.S Supreme Court in *Eisenchimi* Vs. *Fancett Publication*, rightly observed:

> "An infringement is not confined to literal and exact repetition or reproduction; it includes also the various modes in which the matter of any work may be adopted, imitated, transferred, or reproduced, with or less colorable alterations to disguise the piracy. Paraphrasing is copying and an infringement, if carried to a sufficient extent. . . . The question of infringement of copyright is not one of quantity but of quality and value."[18]

On a reading of the various judgments referred to in the above decision, it is clear that in order to constitute infringement of copyright two elements are essential. First, there must be sufficient objective similarity between the infringement work and the copyright work must be the source from which the infringement work is derived, but, it need not be the direct source.

In the case of *Fracis Day and Hunter* Vs. *Bron*[19] it was held that infringement of copyright in musical work is not to be determined by a note for note comparison, but should be determined by the ear as well as the eye.

Painting, sculpture, drawings, engraving, photograph architecture and works of craftsmanship constitute artistic works. Questions about infringement in paintings and pictures require somewhat different criteria of "substantial reproduction." If a painting or a picture in its "plan design arrangement of all important component parts which help an artist to obtain a representation of the idea—on plastic material" are all substantially similar to the copyrighted work, then there would substantial reproduction.[20]

In the case of *Associated Electronics and Electricals* Vs. *Sharp Tools*,[21] it was held that the surest test to determine whether or not there has been a violation of copyright is to see if the reader, spectator or viewer after reading or seeing both the works would get an unmistakable impressions that the subsequent work appears to be a copy of the first.

Sound recording means a recording of sounds from which sounds may be produced regardless of the medium on which such recording is made or the method by which such sounds are produced as defined by Section 2(XX) of the Act.

A sound recording may be of a literary work. Home taping of sound recording is the most common form of infringement of copyright in sound recording. It is practically difficult to take any action against such infringement. Under English law it is not a breach of copyright but this is not so under Indian.

CONFIDENTIAL INFORMATION AND COPYRIGHT

Copyright is a bundle of exclusive rights of the owner of the copyright to authorize other to use the protected work. Copyright Law, however, normally state the action in relation to the work which the copyright owner can exclusively do. In effect, it means that other persons can not do the same thing otherwise they infringe the copyright. The basic rights of the owner of copyright are the reproduction right, adaptation right and publication right. The subject matter of copyright is another essential element in copyright law. Basically the subject matter, which usually referred to as "work" must be an expression of idea in a material form.

The law on confidential information extends the protection to some subjects which are not protected by the copyright law. The expression which is not expressed in material form is outside the scope of copyright protection that is ideas, plots, concepts, scheme, lectures, delivered orally, etc. On the other hand, some subjects which are shown in tangible medium but may not be protected by copyright law, are tables, programs, directions, charts, etc. However, these non-copyright subjects may fall within the coverage of law on confidence if they bear the characteristics of confidential information. These observations *supra* were made in the following cases:

1. *Gilbert* Vs. *Star News Papers Co. Ltd.* (1884) 11 TLR 4 (Plot of comicopera).
2. *Talbot* Vs. *General Television Corporation Pvt. Ltd.* (1980) V.R. 224 (Idea for a series of TV programmes).
3. *Caird* Vs. *Sime (1887) GLP 526, Abernethy* Vs. *Hutchinson (1825)* 3 LJ Ch 209 and *Micols* Vs. *Pitman (1884)* 26 Ch.D. 374 (Lectures delivered orally.)

COPYRIGHT AND THE INTERNET

Digital technology and new communication systems have made dramatic changes in our lives. Business transactions are being made with the help of computers. Business community as well as individuals is increasingly using computers to create, transmit and store information in the electronic form instead of traditional paper documents. Information stored in electronic form is cheaper. It is easier to store, retrieve and speedier to communicate. People are aware of these advantages but they are reluctant to conduct business or conclude transactions in the electronic form due to lack of legal framework. The United Nations Commission on International Trade Law adopted the Model Law on Electronic Commerce in 1996. India being signatory to it has to revise its laws as per the said law. Consequently, the Information and Technology Bill, 1999 was introduced in the Parliament and came into being as The Information Technology Act, 2000.

Copyright works of many different kind appear on the Internet *inter-alia* information on internet web pages—these might be artistic works, drawings, and design, business brochures, product specifications; information which can be downloaded from web pages such as music or computer software or literary, artistic or other works, computer software which is protected by copyright itself and which enables the software and systems to work; and postings to bulletin boards and newsgroups by individuals.

In India, though the IT Act, 2000 has been passed but Internet jurisprudence yet to emerge at par with the west. In England, all the information available on the Internet comes under the Copyright Designs and Patents Act, 1988.

The New IT Act empowers policeman to enter and search premises where they suspect a Cyber Crime is being committed or is being plotted. This is a carry over from the IPC with a tweak that only senior policeman under the Act—a Dy. S.P. can investigate Cyber Crimes. This is too draconian. Most of police officers are not well versed with the computer literacy. It is necessary that the government should dilute the search and seizure clauses so that raids can only take place after complaints are lodged and to make it mandatory for investigators to produce a warrant. This will limit investigator's powers.

Fair Use Vs. Theft: Napster Case

In a landmark judgement of *Recording Industry Association of America* Vs. *Napster*, 2001, the Court has issued injunction against Napster which acted as a felicitator by allowing swapping digitally compressed songs with one another by the user. The court found that Napster is liable for infringement of Copy Right. The brief facts of the case that Napster, accompany formed around a computer programme developed by a teenage college dropout news of the ruling immediately set-off a feeding frenzy as the service as millions of users tried to download as many songs as possible before the looming shutdown. The appeals court decision after four months in October 2 hearing in which the recording industry asked the appeals court to lift its stay on injunction ordered in July against Napster by U.S. District Court (SIC). The appeals court observed:

> "The District Court correctly recognized that a preliminary injunction against Napster participating in copyright infringement is not only warranted but required Napster may be held liable for the copyright infringement by its users to the extent that it knew of specific material and its system is failed to act to prevent its distribution."

The U.S. Court of appeals sent the case back to craft, a new injunction against Napster, that less Broad. It is unclear at the present time what the next legal step might be, but in the mean time, Napster continues to operate as before.[22]

Judge Beezer summarized the central features of the new decision by stating the following:

> "The district court correctly recognized that a preliminary injunction against Napster's participation in copyright infringement is not only warranted but required. We believe, however, that the scope of the injunction needs modification in light of our opinion. Specifically, we reiterate that contributory liability may potentially be imposed only to the extent that Napster:
>
> (1) Receives reasonable knowledge of specific infringing files with copyrighted musical compositions and sound recording;
> (2) knows or should know that such files are available on the Napster system; and
> (3) fails to act to prevent viral distribution of the works."

The mere existence of the Napster system, absent actual notice and Napster's demonstrated failure to remove the offending material is insufficient to impose contributory-liability.[23]

"Conversely, Napster may be vicariously liable when it fails to affirmatively use its ability to patrol its system and preclude access to potentially infringing files listed in its search index. Napster has both the ability to use its search function to identify infringing musical recordings and the right to bar participation of users who engage in the transmission of infringing files. The preliminary injunction, which we stayed, is overbroad because it places on Napster the entire burden of ensuring that no "copying, downloading, uploading, transmitting, or distributing" of plaintiffs' works occur on the system. As stated, we place the burden on plaintiffs to provide notice to Napster of copyrighted work and files containing such works available on the Napster system before Napster has the duty to disable access to the offending content. Napster, however, also bears the burden of policing the system within the limits of the system. Here, we recognize that this is not an exact science in the files are user named. In crafting the injunction on remand, the district court should recognize the Napster's system does not currently appear to allow Napster access to users' MP3 files. On July 28, 2000, the appellate court had granted Napster an eleventh hour stay, enabling the company to keep operating as before while its appeal is heard. Napster was appealing the July 26, 2000 decision by judge Marilyn Patel, U.S. District Court for the Northern District of California, granting the record industry's request for a preliminary injunction.

Napster's Legal Arguments

In response to Judge Patel's ruling, Napster had set forth a number of key legal arguments under US Copyright Law. In general, the company insisted that:

- Napster users are not direct copyright infringers, because they are either covered by the immunity granted by the Audio Home Recording Act (AHRA) and/or their use is a fair use; and
- Even if there is direct copyright infringement, the elements of contributory copyright infringement and vicarious liability have not been shown.

Specifically, Napster's attorneys set forth the following points in their briefs. . . .

The AHRA, Section 1008, immunizes all non-commercial consumer copying of music in digital or analogous form—

1. The district court erred in concluding that generalized knowledge is that is required under the contributory infringement doctrine.
2. Under the substantial non-infringing uses exception set forth in *Sony* Vs. *Universal*, contributory copyright

infringement will be found if the product in question is capable of "substantial non-infringement."

(a) Millions of authorized uses of Napster, by tens of thousands of artists, render Napster capable of substantial non-infringing uses.
(b) Future authorization and sharing of secured files render Napster capable of substantial non-infringing uses.
(c) Space shifting of copyrighted music is a fair use.
(d) Sampling of copyrighted music is a fair use (and indeed helps increase sales of CDs).

3. Under the rules for vicarious liability, Napster neither has a specific right and ability to control or supervise direct infringers, nor does it have a direct financial benefit which depends on the infringing nature of the activity (cf. Fonovisa).
4. In addition, in cases where vicarious liability has been imposed, the direct infringer and the vicarious infringer were both commercial parties to a commercial endeavour.

Napster's Policy Argument

Many commentators have argued in favour of Napster on Policy grounds. Recurring contentions rely on one or more of the following points:

1. The importance and inevitability of peer-to-peer technology.
2. *Sony* Vs. *Universal* stands for the principle that you do not outlaw new technology before all the implications and potential uses of the technology can be ascertained.
3. Even if Napster loses, the technology—and the file sharing that accompanies it—will not disappear.

This highly publicized dispute has been documented in great detail in both the national and international media, and the ongoing developments continue to be watched very closely by internet stakeholders and members of the legal and public policy communities.

It is really a monumental decision in a sense that Napster is going to be relegated to the dustbin, but it is a real shot across the bow against other Internet sites that hope to profit without acquiring the rights to the content they hope to use.

The world's biggest record labels—including Vivendi, Universal's Universal Music, Sony Music, Warner Music and EMI Group Plc—who were involved in the suit against Napster have hailed the ruling.

COPYRIGHT IN COMPUTER SOFTWARE

Now these days Software is one of the most important technologies of the information age. Software is defined "as a set of instructions which when incorporated in a machine readable form is capable of causing a computer to perform a particular task." The definition under WIPO, draft model provisions for the protection of computer software comprises of three components:

(i) Computer Programme,
(ii) Programme descriptions, and
(iii) Supporting material.

"Software" is a general term for what is fed into a computer, whereas the machines themselves are known as the hardwares. Thus, the question of the extent to which proprietary rights may exist in computer programmes has becomes an important issue. But the U.K. Copyright Act, 1956 and its Indian counterpart, Copyright, 1957 and similarly the American Copyright Law prior to 1976 revision, were all silent on the question of computers probably as it were still days for computers. But 1994 Amendment has significantly changed the position. These changes are of particular importance to the computer industry in that a new "rental right" of computer programs has been created, the traditional fair dealing exceptions has been eliminated and radical new penalities have been imposed on users of infringing programs. India has a most stringent copyright laws in the world. The term 'literary work,' includes computer programmes, tables and compilations including databases. Section 14(a)(i). Copyright (Amendment) Act, 1994, which confers on the authors of a literary, dramatic or musical work, the exclusive right to reproduce the work in any material form including the storing of it in any medium by electronic means. This extend to computer programmes. As provided vide section 2(0) as provided in section 14(a)(i). The definition of 'cinematograph film' and 'sound recording' contained in Section 2 are also include 'digital' copies of such work. The law is crystal clear about the rights of licensee. A computer programme licensee does not have a right to lend on other wise transfer programme copy, unless authorized by the copy right owner. The Copyright Act, 1957 was extensively Amended in 1999 and covered a remaining gaps and make it ensuring compliances with TRIP's: WIPO copyright treaty, and WIPO Performances and Phonograms Treaty. (NASSCOM) and BSA has taken a case against two well known Computer Training Center in New Delhi, this is the first Anti-Piracy action against user. The settlement included the payment of damages to the BSA and an agreement to legalize all software used at the centers. The infringers also Provided and undertaking that they would not in future use, Copy, sell, offer for sale or deal in any NASSCOM and BSA members software illegally.

COPYRIGHT IN DATABASE LAW AND MORAL RIGHTS

Examples of databases on the Internet include alphabetical list of names and addresses and lists of hypertext limits and website addresses. Such collations of data may not be sufficient to amount to separate copyright works under the copyrights, Designs and Patents Act, 1988 where created after the EU Database Directive (96/9 of 1996) came into force. However, some databases created before that date did not benefit from copyright under the old English Law. But after 1 January, 1998 database rights were given protection under English Law. In India also these rights are protected under IT Act, 2000 and by 1994 Amendment of Copyright Act, 1957.

Database right is infringed if someone extracts or re-utilises all or substantial part of the contents of the database. Repeated and systematic extraction or re-utilisation of insubstantial parts of the contents of a database may amount to extraction and re-utilisation substantial part of the contents. But if an insubstantial part is taken, there is no infringement provided that database has been made available to the public.

There are no moral rights in computer software by virtue of Sec. 79(2) of the Copyright Designs and Patents Act, 1988 in Britain nor to computer generated works (S. 79)(2)(c). However, the appearance of the website is an artistic work in which moral rights exist. The moral rights can not be assigned but they can be passed on death to heirs of an estate under English Law.

REMEDIES IN INTELLECTUAL PROPERTY

"Ubi jus, ibi remedium" this the common lawyer's view that there is no right without a remedy, is particularly appropriate in the field of intellectual property where the intangible nature of the property means that protection of one's right by mere possession is much more difficult than in respect of most other forms of property.[24]

There are three[25] kinds of remedies against the infringement of copyrights discussed *supra*, namely:

(a) Civil Remedies.
(b) Criminal Remedies.
(c) Administrative Remedies.

Injunction, Damages, or account of profit, Delivery of infringing copies and Damages for conversion are civil remedies.

Imprisonment of the accused or imposition of fine or both. Seizure of infringing copies are criminal remedies.

Administrative remedies consist of moving the Registrar of Copyright to ban the import of infringing copies into India when the infringement is by way of such importation and the delivery of the confiscated infringing copies to the owner of the copyright and seeking the delivery.

A. Civil Remedies Against Infringement

(i) Anton Pillar Order

The procedural law always provides equal opportunities to both the parties to present their case. However, in certain cases court may pass an *ex-parte* order requiring the defendant to allow the plaintiff accompanied by attorney to enter his premises and make an inspection of relevant documents and articles and take copies thereof or remove them for safe custody. Such order is called Anton Pillar Order. It is also known as "Civil Search Warrant."

(ii) Interlocutory Injunction

Interlocutory injunction secures the immediate protection of copyright from an existent infringement or from the continuance of infringement or an anticipated infringement. A plaintiff may pray an interlocutory injunction punishing trial or further orders.

An interesting recent case, *Oxy Electric* Vs. *Zainuddin,* 1990, 2 All ER 902 shows that a plaintiff claiming an injunction is entitled to sit back and wait for trial and is under no duty to seek an interlocutory injunction in the meantime. The significance of this is that the defendant is put under pressure to desist by the pending litigation.

(iii) Damages on Account of Profit

A plaintiff can claim two types of damages viz., one for infringement of his copyright and the other for conversion of his copyrighted work into form.

B. Criminal Remedies

The infringement of copyright has been declared as an offence,[26] punishable with imprisonment which may extend for minimum period of six months to a maximum of three years and with a fine of Rs. 50,000 to Rs. 2 lakh. The power and scope of the remedies for intellectual property infringement means that the mere threat of proceedings can have a very serious effect on a potential defendant.

CONCLUSION

The experience of last around forty years shown that there is an urgent need of adequate information and awareness regarding the copyright law and ramifications of its infringements. There should be a empirical investigation and evaluation of the functioning of the office of the registrar and Copyright Board. Probable copyrights infringement must be assessed and out of court settlements must also be examined. There are certain problems in India with regard to copyright awareness such as ignorance of rights, problems of access to courts, absence of an organized copyright base and administrative red-tapism. These must be addressed in a pragmatic order.

Time has certainly come in India for a more mature appreciation of the fact that copyright law and justice are more than market and property. Aims of legislation on copyright should be to protect rights of intellectuals, jurists and cultural labourers who constitute the bedrock of India as a thriving nation. Moreover, the present IT Act has regulates e-Commerce over the Internet. In new millennium it is needed a law to regulate transaction in Cyber space without such a law, e-Commerce, e-Trading, Pirated goods, Copyrighted Material, and other economic transaction over the Net would have been open to fraud and infringement without the option of judicial redressal.

Efficient e-Commerce and e-Trading requires secure servers and digital signatures devices and algorithms that secure transaction against fraud. Yet in a climate of rapid technological change, no gimenack is proof against smart crooks and pranksters. So IT Act, 2000 should be enforced effectively is the only way to make the Internet secure against the Cyber Crime.

Notes and References

1. Vishwanathan, Aparna, "Beware of the New Copyright Act," *Computer Today*, Vol. II, No. 123 (1995), p. 116.
2. *Supra* note 1, p. 505.
3. *R.G. Anand* Vs. *Delux Films,* AIR 1978 SC 1613. Followed in *Manju Bhardwaj* Vs. *Zee Telefilms Ltd.,* (1996) 22 CLA 72 (MRTPC).
4. *Civic Chandran* Vs. *Ammini Amma,* 1996(1) KLT 608 (Ker HC).
5. *Gramophone Co. of India Ltd.* Vs. *Shanti Films Corpn.*, AIR 1997 CAL. 63.
6. B.L. Wadehra, Law Relating to Patents, Trade Marks, Copyright, Designs and Geographical Indications, Chp. 36, Universal Law Publishing Co. Pvt. Ltd. (2000), pp. 361-62.
7. (1964) 1 WLR 273.
8. (1857)3 K&J 708.
9. *Supra* note 9, p. 351.
10. *Govindan* Vs. *Gopalkrishnan,* AIR 1955 Mad. 391 at 393.
11. *S.K. Dutt* Vs. *Law Book Co.,* AIR 1954 All. 570.
12. *Supra* note 1, p. 529.
13. AIR 1978 SC 1613.
14. *Ibid.*, pp. 1631-32.
15. AIR 1978, SC, 1613 at page 1627.

16. *Hanfstaengle* Vs. *W.H. Smith* (1905) 1 Ch.D. 519, *Oliver Wendell Holmes* Vs. *George D. Hurst* (1898) 174 U.S. 82. *Machael* Vs. *Morethi People of the State of Illino*, (1960) 356 U.S. 947.
17. (1907) 210 US 339.
18. (1958) 355 US 907.
19. (1963) 2 All ER 16.
20. *D.C. Bureau* Vs. *United Concern*, AIR 1967 Mad. 381.
21. (1995) PTC 85.
22. Prof. S.K. Verma, Director, Indian Law Institute, Delhi, Liability of Internet Service Providers (ISPs).
23. See for detailed study Charu Mathur Copyrights of Multimedia Products on the Internet. Protection and Enforcement at p. 17.
24. Prof. Richard Taylor, Lancashire Polytechnic, Lancashire, U.K., a Seminar on IPR Teaching at Delhi, Oct. 21 to 25, 1991.
25. *Supra* note 9, p. 376.
26. Section 63 of Copyright Act, 1957.

Compatibility of Enforcement Measures of Copyright Act with the TRIPS Agreement*

K.C. JOSHI

INTRODUCTION

The disastrous effect of Second World War on the United Kingdom and its allies as well as on the United States of America was responsible for the negotiation of the General Agreement on Tariffs and Trade (GATT). It was a multilateral agreement which envisaged the establishment of an International Trade Organization (ITO). This organization, however, could not be established because the United States Congress did not approve of it. Therefore, GATT was negotiated as an interim arrangement in 1947 but it continued with success for more than four decades

* Paper presented in National Seminar on 'New Dimension of Human Creative Activities and their Protection under Copyright Law—A Human Approach', organized by Faculty of Law, Kumaun University, SSJ Campus, Almora- 263601 (Uttaranchal) on Sept. 10-11, 2005.

and in 1995, the World Trade Organization (WTO) was established. The WTO provides for the institutional framework for implementing the Uruguay Round Agreements, negotiating news trade rules and settling disputes between member-countries.

The WTO aims at developing an integrated and reasonable multilateral trading system comprising the GATT and Uruguay Round results of multilateral trade negotiations. Unlike the GATT, WTO in Article III provides that legal instruments and agreements are binding on all the members. The current WTO system operates under agreements negotiated during the Uruguay Round 1986-94. The Final Act of Uruguay Round was signed in Marrakesh on 15 April, 1994 and came into force on 1 January, 1995. It contains a package of about 60 Agreements, annexes, decisions and understandings including the WTO Agreement (Marrakesh Agreement) establishing the WTO, the GATT, 1994, other Agreements on services and the Agreements on Trade-Related Aspects of Intellectual Property Rights (TRIPs).[1]

INTELLECTUAL PROPERTY RIGHTS (IPRs)

Property has been closely associated with life and liberty. The Constitution of the United States of America provides that no person shall be deprived of life, liberty, or property, without due process of law and nor shall private property be taken for public use, without just compensation.[2] Bentham rejected the idea of natural rights yet accepted liberty, equality or property as components of greater happiness Locke also accepts private property through the concept of labour.

Similarly, J.M. Finnish supports the regime of private property.[3] It was socialism which proposed restrictions on private property and Marx believed that private property was a source of exploitation of labour[4] and denounced it. The devastation caused by war and untold sufferings of human beings ignited the human conscience and the Charter of the United Nations expressed great concern for human rights and fundamental freedoms. The new thinking, however, separated life and liberty from property. The Universal Declaration of Human Rights, 1948 therefore states:

Everyone has a right to life, liberty and security of person.[5]

The right to property has been recognized individually as well as collectively and there is a restriction that no one shall be deprived of his property arbitrarily.[6] The International Covenant on Civil and Political Rights, which is binding on the State parties in Article 6(1) recognizes the human right to life. The right to liberty and security has also been accepted.[7] But there is no mention of right to property. The European Convention for the Protection of Human Rights, 1950 affords protection to property.[8] The British Human Rights Act, 1998 follows this pattern.[9] The Uruguay Round has put the right to property at the central place. The TRIPS Agreement recognizes that "IPRS are private rights".

Property may be either tangible or intangible. Intellectual property means that property which has no tangible form but which represents the product of creative work or invention. The TRIPS Agreement does not give precise definition of intellectual property. It simply states that the term "intellectual property" refers to all categories of intellectual property that are the subject of Section 1 through 7 of Part II.[10] The categories of such rights mentioned therein are copyright and related rights (i.e. computer programmes and compilation of data, rental rights of performers, producers of phonograms (sound recordings and broadcasting organizations), Trade Marks, Geographical Indications, Industrial Designs, Patents, Layout Designs (Topographic) of Integrated circuits and undisclosed information.

India is a party to WTO Agreement. This Agreement[10A] as already stated also contains TRIPS Agreement which is in force from January 1, 1995. It, *inter alia,* lays down minimum standard for protection and enforcement of IPRs with a view to reducing distortions and impediment to international trade. The obligation under TRIPS Agreement relate to provision of minimum standards of protection within the Members legal systems and practices.

ENFORCEMENT OF IPRs

(a) General Obligations

Part III of TRIPS Agreement deals with the enforcement of IPRs. Section I provides that members shall ensure to make available under their domestic law effective action against any act of infringement of IPRs including expeditious and deterrent remedies to prevent infringements as is specified in Part III of

TRIPS Agreement. The decisions on merits are preferably to be given in writing with reasons. Such decisions are to be based on evidence in respect of which parties were given the hearing. Barring the cases of acquittals in criminal cases, the parties to a proceeding are to be given an opportunity for judicial review of final administrative decision[11]

(b) Civil and Administrative Procedures and Remedies

Section 2 (Part II) of TRIPS Agreement makes provision for civil and administrative procedures and remedies. The procedure must be fair and equitable. The defendant shall have the right to detailed notice and representation by an independent legal counsel. He will be exempted from mandatory personal appearance subject to the national constitutional provisions of the Member. Identification and protection of confidential information will be permitted. Further, subject to protection of confidential information, court shall be permitted to summon the relevant evidence in possession of the opposing party.[12]

Provision also exists for grant of injunctions to stop infringement of an IPR of imported goods. The judicial authorities shall have power to award damages to the right holder against the infringer. Such damages will also include other expenses incurred by the right holder including the attorney's fees.[13]

In order to create an effective deterrent to infringements, the judicial authorities shall have the power to order the disposal of infringing goods outside the channels of commerce in such a manner as to avoid any harm caused to the right holder. The materials and implements used in creating infringing goods are similarly to be dealt with. The infringer can also be asked to inform the right holder of the identity of third persons involved in production and distribution of the infringing goods or services.[14]

In view of the human nature it is not improbable that false cases may be instituted against the defendants. To meet such a situation Art. 48 of the TRIPS Agreement provides that adequate compensation shall be awarded to such defendants. The public authorities and officials, however, have been exempted from liability for actions taken in good faith in administration of IPRs.

(c) Interim Measures

The TRIPS Agreement in Section 3 of Part III makes provision for provisional measures to prevent an infringement of any IPR in particular for preventing the entry into the channels of commerce including imported goods immediately after customs clearance and for preserving relevant evidence in regard to the alleged infringement. In such cases the judicial authorities are bound to adopt provisional measures even without hearing the other party *(inaudita altera a parte)* where any delay is likely to cause irreparable harm to the right holder.[15] In such cases the applicant is required to give such evidence which may satisfy the judicial authority about his identity as the right holder and imminent infringement The applicant will also give security to protect the defendant and prevent the abuse of the process. Consequent upon preventive measures and, where the measures have been taken *inaudita altera parte,* the affected parties shall be given notice and a review will be undertaken upon the request of the defendant and, thereupon the provisional measures may be confirmed, modified or revoked. Subject to the member country's law the provisional measures will be revoked or cease to have effect if proceedings leading to decision on merits of the case are not initiated within a reasonable time subject to maximum period of twenty working days or thirty-one calendar days, whichever is longer. Where it is found that there was no infringement of IPR, the applicant be ordered to pay appropriate compensation to the defendant.

(d) Requirements Related to Border Measures

A right holder who has valid grounds for suspecting that the importation of counterfeit trade mark or pirated copyright goods may take place, can make an application in writing with the competent authorities for the suspension by the customs authorities of release into free circulation of such goods. Similar provision is also to be made by members relating to suspension by the customs authorities of the release of infringing goods destined for exportation from their territories.[16] A right holder making such an application will provide sufficient evidence in support of *prima facie* infringement of his IPR. The applicant may be asked to provide a security or assurance sufficient to protect the defendant and to prevent abuse. Where the custom authorities have suspended the free circulation of goods without the decision of a judicial or independent authority and the applicant has not initiated proceedings leading to decision on merits of the case within ten working days extendable to further ten such days and no provisional order has been passed by the competent authority, the owner, importer or consignee of such goods shall be entitled to their release on depositing a security sufficient to protect the right holder for any infringement.[17] These provisions may be made inapplicable to small quantities of goods of a non-commercial nature contained in traveler's personal luggage or sent in small consignments.

Criminal Procedure and Penalties

States, which are parties to the TRIPS Agreement, are required to provide for punishments for wilful trademark counterfeiting or copyright piracy on commercial scale. Such penalties shall include imprisonment and/or monetary fines sufficient to provide a deterrent equivalent to penalties applied for crimes of a corresponding gravity. This may also include seizure, forfeiture and destruction of the infringing goods and accessories used in the commission of the offence. Similar penalties and criminal procedure may be made for other cases of infringement of IPRs when they are committed wilfully and on a commercial scale.

INDIAN COPYRIGHT LAW

The invention of printing gave rise to book trade and necessitated protection of copyright. Copyright is the right which a person acquires in a work which is the result of his intellectual labour. The primary function of copyright law is to protect the fruits of a man's work, labour, skill or test from annexation by other people.[18] The first enactment in India the Copyright Act, 1914 was based on the British statute of 1911. Statutory recognition to copyright was given in England in 1709 by the Statute of Anne. After independence, the Copyright Act, 1957 (Act No. 14 of 1957) was enacted in India repealing and replacing the 1914 Act. The 1957 Act has been amended in 1983, 1984, 1992, 1994 and 1999 to meet the challenges of new technology and to conform to international standards and norms laid down by international conventions.

The principal global conventions relating to copyright include the Berne Convention, 1886 (as in 1971), Universal Copyright Convention, 1952, Rome Convention, 1961, Geneva Convention, 1971, Treaty on Intellectual Property in Respect of Integrated Circuit (IPIC), 1989 and the Uruguay Agreement, 1994. The TRIPS Agreement is an annex to the Uruguay Agreement. Besides the above, convention for establishment of World Intellectual Property Organization (WIPO) was signed at Stockholm in 1967 which came into force in 1970. WIPO is a specialized agency[19] of the United Nations. WIPO is based on Berne Convention for protection of copyright. To further strengthen this international protection of copyright, it has entered into two treaties in 1996. These are WIPO Copyright Treaty and WIPO Performances and Phonograms Treaty. A noval aspect of WTO is that it has linked intellectual property with trade and TRIPS Agreement containing 73 Articles[20] deals with it.

Part II of TRIPS Agreement[21] deals with copyright and related rights. The Berne Convention is the basic international treaty based on the principles of non-discrimination and national treatment. Art. 9 of the TRIPS Agreement specifically provides:

"Relation to the Berne Convention:

1. Members shall comply with Article 1 through 21 of the Berne Convention (1971) and the appendix thereto. However, Members shall not have rights or obligations under this Agreement in respect of the rights conferred under Article 6 *bis* of that convention or of the rights derived therefrom.
2. Copyright protection shall extend to expressions and not to ideas, procedures, methods of operation or mathematical concepts as such."

Art. 6 *bis* deals with what is unknown as author's moral rights and Sec. 57 of the Copyright Act, 1957 incorporates this right in Indian law.

India is a party to the Berne Convention and has ratified the TRIPS Agreement. An attempt has been made in this article to examine in brief the enforcement measures in TRIPS Agreement and the Copyright Act as amended up to 1999.

(a) General Obligations

Part III of TRIPS Agreement relates to enforcement measures. Such measures are to be provided by members which are required to be effective, expeditious and deterrent to prevent infringement of IPR. The members are obligated to provide procedures which are consistent with basic principles of fairness coupled with judicial objectivity

The copyright law of India (hereinafter referred to as Copyright Act) provides for three types of adjudicative procedures. There is a Copyright Board.[22] District Courts, Courts of Metropolitan Magistrates/Judicial Magistrate of Ist Class and the High Courts. The Registrar of the Copyright Board, who is Secretary of the Board,[23] need not possess legal qualifications. The members of the Copyright Board also have no prescribed legal qualifications *albeit* in practice most of them are appointed from the Union Law Ministry or State Law Departments. The Chairman of the Copyright Board however must be a person who is, or has been a Judge of a High Court or is qualified for appointment as a Judge of a High Court.[24]

(b) Administrative and Civil Procedures

Copyright Board and the Registrar of the Board are principal authorities discharging administrative and quasi-judicial functions. Except the Chairman of the Copyright Board, the Act does not provide for judicial qualifications of the Registrar and the members (not less than two and more than fourteen) of the copyright Board. The main function of the Registrar of the copyright Board and of the copyright Board is to grant licenses.[25] The copyright Board have certain adjudicative functions also. Thus, under Sec. 19A, disputes with respect to assignment of copyright are determined by the Board. Under this provision it can revoke the assignment of copyright and order for the recovery of royalty payable to the owner of the copyright. The Board can revoke the assignment "after holding such inquiry as it may deem necessary." Under Sec. 52(j)(iv), Proviso, if a complaint is made to the Copyright Board that the owner of sound recording has not been paid in full on being *prima facie* satisfied about the genuineness of the complaint, the Board may even pass an *ex parte* order directing the person making the sound recording to cease from making further copies. In case of resale share right in original copies, the share of the first owner is to be determined by the copyright Board and its decision is final.[26] The question of existence of a right or otherwise of share is also finally decided by the copyright Board.[27]

For certain matters, Registrar of copyright and the Copyright Board have been conferred powers of civil court,[28] when trying a suit under the code of Civil Procedure, 1908. Such powers are available for summoning and enforcing the attendance of any person and examining him on oath, requiring the discovery and production of any documents, recording evidence on affidavit, issuing commissions for the examination of witnesses and documents, requisitioning any public record or copy thereof from any court or office and other matters as may be prescribed. The orders passed by the Registrar of the Copyright Board and the Copyright Board are in the nature of a decree passed by a civil court and are executable in the same manners.[29] The Copyright Board is deemed to be a civil court for the purposes of Sections 345 and 346 Code of Criminal Procedure, 1973 for the purposes of contempt. Provisions of the Indian Penal Code, 1860 dealing with false evidence[30] and intentional insult to public servant sitting in judicial proceedings[31] are also applicable to the copyright Board.[32]

(c) Infringement of Copyright

Chapter XI of the Copyright Act deals with infringement of copyright. Copyright in a work is deemed to be infringed when any person without authority does anything to interfere with the owner of the copyright or permits for profit communication of the work to the public with knowledge that such communication constitutes infringement of copyright or makes for sale or hire or by way of trade, displays or offers for sale or hire or distributes for trade or to adversely affect the owner of the copyright or imports copies of work into India which infringe copyright.[33] The Supreme Court in *R.G. Anand* Vs. *M/s Delux Films*[34] has laid down test of infringement of copyright. If the reader, spectator or the viewer after having read or seen both the works is clearly of the opinion and gets an unmistakable impression that the subsequent work appears to be a copy of the original, it is a case of violation of copyright.[35]

(d) Remedies for Prevention of Infringement

The TRIPS Agreement envisages administrative, civil and compensatory measures to be adopted by Members. The Copyright Act provides for civil remedies in Chapter XII[36] and makes infringement of copyright or other rights conferred by the Act offences punishable with imprisonment and fine under Chapter XIII, and confers certain powers of civil courts on the Registrar of copyright Board and the copyright Board. It also lays down procedure for trial of cases of infringement and provides judicial machinery therefor.[37]

(i) Civil Remedies

As per Sec. 55 where copyright in any work has been infringed, the owner of copyright shall be entitled to all such remedies by way of injunction, damages, accounts and otherwise. The cost will be decided by the court at its discretion, Sec. 57 of the Act deals with author's special rights known as *Droit Moral* or moral rights of author. The Berne Convention (Paris Text, 1971) in Article 6 bis provides for such rights *albeit*, this Article does not form binding part of the TRIPS Agreement.[38] *Droit Moral* is independent of the author's economic rights and, even after transfer of the said rights, the author enjoys the right to claim ownership of the work and to object to any distortion, mutilation or other modification in relation to the said work, which would be prejudicial to the owner or his reputation. The author has the remedy of restraining or claiming damages in respect such distortion, etc. under section 57(1)(b) of the Copyright Act. The first case on author's moral right is *Manu Bhandari* Vs. *Kala Vikas Pictures Pvt. Ltd.*[39] In this case, there was a contract between Smt. Manu Bhandari, a reputed author in Hindi Literature and Kala Vikas Pictures Pvt. Ltd., Bombay whereby she sold the filming rights of her Hindi novel "Aap ka Bunty" for their film. The producer and Director of the Kala Vikas Pictures produced a motion picuture "Samay ki Dhara." The author alleging distortions and mutilation in her novel sought an injunction against the screening and exhibition of the film on the ground of Sec. 57 of the Copyright Act. Her suit was dismissed by the trial court and she appealed to the Delhi High Court. The case was heard by Justice S.B. Wad. When the judgment was ready for pronouncement, the parties informed the court that they have reached an agreement and the suit in the lower court and appeal in the High Court may be dismissed. But the Counsel of the parties requested the court to pronounce the judgment as there was no decision of any court of law on the interpretation of Sec. 57 of the Act.

The court has noted the importance of intellectual property rights which is "hallmark of any culture." "Quality" of creative genius of artists and authors determine the maturity and quality of any culture. Art needs healthy environment and adequate protection. The protection which law offers is thus not the protection of artists as author alone Enrichment of culture is of vital interest to each society. Law protects this social interest. Section 57 of the Copyright Act is one of such examples of legal protection. Sec. 57 lifts authors status beyond the material gains of copyright and gives it a special status."[40] Interpreting the scope of Sec. 57, the court held that it confers additional rights on the author of a literary work as compared to the owner of a general copyright. In other words, even after the assignment either wholly or partially of the copyright the rights under Sec. 57 remain in tact. It even overrides the terms of the contract of assignment of copyright. The contract of assignment is subject to the provisions of Sec. 57. The language of Sec. 57 is very wide and it cannot be restricted to literary expression only. Visual and audio manifestations are directly covered by it.[41]

Sec. 58 of the Act also provides that infringing copies of any work in which copyright subsists and all plates used or intended to be used shall be deemed to be the property of the owner. This meets the requirement of Art. 46 of the TRIPS Agreement to a better extent. Sec. 60 of the Act which provides for remedy of declaration, injunction or damages in cases of groundless threat of legal proceedings is similar to Art. 48 of the TRIPS Agreement.[42]

(ii) Criminal Procedure and Penalties

The TRIPS Agreement in Art. 61 states that Members shall provide for criminal procedures and penalties to be applied at least in cases of wilful trademark counterfeiting or copyright piracy on a commercial scale. Remedies available shall include imprisonment and/or monetary fines sufficient to provide a deterrent ... and shall also include the seizure, forfeiture and destruction of the infringing goods and of any materials and implements. . ."

Chapter XIII (Ss. 63-70) of the Copyright Act provides for criminal procedures and penalties. Wilful infringement or abatement of infringement of copyright is punishable with imprisonment which shall not be less than six months and may be extended to three years and a fine not less than fifty thousand rupees extendable to two lakh rupees. Thus, the parliament has prescribed both the lower and upper limits. The quantum of punishment was enhanced by the 1994 amendment. The object seems to make the offence of copyright infringement more serious. But the Delhi High Court in its 2001 ruling in *Siyaram Silk Mills Ltd*. Vs. *State*[43] compromised a case under Sec. 63 by applying Sec. 482 of the Code of Criminal Procedures, 1973.[44] The power of the High Court under Sec. 482 Cr. PC is in the nature of an exception. This inherent jurisdiction can be exercised in three situations namely: (i) to give effect to an order under the code; (ii) to prevent abuse of process of the court; and (iii) to otherwise secure the ends of justice.[45] The ruling in the *Siyaram Silk Mills*, seems contrary to the intention of the legislature as well as to the provisions of TRIPS Agreement, which forms part of Indian Law.

Sec. 64 confers power on any police officer not below the rank of Sub-Inspector to seize without warrant all copies of work and all plates used for making infringing copies of the work and produce them before a Metropolitan Magistrate or Judicial Magistrate of First Class. This provision is consistent with the spirit of Art. 61 of the TRIPS Agreement. The constitutional validity of Sec. 64 of the Copyright Act was examined by a two Judges Bench of the Rajasthan High Court in *Girish Gandhi* Vs. *Union of India*.[46] In this case writ petitions were filed in the Rajasthan High Court on the apprehension that police may initiate action against them under Sec. 64 of the Copyright Act which confers unguided and uncannalised power on the police. Being owner of video parlour, the petitioner might be harassed by the police. It was claimed that this section was hit by Art. 14 of the Constitution and was unconstitutional.[47] The court dismissed the petition on the ground that "until and unless, some injury is caused to the petitions, the petitioner cannot move an application under Articles 226 and 227 of the Constitution of India for issuance of writ only on the apprehension."[48] Nevertheless the court examined the constitutionality of Sec. 64 of the Act and found "certain guidelines and safeguards" in Sections 51, 52, 52A and

64(2) of the Copyright Act, which prescribe the procedure in seizing the material as per satisfaction of police officer.[49] It was concluded that Sec. 64 is valid and is not hit by Art. 14 or any other articles of the Constitution.[50]

(iii) Appeals

The Copyright Act also makes provision for appeals in Chapter XIV (see 71-73). Orders of the Registrar, Copyright Board are appealable to the Copyright Board and the orders of the later are made appealable to the High Court under Sec. 72 of the Act. Appeals from the order of the Magistrate made under Sec. 64(2) and decision of trial courts made under Sec. 66, are appealable to the court to which appeals from the court making the order ordinary lie.[51] Besides, any aggrieved party may involve the extra-ordinary jurisdiction of the High Courts under Art. 226 and of the apex court under Art. 136 of the Constitution.

CONCLUSION

The importance of IPRs is now acknowledged. India already had a law on copyright prior to independence which was based on English law of 1911. In 1957, the present Copyright Act was enacted by the Parliament. The information technology revolution and associated developments necessitated amendments in the law. Five amendments have been made in this Act till 1999. Establishment of WTO by the Marrakesh Agreement 1994[52] is a radical change in international trade. The WTO Agreement contains a package of about sixty Agreements, Annexes, Decisions and Understandings. Agreement on Trade Related Aspects of Intellectual Property Rights is an Annex to WTO Agreement.[53] IPRs have been linked with international trade and recognized as private rights. Under the provisions of the Agreement, Members are obligated to make their national laws consistent with TRIPS and other Agreements. India is a member of WTO and as such a party to the TRIPS.

The TRIPS Agreement *inter alia* provides for enforcement of IPRs. These enforcement measures are aimed at to provide effective actions against any act of infringement of IPRs including deterrent steps. The Copyright Act meets all the measures provided in the TRIPS Agreement and in certain cases of infringement of copyright and other rights under the Act it makes provisions for drastic punishments.[54] The judicial interpretation of the Act has also been in harmony with the intention of the law.[55] There are not many decisions of the courts on Copyright.[56] But the ever increasing and copious use of computer, internet and other electronic media is bound to develop the jurisprudence of copyright in India. Various amendments made in the Act since 1984 are pointer to this direction. It is expected that the enforcement process and procedures will stand the test of the time. The enforcement measures given in the Act are effective, equitable and controlled by judicial process as envisaged by the TRIPS Agreement.

NOTES AND REFERENCES

1. It is Annex. IC.
2. Const. of USA, Fifth Amendment and Fourteenth Amendment.
3. See, Lloyd's Jurisprudence 254, 120 and 140 (Fifth ed.)
4. *Ibid* at 973.
5. Universal Declaration of Human Rights, Art. 3.
6. *Id* Art. 17.
7. Art. 9
8. Protocol No. 1, Art. 1.
9. Wade and Forsyth, *Administrative Law*, 186 (8th ed., 2000).
10. TRIPS Agreement, Art. 1(2).

10A. See also Jayant Bagchi, *World Trade Organisation* (2000); Birnie and Boyle, *International Law and the Environment*, 697-98, 732 (First Indian ed. 2004), K.C. Joshi, *International Law and Human Rights*, Chapter 18 (2006).

11. *Supra* note 10, Art. 41.
12. *Id.*, Arts. 42 and 43.
13. *Id.*, Arts. 44-45
14. *Ibid.*, Arts. 46-47.
15. *Id.*, Art. 50(2)
16. *Id.*, section 4, Art. 51.
17. *Id.*, Arts. 53 and 55.
18. *Sulamangalam R. Jayalakshmi* Vs. *Meta Musicals, Chennai*, AIR 2000 Mad. 454. 463. Sec. 14 of the Copyright Act., 1957 gives an illustrative definition of copyright.
19. Under Art. 57 of the UN Charter.
20. As modified in April 1995; www@uspto.gov
21. Art. 9-14.
22. The Copyright Act, Sec. 11.

23. *Ibid.*, Sec. 11(4).
24. *Id.*, Sec. 11(3).
25. *Id.*, Secs. 31.31A, 32 and 32A.
26. *Id.*, Sec. 53A(2).
27. *Id.*, Sec. 53A (3).
28. *Id.*, Sec. 74.
29. *Id.*, Sec. 75.
30. IPC Sec. 193.
31. *Id.*, Sec. 228.
32. Copyright Act, Sec. 12(7).
33. *Id.*, Sec. 51.
34. AIR 1978 SC 1613.
35. *Id.*, at 1627.
36. Copyright Act, Secs. 54-62.
37. *Ibid.*, Secs. 63-70.
38. TRIPS Agreement, Art. 9, Part II, Sec. 1.
39. AIR 1957 Del. 13; see also, *Amar Nath Sehgal* Vs. *Union of India*, 19 IPLR 160 Del (1994).
40. AIR 1987 Del. at 15.
41. *Id.*, 16-17 paras 9 and 13
42. Clause (1), "Indemnification of the Defendant" provides for adequate Compensation for abuse of process by plaintiff.
43. 2001 PTC 600, comments in XXXVII ASIL (2001) 392-93.
44. Inherent jurisdiction of the High Court.
45. *Jandu Pharmaceutical Works Ltd.* Vs. *Sharaful Haque* (2005) Cr LJ 92 (SC). For details see, S.N. Misra, *The Code of Criminal Procedure*, 592-602 (Twelfth ed., 2005).
46. AIR 1997 Raj 73.
47. In *E.P. Royappa* Vs. *State of Tamil Nadu*, AIR 1974 SC 555, where the court held that Art. 14 also embodies a guarantee against arbitrariness.
48. AIR 1997 Raj at 85 para 26.
49. *Id.*, para 24.
50. *Id.*, para 26.
51. The Copyright Act, Sec. 71.
52. Effective from 1st January 1995.
53. Annex IC.
54. The Copyright Act, Secs. 63, 63A, 63B and 65.
55. Siyaram Silk Mills ruling, *supra* note 43 is an exception.
56. *Barabara Taylor Bradford* Vs. *Sahara Media Entertainments*, (2004) PTC 474 (Cal.), comments in XLASIL (2004) 397-99.

Evolution, Protection and Enforcement of Knowledge Based Creations—Some Issues*

PRITI SAXENA

INTRODUCTION

No doubt, one of the most developed species of the animal kingdom is, none else, but the human being, endowed by the nature with reason, intellect and knowledge. His intellect plays a crucial role in keeping pace with the time. Brain and brawn are the two sources of human being which can be considered the prime input in the production of knowledge-based creations, i.e. intellectual properties. This is the knowledge and ingenuity of human being that forms the very basis of development in science, technology and information of the nation. The skill and talent of

* Paper presented in the National Seminar on 'New Dimension of Human Creative Activities and their Protection Under Copyright Law—A Human Approach', organized by Law Faculty, SSJ Campus, Kumaun University, Almora, on September 10-11, 2005.

man has played a vital role in most of the progress that world has witnessed overtime. Therefore, the society (state) in its obligation to reward the human being for the product of his brain has provided certain legislative measures to protect the intellectual property rights including copyrights.

EVOLUTION

The very foundation and philosophy of copyright law or the moral basis of protecting the knowledge-based creations, is the maxim, *"thou salt not steal."* The law does not permit to appropriate what has been produced by the labour, skill and capital of another. An artistic literary or musical work is the brain child of the author, the fruit of his labour and so, considered to be his property. So highly prized by all civilized nations that it is thought worthy of protection by national laws and international conventions.[1]

The first international convention relating to copyright was the Convention of International Union for the Protection of Literary and Artistic Works which was signed at Berne on 9th September, 1886, and is known as 'Berne Convention'. This convention was modified in 1896 by the Additional Act of Paris and in 1908 a revised convention was concluded at Berlin. In 1928, the convention was replaced with modifications and additions by Rome Convention.[2] In 1948, the Rome Convention was further revised at Brussels, known as Brussels Copyright Convention. In 1952, under the auspices of UNESCO, a Universal Copyright Convention was formulated in Geneva, which was further revised in 1971 at Paris.

Besides these, there are several other international agreements on copyright protection. These are Rome Convention for the Protection of Performers, Procedures of Phonograms and Broadcasting Organisations, 1961, The WIPO Copyright Treaty, 1966, The WIPO Performances and Phonograms Treaty, 1966, The World Trade Organisation (WTO) Agreement on Trade Related Aspects of Intellectual Property Rights (TRIPS) 1994.

At national level, the English Copyright Act, 1842, was held to be applicable in India.[3] The Copyright Act, 1911, of England was extended to India but in 1914, Indian legislature passed Copyright Act and 1914 Act stood repealed. This Act of 1914 continued up to 1947,[4] thereafter, the constitution of India came into force in January, 1950 by virtue of Article 372(2), the Copyright Act, 1914 was 'adopted' though this was confined to that portion enacted by Indian Legislature.

In 1957, Parliament enacted Copyright Act. On the necessity of copyright law Krishna Iyer J. observed, "The creative intelligence of man is displayed in multiform ways of aesthetic expression but it often happens that economic system so operate that the priceless divinity which we call artistic or literary creativity in man is exploited and masters, whose works are invaluable are victims of piffling payments. World opinion in defence of human rights to intellectual property led to international and municipal laws, commissions, codes and organizations, calculated to protect works of art. India responded to this universal need by enacting the Copyright Act, 1957."[5]

PROTECTION

"What is worth copying is *prima facie* worth protecting"[6] may be the reason behind copyright protection. Indian Copyright Act, 1957, was basically enacted to encourage and protect authors, composers, artists of their rights from the apprehension of being stolen. As we know that intellectual property differs from other kinds of property. There is no certainty as to the value of intellectual property and how it is to be used. Neither this property can be locked up in safe place, nor can it be deposited in a bank. Due to technological advancement it is very easy to have an access to this property which is readily available, therefore, more easy to steal also. This, definitely, results in difficulty to protect the knowledge-based creations. To overcome the evils of commercial piracy, which is a big business today, the Act of 1957 was first amended in 1984. To give more teeth, two amendments were made in the Copyright Act, 1957 in the year 1994 and 1999. The 1994 amendment widened the area of protection to include Performers' rights, assignment of copyrights by authors and artists, protection of computer programmes, cinematography of films and sound recordings known as neighbouring rights. In 1999, the definition of literary work and the meaning of copyright relating to computer programmes, was amended with other insertions. But, this knowledge-based creation is not easy to protect, not in India but in the world, where there is hardly any country where pirated articles are not being sold.

The rapidly growing international trade makes it imperative that "intellectual property rights are properly recognized and managed in different countries of the world. National protection is no longer adequate to safeguard intellectual property rights which can easily be pirated or copied by nationals of other countries and exploited in their own market or even in international markets. International remedies for such infringement are necessary. The earlier conventions which are administered by WIPO and the provisions of TRIPS Agreement are a step towards such international protection of intellectual property rights.[7] In the field of copyright India is a signatory to the Berne Convention passed the International Copyright Order, 1958, which is now replaced by the International Copyright Order, 1991. It provides the same protection to nationals of member-states as its own nationals."[8]

ENFORCEMENT

The purpose of any law, passed by a competent authority is, its proper and meaningful enforcement, so that the very purpose, for which it is enacted, be fulfilled. The Indian Copyright Act is considered to be a very effective piece of legislation[9] providing also for remedies against the infringement of copyright. These remedies are civil, criminal and administrative in nature. Sections 54-62 deal with 'civil remedies'.[10] Sections 63-70 deal with various offences resulting in different punishments.[11] Section 53 deals with administrative remedies.

In a civil suit, injunction,[12] account of profits, damages and delivering the infringing copies to the copyright owner can be sought. Wilful infringement or abetment of infringement of copyright is a criminal offence under Copyright Act, punishable with imprisonment which may be from six months to a maximum of three years and with a fine ranging from minimum Rs. 50,000 to a maximum of Rs. 2,00,000. For repeated offence, the minimum punishment is one year which may extend up to three years and the fine shall not be less than one lakh extendable to Rs. 3 lakhs.[13] Criminal remedy and civil remedy can be availed simultaneously.

A sub-inspector of police has the power to seize infringing material without a warrant. Section 53 deals with administrative remedies, consist of moving the Registrar of Copyright to ban the import of infringing copies in India and transfer such confiscated imported material to the copyright owners. There is also provision for appeals against the order of Registrar, to Copyright Board and against the Copyright Board to the High Court.[14]

CONCLUSION

Though, various remedies are available under the Act to protect the owner of copyright against infringement thereof but we are lacking in the area of enforcement of copyright laws. The reason may be, either less understanding of existing laws or poor enforcement of legal provisions or lacunae in protecting rights. But whatever may be the cause, the position is not very good of a country, governed by rule of law, witnessing negation of law in the arena of intellectual property rights. The need, therefore, is to ensure a proper enforcement of existing law, which is, of course, most effective piece of legislation with sharp teeth, and to create awareness thereof. For this purpose some points may be appreciated:

- Police officials, conferred with the power of seizure etc. under the Act, should be given a periodical training so that infringement of copyright law may be checked and controlled properly. A separate wing in the police force be created amongst those officers having knowledge and interest in intellectual property laws.
- For judicial officers, workshops, seminars and symposia be conducted for latest developments in intellectual property laws.
- For all those concerned with intellectual property laws awareness program must be carried out so that they may be able to know what the law is? The media, magazines, newspapers may be helpful in creating awareness. Documentary pictures may be shown to inculcate Copyright Literacy.
- For teachers, at all level, compulsory training/refresher courses be organized on intellectual property laws

because one of the biggest area where this infringement is being committed, is teaching fraternity. They should, particularly be trained on the question of fact, as to how much or to what extent they can borrow from others' writings under *fair use exception* because they write research paper and articles in order to improve their *Bio-Data* for the purpose of their future/further promotions/elevations.

- For students, the knowledge of copyright is to be developed by incorporating a new topic as their course curriculum in the Research Methodology paper, because the research scholars in order to compile their thesis by collecting the work of other authors and copyright owners, (as their own) do not appreciate the line of demarcation—between *use and fair use*.
- Finally, copyright piracy is a world wide phenomenon, which not only affects creativity of authors but also denies them for what they are eligible under law (legitimate dues as copyright owner). For this separate machinery be developed, in the *era of specialisation*, to protect *human talent* under *copyright jurisprudence* which can fuel future knowledge-based creations.

NOTES AND REFERENCES

1. *Gramophone Co. of India* Vs. *B.B. Pandey*, AIR 1984 SC 667.
2. This convention provided that the instruments previously should continued to be applicable in regard to relations with countries which did not ratify the Rome Convention and that the countries on whose behalf the Rome Convention was signed might retain the benefit of the reservations which they had previously formulated.
3. *MacMillan* Vs. *Khan Bahadur Shamsul Ulama Zaka*, ILR (1895) 19 Bom. 557.
4. Till India attained independence on 15th August, 1947.
5. *Indian Performing Rights Society Ltd.* Vs. *Eastern India Motion Picture Association*, AIR 1977 SC 1443.
6. Paterson Justice in *University of London* Vs. *University Tutorial Press Ltd.*, (1916) 2 Ch. 601.
7. Intellectual Property Rights—The Indian Experience, Dr. Justice A.S. Anand (1997) 6 SCC J.S. 1 (in 1999, Indian Copyright Act, 1957 was amended to protect rights more effectively.)

8. The States so covered are the Berne Convention signatories, the Universal Copyright Convention Countries, the Phonograms Convention Countries.
9. Chapter XI, of Copyright Act, 1957, deals with Infringement of copyright.
10. Chapter XII, of Copyright Act, 1957.
11. Chapter XIII, of Copyright Act, 1957.
12. See, Interlocutory Injunction—*American Cyanamid K.C.* Vs. *Manufacturing Process Ltd.*, (1976) Ch. 55; Ethicon Ltd., 1975 A.C. 396; Anton Pillar and Mareva injunction.
13. The very object is liberalized by Delhi H.C. in *Siyaram Silk Mills Ltd.* Vs. *State*, 2001 PTC 600, see also K.C. Joshi, 'Compatibility of Enforcement Measures of Copyright Act with TRIPS Agreement', Paper presented in National Seminar on 'New Dimension of Human Creative Activities and their Protection Under Copyright Law—A Human Approach', organized by Law Faculty, SSJ Campus, Kumaun University, Almora, on September, 10-11, 2005.
14. Besides this the aggrieved party has, of course, extra-ordinary remedy under Article 226 of the Constitution of India in High Court and under Article 136 of the Constitution of India in Supreme Court of India.

Copyright vis-a-vis Societal Rights: The Indian Perspective of Social Engineering

D.K. BHATT

Human creative activities involving intellect and ingenuity play the most vital role in the all-round development and progress of any society. Creativity, however, relies heavily on the rich common heritage of prior works. Innovations do not bloom in an intellectual vacuum where access to knowledge is inhibited. Sir Issac Newton, expressing his gratitude to his predecessors said, "If I have seen further, it is by standing on the shoulders of giants." In science and art, revisiting, revising, reusing and transforming ideas from prior works is an age-old phenomenon. New works essentially draw ideas and inspiration from tens, even hundreds, of prior works. The original element of every new work, however, needs protection so that the interest of the creator or publisher thereof is not unscrupulously damaged. This necessitates recognition and protection of the intellectual property rights, viz., copyright and neighbouring rights of the authors, creators and performers through the mechanism of law. But the conferment of exclusive proprietary right on the author/creator/performer and/

or his publisher carries with it a risk of undue obstruction to the access of knowledge and information to the general society. According to great sociological jurist Dean Rosco Pound, the task of any law in society is "social engineering", that is, balancing and harmonizing of competing interests. In the opinion of another jurist Ihring, law does not exist for the individual as an end in himself, but serves his interest with the good of society in view. Any copyright law, therefore, involves a delicate balancing between the monopolistic proprietary interest of the author/creator and the society's interest in easy access to the copyright work. Whereas these rival interests inherent in the concept of copyright have received explicit international recognition in major human rights instruments as well as in treaties and declarations on copyright, the task of social engineering between the two competing interests is left to the national legal systems of individual countries.

The present paper traces the dichotomy between the human rights of the individual and those of the society inherent in the concept of copyright as recognized in the international instruments; supplements these with relevant provisions in the Constitution of India and humbly ventures to elucidate how the human rights of the society have been harmonized with the rival monopolistic human rights of the creator and the publisher in the (Indian) Copyright Act of 1957.

INTELLECTUAL PROPERTY RIGHTS AND HUMAN RIGHTS

The concept of intellectual property rights is basically concerned with individual rights of the creator of a work. However, it has been recognized universally that the intellectual property system ought to serve as an engine for the economic, social and cultural progress of the world's diverse populations too. It should thus be in consonance with human rights where it has interface with them, for instance, the human right to health, science and technology, access to knowledge in works of art and literature, non-discrimination, etc. As a matter of fact, all members of intellectual property treaties such as the *Berne Convention, 1886, World Intellectual Property Organization (WIPO) Convention, 1967*, and the *Agreement on Trade-Related Intellectual Property Rights (TRIPS) 1994* are also members of the principal treaties on human rights. There has been a growing consciousness towards the nexus between intellectual property rights and human rights in general and the likely impact of *TRIPS (Agreement on Trade Related Intellectual Property Rights)* on human rights in particular. The *Sub-Commission on the Promotion and Protection of Human Rights* of the *UN Commission on Human Rights* also adopted a resolution on 'Intellectual Property and Human Rights' in the year 2001, which reaffirmed the significance of the goal of realizing economic, social and cultural rights for every human person. The essential emphasis of any intellectual property law, e.g., the copyright law, is on the balancing of rights of the creators/authors with those of the society at large. Several international human rights instruments complement the intellectual property law in this regard.

Article 27 of the *Universal Declaration of Human Rights (UDHR)* provides:

(1) Everyone has the right freely to participate in the cultural life of the community, to enjoy the arts and to share in the scientific achievements and its benefits.
(2) Everyone has the right to the protection of the moral and material interests resulting from any scientific, literary or artistic production of which he is the author.

All these rights are considered to be universal in application, vesting in each person by virtue of his common humanity, and independent of their recognition in the municipal laws of different countries. As Art. 28 of UDHR states:

> Everyone is entitled to a social and international order in which the rights and freedoms set forth in this Declaration can be fully realized.

One of the most significant provisions recognizing the human rights inherent in intellectual property is Art. 15 of the *International Covenant on Economic, Social and Cultural Rights* (ICESCR). Paragraph (1) of Art. 15 of ICESCR recognizes the following rights of everyone:

(a) to take part in cultural life;

(b) to enjoy the benefits of scientific progress and its application; and

(c) to benefit from the protection of the moral and material interests resulting from any scientific, literary or artistic production of work of which he is the author.

It thus categorically recognizes the protection of moral and material interests regarding the literary, scientific and artistic works of the authors, while conceding right of the society in general to participate in cultural life, to enjoy scientific progress and application.

The *UN Declaration on Right to Development, 1986* enunciates:

> "The right to development is an inalienable human right by virtue of which every human person and all peoples are entitled to participate in, contribute to and enjoy economic, social, cultural and political development, in which all human rights and fundamental freedoms can be fully realized."[1]

The right to development is a right of communities as well as individuals and is addressed in the *Vienna Declaration of 1986*.[2] It seeks to promote the full realization of all human rights—political, economic, social and cultural—so as to improve the potentialities of the overwhelming majority of humans.[3] Since an encroachment or deprivation of economic, social or cultural rights tantamount to violation to human dignity—the right to development becomes an essential facet to the basic 'right to life'. Both these rights viz. to life and to dignity are key concepts in all human rights instruments adopted by the international community, beginning with the *Universal Declaration of Human Rights, 1948*. The right to development is more relevant to the developing and under-developed countries of the world as well as to the underprivileged sections of the people even in developed countries. In 1993, the *World Conference on Human Rights* established the 'right to development' as a basic human right when it proclaimed that human rights—both individual and collective—are intrinsically linked to the full realization of the right to development. The same conclusions were reaffirmed by the *World Summit for Social Development, 1995* at Copenhagen.

Thus, the concept of right to development as a basic human right signifies that all individual human rights should ultimately aim at and be subject to the larger societal right of development.

The major international human rights instruments, therefore, recognize certain societal rights relevant for the purposes of intellectual property laws and in particular, the copyright law. These might be summarized as follows:

- Right of every human being freely to participate in the cultural life of the community including right to enjoy the arts;
- Right to share in scientific achievements and to enjoy the benefits of scientific progress and its application; and
- Right of every human being and all peoples to participate in, contribute to and enjoy economic, social, cultural and political development.

THE BASIC CONCEPT OF COPYRIGHT

The conception of copyright is two-fold: economic and moral. From economic conception, copyright law rewards the creator with exclusive proprietorship over his work. The gamut of such economic right(s) pays for the creator's skill and labour as well as the investment that the entrepreneur has risked in producing and marketing the copyright work.[4] In today's world, regulation and protection of copyright has become a pertinent issue in international trade and exchange of books, periodicals, movies, computer software and database and other objects of copyright. There exist a global awareness to recognize the economic rights of the creator and publisher, and to modify municipal legal systems to embody adequate safeguards for protecting copyrights, so that the blatant unauthorized reproduction and piracy of copyright works might be curbed effectively. It is a known fact, both at the national and international level, those rampant violations of copyrights cost the authors/creators and publishing and producing companies billions of dollars every year.

The moral conception of copyright aims to protect the credit, honour and reputation of the creator/author. Every copyright work—be that a book, a record, a painting or a software—is a form of self-expression and a manifestation of originality. It is, therefore, an obligation of justice that legal systems should build effective bulwarks to protect the authorship, the credit for the expression and its originality, and the distinct reputation of the author/ creator. Art. 6 of the Berne Convention for the Protection of Literary and Artistic Works, 1886 acknowledges two moral rights of the author, namely, the right to claim authorship of the work and to object to any distortions, mutilation or other modification of the work which would be prejudicial to his honour and reputation.

INDIAN CONTEXT: RELEVANT PROVISIONS

The Constitution of India, which is the supreme law of the country, grants recognition to numerous civil, political, economic and cultural rights of the people. Of these, whereas certain basic human rights and freedoms are guaranteed under Part III thereof, under the rubric of Fundamental Rights, certain social and economic rights are embodied in Part IV under 'Directive Principles of State Policy' as non-justiciable but equally fundamental in the governance of the country. The Preamble to the Constitution of India outlines the grand objectives of the Indian polity in these terms to secure to all its citizens social, economic and political justice; liberty of thought, expression, belief, faith and worship; equality of status and opportunity and to promote among them fraternity so as to secure the dignity of the individual and the unity and integrity of the nation.

The fundamental right to freedom of speech and expression under Art. 19(1)(a) has been interpreted by the apex court to include the right to acquire information and disseminate it through any available media whether print or electronic or audio-visual. It thus includes freedom of the press and invalidates imposition of pre-censorship prohibition of disseminating or circulating one's views either orally or in writing or through audio-visual instrumentalities. The right to freedom of speech and expression includes the right to educate, to inform and to entertain and also the right to be educated, informed and entertained. It guarantees and comprehends the right of the citizens to know the right to receive information regarding matters of public concern. Thus, Article 19(1)(a) covers right of the creator or owner to publish, record, perform, translate, broadcast recite or adapt the work. Article 19(1)(g) guarantees to all citizens the right *inter alia* to carry on any profession, occupation, trade or business, subject to reasonable restrictions by the State under Article 19(6) in general public interest. The rights of the owner or his assignee under this article to exploit the copyright work financially are covered. Life and personal liberty are guaranteed to every person under Article 21 and the Supreme Court has declared that 'life' here does not connote mere physical or animal existence but a life with human dignity and all that goes along with it,"[5] i.e. which allows him to grow in all aspects—physical, mental and intellectual.[6] Similarly, prohibiting a person from writing a book of his choice without these being any law to that effect has been held to be unconstitutional[7] for violating 'personal liberty' of the author. The moral rights of the author viz. right to ascribe, amend, delete, withdraw, etc. are also covered by Article 21 of the Constitution.

Under the Directive Principles, Article 38(1) enjoins the State to secure and protect a social order informed with social, economic and political justice. Social justice equality and dignity of the person are cornerstone of social democracy. In the same vain. Article 39(b) obligates the State to secure that ownership and control of the material resources of the community are so distributed as best to sub-serve the common good. Here, the term material resources of the community is wide enough to cover all the nation wealth, not merely natural or physical resources but also movable and immovable properties.[8] Everything of value or use in the material world in material resource and the individual being a member of the community his resources are part of those of the community.[9] Obviously this cover intellectual properties including copyright and neighbouring rights. Article 39(c) envisages that the State should secure the operation of the economic system is a way not to result in the concentration of wealth to the common detriment. Thus, here the intellectual property laws are also required to leave amble scope for promoting social interests and not to result in individualistic monopolies.

The State under Art. 47 is obligated towards raising the standard of living of the people and the improvement of public health. The State while enacting or modifying IPR laws must therefore keep this basic duty in view.

The 42nd Amendment of the Constitution introduced the

innovative concept of Fundamental Duties of the Indian citizens in the Constitution. Thus, it is the fundamental duty of citizen *inter alia:* (i) to develop the scientific temper, humanism and the spirit of enquiry and reform, and (ii) to strive towards excellence in all spheres of individual and collective activity so that the nation constantly rises to higher levels of endeavour and achievement. Such developing of scientific temper and inquisitive spirit, and pursuit of excellence can be possible only if there is smooth access to existing knowledge and information to citizens. It, therefore, underlines the significance of societal interest even in intellectual property laws including copyright law.

India is a signatory to most of the major human rights instruments and has therefore an international obligation for the observance of the same in the country's legal system.

HARMONY OF INDIVIDUAL AND SOCIAL INTERESTS UNDER THE COPYRIGHT LAW IN INDIA

In India the Copyright Act, 1957 as amended upto date embodies elaborate provisions regarding the recognition and protection of copyright and its neighbouring rights. The original Act of 1957 followed the provisions of the *Berne Convention for the Protection of the Literary and Artistic Works, 1886* (to which India is a signatory), and the *Universal Copyright Convention, 1952.* In the course of time, certain modifications have been incorporated therein by means of amending Acts of 1983, 1984, 1994 and 1999. Consequent upon India signing the General Agreement on Trade and Tariff (GATT) and the later the World Trade Organization (WTO), the copyright law in India has been modified in consonance with the law in many developed countries.

First and foremost, the Copyright Act of 1957 grants exclusive proprietary rights to authors or creators of works such as books, films or computer programmes to control the copying or other exploitations of such works. Unlike other intellectual property rights, copyright begins automatically on the creation of the work[10] provided that it falls in the category of 'work' in which copyright can subsist[11] viz., (a) original literary, dramatic, musical and artistic works, (b) cinematograph films, and (c) sound recording; and that either the author is a 'qualifying person' or the work has been published or broadcast in an appropriate manner, in case of certain type of works, including literary works such as books and computer programmes, the work must be 'original' and must be 'recorded' in some form. Besides controlling the making of copies, the owner of copyright in a work has the exclusive right to control publication, performance, broadcasting and adaptations of the work. Apart from these 'economic rights', the author, director or commissioner of a work, may in certain cases, be entitled to exercise some 'moral rights' which include the right to be identified with the work and to object to distortion or unjustified treatment thereof. Where any of the various exclusive rights which collectively make up copyright in a work have been exercised without permission, civil remedies may be available to the owner or author. In certain cases criminal sanctions may also be brought to bear, principally where copyright is being infringed with a view to commercial gain.[12]

Insofar as the societal interest in uninhibited access to copyright works even in absence of the author's consent is concerned, the Copyright Act of 1957 in India also contains provisions for ensuring the copyrights to play a balanced role in the overall economic, social, educational and cultural development of the society. Sections 52 and 52(1)(aa) embody elaborate provisions enabling the reproduction of copyright work for certain public purposes in this regard, some of which may be epitomized as follows:

1. A fair dealing with a literary, dramatic, musical or artistic work, not being a computer programme, for purposes of private use including research, criticism or review.
2. Reproduction for judicial proceedings and reports thereof, or for exclusive use of legislative members.
3. Publication, reproduction or performance for educational purposes in certain circumstances:
   (a) Publication in a collection for use of educational institutions;
   (b) Reproduction by teacher or pupil in the course of instructions or in question papers;
   (c) Making maximum 3 copies for the use of a public library; and

(d) Reproduction of unpublished work kept in a museum or library for purposes of study or research.

4. Reproduction in newspaper and magazine of an article on current economic, political, social or religious topics in certain circumstances.
5. Publication in newspapers or magazines a report of a lecture delivered in public.[13]
6. If the copyright work is a computer programme, then making of copies or adaptation in order to:
   (a) Make back-up copies for protection against loss, destruction or damage;
   (b) Study or observe functioning of the computer programme; and
   (c) Make non-commercial personal use thereof.[14]

The Indian copyright law also recognizes grant of non-voluntary or compulsory licenses in pursuance of the *Berne Convention, 1886, Universal Copyright Convention, 1952, Rome Convention, 1961, Stockholm Convention Establishing WIPO, 1970, WIPO Copyright Treaty, 1996* and *WIPO Performers and Phonograms Treaty, 1996*. Under these treaties such licenses are:

(i) Confined to countries recognized as developing countries, only so long as those countries are ranked that way; and
(ii) Confined only to the translation and reproduction rights in case of author's copyright works and to the broadcasting and recording rights in case of performers' works.

Under the Copyright Act, 1957 Sections 31, 31-A, 32 and 32-A deal with non-voluntary or compulsory licenses in relation to Indian published and unpublished works and foreign works.

Under Sec. 31 of Copyright Act, 1957 where author of a published/performed Indian work refuses to republish or to allow republication/performance in public, due to which the work is withheld from public, the Copyright Board may grant compulsory license for its republication or performance. Under section 31-A the Board may grant compulsory license for publication or translation to any person on his application regarding unpublished work of an Indian author who is dead, unknown or untraceable. Where the work is not Indian, any person may apply under Sec. 32 to the Board for a license to produce and publish a translation of a literary or dramatic work after three years since its original publication if such translation is required for purposes of teaching scholarship and research. The license compulsorily restricts distribution of such translated work to India only, except where the work is translated in a language other than English, French or Spanish and such export, effected by the Government, is to NRIs or is meant strictly for teaching, scholarship or research purposes only. Almost similar provisions cover compulsory license to broadcasting authorities as well.

CONCLUSION

Free flow of ideas, knowledge and information is a *sine qua non* for a rich blooming of human creative and inventive activities in the society. The society has a benevolent interest in unobstructed access to knowledge and creative works that ensures participation in and enjoyment by all the peoples the economic, social, cultural and political development of the society. But the need for the adequate recognition and protection of the economic and moral interests of the author/creator in his work against unauthorized exploitation thereof by unscrupulous persons leads to the grant of monopolist proprietary rights to the author/creator of the work. These two rival interests, viz. social interest in free access and individual interest in proprietary monopoly have been duly been recognized in major human rights instruments such as the *Berne Convention, 1886* also grant recognition to this dual object of copyright law, namely, to protect author's interests in his work as well as to safeguard society's interest in easy access to all such works. The task of social engineering regarding these conflicting interests is however left to legal systems of individual countries.

From Indian perspective, the requirement for reconciling these competing interests also finds sustenance in our constitution scheme. Not only the Preamble enunciates the trinity of justice, liberty and equality coupled with dignity of individual as noble ideals of the Indian Republic, but numerous provisions in Parts III, IV and IV-A of the Constitution confer an overt or covert recognition to the individual as well as societal rights involved in the concept of copyright. Thus, Arts. 19(1)(a) and (g), 21, 38(1), 39(b) and (c), 47 and 51-A(h) and (j) lay down constitutional foundation for the moral or economic concept of copyright as well as for the distinct requirement of the social interest in easy access to copyright works aimed at securing social, economic and political justice.

The Copyright Act, 1957 aptly balances the competing interests of the author/owner/performer/creator with those of the society as it embodies multiple provisions both for recognition and protection of author/performer/publisher's copyright as well as for securing smooth societal access to copyright works so as to promote overall social, cultural, economic and political development. The Act also incorporates special provisions in relation to translation and reproduction of foreign copyright works in India in pursuance of the *Berne Convention, Rome Convention,* etc. and in furtherance of the objectives of *WIPO* regarding its cooperation with developing countries. The amendments of 1994 in the Act have also brought it in tune with giant advances of information technology, which have revolutionized the collection, storage, processing, and exchange of information. The foregoing discussion establishes that the (Indian) Copyright Act, 1957 forges a fine balance between the individual rights *vis-a-vis* societal rights.

Notes and References

1. General Assembly Resolution 41/128 (1986), Art. 1.1.
2. *Ibid.*
3. Ahmed Aoued, 'The Right to Development as a Basic Human Right' in Lucy Williams etc. (ed.), Law and Poverty, p. 11.
4. Akolda M. Tier, Rights conferred by Sudanese Copyright Protection Act, 1974: *JILI*, 38 (3) at p. 331.
5. Francis Coralie, AIR 1981 SC 746.
6. *Shantisar Builders* Vs. *N.K. Totame,* AIR 1990 SC 630.
7. *State of Maharashtra* Vs. *Prabhakar Pandurang,* AIR 1966 SCC 424.
8. *Tamil Nadu* Vs. *L. Abu Kavur Bai,* AIR 1984 SC 326.
9. *State of Karnataka* Vs. *Ranganatha Reddy,* AIR 1978 SC 215, 250.
10. Sec. 17 of Copyright Act, 1957.
11. Sec. 13 of Copyright Act, 1957.
12. Dr. G.S. Karkara, 'Copyright of Intellectual Property', *Journal of the Legal Studies,* 2000.
13. Sec. 52.
14. Sec. 52(1)(aa).

Relation of Copyrights and Human Rights under TRIPS

RAM NARESH CHAUDHARI

It is a pleasure for me to present this paper entitled "Relation of Copyrights and Human Rights under TRIPS" in National Seminar on "New Dimension of Human Creative Activities and their Protection under Copyright Law—A Human Approach" organised by faculty of Law, Kumaun University, Almora (Uttranchal).

Copyright is one of the specie of intellectual property system which has been termed as one of the cornerstone of modern economic policy and may also be termed a catalyst for improvement of national trading capacities, i.e., economic development of the country.

Copyright law was passed in 1957 which provides for protection of literary and artistic works. This includes literary works such as books, short stories, poems, other writings, instruction mannuals, catalogues; dramatic works, including plays, films, scripts, scenarios and others intended to be performed such as choreographic works; musical works, artistic works including paintings, sculptures, engravings, maps, drawings, photographic works and audio-visual works including documentaries, television programmes, news reels, videotapes, videocassettes, etc. In 1984, computer programme were also included as literary works.

The latest amendment of the Indian copyright law was passed by Parliament on May 1, 1994; which came into force on and from May 10, 1995. This widens the scope of the Act too much.

Now, Copyright Act is one of the most modern copyright legislations in the world as it amends the earlier Copyright Act and modernises it covering with emerging new technologies. Items covered by the new law include, *inter alia,* satellite, broadcasting, digital technology, protection of computer programmes, modernisation of rules concerning Cinematographic films and Sound recordings. It also improves the protection of works of fine art; introduces new rights for performers of works and establishes new rules concerning the collective administration of rights.

Particularly after the amendments to the Copyright Act in 1994, India has no special problem with the copyright provisions of the TRIPS agreement. In several cases, the Indian legislation is more stringent that what is required under the Urguay Round. These provisions also imply better copyright protection in all members countries of the W.T.O. Since India is a major exporter of software, it should be in India's interests to have such better across the globe.

Ecocouragement of creativity in literary and artistic works, its protection through national copyright-legislation and the determined enforcement of such legislation in the face of emerging technologies, is an important contributory factor in socio-economic and cultural development and in encouraging, attracting and sustaining investment in what has come to be known as the cultural industry. This includes institutions and enterprises that undertake the production and distribution of educational, scientific and cultural material as well as that covering information technology, sophisticated high technologies, computer software and entertainment.

Copyright industry, another name of cultural industry which depends for its sustenance on an updated, modern, effective and well enforced copyright legislation. Copyright industry is growing rapidly in developed as well as in a number of developing countries.

Since copyright law covers mass media communication, including virtually all forms and methods of public communication, not only printed publications but sound and television broadcasting, films as well as computer programmes. This very much established the importance and utility of the act for the public at large and for the nation itself.

The core of this industry is book publishing, newspapers, periodicals, printing and publishing; advertising, radio and television, broadcasting, sound recordings, music and audio-visual works, motion pictures and films, and computer software and data processing industry. Most of each industries deal with the generation of new copyright material. The software and data processing companies deal both with the generation of copyright material and its application.

There are related non-core industries and institutions whose activities are in some measure copyright dependent. These include those industries that deal with the production of equipment or hardware needed for the use of copyrighted material (radios, television sets, computers, recording and listening devices, etc.) as well as the output of printers, binders, paper and printing machine manufacturers to the extent of their contribution to output needed for copyright industries and, of course, such institutions as libraries, theaters, etc.

These copyright industry represents, the fastest growing sector of the economy, creating considerable employment generation and having an increasing export performance and potential and in turn these industries may have immense contribution to the Gross National Product (GNP). So, economic importance of copyright and of the copyright industry is well established. The employment potentiality of the copyright industry is of great importance for any country. The Indian Book industry, which ranks amongst the top ten in the world. The Indian film industry the biggest Hollywood on earth. In recorded music India is a very major producer. The computer software (which is protected since 1984 as a literary work under the copyright law, is now one of the foremost in the world.

In a world of hyper-competition, how could and should be protect, foster and promote creativity in our countries particularly copyright-related industrial sector which has not only vast employment potential, but contributes substantially to socio-economic growth is a vital question. Now, technology is emerging as a valuable commercial or tradeable assets, and a dominant factor in determining international competitiveness.

Provisions of the Act require to be effectively and efficiently enforced effective enforcement helps national creativity and contains piracy. Piracy of literary and artistic works has to be sternly checked. Piracy of intellectual works in plain and simple theft. Piracy of cassettes, CDs and LPs has become common. Anti-piracy measures need to be directed not only of the person making infringing copiers but also those who are directly involved in the sale or distribution of such copies.

Encouragement of the following: facilitation of licensing, negotiated royalty payments, identification and reduction of obstacles, facilitation of access to copyright works under fair and reasonable terms, strict enforcement of protection for copyright works and tax incentives and remissions for author's works to be taken up with the governments as these will certainly be an incentive to creativity.

It would be appropriate to stress the need for institutionalised awareness-building with institutions for the purpose being set-up at national and/or sub-regional levels. It is essential, imperative and urgent that is intellectual property rights and their protection not only should a programme new culture be developed in business research and development and in University circles, but also that the mindset among the community at large be helped through awareness building.

We may utilize the intellectual property and copyright system for further sophisticated and qualitative growth in industry, trade, and overall socio-economic development and higher growth would help to tackle the problems of unemployment, poverty and deprivation in the country.

It calls for knowledge-based growth, greater concentration on and spread of education, requiring its own reservoir of scientists, technologists, inventors, innovators and creators who will constantly strive to produce tangible goods from scientific ideas and human creativity. It is the duty of national government and of societies as a whole to provide effective protection for such creativity the must rise to the occasion, we must think a new and act a new.

Copyright which is one of the constituent of intellectual

property is a legal right creation of human intellect is easy enough to grasp but difficult to define in a precise way since by its very nature it refers to property that is intangible. It encourages innovation and inventive activity. Legally, the right to property confers a right of ownership. In the context of intellectual property, this means a right to exclusive use of applications, of ideas and information that one of commercial value. It is, therefore, confers a right of ownership. So, copyright's owners have the right to exclude others from using the work without their authorisation. These rights are known as exclusive rights. It includes:

(i) Reproduction rights: copying and reproducing the work.
(ii) Performing rights: performing the work in public.
(iii) Recording rights: making a sound recording of the work.
(iv) Motion picture rights.
(v) Translation and adoptation rights.
(vi) Broadcasting rights.

These are known as economic or market rights, countries are required to comply with the provisions of Berne Convention, 1971. The Berne Convention makes provisions for non-economic, non-market or morale rights and protects authors even after they have transferred economic rights against distortions and acts that are prejudicial to their honour or reputation. Authors can also continue to claim authorship of their work, even after economic rights have been transferred. Preamble of the agreement on trade-related aspects of intellectual property rights requires the members to reduce distortion and impediments to international trade, and taking into account the need to promote effective and adequate protection of intellectual property rights.

Recognising to this end, the need for new rules and disciplines concerning:

(a) The provisions of adequate standards and principles concerning the availability, scope and use of trade-related intellectual property rights.
(b) The provisions of affection and appropriate means for the enforcement of trade-related intellectual property rights, taking into account differences in national legal system.

Part I contains general provisions and basic principles. Article 2(1) provides members shall give effect to the provisions of this Agreement. Members may, but shall not be obliged to implement in their domestic law more extensive protection than is required by this Agreement, provided that such protection does not contravene the provisions of this Agreement. Members shall be face to determine the appropriate method of implementing the provisions of this agreement within their own legal system and practice.

Article 7 in its objectives provides the protection and enforcement of intellectual property rights should contribute to the promotion of technological innovation and to the transfer and dissemination of technology, to the mutual advantage of procedures and users to technological knowledge and in a manner conducive to social and economic welfare and to a balance of rights and obligations.

Art. 8 provides principles; "Members may, in formulating or amending their national laws and regulations, adopt measures necessary to protect public health and nutrition, and to promote the public interest in sectors of vital importance to their socio-economic and technological development, provided that such measures are consistent with the provisions of this Agreement.

As mentioned above the Indian Copyright Act is one of the most modern copyright legislation in the world. The Copyright Law of 1957 was revised in 1983 and in 1984 to provide for enhanced penalties for infringement and against the piracy of works, as well as to protect computer programmes as literary works, in fact India was one of the first few countries to so protect computer programmes. Besides civil remedies for infringement of copyright by way of injunction, damages[1] and declaratory remedy,[2] there are penalties for infringement include imprisonment which shall not be less than six months, but which can extend to three-years and a fine which shall be not less than Rs. 50,000 but which may extend to Rs. 200,000.[3] There is also enhanced penalty on second and subsequent convictions with imprisonment for a term which shall not be less than one year but which may extend to three years and with fine which shall not be less than one lakh rupees but which may not extend to two lakh rupees.[4]

This new legislation which, in important respects, amends the earlier Copyright Act, not the least by modernising some of its sections which deal with emerging new technologies, is now one of the most modern copyright legislation in the world. Issues covered by the new law includes, *inter allia*, satellite broadcasting, digital technology, protection of computer programmes, where if modifies the definition of such programmes, modernisation of rules concerning cinematographic films and sound recordings. It also improves the protection of works of line art; introduces new rights for performers of works and establishes new rules concerning the collective and ministration of rights. The duration of protection has also been increased from 50 years to 60 years after the death of the authors.

Thus, this legislative back-up provides for fairly strong copyright protection. In many respects the new Indian legislation is well ahead of the provisions in the Agreement on Trade Related Aspects of Intellectual Property (TRIPS).

Notes and References

1. Article 55.
2. Article 60.
3. Article 63.
4. Article 63A.

Copyright: Remedies and Protection Against Infringement

J.S. BISHT

What is worth copying is *prima facie* worth protecting.[1]

The natural creative instinct inherent in the human psyche has always been a catalytic urge behind all the inventions, discoveries, innovations and original writings. The brawn of the brain has enhanced the rights' regime and a new right under the catalogue of 'intellectual property rights' appeared on the legal horizon. IPR is a concept and practice evolved by the industrialized western countries in 19th century to allow monopolistic ownership and control over intangible products. IPR may be defined as "property rights—intangible or incorporeal—covering all the creations, which emanate from the exercise of human brain" and are protected by a basket of legal rights developed by different jurisdictions. These creations of the author are recognized as "work" and includes within their gamut literary, dramatic and musical work, artistic work, cinematographic film, sound recording and computer programmes. These intellectual creations bestow various rights in the rubric of human rights on the creator. These are private rights entitling their public protection against their breaches. If these rights are not protected then the zeal of human efforts to create the new will be dampened, and the pace of progress and development will take a slow pace, if not to a grinding halt. Therefore, on the larger public interest and development, it is the imperative need of the hour that these economic and property rights be protected. This right emerging from the municipal field is the concern of international law and efforts to protect these rights on global basis have been realized with uniformity under the TRIPS Agreement. The State, having a welfare perception in the municipal law, is under an obligation to protect these rights as it does to protect the property rights of the individual.

CONTOURS OF THE COPYRIGHT

Copyright is not a single right but brings within its ambit a bundle of rights, which can be classified under various categories. The rights and rationale for their protection is as under:

(1) Economic Rights

The author is ensured of some financial gain by exploiting the economic rights inherent in copyright. These economic rights may be availed of as reproduction right, performance right, publication right, right to communicate to the public, cinematographic and sound recording right, translation, adaptation and right to claim ownership of the work, which result into monetary returns to the owner or a third person by way of assignment[2] or license.[3]

The authors are entitled to all these economic rights pertaining to literary, dramatic and musical works. The term literary work includes works expressed in writing or in print irrespective of the question whether their quality or style is high.[4] Writing does not mean that it should be contained in alphabets only but it includes codes, symbols, notations, numerals or combination of them, which are used as medium of instruction, computer programmes. What is required is not the merit of the work but the originality and originality connotes that the work has originated from the author and is the product of his intellectual labour and skill.[5] Thus, compilation,[6] abridgement,[7] translation,[8] etc. are derived from an original work also qualify for protection provided it involves the judgment, skill and labour of the author. The 1994 amendment to the Copyright Act, 1957 also includes 'computer programmes' within the definition of 'literary work'. 'Literay work' includes computer programmes, tables and compilations including databases. Author means a person who causes the computer generated work to be created. Thus, the author of the computer programme is also given protection under the Copyright Act, 1957.

The authors of celluloid works are entitled to make a copy of the film or recording, sell or give on hire or offer for sale or hire copy of the film or recording and to communicate the work to the public.[9] Cinematograph film has been defined as "a work of usual recording on any medium produced through a process from which a moving image may be produced by any means and includes a sound recording accompanying such visual recording and cinematograph shall be construed as including any work produced by any process analogous to cinematography including video film."[10] Similarly, a "sound recording"[11] means recording of sounds from which such sounds may be produced regardless of the medium on which such recording is made or the methods by which the sounds are so produced.

(2) Moral Rights

The Copyright Act protects the financial interests of the author as well as the moral rights,[12] which includes the name and fame of the author. The author enjoys societal recognition and respect for the contribution of his intellectual creations to the society, therefore, a third person should not be allowed to take benefits by distorting or altering the original work of the author. Such acts are prejudicial to the personality of the original author. The loss caused to him by alteration or distortion of his work cannot be measured in terms of money. Such special rights are called 'moral rights' in English law and 'droit moral' under the French law. Section 57 of the Act provides for these special rights independent of the economic rights during the subsistence of copyright.

Every author has a right to be ascribed with his work, therefore, a third person cannot ascribe his name with author's work. The author can restrain or claim damages for any distortion, mutilation, modification of his work, if such work is prejudicial to his honour or reputation.[13]

(3) Author's Resale Right

The value of paintings, sculptures, drawing or original copies of literary, dramatic or musical work lies in the original copy rather than in the number of copies and the value of this original copy increases with the passage of time. Sometimes these works are resold or auctioned at exorbitant prices but the authors do not receive any share in the profits incurred in the successive sales. Recognizing this fact, the civil law countries including Italy, France and Germany provide for an artist's resale right in unique works of art, such as paintings and sculptures.[14] This right which is known as 'droit de suite' is recognized by the Berne Convention.[15] This right enables the artist or his heir to get a proportion of resale prices. This right has been incorporated under Section 53A of the amended Act of 1994, which provides that the authors of the above said works if they are the first owners of the right or their legal heirs have a right to share in the resale price of the above even though such works are assigned. The quantum of share will be decided by the Copyright Board. However, the maximum amount of such share shall not exceed ten per cent of the resale price.

(4) Right to Prevent the Import of Infringing Copies of Work

Copies of a work made without the authority of the author are the infringing copies which will cause injury to the economic interest of the author. To safeguard this monetary interest Section 53 of the Act empowers the author to apply to the Registrar of Copyright to prevent the import of such infringing copies of the work. Supreme Court while clarifying the meaning of the term 'import' held that the term import as used under Sections 51 and 53 means bringing the infringing copies in India from outside and is not limited to importation for commerce only, but includes importation for further transit of the above work across the country.

INFRINGEMENT OF COPYRIGHT

Copyright is a right given to authors or creators of 'works', such as books, films and computer programmes, to control the copying or other exploitation of such works.[16] Infringement of a copyright is a trespass on a private domain owned and occupied by the owner of the copyright, and, therefore, protected by law.[17] Copyright begins automatically on the creation of a 'work' without the need for compliance with any formalities.[18] The only condition for protection which apply to all works is that the work must be of a type in which copyright can subsist.[19] In case of literary works such as books, the work must be 'original' and 'recorded'. The author or owner of copyright in a work has the exclusive right to control publication, performance, broadcasting and the making of the adaptations of the work.[20] The author has the exclusive right to publish the translation and no other person has the right to translate his works.[21] However, there cannot be a copyright in an event which has actually taken place. Ideas, information, natural phenomena and events on which an author expands his skill, labour, capital, judgment and literary talent are common property and are not subject of copyright.[22] If any of the various exclusive rights which collectively constitute copyright in a work is exercised without permission, civil and criminal remedies are available to the author or owner against such infringement.

Chapter XI of the Copyright Act provides for the measures against infringement of copyright. Copyright in a work shall be deemed to be infringed when any person without an authority does anything against the exclusive right of the owner of the copyright or permits for profit communication of the work to the public with the knowledge that such communication constitutes infringement of the copyright and makes for sale or hire, or by way of trade displays or offers for sale or hire, or distributes for trade to affect prejudicially the owner of the copyright or imports into India copies of the work infringing copyright.[23] According to Justice Kekewich, 'a copy has been defined as that which comes so near the original as to suggest the original to the mind of the spectator.'[24] It is always a question of fact that the court will examine the degree of resemblance[25] to determine the infringement. Infringement can be established if the published work is 'almost identical' and 'certainly deceptively similar'[26] to the original work. In *R.G. Anand* Vs. *M/s Delux Films*[27] the Supreme Court while laying down the test of infringement observed that 'one of the surest and safest test to determine whether or not there has been a violation of copyright is to see if the reader, spectator or the viewer after having read or seen both the works is clearly of the opinion and gets an unmistakable impression that the subsequent work appears to be a copy of the original'.[28] In order to be actionable the copy must be a substantial and material one which at once leads to the conclusion that the defendant is guilty of an act of piracy.[29]

REMEDIES AGAINST INFRINGEMENT

The Copyright Act under Chapter XII provides for civil remedies for infringement of copyright and under Chapter XIII for criminal remedies and declares infringement of copyright and other rights conferred by this Act as offences punishable with imprisonment and fine. The Act confers certain powers of civil courts on the Registrar of the Copyrights and the Copyright Board itself. The mechanism of protection of copyright in India has been devised in conformity with the TRIPS Agreement.

(1) Civil Remedies

According to Section 55 of the Act where copyright in any work has been infringed, the owner of the copyright shall be entitled to all such remedies by way of injunction, damages, accounts and otherwise. For the purposes of the section, the person (author or publisher) whose name(s) appears on the copies of the work as published shall be presumed to be the author or publisher of the work. Section 57 of the Act deals with the author's special rights christened as 'moral rights'. These rights can be claimed by the author ever after the assignment of the copyright and enjoys the right to claim authorship of the work and to restrain any distortion, mutilation, modification in relation to such work, which would be prejudicial to his honour or reputation. The section enables the author to claim damages in respect of any distortion, mutilation or modification. These rights, except the right to claim authorship, can be exercised by the legal representatives of the author. Section 58 of the Act entitles the owner to recover the possession of all infringing copies of any work in which copyright subsists and all plates used or intended to be used for the production of such infringing copies and shall be deemed to be the property of the owner. As such the owner is given a right to claim the possession of the physical material bearing the infringing work. Section 60 of the Act provides for the remedy of declaration by way of injunction or damages in cases of groundless threats of legal proceedings.

(2) Penal Remedies

Chapter XIII of the Copyright Act provides for penal remedies against the infringement of copyright and other rights conferred by the Act. The legislative scheme of the chapter makes infringement and abetment of infringement a penal offence punishable with imprisonment and fine. Section 63 of the Act provides that an offence of infringement or abetment of infringement shall be punishable with imprisonment which shall not be less than six months but may extend to three years and a fine not less than fifty thousand rupees and extending up to two lakh rupees. However, as a deterrent measure to prevent the recurrence in the offence, the parliament has constricted the judicial discretion in awarding the punishment, where on a subsequent conviction the court shall award the imprisonment for a term not less than one year extendable to three years and a fine not less than one lakh rupees extendable to two lakh rupees.[30] The computer programmes are also protected with the same measure of punishment except the lower limit of imprisonment, which shall not be less than seven days.[31] The Act confers power on any police officer not below the rank of a sub-inspector to seize without warrant all copies of the work and all plates used for making infringing copies of the work and to produce them before a Magistrate at the earliest. Any person having an interest may apply to the Magistrate for the restoration of the seized material to him.[32] The Act makes the possession of any plates for making infringing copies in which copyright subsists an offence punishable with imprisonment extendable to two years and fine.[33] Section 66 of the Act provides that the court may order the delivery of all copies of the work and all plates to the owner of the copyright irrespective of the conviction of the offender.

(3) Appeals

Chapter XIV of the Act provides for appeals against the orders of Magistrate, Registrar of Copyrights and Copyright

Board. An appeal against the orders of the Magistrate passed under Sec. 64(2) and Sec. 66 shall lie to the court to which appeals from the court making the order ordinarily lie.[34] Appeal against the decision of the Registrar of the Copyrights shall lie to the Copyright Board[35] and an appeal against the orders and decisions of the Copyright Board shall lie to the High Court within whose jurisdiction the aggrieved party resides or carries on business.[36] Writ jurisdiction of High Courts can also be invoked against the orders of the Copyright Board apart from the appellate remedy.

CONDITIONS AND EXTENT OF PROTECTION

The protection under the Copyright Act, 1957 is not subject to any formalities like registration of the work and deposit of the copy with the Registrar of Copyrights. However, certain minimum conditions are to be satisfied to bring the work under the protective cover of the law. First, it must be an original work. Secondly, the work must have been published in India. Thirdly, if the work is published outside India or is an unpublished one, the protection is available if the author is a citizen of India. Thus, the Act protects the work of an Indian author whether the work is published or unpublished.

Perpetual protection to a work is not granted by the Act. If the work is created by an individual the protection extends for the life time of the author and sixty years after his death. But if the work is created by an institution then the protection is available for sixty years from the date of the publication.[37]

The Copyright Act is territorial in operation but India's membership to Berne Convention and Universal Copyright Convention facilitates the Indian author to avail international protection on the principle of "national treatment". The TRIPS Agreement provides that members of WTO even if they are not party to the Berne Convention must comply with the substantive law provisions of the Berne Convention. However, the WTO members, who are not party to the Berne Convention, are not bound by the moral rights provisions of the Berne Convention.[38] Thus, the Indian work enjoys national as well as international protection.

CONCLUSION

The Copyright Act confers a variety of rights on the author, which is a sincere legislative attempt to protect his legitimate interests. At the same time public interest to have an access to knowledge as against the private interests of the author has also been envisaged to the noble cause of societal development, which does not amount infringement of copyright. But it is also necessary that the intellectual labour and skill of the author should be rewarded. India has a large market of pirated books, computer software, audio-visual discs and music cassettes causing recurring losses to authors, creators, owners, publishers and cinema industry, which depict as to how rampant is the infringement of copyright in India. This state of affairs reveal the inadequacy of penal provisions and half-hearted enforcement measures. Therefore, it is an urgent need of the hour that penal provisions be made more stringent to prevent the infringement and unauthorized exploitation of the precious economic and moral rights of the authors. Since information technology has taken a giant leap and the process of globalization and liberalization of economy has already commenced, therefore, in the impending future as a result of globalization, there will be an explosion in IPR litigation. The civil and criminal courts dispensing justice under the existing adjudicatory framework, already suffering from dilatory justicing, will fail in the docket management and quick disposal of IPR cases. To cope with this eventuality, it is submitted that special IPR tribunals should be constituted at the district and the state level with final appeal to the Supreme Court.

NOTES AND REFERENCES

1. Paterson, J. in *University of London Press* Vs. *University Tutorial Press*, (1916) 2 Ch. 601.
2. Secs. 18 to 21 of the Copyright Act, 1957.
3. Section 30 of the Act.
4. As per Paterson, J., *University of London Press* Vs. *University Tutorial Press*, (1916) 2 Ch. 601.
5. *Ibid*.
6. *Stasang* Vs. *Kiron Chandra*, AIR 1972 Cal. 533.
7. *MacMillan* Vs. *Cooper* (1923) 93 LJ PC 113.
8. *Collins* Vs. *Bond* (1927) 1 Ch. 167.

9. Sec. 14 of The Copyright Act, 1957.
10. Sec. 2 (f).
11. Sec. 2 (xx).
12. 'Moral Rights', 53 *Harv. L. Rev.* 554.
13. Sec. 57 of the Copyright Act, 1957.
14. M.E. Price, 'Government Policy and Economic Security for Artists: The Case of the Droit de Suite', *Yale L.J.* 1333 (1968).
15. Article 14 of the Convention.
16. G.S. Karkara, 'Copyright of Intellectual Property', *Journal of the Legal Studies*, 2000, p. 1.
17. *Bobbs Merrill Company* Vs. *Isidor Straus and Nathan Straus* (1907) 210 US 339.
18. Sec. 17 of the Copyright Act, 1957.
19. Sec. 13 of the Copyright Act, 1957.
20. *Supra* Note 16.
21. *Cherian P. Joseph* Vs. *K. Prabhakaran Nair*, AIR 1967 Ker. 234 at p. 235.
22. *Indian Express Newspapers* (*Bombay Pvt. Ltd.*) Vs. *Dr. Jagmohan Mundhara*, AIR 1985 Bom. 229.
23. Sec. 51 of the Copyright Act, 1957.
24. (1905) 1 Ch. 519.
25. *Mohendra Chundra Nath Ghosh* Vs. *Emperor*, AIR 1928 Cal. 359 at p. 360.
26. *Khem Raj Shri Krishna Dass* Vs. *M/s Garg & Co.*, AIR 1975 Del. 130.
27. AIR 1978 SC 1613.
28. *Ibid.*, p. 1627.
29. *Ibid.*
30. Section 63-A, The Copyright Act, 1957.
31. Section 63-B of the Act.
32. Sec. 64 of the Copyright Act, 1957.
33. Sec. 65 of the Copyright Act, 1957.
34. Sec. 71 of the Act.
35. Sec. 72 (1).
36. Sec. 72 (2).
37. Secs. 22-29 of the Act.
38. Article 9.1, TRIPS Agreement.

Computer Applications and Protection of Copyright

KAILASH CHANDRA SODANI AND SUNIL ASOPA

Today, protection of Intellectual Property especially copyright, on computer and related applications is one of the biggest problems. There are three main areas of computer applications in which it is very difficult to protect, especially copyright, that is:

1. Internet,
2. Software, and
3. Databases.

1. Internet

The Internet is a vast, fluid and boundless universe. Even though it is at an incipient stage, the net is becoming one of the most-favoured and convenient places to do business[1] because Internet is the largest and the most efficient mechanism for distribution of knowledge. It works on various computer programs or software developed specially for it. Internet has been understood as having a potential to change society in a revolutionary way. It is also place where is ever increasing threat of violations of various laws including intellectual property laws. Business activities over the net, popularly termed as "E-Commerce", are growing by leaps and bounds. Just half a century ago, nobody would have probably imagined something like the Internet and today it occupies a vital part of the world's economy.

2. Software

A Computer is essentially a series of electronic circuits that are arranged in various complex structures, so as to provide a high degree to function, though it needs requests from the operator. This method of communication is carried through a set of instruction, known as software. It is thus a series of command arranged in a structure or a language, which the computer will understand and translate into the actions that are required to produce a result that could be communicated to the operator. In other words, software is essentially a series of commands strong together in a language, which is understandable by the programmer or the operator on the one hand and which can be translated into a language understandable by the computer on the other.

To make the program effective, the sequence of commands must be physically stored on a portion of the computer that can be readily accessed by the processing unit of the computer. Thus, the program should be reduced to a physical form that is capable of being so stored. Most of these programs or software, more particularly those which are good enough to be commercially distributed are normally brought and sold in CD-ROM or floppies from where they can be downloaded to the hard disc of a computer.

Though these CD-ROM or hard disc are each tangible commodities that could be bought, sold and resold. The software embedded in these media is intangible and fall into a very different category. To ease out the tilings, let us take the example of the most common and widely used software WINDOWS. As a program, it is stored on a CD-ROM and sold across the shelf. The buyer can install the program by carrying out installation process by downloading the essential copies through various command routines from the CD-ROM. The buyer can, with the help of commands, use this program.

It is this simple procedure by which the buyer can install this program on other computers. Since the price paid for the software is actually the price paid for the intangible command routines contained in the CD-ROM. By reproducing, for the benefit of others without the payment of adequate compensation to the developer of the software would tantamount to profiting unfairly from the purchase of software. Here, we can say that this unfair downloading or installing may amount to infringement of certain rights of the developers and distributors. Since the software program is essentially an intangible item, it is safe to presume that the protection granted to other types of intangible products could just as easily be granted to the software programs.

3. Databases

Database as a concept has undergone a change after Internet has narrowed the distances for transacting businesses.[2] Databases were initially seen primarily as stored information, say in the form of share prices, details of employees, products and such other information.[3]

This information was restricted in terms of the number of persons who could get access to it and the holder or the proprietor of the information had a control over the information by and large.[4]

Today the term databases constitute data stored in the world wide web, CDs, multi-media products, networks and so on. Databases can be identified by two special features:

A. Accessibility to the data.
B. Speed of accessibility.

Accessibility of databases is no more limited to a few or a restricted number of people. Networking and eventually the Internet in itself has widened the horizon of accessibility of all the databases. Unlike earlier times when a document took days to reach the recipient across the country, it now takes a matter of few seconds to travel across the globe.

The result is that the volume of data processed every day as well as the number of people connected has increased. A wide range of material in a wider medium for propagation is being accessed or is accessible to a much higher number of people.[5] Both the quality and quantity of the data has gained a lot of significance with the development of knowledge sharing which evolved with the computer era.

Even Governments publish what at one time would have been confidential information. Hence data have become extremely important for all walks of life. The humongous information being created everyday has highlighted the need for protection of databases. On account of these reasons, adequate protection of databases has become very important.

The consequences of inadequate protection have been emphasized by various fact situations that have affected huge corporations. In order to provide such a protection, the first step is to analyze and arrive at the possible kinds of protection that can be provided. The object of such a protection is to ensure:

(a) that the owner gets his right to protect the data adequately;
(b) accessibility of data for all those who legitimately wish to use the same; and
(c) Prohibition of unauthorized use of data.

4. Protection of Copyright on Internet

Copyright is an intellectual property right that subsists in literary and artistic creations. However, the protection of this right is endangered over the Internet. Illegal and unauthorized distribution of copyrighted works on internet is the greatest grievance of copyright owners.

A copyright owner may place his work on the World Wide Web with the intention of sharing his creations with the public. However, that does not mean that people will not misuse his work or exploit his creations for personal economic gains. Furthermore, though copyright protection technologies such as encryption and digital watermarking are likely to prevent much of the infringement, they will not be able to preclude the "scanning" of hard copy images onto the Internet.

Moreover, it would be difficult and unreasonable for the Internet Service Providers (ISPs) and Online Service Providers (OSPs) to monitor all the numerous transactions and activities over the net. However, in several cases, when the ISPs and OSPs have encouraged or aided in infringing activities, they have been held guilty of vicarious or contributory infringement.

Courts are moving away from imposing direct liability on service providers. Courts scrutinized the conduct of these service providers through the theories of contributory and vicarious liability. These changes can be observed in the rulings of US Courts in several cases.[6] Furthermore, as indicated by the US Court in a leading case of[7] *MAI Systems*, the using of hypertext to link websites without prior permission or consent may also amount to copyright infringement. The Court of Session passed a judgement on similar line in a Scottish case.[8]

As the communication media over the Internet is vastly different from the normal methods to which copyright law is applied, several nations have amended their copyright laws in order that they may be applied to activities on the Internet.

It is submitted that there are many problems in protecting Intellectual Property on Internet. One of the problem is lack of concrete laws. Starting from commercial enterprises to professionals, all of them have started utilizing the Internet to increase their avenues and incomes. With the increase in business transactions over the Internet, it has become incumbent to have laws that will discipline these transactions and activities.

Another problem coming in the way of protecting copyright on the Internet is due to the difficulty in formulating laws for the Internet in the field of territorial jurisdiction. It is a well-recognized concept that laws on any particular topic govern the range of activities concerning that topic within the geographical limitations of a particular region.

Since Internet is a world without any boundaries or demarcations, therefore, activities over the net cannot be compartmentalized according to the country in which they take place. Thus, it would be troublesome to decide as to where the crime has taken place and which courts have jurisdiction to decide. Moreover, it would be impracticable to form an international law governing the Internet. It would be virtually impossible for the world community to arrive at a consensus on regulations governing Internet. The activities over the net are at a nascent stage, therefore, it is not possible to have a concrete set of rules to control them. Even if an international law is formed, several countries will not have the capacity to enforce the newly formed law and that would result in an ineffective implementation.[9]

The first step taken in this direction was by the United Nations Commission on International Trade Law (UNCITRAL) in drafting a model law on Electronic Commerce in December 1996. This model law has become the basis for the adoption of cyber laws by individual countries. However, due to the lack of any other concrete laws, the Internet has become a breeding ground for several crimes most of them related to intellectual property rights, namely, copyrights and trademarks. Activities over the net have greatly threatened these intellectual property rights.[10]

Keeping these vandalistic operations in mind, several countries are using and modifying intellectual property laws to curb cyber-crimes and regulate activities on the net Laws concerning copyrights.

5. Protection of Copyright on Software

Copyrights were originally developed to prevent unauthorized copying of printed text, graphics, and audio-visual recordings. Their protection has been extended to computer software, in part because the physical process of copying software is similar to copying text or recordings, and in part because the availability of patents for software was uncertain.

A copyright is easy to acquire. As soon as the employer or the employee creates something, either of them can own copyright to it. The distinction between what's the 'idea' and what's the 'expression' is one of the important question that hadn't been clearly answered for copyright protection of interfaces.

The copyright statute provides very little guidance, so the courts have to decide each individual case by analyse to previous court decisions, most of which don't deal with software. One principle is that court should rely on the functional part of the design qualify as idea not as expression.

6. Protection of Copyright on Databases

As we know copyright is the monopoly right that vests on an author or the owner of a material/literature to prevent copying by third parties of the work of the author. In databases, copyright vests as soon as a database or any data for that matter is created. The issue in question is the prevention of infringement of already available work or the unauthorized use of a third party's work.

In India, copyright is available in the form and for the substance of the matter. However, any person who makes infringement can intelligently change the arrangement of a pre-existing database and re-use the same material thereby avoiding the copyright law. Sec. 2(v) of the Indian Copyright Act, 1957, as amended in 1994, defines 'adaptation' in relation to any work as 'any use of such work involving its rearrangement or alteration'. Sec. 52 specifically states that:

> "the making of copies or adaptation of a computer program by a lawful possessor of the program to utilize the program for the purposes for which it is supplied is not an infringement."

It should be noted that the form and manner of adaptation in itself could be a subject-matter of a copyright. As per our laws today, compilations of data or documents, including materials from the public domain, can receive protection by a copyright if the creator of the compilation can show originality in the selection and arrangement of the data.

However, the author has to still prove originality in terms of the selection of the materials. The protection under copyright law is not necessarily the best form of protection. Today e-commerce being the major business generator, varied data are stored in the world wide web. The wide accessibility to information is the advantage but flip side is the misuse of such information for purposes other than for those for which it is intended.

CONCLUSION

It is universally acknowledged that the free and unrestricted exchange of materials and related data should be assured to all human beings.[11] However, the need was also felt for prohibition of unauthorized use and claim of benefits.

Many important civil law issues like the issue of jurisdiction and such other issues[12] also arise which could involve issues of privacy, issues of violation of local laws at national level and international level. The international opinions seem to favour the view that any protection so envisaged ensures that there is no restriction of certain non-commercial and important information. In modern society, question arises to what extent a person should be permitted to enjoy exclusive intellectual property rights concerning its exploitation?[13]

The Courts of the United Kingdom in various cases[14] have qualified cyber squatting activities as those under the tort doctrine of passing off. In a recent case, the Court of Appeal (UK) laid down that in a successful action of passing off, the Claimant must establish the following ingredients:

- There is a goodwill or reputation attached to the goods or services supplied by the Claimant in the mind of the public to the extent that the identifying "image" used by the Claimant is recognised by the public as distinctive of the claimant's goods or services.
- There is a misrepresentation by the Defendant leading or likely to lead the public to believe that the goods or services that are being offered by the Defendant are those of the Claimant, whether or not that misrepresentation is intentional.
- There is some likelihood of damage being suffered by the Plaintiff because of this misrepresentation.

Therefore, according to this explanation, cybersquatting activities may come under the purview of passing off. In such cases the remedies, which the aggrieved party has may either take the form of damages or compensation, injunctions (interlocutory or permanent) or both.

In some areas, the attempt has been made to develop new, specialized forms of protection.[15] In the fields of databases, where a European directive established a new form of right—the database right and semi-conductor chip design protection.

Inspite of various efforts at national and international platforms, the intellectual property rights are not fully safe on computer applications. With the advancement of technology infringement of IPRs has become rampant, therefore, much have still to be done in IPR regime for the protection of intellectual on computer applications.

NOTES AND REFERENCES

1. Law of Copyright: from Gutenberg's Invention to Internet, 1999, Butterworths India, 2000.
2. Law relating to Patent, Trade Marks, Copyright, Designs and Geographical Indications Intellectual Property Law Handbook, B.L. Wadharea, 2nd revised Edition, 2000, Universal Law Publishing Co. Ltd.
3. IT Encyclopedia—Parag Diwan, R.K. Suri, S. Kaushik, Ist Edition, 2000, Pentagon Press.
4. www.ipf.ai.mit.edu/links
5. Guide to IP in the IT industry, Baker and Mikangic and Robot J. Hort Snert and Maxwell, 1998, 1st edition.
6. *Religious Technology Center* Vs. *Netcom On-Line* (1995), *Sega Enterprises Ltd.* Vs. *Maphia* (1996) and *Sega Enterprises Ltd.* Vs. *Sabella* (1996).
7. *MAI Systems Corp.* Vs. *Peak Computer Inc.* (1993).
8. *Shetland Times* Vs. *Dr Jonathan Wills and Zetnews Ltd.* (1997).
9. IT Encyclopedia, Parag Diwan, R.K. Suri, S. Kaushik, 1st Edition, 2000, Pentgon Press.
10. The Law relating to Computers and The Internet by Rahul Matthan, Buttorworths India, 2000.
11. Protection of IP in India—Role of Courts, Rodney D. Ryder, 1999, 35 Corp. L. Ad. 93-97.
12. IPR in India, the next millennium, Naresh Kumar, 1999 (Ja) 32 Corp L. Ad. 50-58.
13. The Law Relating to Computers and the Internet by Rahul Matthan, Butterworths India, 2000.
14. *Glaxo Plc.* Vs. *Glaxwellcome Ltd.* (1996) and *Marks & Spencer and Others* Vs. *One in a Milion* (1998).
15. *Computer Law* by Chris Reed First, Reprint 2000, Universal Publishers.

Copyright-Cultivation of Mind: An Exclusive Human Right

NIDHI DEEPAK

INTRODUCTION

In the primitive ages of human culture there was not any recognition of copyright, but gradually it came to be recognized as such. Now-a-days copyright has become a very valuable right.

In ancient time creative writers, musicians and artists wrote, composed or made their works especially for fame and recognition rather than to earn money or any other kind of benefit or profit. Copying was a very laborious and expensive process. The concept of copyright protection was recognized only after the invention of printing press in the 15th Century. The task of publishing and republishing of literature and books, etc. in large number was made practicable by the invention. All of this led a great change in the society, and copyright has emerged as an important right. This gradual change has opened the door of new era, i.e. the era of copyright. According to C. Wilfred Jenks (in social justice in the law of nation):

"Change is the law of nation everything except of course the law of changes itself is subject to change. Law being no exception to this rule is inherently of dynamic character. Today the same trend is continuing with greater acceleration."

NEW ERA OF COPYRIGHT

Copyright is a kind of intellectual property the importance of which has increased enormously, and reason behind this is rapid technological development in the field of music, printing, and entertainment and computer industries.

The subject-matter of copyright is the work produced by the intellectual labour of a person that's why the copyright is a right to intellectual property of a person. Locke said.

"Every man has a property in his own person and also. *The man has the right to preserve his property,* i.e. the man has such human right to preserve or save his property."

In *R.C. Cooper* Vs. *Union of India,* AIR 1970 SC 564, it was quoted that,

> Property means the highest right a man can have . . . which does not depend on another courtesy; it includes ownership estate and interest in corporeal things and also rights such as trade marks, copyright patents. . . .

The jurists who propounded the contract theory of the origin of the state are in the opinion that the state and law come into existence only for the protection of the property. It can be deduced that the state is major component, which is highly responsible for any infringement of copyright, if the person is not aware or there is no such remedy available for prevention of violations.

The law of copyright in India is conferred and protected by the Copyright Act, 1957, but the present law of copyright was brought into force with large-scale amendment by Copyright Amendment Act, 1994, on May 10th, 1995.

The law of copyright gives protection to creative human generic including works of art and literature. This expression refers to an economic right vested in the owner. The economic rights include such rights, which have pecuniary value. Exploitation of the work by the exercise of these rights brings economic benefits to the owner of the copyright. The owner of the work may exploit the work himself or license others to exploit any one or more of the rights for consideration, i.e. to say that owner of the copyright in a literary, dramatic or musical work enjoys the exclusive right or to do authorize the doing of the listed acts. These rights are in his exclusive domain; it is a bundle of negative rights. These rights are negative right in the sense that the owner has a right to prohibit others not to do any such action with the work of the owner or it can be said that others can't do any of such acts without the permission license or consent of the person concern. The law does not permits one to appropriate to himself what has been produced by the labour skill and capital of another. The object of copyright law is to protect the author of the copyright from an unlawful reproduction because of his human right.

ETHICS OF COPYRIGHT—AN EXCELLENT PORTRAIT OF HUMAN RIGHT

It is too dangerous to compose any thing today, because there is no end of diversity. Slight modification in composition can be prove it to be the different one, and also there is much scope for improvement. There is Plato's seventh epistle that no intelligent man will be so bold as to put into language those things which his reason has contemplated. If he shows be betrayed into so doing then surely no the gods but mortals have utterly blasted his wits. However, there is increasing acceptance and tolerance in the knowledge sector that nobody may right the last word and if perfection is pursued as test, the writing would become scarce, knowledge shall flourish in the society only if it is shared. (Prof. Ashwani Bansal in his materials on copyright law).

Ars longa, vita bresis, i.e. art is long life is short. This is the human tendency to express himself in few words, composition, drawing, work of architecture, music, etc. Simultaneously this is the duty of the state to safeguard the art or expression from any kind of piracy or copying and to save them from the ghost of infringement of intellectual property right or copyright or his human right. What the words human right reflects. Human rights says the united nations could be generally defined as those rights which are inherent in our nature and without which we can't live as human being.

Human rights and fundamental freedom guaranteed by the constitution of India allows us to fully develop and use our human qualities, our talent and our conscience, and to satisfy our spiritual and other needs. These rights are based on mankind's increasing demand for a life in which the inherent dignity and worth of each human being will receive respect and protection.

Art. 19(i)(a) of the Constitution of India, 1950 also secure to every citizen the freedom of speech and expression, which means the right to express one's convictions and opinions freely by word of mouth, writing, printing, picture or any other mode.

A democratic government attaches great importance to his freedom because without the freedom of speech appeal to reason, which is the basis of democracy can't be made.

(V.N. Shukla's Constitution of India).

The infringement of copyright of a person leads to violation of his freedom guaranteed under the Constitution of India, 1950, i.e. freedom of speech and expression U/A 19(i)(a) along with freedom to practice profession U/A 19(i)(g). Simultaneously, the state enters into the liability for such infringement from the window. The human right of human being is big responsibility of the state. The copyright is one of the important human rights of the owner of the property.

The Constitution of India guarantees the vested substantive power to enact laws to recognize the creative process and to promote the progress of science arts by securing the exclusive right, as a resultant several attempt have been made like enforcement of Copyright Act. But it must be kept in mind that right claiming under Copyright Act should be in conformity with the provisions of Constitution of India, 1950.

The Copyright is a subject, which traverses, national boundaries. The government of several nations has entered into various Conventions and agreements. International treaties such as the Berne Convention for the protection of literary and artistic works and the agreements on trade-related aspects of intellectual property rights are the major International instruments in this regard.

The copyright and human rights are the same expressions or interchangeable expression. What a copyright secures to a person is same as secured by human right to him. Human rights are not only the rights but also an opportunity to live as a human being. . . A Soviet International scholar Vladimir Kud Kulrygulse stated that *Human rights are an opportunities guaranteed by the state to its citizen to enjoy the societal benefits and values existing in the given society.*

Human rights are birth right of people the world over. Hence, their fulfilment does not lie in the reproduction of institution of the advanced world, but on the consciousness in the developing world, to ensure the respect and protection of human right.

Prof. Edgs Boden Heimer said, "Law being the cement which holds the social structure together must intelligently link the past with the present without ignoring the pressing claims of future (Jurisprudence—the philosophy and method of law; Harward University Press, Cambridge Mass Achusells (1962, p. 6).

CONCLUSION AND SUGGESTIONS

Digital environment and technological growth has made it easy and cheap to reproduce the things, i.e. it has made piracy very simple and uncontrollable. This reflects that a copyright infringement unanswerable.

The origin and growth of intellectual property assumed its shape with the development of commercial relations in various branches of digital stage. Earlier intellectual property was known as "Vidyaa" they created their works for his soul's enjoyment and not for money or property and it was supposed to be a sin to sell the knowledge. Then the question arises why the copyright of person should be made protected. The gradual change in India answers, i.e. if their interests are not protected they would not find any encouragement for undertaking researches inventions, studies in their respective field or they will loose the cultivation of mind. To save this brainpower the copyright of human being must be safeguarded. To sort out this problem some suggestions are given below:

1. The knowledge of law of copyright is scanty. Neither the beneficiaries knows their rights nor the persons bearing the liability are aware about the necessity to pay for the work done so 1st of all some programmes must be held for causing awareness among them, like seminars, symposias, etc.

2. The subject matter of copyright lies in the entertainment industry, music cinematography. The soul of the work is its content and without appreciating the demand of powerful media not one can be able to give any assistance to original works.
3. The emphasis must be place upon the protections of copyright as well as intellectual property right not only in India but also outside the India, as Pirates copies of Indian movies, sound recordings and classical music of Indian celebrities has been sale in U.S.A. without any authorization of person concerned.
4. India has large film industry, software industry, India is much good in literary, dramatic or musical product, still we are lacking. The foreign rights holders are benefited due to loose Copyrights Act, i.e. the Copyright Act is in urgent need of amendment accordingly.
5. We the Indians are not in such a position to reap much of the benefits by Intellectual property rights protection, the Government has to expend the Intellectual Property Right system.
6. The role of Judiciary is much expedient to interpret the copyright in such manner as should be exclusively beneficial to the owner of property.
7. The relevant sector of intellectual persons needs to train; also there must be a separate legal framework to deal with copyright infringement.

Judicial Development and Interpretation of Moral Rights in India

SATISH CHANDRA

In material world, laws are geared to protect the right to equitable remuneration. But life is beyond the material. It is temporal as well. Many of us believe in the soul. Moral rights of the author as flowing from Section 57 of the Copyright Act, 1957 (which speaks of "author's special rights") are the soul of his works. The author has a right to preserve, protect and nurture his creations through his moral rights.

When an author creates a work of art or a literary works, it is possible to conceive of many rights, which may flow. The first and foremost right, which comes to one's mind, is the "Paternity Right" in the works, i.e. the right to have his name on the work. It may also be called the 'identification right' or 'attribution right'. The second right which one thinks of is the right to disseminate his work, i.e. the 'divulgation or dissemination right'. It would embrace the economic right to sell the work for valuable consideration. Linked to the paternity right, a third right, being the right to maintain purity in the work can be thought of. There can be no purity without integrity. It may be a matter of opinion, but certainly, treatment of a work which is derogatory to the reputation of the author, or in some way degrades the work as conceived by the author can be objected to by the author. This would be moral right of "integrity". Lastly, one can conceive of a right to withdraw from publication one's work, if the author feels that due to passage of time and changed opinion it is advisable to withdraw the work. This would be the author's right to "retraction". Except for the 'divulgation or dissemination right' which perhaps is guided by commercial considerations, the other three rights originate from the fact that the creative individual is uniquely invested with the power and mystique of original genius, creating a privileged relationship between a creative author and his work. This is the source of the last three rights and therefore, could be captioned under the banner, "The Author's Moral Rights."[1]

The significance of 'author's special rights' has been articulated by Prof. Upendra Baxi.

"The Act reaches out, in its solicitude for author's rights, even after part or whole assignment, and "independently of author's copyright" to confer upon her certain special rights. An author will have the special right to claim the authorship of the work as also the right to restrain, or claim damages in a situation where there occurs any "distortion, mutilation or any other modification" of the work and "any other action in relation to said work which would be prejudicial to his honour or reputation. This right is also made exercisable by the legal representative of the author."[2]

"AUTHOR'S SPECIAL RIGHTS" IN INDIA

Though our copyright statute is of British mould, we took a step ahead of Britain in incorporating Section 57 in the Copyright Act, 1957 and thereby giving recognition to moral rights of the authors.[3] The bundle of rights and remedies provided by Section 57 is in tune with the modern development in law relating to protection of intellectual property of author and the international agreements and treaties in this regard.[4]

Section 57 of the Copyright Act, 1957 as amended by Act 38 of 1994 runs as under:

57: Author's Special Rights:

1. Independently of the author's copyright and even after the assignment either wholly or partially of the said copyright, the author of the work shall have right—
   (a) to claim authorship of the work; and
   (b) to restrain or claim damages in respect of any distortion, mutilation, modification or other act in relation to the said work which is done before the expiration of the term of copyright if such distortion, mutilation, modification or other act would be prejudicial to his honour or reputation:
   Provided that the author shall not have any right to restrain or claim damages in respect of any adaptation of a computer programme to which clause (aa) of sub-section (1) of section 52 applies.
   Explanation—Failure to display a work or to display it to the satisfaction of the author shall not be deemed to be an infringement of the rights conferred by this section.
2. The right conferred upon the author of work by sub-section (1), other than the right to claim authorship of the work, may be exercised by the legal representatives of the author.

Section 57 speaks of "author's special rights". It does not speak of publishers or owner's rights. "Action prejudicial to his honour or reputation" within the ambit of Section 57(1)(b) is also referable to the author only.[5]

Under Section 57 the author shall have a right to claim the authorship of the work. He has also right to restrain the infringement or to claim damages for infringement. These rights are independent of author's copyright and the remedies open to the author under Section 55. In other words, Section 57 confers additional rights on the author of a literary work as compared to the author of general copyright. The special protection of the intellectual property is emphasised by the fact that the remedies of a restraint order or damages can be claimed "even after the assignment wholly or partially of the said copyright."[6]

Section 57, thus, clearly overrides the terms of contract of assignment of copyright. To put it differently, the contract of assignment would be read subject to the provision of Section 57 and the terms of contract cannot negate the special rights and remedies guaranteed by Section 57. This is a special provision for the protection of special rights of the authors. The object of this section is to put the intellectual property on a higher footing, than the normal objects of copyright. The language of Section 57 is of widest amplitude. It cannot be restricted to 'literary' expression only. Visual and audio manifestations are directly covered.[7]

Under the Copyright Act, 1957 no particular mode is prescribed to acquire special rights. The author of work inheres these rights independently of copyright in his work in which he has copyright. The special rights are inalienable but sub-section (2) of Section 57 permits the exercise of rights conferred upon an author of a work by sub-section (i) by legal representatives of the author except to claim authorship of work.

In substance, Section 57 confers two special rights in favour of the author of the work. Firstly, to claim authorship of the work and secondly, to restrain or claim damages in respect of any distortion, mutilation, modification or other act in relation to the said work which is done before expiration of term of copyright if such distortion, mutilation, modification or other act would be prejudicial to his honour or reputation.

One peculiar feature of these rights is that though they exist independently of ownership of copyright and vest only is respective authors, yet there can be no occasion for them to arise unless there is or has been a copyright in any particular work.[8]

INFRINGEMENT OF AUTHOR'S SPECIAL RIGHTS

This section (Sec. 57) provides an exception to the rule that after an author has parted with his rights in favour of publisher or any other person, the latter alone is entitled to sue in respect of infringement. The author retains the special right even after the assignment of the copyright. The principle underlying this section is that damage to the reputation of an author is something apart from infringement of the work itself.[9]

Although many authors complain of the distortion, very few have sought judicial protection. The Delhi High Court in the case of *Mannu Bhandari* Vs. *Kala Vikash Picture Pvt. Ltd.*[10] got an occasion to interpret infringement of author's special right as enshrined under Section 57 of the Copyright Act, 1957 after 30 years of the commencement of this Act. In this case,[11] plaintiff Smt. Mannu Bhandari brought a suit against M/s Kala Vikash Pictures Pvt. Ltd. and its producer and director. Kala Vikash had produced motion picture 'Samay Ki Dhara' under assignment of filming rights of the plaintiff's novel 'Aap ka Bunty'. Her complaint was of mutilation and distortion of the novel. She pleaded for permanent injunction against the screening and exhibition. Although before the court's decision, parties interested into a settlement agreement, the court passing the final order passed some important observations:

> "The court does not sit as a sentinel of public morals or super sensor in exercise of its powers under the said section. It cannot impose its own views (prudish or liberated) on sex or its depiction in the works of Art. The concern of the court is to examine how for the new 'avatar' is true and authentic and what changes are necessary due to constraints of a medium."[12]

It is pertinent to note that even the plaintiff preferred to settle her dispute with the defendant film producer out of court before judgement was pronounced by the High Court. It became, therefore, unnecessary to decide the dispute between them. The findings of fact and the directions in the judgement thereby became infructuous. Nevertheless, at the request of the parties S.B. Wad, J., delivered his "judgement", giving us the benefit of his considered views on the scope and applicability of Section 57.

Interpreting Sec. 57 (as stood before amendment in 1994) the court observed:

> "The words 'other modification' appearing in sub-clause (a) will have to be read *ijusdem generis* with the words 'distortion' and 'mutilation'. The modification should not be so serious that the modified from the work looks quite different work from the original."[13]

Dealing with the purpose and ambit of Section 57, the learned judge points out that the object of that Section is to put intellectual property on a higher footing "than the normal objects of copyright,"[14] lifts author's status beyond the material gains of copyright and give it a special status.[15]

Again a suit for the infringement of the author's special right under Section 57 (as amended in 1994) came before the court in *Phoolan Devi* Vs. *Shekhar Kapoor*,[16] where the plaintiff sought restraint order against the defendants from exhibiting publicly or privately, selling, entering into film festivals, promoting, advertising, producing in any format or medium, wholly or partially, the film 'Bandit Queen' in India or elsewhere. She (the plaintiff) claimed to be a public figure, rather a legendary by figure and contended that the basis of the film being a novel dictated by the illiterate plaintiff herself had been considerably mutilated by the film producer in their film bearing the title 'Bandit Queen'. It was held that from the documents or record it can not be said that plaintiff had consented and given licence to the defendants to make the film in any manner they like including exhibiting sexual abuse which has been shown in graphic detailed by the defendants in the film. It was observed:

> ". . . the defendants have no right to exhibit the film as produced as has been filed in this court violating the privacy of plaintiff's body and person. . . . No amount of money can compensate the indignities, torture, feeling of guilt and shame which has been ascribed to the plaintiff in the film."[17]

In *K.P.M. Sundaram* Vs. *Rattan Prakashan Mandir*,[18] the plaintiff and his co-authors entered into an agreement with the defendant giving them sole and exclusive licence to print and publish their works. The plaintiff claimed that the defendants mutilated and distorted the original works by publishing various looks in modified form. The defendants admitted the modifications made. The plaintiff revoked the agreement. It was held that with the revocation of agreement by the plaintiffs, no right was left with the defendants to continue to publish and sell in works. Interim injunction was also granted. Therefore, the moral rights remain with the author and are enforceable even if all the economic rights have been licensed or assigned.

In *Ganapati Prasad* Vs. *Parmanandi Saroja*,[19] the plaintiff claimed to be the writer of a TV serial. She objected the telecast of serial without referring the name of plaintiff as writer. The court held that it is not established that reputation of the plaintiff will be affected in such a case. Also it cannot be said that she would suffer mental agony or anguish. If ultimately the plaintiff succeeds in establishing that she got a copyright and due to the act of defendants there was infringement of her copyright, she can be compensated. It is not unreal for the writer to sell their stories for production for a picture or a TV serial. So she can be sufficiently compensated by way of damages if she succeeds the suit. Accordingly, the temporary injunction restraining the further telecast of the serial was refused.

The question whether author's special rights are independent of any contractual assignment of economic rights in an artistic work came up for consideration before the Delhi High Court in *Amar Nath Sehgal* Vs. *Union of India*.[20] The case involved a bronze mural, and acclaimed piece of artistic work, created by Amar Nath Sehgal, the plaintiff, for the Government of India for display at Vigyan Bhawan, one of New Delhi's prominent buildings accommodating many important public offices. The plaintiff had assigned his copyright in the mural to the Union of India, the defendant. In 1979, during partial reconstruction of Vigyan Bhawan, the mural was pulled down without the permission of Amar Nath Sehgal and dumped, impairing its aesthetic and market value and resulting in its dismemberment with part of the Sehgal's name disappearing altogether. Failing in his attempts to seek redress through written and verbal representations, Sehgal was constrained to file a suit seeking damages for infringement of his special rights or moral rights as embodied under Section 57 of the Act. The Union of India principally relied upon its unfettered rights as the copyright owners pursuant to Sehgal's assignment of the copyright in their favour. Rejecting the defence raised by the Union of India, Pradeep Nandrajog, J. held that the defendants have not only violated the plaintiff's moral right of integrity in the mural but have also violated the integrity of the work in relation to the cultural heritage of the nation.[21]

Furthermore, the learned judge passed four directions as under:[22]

(a) A mandatory injunction directing the defendants to return to the plaintiff the remanents of the mural within 2 week from today.

(b) Declaration is granted in favour of the plaintiff and against the defendants that all rights in the mural shall henceforth vest in the plaintiff and the defendants would have no right whatsoever in the mural.

(c) Declaration is granted in favour of the plaintiff that he would have an absolute right to recreate the mural at any place and would have the right to sell the same.

(d) Damages in sum of Rs. 5 lacs are awarded in favour of the plaintiff and against the defendants. If not paid within one month from today, the damages shall carry simple interest @ 9% p.a. from today till date of payment.

Nandrajog, J., made an important observation articulating physical condition of the mural when he pointed out:

> "I am of the opinion that the mural, whatever be it's form today is too precious to be reduced to scrap and languish in the warehouse of the Government of India. It is only the plaintiff who has a right to recreate his work and, therefore, has a right to receive that broken down mural."[23]

The learned judge, perceptively, held that authorship is a matter of fact. It is history. Knowledge about authorship not only identifies the creator, it also identifies his contribution to national culture. It also makes possible to understand the course of cultural development in a country. Linked to each other, one flowing out from the other, right of integrity ultimately contributes to the overall integrity of the cultural domain of a nation. Language of Section 57 does not exclude the right of integrity in relation to cultural heritage. The cultural heritage would include the artist whose creativity and ingenuity is amongst the valuable cultural resources of a nation. Through the telescope of Section 57 it is possible to legally protect the cultural heritage of India through the moral rights of the artist.[24]

It is highly significant that the learned judge has referred and relied upon India's Vision for Art and Culture (10th Five Year Plan, 2002-7); Convention on means of Prohibiting and Preventing the Illicit Import, Export and Transfer of Ownership of Cultural Property adopted by 102 State Parties on 14th November, 1970; Declaration of the Principles of International Cultural Cooperation proclaimed by the General Conference of the United Nations Educational, Scientific and Cultural Organization at its 14th Session on 4.11.1996; Convention Concerning the Protection of the World Cultural and Natural Heritage on 16.11.1972 and International Covenant on Economic, Social and Cultural Rights, 1966 and reminded the Government of India of their minimum obligations, India being a signatory to aforesaid Conventions. Further, the learned judge has relied upon the decision in *Vishaka & Ors.* Vs. *State of Rajasthan,*[25] when the Supreme Court read International Conventions not being inconsistent with our laws to interpret the guarantee of gender equality under our Constitution and in the absence of domestic law occupying the field, formulated guidelines.

It is submitted that this is indeed a very major and welcome enunciation of the protection of moral rights both in its rationale and provenance. This division, further, assumes significance for the fact that it is the first time that an Indian High Court has dealt with the moral rights of the author of an artistic work.

To conclude, it may be observed that the Indian High Courts have interpreted Section 57 in ways which redeem the Indian law of Copyright as an authentic protector of the author's moral stature and let us hope the present trend will be followed by all other High Courts in the country.

EXCEPTIONS OF THE INFRINGEMENT

Section 57 itself provides the exception to the special rights of the author. By amending Act 38 of 1994 a significant change was made in Section 57 when by substituting old sub-section (1) a proviso was added to it which reads that the author shall not have any right to restrain or claim damages in respect of any adaptation of a computer programme to which clause (aa) of sub-section (1) of Section 52 applies. The said clause (aa) which was inserted by Act 38 of 1994 reads as under:

(aa) The making of copies or adaptation of a computer programme by the lawful possessor of a copy of such computer programme, from such copy:

(i) in order to utilize the computer programme for purpose of which it was supplied; or

(ii) to make back-up copies purely as a temporary protection against loss, destruction or damages in order only to utilize the computer programme for the purpose for which it was supplied.

Also, the explanation appended to sub-section (1) of Section 57 serves as a saving provision, stating that failure to display the work or failure to display the work to the satisfaction of author shall not be deemed to be an infringement of the rights conferred by this section.[26]

Further, if an employee is paid for his work during the employment he cannot claim special rights in those works as he has no copyright in such work.

Notes and References

1. Vide opinion of Mr. Justice Pradeep Nandrajog in *Amar Nath Sehgal* Vs. *Union of India*, 2005(30) PTC 253 (Del.) at 260-61.
2. Upendra Baxi, "Copyright Law and Justice in India", J.I.L.I., 1986 at 523.
3. Surendra Yadava, "Moral Rights in Copyright Law of India", *Id.* at p. 61.
4. *Smt. Mannu Bhandari* Vs. *Kala Vikash Pictures Pvt. Ltd.*, AIR 1987 Del. 13 at p. 16.
5. *Wiley Eastern Ltd.* Vs. *Indian Institute of Management*, 1995 PTR 53.
6. *Smt. Mannu Bhandari* Vs. *Kala Vikash Pictures Pvt. Ltd., supra* n. 1513 at pp. 15-16.
7. *Ibid.*
8. Iyengar's, "*The Copyright Act, 1957,*" (6th Ed.), New Delhi, Butterworths India, 2000 at p. 11.
9. Anurag K. Agrawal, "*Moral Rights in Copyright Law*", (2003) 8 SCC (J) at 3.
10. AIR 1987 Del. 13.
11. *Ibid.*
12. *Id.*, at p. 19.
13. *Id.*, at p. 16.
14. *Ibid.*
15. *Ibid.*
16. 1995 PTC Del.
17. *Ibid*
18. AIR 1983 Del. 461.
19. 1990 (1) Andh. L.T. 624, at pp. 629-30.
20. 2004(30) PTC 253 (Del.)

21. *Ibid*, at 268.
22. *Ibid*.
23. *Ibid*.
24. *Ibid*., at 263.
25. (1997) 6 SCC 241.
26. Iyengar's *supra* n. 8 at p. 491.

Creative Activities and their Protection under Copyright in Fine Arts

SHEKHAR CHANDRA JOSHI

Copyright and neighbouring rights are essential to human creativity, by giving creators incentives in the form of recognition and fair economic rewards. Under this system of right, creators are assured that their works can be disseminated without fear of unauthorized copying or piracy. This in turn helps increase access to and enhances the enjoyment of art, culture, knowledge and entertainment all over the world.

First of all, I would like to share with you a question on copyright first raised in my mind long back when I was studying in Intermediate. One of my paintings was exhibited by my younger sister. She wrote her name cutting or removing my signature from the paintings which I painted in early school days. These paintings were copied by me from calendars. Nevertheless I could not excuse her until I could understand the importance of the signature put on any creative work done by the artist.

It shows that there may be several examples that need the protection of their work of art under copyright. Although all work is copyrighted at the moment of creation, not all work is protected equally. Every artist is worried about duplicity without having sufficient copyright. It is presumed that due to inadequate knowledge of the protection of creators' rights and its copyright regarding unauthorized copying or piracy of their creativity in fine arts there is a need to bring out the truth and facts in general. The present paper highlights these aspects with sufficient examples and suggestions including the major safety points towards the production of creators' human rights under copy right law.

Recently I experienced great joy in giving the copyright to Lalit Kala Akademi, New Delhi of one of my oil paintings entitled "Uttarakhand ka Sangharsh" when it was purchased by them for Rupees four thousand in the year 1996. Unfortunately, I don't have any copyright with me for the same painting that could be a matter of pride for me in the future. Many artists sell their work of art in hurry without thinking of the future prospects. So there is a trend to buy the work of artists in their early stages to get big prices after a long period.

The kinds of works covered by copyright in the field of fine arts are drawings, paintings, sculptures, architectures, music, dances and plays, etc., the reproduction of various forms either as printed publication of these visual images or sound recording of a play or musical work of creators. In India the Copyright Act, 1957 (14 of 1957) exists specially for the fine arts and literature in Appendix 4 amending by subsequent Amendment Acts including the Copyright (Amendment) Act, 1999 enacted by Parliament in the Eighth Year of the Republic of India as follows:

1. Short title, extent and commencement.—(1) This act may be called the Copyright Act, 1957.

(2) It extends to the whole of India.

(3) It shall come into force on such date as the Central Government may, by notification in the official Gazette, appoint.

2. Interpretation.—In this Act, unless the context otherwise requires,

(a) "adaptation" means—

(i) in relation to a dramatic work, the conversion of the work into a non-dramatic work;

(ii) in relation to a literary work or an artistic work, the conversion of the work into a dramatic work by way of performance in public or otherwise;

(iii) in relation to a literary or dramatic work, any

abridgement of the work or any version of the work in which the story or action is conveyed wholly or mainly by means of pictures in form suitable for reproduction in a book, or in a newspaper, magazine or similar periodical;

(iv) in relation to a musical work, any arrangement or transcription of the work; and

(v) in relation to any work, any use of such work involving its rearrangement or alteration;

(b) "work of architecture" means any building or structure having an artistic character or design, or any model for such building or structure;

(c) "artistic work" means—

(i) a painting, a sculpture, a drawing (including a diagram, map, chart or plan), an engraving or a photograph, whether or not any such work possesses artistic quality;

(ii) a work of architecture; and

(iii) any other work of artistic craftsmanship;

(d) "author" means—

(i) in relation to a literature or dramatic work, the author of the work;

(ii) in relation to a musical work, the composer;

(iii) in relation to an artistic work other than a photograph, the artist;

(iv) in relation to a photograph the person taking the photograph;

(v) in relation to a cinematography film or sound recording, the producer; and

(vi) in relation to any literary, dramatic, musical or artistic work which is computer-generated, the person who causes the work to be created;

(dd) "broadcast" means communication to the public,—

(i) by any means of wireless diffusion, whether in any one or more of the forms of signs, sounds or visual images; or

(ii) by wire, and includes a re-broadcast;

(e) "calendar year" means the year commencing on the 1st day of January;

(f) "cinematograph film" means any work of visual recording on any medium produced through a process from which a moving image may be produced by any means and includes a sound recording accompanying such visual recording and "cinematograph" shall be considered as including any work produced by any process analogues to cinematography including video films;

(ff) "communication to the public" means making any work available for being seen or heard or otherwise enjoyed by the public directly or any means of display or diffusion other than by issuing copies of such work regardless of whether any member of the public actually sees, hears or otherwise enjoys the work so made available;

(ffa) "composer" in relation to a musical work, means the person who composes the music regardless of whether he records it any form of graphical notation;

(ffd) "copyright society" means a society registered under sub-section (3) of Section 33;

(h) "dramatic work" includes any piece for recitation, choreographic work or entertainment in dumb show, the science arrangement or acting form of which is fixed in writing or otherwise but does not include a cinematograph film;

(m) "infringing copy" means—

(i) in relation to a literary, dramatic, musical or artistic work, a reproduction thereof otherwise then in the form of a cinematograph film;

(ii) in relation to a cinematographic film, a copy of the film made on any medium by any means;

(iii) in relation to a sound recording, any other recording embodying the same sound recording, made by any means;

(iv) in relation to a programme or performance in which such a broadcast reproduction right or a performer's right subsist under the provisions of this Act, the sound recording or a cinematographic film of such programme or performance, if such reproduction, copy or sound recording is made or imported in contravention of the provisions of this act;

(p) "musical work" means a work consisting of music and includes any graphical notation of such work but does not include any words or any action intended to be sung, spoken or performed with the music;

(q) "performance", in relation to performer's right, means any visual or acoustic presentation made live by one or more performers;

(s) "photograph" includes photolithograph and any work produced by any process analogous to photography but does not include any part of a cinematograph film;

(t) "plate" includes any stereotype or other plate, stone, block, mould, matrix, transfer, negative, duplicating equipment or other device used or intended to be used for printing or reproducing copies of any work, and any matrix or any appliance by which sound recording for the acoustic presentation of the work are or are intended to be make;

(uu) "producer", in relation to a cinematograph film or sound recording, means a person who takes initiative and responsibility for making the work;

(x) "reprography" means the making of copies of a work, by photocopying or similar means;

(y) "work" means any of the following works, namely:—
   (i) a literary, dramatic, musical or artistic work;
   (ii) a cinematograph film;
   (iii) a sound recording;

(za) "work of sculpture" includes casts and models.

Finally, it can be said that the Copyright Act works in above said class in the field of fine arts such as dramatic, musical and artistic works; cinematograph films; and sound recording which copyright subsist throughout India except in any work specified in sub-section (1), other than a work to which the provisions of Section 40 or Section 41 applying. However, the terms of copyright shall subsist in these works published within the life time of the author until sixty years from the beginning of the calendar year the next following the year in which the author dies. In this section the reference to the author shall, in the case of a work of joint authorship, be construed as a reference to the author who dies last. In the case of anonymously or pseudonymously works publication, copyright shall subsist until sixty years from the beginning of the calendar year next following the year in which the work is first published; and many more terms exists for copyright in the field of fine arts. The owner of the copyright in any existing work or the prospective owner of the copyright in any future work may grant any interest in the right by license in writing signed by him or by his duly authorized agent provided that in the case of a license relating to copyright in any future work, the license shall take effect only when the work comes into existence.

There is a provision to keep the register at the Copyright Office in the prescribed form entering the names or titles of works and the names and addresses of authors, publishers and owners of copyright and such other relevant particulars. Every entry made in the Registar of Copyrights or the particulars of any work entered under Section 45, the correction of every entry made in such register under Section 49, and every rectification ordered under Section 50, shall be published by the Registrar of Copyrights in the Official Gazette or in such other manner as he may deem fit. There is also a provision for the infringement of copyright by law for the infringement of a right.

In Tanzania the Copyrights and Neighbouring Rights Act No. 7 of 1999 deals with the protection of these rights and also protect expressions of folklore. The Act has come into operation from 31st December, 1999. The copyright office of United States is registering the case of photographers. Alike these registrations we should try our best to register ourselves in each branch of fine arts in the Copyright Office of India. Maximum registration and complaints of fine artists related to copyright will bring out with new solutions to create everlasting works of art.

Finally, I suggest it is best to consult a lawyer before submitting all the documents of copyright in each field of fine arts and its claim of infringement. In case of any new creation and even any theft of artistic work there is a need to register immediately. Copyright Protection does not begin until the copyright office receives your submission and approves it.

References

1. *Intellectual Property Law*, P. Narayan, Eastern Law House, Kolkata, New Delhi.
2. *Ibid.*
3. *Ibid.*
4. *Ibid.*
5. *Ibid.*
6. *Encata Encyclopedia.*
7. *Ibid.*
8. *Ibid.*

Protection of Cultural Rights under Copyright in Relation to Indigenous Peoples

MEENA PATHANI

Whenever dominant neighbouring peoples have expended their terrories and encroached upon the new territories, the very existence of the indigenous peoples of the land have been endangered. Their science, ideas, arts and cultures have been at stake. Presently the outside world is taking more and more interest in indigenous peoples' traditional knowledge and cultures resulting in its continuous exploitation. The commercialisation of indigenous art and culture is fastly growing. Their medical knowledge, their skills in biodiversity, forest conservation and environment protection are widely used but they themselves are not getting profit out of it, the present paper deals with the steps taken in the direction of the protection of human rights of indigenous peoples by different international organisations. As the culture right is also an important human right, the emphasis will be on the protection of their cultural rights and their traditional knowledge system specially, the protection of the Expression of Folklore and the efforts taken in this concern.

For indigenous peoples all over the world the protection of their cultures, intellectual property and other human rights has taken on a growing importance and urgency the International Labour Organisation (ILO) was the first international body to take action on indigenous issues since its creation in 1919, ILO has defined the social economic rights of the groups whose customs, traditions, institutions or language set them apart from other sections of national communities in 1957, ILO adopted Convention No. 107 and recommendation No. 104 on the protection and integration of indigenous and tribal populations. These were the first international legal instruments specially created to protect the rights of the peoples whose ways of life and existence were—then as now—threatened by dominating cultures. (Human Rights: UN Initiatives by Rahul Rae, Author's Press, N.D. 2000, pp. 235-36)

The working group on Indigenous Populations in the centre of indigenous rights activity in the United Nations. The need for the fresh attitude towards the issue of indigenous peoples was felt by the General Assembly when, by its resolution 45/164 of 18 December, 1990, it proclaimed 1993 the International Year of the World's Indigenous Peoples.

The United Nations Conference on Environment and Development, held at Rio de Janerio in June 1992, recognised that indigenous peoples and their communities have vital role in environment management and development because of their traditional knowledge. One of the outcome of the Earth's Summit was signing of the Convention on Biological Diversity (CBD) which includes provisions and the protection of their Intellectual Property Rights: Article 8(j) of the CBD has specially determined that subject to national legislation, contracting parties should "[. . .] respect, preserve and maintain knowledge, innovations and practices of indigenous and local communities embodying traditional life styles relevant for the conservation and sustainable use of biological diversity and promote their wider application with the approval and involvement of the holders of such knowledge, innovations and practices and encourage the fair and equitable sharing of the benefits arising from the utilisation of such knowledge, innovations and practices."

Thus, CBD was the first genuine effort in the direction of the preservation and conservation of cultural rights of indigenous peoples and their traditional knowledge.

Most noticeably, the World Intellectual Property Organisation (WIPO) Inter-governmental Committee on Intellectual Property and Genetic Resources, Traditional Knowledge and Folklore (GRTKF) was created as a result of CBD Articles 8(j) and 15 discussions and by Members of WIPO realising the conveniency of WIPO hosting an inter-governmental forum to discuss IPR, genetic resources, traditional knowledge and folklore-related issues. These same issues have been part of agendas of other international organisations (e.g. UNCTAD, UNESCO), regional blocs (e.g. Andean Community, Organisation of African Unity), indigenous peoples' forums (e.g. COICA), among many others. The focus of these forums has basically being to assess: how to legally protect traditional knowledge and folklore.

The Folklore is an important element of the cultural heritage of every nation. Folklore is commercialized without due respect for the cultural and economic interest of the communities in which it originates. There are so many evidences of indigenous music and dance being sampled by record companies and performance groups, which are presented to the public as original composition or coreography. Babacar N. Doye, a former director of copy right office of Senegal, cites an example of an African Folklore Group's European Performance of Composer who arranged and registered the recording as his original work. The work was a phenomenal success, all profits went to the composer without any compensation to the community from which the Folklore originated. (Quoted by Justice R.K. Abichandani, Judge HC Gujarat in his key note address to Judicial Round Table on IPR Development and Abjudication.)

The technological advancement has increased the chances of commercial exploitation of works of arts, crafts and knowledge of indigenous communities. The need for protection of folklore as copy right has been internationally recognised. Folklore as understood within World Intellectual Property Organisation (WIPO) and the United Nations Educational Scientific and Cultural Organisation (UNESCO) from 1978 and defined in 1982 in " Model Provisions for National Laws on the Protection of Expressions of Folklore Against Illicit Exploitation and Other Prejudicial Actions" to include "characteristic elements of the traditional artistic heritage developed and maintained by a community or by individuals reflecting traditional artistic expectations of such a community."(WIPO/GRTKF/IC/4/INF/2, Annex iv, pp. 211-13).

Current laws for copyright protection are unsuitable for protection of folklore, as copyright is individualistic or authorcentric and in the case of folklore there is no particular author or individual behind it. Measures should be taken for the development of *sue generis* legislation for protection of folklore. Model provisions prepared by WIPO suggested that the protection of folklore should be at regional and international level. The member-States should encourage extensive research in this respect and should make arrangements for facilitating funds to the concerned institutions.

As the existing Intellectual Property Rights regimes are inadequate to incorporated all the issues in the protection of folklore, WIPO and UNESCO have done a commendable job by offering Model Provisions for the protection of expression of folklore and given guidelines to the member-States for making and amending their national laws in this respect, so that the right to Expression of Folklore can be protected in the way other intellectual property rights are being protected in their respective countries.

New Dimension of Human Creative Activities and their Protection under Copyright Law

BRISKETU SHARAN PANDEY

1. ORIGIN OF COPYRIGHT IN THE PHANTOM OF HUMAN RIGHT

Introduction

The right to culture in human rights law is essentially about the celebration and protection of humankind's creativity and traditions. The right of an individual to enjoy culture and to advance culture and science without interference from the state is a human rights. Under international human rights law governments also have an obligation to promote and conserve cultural activities and artifacts, particularly those of universal value. Culture is overwhelmingly applauded as positive in the vast majority of human rights instruments. However, some statutes recognize that certain kinds of cultural and social practices may have a negative impact on an individual's health and well-being.

Moral rights are a widely accepted concept, incorporated in legislation, in Europe, the UK and North America. Though the exact nature and extent of the moral rights protection in place may vary from country to country, the most widely accepted moral rights are the rights of an artist to be recognised as the creator of a work (the right of attribution) and not have the work altered without prior agreement (the right of integrity).

Intellectual property law and international trading regimes are two salient areas of policy that have a profound impact on the operations of cultural industries such as publishing. This paper reviews the distinctive attributes of seven different forms of intellectual property protection, pointing the way for publishers to expand their thinking about protecting and exploiting their investment in intellectual property. It examines the nature of authorship in an historical context paying particular attention to the concept of moral rights. It then discusses the treatment of intellectual property and moral rights within various international trading regimes.

The purpose of this chapter is to provide some information and analysis of value to cultural analysts, the cultural sector and specifically writers and publishers in this time of expansion. In attempting to encompass these areas I have simplified both the issues and the arguments but, I hope, not so much as to invalidate the arguments put forward and consideration of their implications.

2. MORAL RIGHTS OF AUTHOR

Authors' rights as established in the copyright laws of most countries have two components. First, economic rights, rights to obtain remuneration in return for the right to publish the work, and second, moral rights, rights to prevent mutilation or distortion of the work, to receive authorial credit for the work, to decide when the work is complete and can be sent forth into the world, and, in some countries, the right to withdraw the work. The rights of authors to obtain redress from those who alter or mutilate their work or deny their authorship of it are, in particular, the subject of considerable controversy.

The TRIPS agreement requires that parties to the agreement provide protection equivalent to that of the Berne Convention.[1]

While the moral rights guarantees of the Berne Convention[2] are specifically excluded from enforcement under TRIPS,[3] countries joining the Berne Union will have to meet the moral rights requirement of Article 6 bis, and these rights will be available to foreign authors under the national treatment requirements of Berne.[4] The issue of moral rights is increasingly important to authors, publishers, movie directors, and producers because many countries have joined the GATT, or already are Berne members.

MORAL RIGHTS[5] DEFINED

The Nature and Forms of Moral Rights

The rationale that underlies moral rights is that the rights of an author, in the broad sense of a creator of an original work, in her work include not only rights required to derive financial benefit from it, but also rights to protect the author's investment of her own creative energy and personality in her work. In a classic American exposition on moral rights, one author states that:

> The copyright law, of course, protects the economic exploitation of the fruits of artistic creation; but the economic, exploitive aspect of the problem is only one of its many facets. . . . When an artist creates, be he an author, a painter, a sculptor, an architect or a musician, he does more than bring into the world a unique object having only exploitive possibilities; he projects into the world part of his personality and subjects it to the ravages of public use. There are possibilities of injury to the creator other than merely economic ones; these the copyright statute does not protect. Nor is the interest of society in the integrity of its cultural heritage protected by the copyright statute.[6]

France is normally held up as the model for moral rights law,[7] but many Western European civil law countries espouse the doctrine, with some variation.[8] The doctrine's origin is entirely judicial, perhaps unusual in a legal system that stresses legislative over judicial law-making.[9] There are four basic rights that constitute the *droit* moral; not all systems recognize all of them. They are: the right of publication (*droit de divulgation*), the right of paternity (*droit de paternite or droit an respect du nom*), the right of integrity (*droit de respect de l'oeuvre*), and the right of withdrawal (*droit de repentir or de retrait*).[10] Each of these rights is compound, each consisting itself of a small bundle of rights.

The right of publication is the right of the author to choose whether or not to present her work to the public.[11] The right of paternity is the right to claim authorship of one's work, to prevent others from unjustly claiming authorship, and to prevent having one's name falsely associated with another's work. The right of paternity includes the right to publish pseudonymously.[12] The right of integrity includes the "right to authorize or prohibit any modification of the author's work," and to protect against distortion of the work.[13] It also includes the right to prevent mutilation of or derogatory action toward the work. This was the right at issue in the *Buffet case,* where the buyer of a refrigerator painted by Bernard Buffet attempted to sell the individual painted panels of the refrigerator separately; the court enjoined the sale.[14] The right of withdrawal is the least exercised moral right. There is wider recognition of a right to make corrections, particularly in later editions.[15] The right of withdrawal may exist in common law countries, but only under compelling circumstances and in very limited cases.[16]

Duration and Alienation of Moral Rights

The duration of moral rights varies significantly among nations. In a minority of states, moral rights either have the same duration as the copyright,[17] or endure for a different term of years after the death of the author.[18] Many nations, however, recognize moral rights generally in perpetuity without distinction among works by individual authors or collective works, including France.[19] Other countries recognize the perpetuity only of certain rights, primarily the rights of integrity and attribution. The need for a perpetual moral right is "justified by the longevity of the work, which survives the extinction of the monopoly and continues to carry the expression of the author's personality."[20]

The ability to transfer moral rights varies from country to country. The World Intellectual Property Organization's definition of moral rights states that "most of the copyright laws recognize moral rights as an inalienable part of the copyright, distinct from the so-called 'economic rights'."[21] The Berne Convention apparently does not require inalienability, however. Berne requires that moral rights not pass as part of copyright; it does not expressly require that the rights be inalienable.

Moral Rights Laws outside Europe

While there is universal recognition of the author's right "to affirm his paternity in a work, or to defend his integrity in it," there are two approaches to enforcement of these rights. The civil law countries of Latin America, Africa, and East Asia spell out the right with particularity in their copyright laws, while the common law countries generally leave moral rights to the protection of the courts. Statutory recognition of moral rights has grown, however, in common law countries.[22] For example, India,[23] Israel,[24] and other nations have adopted moral rights legislation within their copyright law, while the United States has adopted the Visual Artists Rights Act.[25] The United States has consistently objected to the express recognition of moral rights,[26] and moral rights were a longstanding reason that the United States did not join the Berne Convention until 1989.[27] U.S. common law and trademark causes of action do provide some analogous protections.[28] In addition, some individual states have enacted moral rights laws giving limited protection.[29] The countries that protect the right of divulgation as part of copyright law are civil law counties and countries whose law derives from the civil law. Common law countries provide such protection under the law of privacy or secrecy, and through the refusal to specifically enforce personal service contracts.[30]

Fewer countries, as noted above, recognize the right of withdrawal.[31] Some other countries, including Spain, which historically adopted the French model in many respects,[32] adopt a more limited right to make changes or corrections. The right of retraction, to fully cancel an assignment of rights to publish, is the least recognized of the four moral rights. The method of executing the right is seldom detailed in statutory law. In all countries recognizing the right, the author must pay full compensation. Indeed, in Spain, for example, if the author later decides to publish the work, she must offer it to the original assignee on the original terms.

The precise terms of the moral rights statutes are probably less important than several other characteristics in determining the actual efficacy of moral rights in any country. Widespread adherence to the Berne Convention means that most countries have had to provide moral rights protection to meet its minimum standard protecting the rights of integrity and paternity. However, the existence of substantial industries dependent in some measure on copyright and authorial originality, and the existence of a legal system that provides effective (though not necessarily speedy) protection are better indicators of the availability of substantive remedies and the development of a significant jurisprudence of moral rights than membership in the Berne Union.

MORAL RIGHTS IN INTERNATIONAL DOCUMENTS

The Berne Convention

Paragraph 1 of Article 6 bis of the Berne Convention protects the rights of paternity and integrity.[33] While the rights are separate from and not transferred with the copyright, they are not clearly inalienable.[34] The rights of divulgation and withdrawal are not included in Berne. Under the second paragraph of Article 6 bis, moral rights must last at least as long as the economic rights, but countries that did not provide moral rights protection prior to acceding to the Convention are excepted from this requirement. In those countries, protection need only last until the author's death.[35]

The third paragraph of the Article provides that enforcement of the provision is to be through the national law "of the country where protection is claimed."[36] Thus, an American being sued for violation in Israel of moral rights should be subject to Israeli law. An American being sued in Israel for a violation of American copyright law should be subject to American law.

There are a number of explanations for the recent rapid growth of the Berne Union. In the aftermath of the breakup of the Soviet Union, the newly independent states and former socialist nations have attempted to integrate rapidly into the Western economic system. There also may be an increasing belief among countries that had previously eschewed intellectual property protection that such protection has come to be a requirement of foreign investment, or at least a requisite for other gains from the GATT.

Trade-Related Aspects of Intellectual Property Rights (TRIPS)

The Agreement on Trade-Related Aspects of Intellectual Property Rights (TRIPS) is one of six major trade agreements of the GATT Uruguay Round.[37] TRIPS requires, *inter alia*, that GATT members give protection to the intellectual property of other members that is equivalent to that of the Berne Convention;[38] the Paris Convention for the Protection of Industrial Property;[39] the Rome Convention,[40] governing performers, record producers, and broadcasters; and the Treaty on Intellectual Property in Respect of Integrated Circuits.[41] Additionally, intellectual property must be granted most favoured nation treatment, subject to certain exceptions.[42] Geographical indications, identifying the origin of a good, must also be protected.[43]

Although compliance with the general substance of the Berne Convention is mandatory under TRIPS, compliance with Article 6 bis was specifically excepted,[44] at the insistence of the U.S. delegation.[45] The agreement instead incorporates the United States' proposed language verbatim.[46] GATT members must guarantee that enforcement of rights guaranteed under TRIPS will be available to rights holders by "civil judicial procedures."[47] Criminal penalties must be applicable for "wilful trademark counterfeiting or copyright piracy on a commercial scale."[48]

From the standpoint of moral rights, it is perhaps most important that the GATT dispute resolution procedures apply to TRIPS.[49] The dispute resolution procedures provide a way to make the Berne Convention powerfully enforceable. The only formal dispute resolution method provided in the Berne Convention is suit in the International Court of Justice.[50] This has never happened.[51] Allowing enforcement of moral rights through the GATT mechanism would thus create a risk that the United States would be penalized for inadequate recognition of moral rights.[52] The language excepting moral rights from TRIPS should fully remove complaints of both over-enforcement and under-enforcement of moral rights from TRIPS.

Economics of Moral Rights

Moral rights are so named to distinguish them from remunerative, "economic" rights. But both moral and remunerative rights are legal rights, and, as legal rights, have economic consequences. Moral rights laws serve to protect national authors against damage by other nationals, as in Mannu Bhandari. Moral rights require indigenous industries to operate at a higher level of sophistication than would otherwise be the case. Although the cost of producing works thereby increases, suggesting lower production, the lower risks to authors might induce more to publish for reduced payment demands. In addition, some externalities might also be viewed as justification, such as improved reputation of indigenous authors and publishers outside the country. It seems likely that the importance of the indigenous protection rationale increases in proportion to the growth of copyright industries.[53]

In fact, however, moral rights represent a means of allocating costs between authors and users. The costs to authors are emotional, as in the mental distress that comes from seeing one's work mutilated,[54] as well as economic, in the reduction in value of one's work caused by the mis-attribution or the false depiction of the mutilated or distorted work.[55] There are costs to users in complying with the requirements of moral rights. The users may lose some part of their audience, as in Mannu Bhandari, where the film-makers recast the film into the mold of the traditional Hindi film,[56] or may have to invest more time and money into creating a better work. The loss to the user may be more personal as well, as the maker of the derivative work is forced to forego some of her own creativity in modifying the work in favour of respecting the author's[57] integrity.

One can envision a number of moral rights regimes, each allocating the costs and risks differently. Most authors, however, probably do not possess bargaining power equal to that of the user. In that case, as also where such rights are uncertain, the user can force the author to bear a disproportionate part of the risk and cost of violation. Thus, it would seem that, in the absence of equal bargaining power between authors and users, inalienable and unwaivable moral rights are the only ones that fully prevent users from externalizing the costs of infringement. However, while inalienable and unwaivable rights protect the weak or risk-averse author, they reduce the possible return to the risk-accepting author. It may be that allowing waiver or alienation of the moral right would result in the greatest net gain over all authors, risk-accepting and risk-averse.

Moral Rights and the Ambiguity in TRIPS

Since 1886, the author's rights have been the subject of the Berne Convention for the Protection of Literary and Artistic Works. It is one of the remarkable conventions as regards copyrights. To a lesser extent, these rights are also subject to the Universal Copyright Convention of 1952 (UCC). The so-called "neighbouring" or "related" rights are partly covered by the Rome Convention for the Protection of Performers, Phonograms and Broadcasting Organizations of 1961.

Considerable concessions for developing countries were moulded into a Protocol to the Berne Convention at the Stockholm Revision in 1967. These proved more than the traditional publishing States — mostly developed countries — could take. As it became clear that the Stockholm version would not be supported, a further revision conference was called in 1971 in Paris. It toned down the special concessions provided earlier in the Stockholm Revision.

At present, Article 6 bis (1) of the Berne Convention provides:

> "Independently of the author's economic rights, and even after the transfer of said rights, the author shall have the right to claim authorship of the work, and to object to any distortion, mutilation or other modification of, or other derogatory action in relation to, the said work, which would be prejudicial to his honour or reputation."

The British incorporated the provision of Article 6 bis (1) through the Copyright, Design and Patents Act, 1988 (British Act).

Upon ratifying the Berne Convention, the American Congress concluded that the existing Federal and State protections satisfied Article 6 bis obligations, however, some of these rights were for the first time recognized in 1990.[58]

Article 9 (1) of the TRIPS Agreement provides:

> "Members shall comply with Articles 1-21 and the Appendix of the Berne Convention (1971). However, members *shall not have rights or obligations* under this Agreement in respect of the rights conferred under Article 6 bis of that Convention or of the rights derived therefrom." (emphasis supplied)

Three main considerations may provide an answer for the non-inclusion of "moral rights" in the TRIPS Agreement:

First, although most common law countries have adopted the moral rights provision, the tensions between copyright and author's rights system have not disappeared. The persistence of conceptual differences about the appropriate form of copyright law is apparent in the incomplete and unsatisfactory codification of moral rights in the common law system.

Secondly, the reason for legislation about moral rights has been a degree of concern about their economic effects. Here, the common law countries have been most fearful about the practical consequences of introducing protection for moral rights into systems that traditionally emphasize economic rights.

Finally, the exclusion of moral rights from international harmonization efforts may have to do with a fundamental incompatibility between the philosophy of moral rights and the commercial thrust of the international copyright regime.

This is a setback to the recognition of moral rights across the globe. It had been after a great deal of intense debates throughout the world that the representative voices of authors insisting that all systems should have a structured set of rules on moral rights in place, the moral rights had found a place in the British and American legislations. Ironically, this provision of TRIPS negates the moral rights and pushes them on the back seat. This trend is quite disturbing because economic rights without being accompanied by moral rights are just like a body without a soul.

PROTECTION OF THE AUTHOR: CASE OF *MANNU BHANDARI*[59]

The Facts of the Case

Mannu Bhandari is a distinguished author of novels in Hindi. Her work is concerned with reconciling the modern with the trimillenial Hindu tradition. Kala Vikas Pictures, a motion picture production company, bought the rights, except the publication right, to her novel *Aap Ka Bunty* for 15,001 rupees.[60] Ms. Bhandari agreed to permit the director and screenwriter, Shri Sirsir Mishra, to make "certain modifications in her novel for the film version, in discussion with her to make it suitable for a successful film."[61] The contract further specified that Ms. Bhandari would receive credit as author of the novel on which the movie was based.

Ms. Bhandari later became concerned by the extent of the changes made for the film, including the name of the film, characterization, "vulgar" dialogue, and the ending of the film.[62] After finding the director unresponsive to her complaints,[63] Ms. Bhandari sued for infringement of her moral rights in the novel, specifically for violation of her right of integrity; that the film-makers had "mutilated and distorted" the novel.

The district court in Delhi denied Ms. Bhandari an "ad-interim restraint order," holding that she had not shown *prima facie* mutilation or distortion, because she had authorized the producers "to make necessary changes in order to make a successful film."[64] In an odd holding, the district judge stated:

> In my view, *prima facie* the film is not at all going to harm the reputation of the plaintiff in any manner. The plaintiff's reputation can be harmed in the eyes of those only who have read her novel and seen the film also. Those who have read her novel and seen the film may change their views about the producer, director of the film but not about the plaintiff.

The trial judge thus suggested that a bad film reflects poorly only on the film-makers, not on the author of the adapted work. It is more likely, however, that those who know the author's work only through its film adaptation are unlikely to distinguish carefully between the film representation of the work and the work itself. The lower court also found laches on Ms. Bhandari's part, arguing that she had waited until after the film had been completed to complain.

On appeal, the High Court in Delhi modified the district court's denial of relief, directing that a number of changes be made to the film before release. The parties settled the case immediately before the High Court handed down its opinion. The film-makers agreed to withdraw Ms. Bhandari's name and the name of her novel from the movie[65] and all attendant publicity, and released the copyright to her.[66] In return, Ms. Bhandari agreed not to "claim any right or interest" in the movie, and not to contest in any way the release of the movie (so long as neither her name nor the title of her novel were used). The parties requested that judgment be pronounced notwithstanding the settlement and attendant dismissal of appeal, citing the complete lack of precedent in the area as the rationale.[67] The High Court did so with apparent glee.

The High Court Decision

The court's resolution of the issues is quite thorough. The decision covers three important concerns: whether an assignment of copyright also transfers the moral right and the interpretation of the copyright assignment in light of the moral right; what constitutes a "distortion, mutilation or other modification" of the work;[68] and what constitutes an "action . . . which would be prejudicial to [the author's] honour or reputation."

Moral Right and Contracts

The Indian copyright law makes the moral rights of paternity and integrity independent of the author's copyright, and provides that assignment of copyright does not assign the moral rights; the author may obtain injunctive relief or damages for infringement of moral rights. The court stated that the moral rights provision overrode the terms of Bhandari's contract, that the contract could not negate the law's rights and remedies, and that "the assignee of a copyright cannot claim any rights or immunities based on the contract which are inconsistent" with the law.[69] Taken literally, a film-maker could never make a derivative work from a novel, for some modification, as broadly defined by the court, would be inevitable. The court, however, does not appear to take its statement quite so literally.

The court found that Bhandari's contract provided that she had agreed "to allow the director/screenwriter to make certain modifications in her novel for the film version in discussion with her to make it suitable for a successful film." The court insisted that this language be read to compliment the moral rights provisions. The court defines the modifications permissible under the contract to include only those permissible under Section 57. The court finds it "obvious" that, under law and contract, the film-makers had the right to make only the certain necessary modifications, and only upon consultation.

Distortion, Mutilation, and Modification

The court at first took an expansive view of the term modification, stating that:

> The words "other modification" appearing in the sub-cl. (a) will have to be read *"ejusdem generis"* with the words "distortion and mutilation." The modification should not be so serious that the modified form of the work looks quite different from the original work. "Modification" in the sense of the perversion of the original, may amount to distortion or mutilation. But, there can be a modification simplicitor such as where "A" is changed to "B", both being quite distinct. Sub-clause (a) thus provides inviolability to an intellectual work.

That is, any modification could be a violation of the author's moral right; the work is "inviolable" even as to apparently minor changes that are nonetheless "distinct." Taken literally, this would present a substantial problem for makers of motion pictures or other derivative works, as it appears to provide no protection for interpretive changes in making the film. If moral rights are entirely inalienable, no maker of a derivative work that modifies the original can be protected from an author's claim of moral rights infringement. In discussing the use of "brash sex" in the movie, the court stated that it did not sit as a censor or to impose its views on sex; its only concern was whether the derivative work is authentic and "what changes are necessary due to constraints of a medium." The court appears to have made moral rights inalienable, while placing outside the prohibition on modifications such changes as are necessary to make the transition to a different medium. This standard seems very protective of the author; however, the court's resolution of specific fact issues in the picture is inconsistent at best.

The Honour or Reputation of the Author

The court found a close relationship between the right of integrity and the right of paternity in this case. The reason for not allowing modifications that distort or mutilate was that Ms. Bhandari was to receive authorial credit for the movie. The court found that the term "credit," as a term of art in show business, means recognition of the work of those who have made credit-worthy contributions to making the work a box-office success. Box office success, however, does not imply that the work done will be a credit to the author's reputation. The court then interprets the contract term "'proper' publicity" as that which does not harm the author's honor and reputation. The author, then, was promised that her reputation would at least not be harmed by the film. The court takes into account the unique conditions of the Indian film business bearing upon the damage to the author's reputation. As the court explains, colourfully:

> It is widely believed that there are investments and collections of crores of rupees in a successful Hindi movie and the heroes and heroines are paid fabulous amounts for their services. If the complaint of the author (of mutilation and distortion of the novel) is correct the lay public and her admirers are likely to conclude that she has fallen prey to big money in the film world and has consented to such mutilation and distortions. The apprehension of the author cannot be dismissed as imaginary. It is reasonable. Her admirers are likely to doubt her sincerity and commitment and she is likely to be placed in the category of cheap screenplay writers of the common run Bombay Hindi films.[70]

K.P.M. Sundhram Vs. Rattan Prakashan Mandir[71]

The plaintiff and his co-authors entered into an agreement with the defendant giving them sole and exclusive licence to print and publish their works. The plaintiffs claimed that the defendants mutilated and distorted the original work by publishing various books in modified form. The defendants admitted the modifications made. The plaintiffs revoked the agreement.

The Court held:

> With the revocation of agreement by the plaintiffs, no right was left with the defendants to continue to publish and sell the works. Interim injunction is also granted.

Therefore, the moral rights remain with the author and are enforceable even if all the economic rights have been licensed/assigned.

Similarly, there is a catena of case-law in support of the author's moral rights. The Indian courts have been sensitive towards the moral rights of authors and the above mentioned cases buttress this fact.

3. INTERNATIONAL CONVENTIONS REGARDING CORRELATION OF HUMAN RIGHTS AND COPYRIGHTS AND CULTURE

A. UNITED NATIONS

1. Universal Declaration of Human Rights (1948) (Article 27)

Cultural rights are incorporated in Article 27: "Everyone has the right freely to participate in the cultural life of the community, to enjoy the arts and to share in scientific advancement and its benefits. Everyone has the right to the protection of the moral and material interests resulting from any scientific, literary or artistic production of which he is the author."

2. International Covenant on Economic, Social and Cultural Rights (1966) (Article 15)

The ICESCR, adopted by the General Assembly in December 1966 and entered into force in 1976. It elaborates the principles laid out in UDHR and is legally binding on all states who have signed and ratified its provisions.

Article 15 upholds the right of everyone to:

"1. (a) To take part in cultural life; (b) To enjoy the benefits of scientific progress and its applications; (c) To benefit from the protection of the moral and material interests resulting from any scientific, literary or artistic production of which he is the author.
2. The steps to be taken by the States Parties to the present Covenant to achieve the full realization of this right shall include those necessary for the conservation, the development and the diffusion of science and culture.
3. The States Parties to the present Covenant undertake to respect the freedom indispensable for scientific research and creative activity.
4. The States Parties to the present Covenant recognize the benefits to be derived from the encouragement and development of international contacts and co-operation in the scientific and cultural fields."

3. The Committee on Economic, Social and Cultural Rights

This was set-up in 1985 and is composed of 18 independent experts to oversee the implementation of the Convention. Reports can be made on violations of economic, social and cultural rights to this committee. It was not established by the Convention but by the UN Economic and Social Council (ECOSOC) for the purpose of monitoring the Convention. State parties are required to submit periodic reports to the Committee. The committee can also receive information from international organisations, NGOs and elsewhere. Since 1990, there has been discussion regarding the adoption of an optional protocol to enable individuals and groups to submit complaints of violations directly to the Committee.

Limburg Principles on the Implementation of the International Covenant on Economic, Social and Cultural Rights (1986)

These were approved by a group of experts in international law meeting in 1986 in Maastricht, Netherlands and give an interpretation of state obligations under the ICESCR. They apply more broadly to economic, social and cultural rights but do have a bearing on the implementation of cultural rights specifically.

4. Maastricht Guidelines on Violations of Economic, Social and Cultural Rights (1997)

These were developed by a group of 30 experts in 1997. The guidelines elaborate the standards contained in the Limburg principles on the implementation of the International Covenant on Economic, Social and Cultural Rights. They apply more broadly to economic, social and cultural rights but do have a bearing on the implementation of cultural rights specifically.

5. Declaration of the Principles of International Cultural Co-operation (1966)

This declaration was adopted by the General Conference of the United Nations Educational, Scientific and Cultural Organization in 1966. It stresses the importance of cultural cooperation at an international level and the benefits in terms of increased understanding between peoples.

6. Recommendation concerning Education for International Understanding, Cooperation and Peace and Education relating to Human Rights and Fundamental Freedoms (1974)

This recommendation was adopted by the General Conference of UNESCO in 1974. It emphasises the importance of ensuring culture forms part of educational programmes as a means of enhancing cultural understanding and combating race relations.

B. EUROPEAN UNION

Charter of Fundamental Rights of the European Union (2000) (Article 22)

The Charter stipulates that member-states of the European Union shall respect cultural, religious and linguistic diversity.

C. ORGANIZATION OF AMERICAN STATES (OAS)

American Convention on Human Rights (1969) (Article 26)

The American Convention on Human Rights, which entered into force in 1978, protects economic, social and cultural rights and places an obligation on states to progressively realise these rights.

Protocol of San Salvador: Additional Protocol to the American Convention on Human Rights in the Area of Economic, Social, and Cultural Rights (1988) (Article 14)

An Additional Protocol on Economic, Social and Cultural Rights (the "San Salvador Protocol") entered into force in 1999 and elaborates on these principles. The treaty recognizes the right of everyone to take part in the cultural and artistic life of the community; enjoy the benefits of scientific and technological progress; benefit from the protection of moral and material interests deriving from any scientific, literary or artistic production of which he is the author. States shall take steps to ensure the full exercise of this "right to the benefits of culture", must guarantee the freedom indispensable for scientific research and creative activity, and should encourages international cooperation in the fields of science, arts and culture.

4. TRIPS AND COPYRIGHT

India's copyright law, laid down in the Indian Copyright Act, 1957 as amended by Copyright (Amendment) Act, 1999, fully reflects the Berne Convention on Copyrights, to which India is a party. Additionally, India is party to the Geneva Convention for the Protection of Rights of Producers of Phonograms and to the Universal Copyright Convention. India is also an active member of the World Intellectual Property Organisation (WIPO), Geneva and UNESCO.

The copyright law has been amended periodically to keep pace with changing requirements. The recent amendment to the copyright law, which came into force in May 1995, has ushered in comprehensive changes and brought the copyright law in line with the developments in satellite broadcasting, computer software and digital technology. The amended law has made provisions for the first time, to protect performer's rights as envisaged in the Rome Convention.

Several measures have been adopted to strengthen and streamline the enforcement of copyrights. These include the setting up of a Copyright Enforcement Advisory Council, training programs for enforcement officers and setting up special policy cells to deal with cases relating to infringement of copyrights.

The report's statement that it would be premature for developing countries to sign the WIPO "Internet" Treaties and should not consider equivalent legislation to DMCA and the EU directive is based on two separate misunderstandings.

First, countries with lower standard of protection for rights will merely become piracy havens, to which illegal operators move, forcing out legitimate businesses who do pay rewards to creators. This would be true for both physical businesses and internet operators who can operate in a borderless environment. The Government is aware of the links between organised crime and counterfeiting and piracy. The Government needs to be aware that encouraging piracy in developing countries will have a potentially disastrous knock-on effect on the economies of developed countries: once unlicensed free copies are available on-line in a copyright unfriendly country the dissemination throughout the world is inevitable, and the Napster case shows how difficult in practice it is to prevent such copies being used.

Secondly, the DMCA and the Directive protect both the technology that will be used to secure modes of distribution on the internet (DRM) and the rights management information which links works in digital form to information about their owners, their terms of usage, etc. The full potential of technological protection measures such as these in the long-term will be to promote access to copyright material. Copyright owners who are confident of secure distribution will be able to make works available on differential terms, i.e. could themselves distinguish between certain purposes and developing country destinations. Countries with no protection for DRM technology risk copyright owners being reluctant to distribute their works there because there is insufficient protection to protect the investment.

We urge the Government not to accept the recommendations in the Commission's report on copyright law. Any IPR policy for developing countries should take a differentiated and specific approach to copyright. Many developing countries have their own very strong musical culture and so this is the one area which they could develop, through copyright, into a business which could contribute to their own economic development (without the requirement of a high technological standard).

More research is needed regarding other tools to enable developing countries to take advantage of their own resources without damaging the whole creative sector.[72]

This demonstrates that human rights are contestable, not immutable concepts. Typically, also, they entail striking a balance between various rights and prioritizing them. Historically, human rights have been most strongly articulated in the 'first generation' civil and political rights, while the 'second generation' economic, social and cultural rights are often considered to be aspirations at best; and 'third generation' collective rights including sustainable development are not easily made legally enforceable. It is significant that the right to property has been considered a civil rather than an economic right, and that this is the only positive economic right usually recognized, the remainder seem to articulate rather broader social or public interests. Thus, the key needs for access to land and natural resources, shelter, food, work, and health, let alone cultural rights are generally aspirational and not enforceable rights.

Certainly, IPRs may be evaluated in relation to the balance

they strike between the more 'public' interests in the enjoyment of cultural life and the benefits of science, and private legally enforceable rights in property. All too often, however, private rights tend to prevail over public interests, especially when claims take a legal form. The key issue is how to define the scope of IP rights according to public welfare criteria, as recognized in all IP regimes, and indeed in Article 7 of the TRIPS agreement itself. The problem is that the TRIPS emphasizes the property rights which states must grant and protect, and it defines rather narrowly the exceptions which states may provide to safeguard the public interest.

Thus, a recourse to human rights does not resolve issues about the substantive content of International economic rules, it merely shifts the debate to a different ground. Indeed, if Human rights norms are limited to liberal concepts of protection of private property and individual liberty, they may inhibit important public concerns such as the alleviation of poverty, disease and hunger. This is well illustrated by the constitutional challenge brought by pharmaceutical firms against South Africa's new medicines laws.[73] Strikingly, this was a claim of human rights violations, especially the deprivation of property without compensation. This case raised echoes of the successful constitutional challenge brought by pharmaceutical companies in Italy in 1978, on the grounds that the exclusion of medicines from patent protection was unfairly discriminatory, which dealt a mortal blow to the once flourishing Italian generic drug manufacturing industry.[74] Certainly, counter-arguments could be made, especially since the South African constitution recognizes rights *inter alia* to health care, and places an obligation on the government to take reasonable legislative and other measures, within its available resources, to achieve the progressive realization of each of these rights. Few other constitutions provide such a basis to balance vested property rights against the rights of the dispossessed. However, the collapse of the case was due to the global attention attracted by the access to medicines campaign, which was able to build international support around the issue of HIV-AIDS, and gave a new impetus to the political debates around the TRIPS agreement. Without this political debate, the South African courts might easily have upheld the 'pharmaceutical companies' rights to their patents.

Ultimately, how the balance is struck between different

conflicting rights-claims must be decided by democratic deliberation. For a supra-national adjudicative body to evaluate the validity of regulations adopted by national democratic states, on the basis of its perception of the proper balance of private rights of individuals, gives insufficient emphasis to democratic decision-making. An important proposal has been made in this respect by Laurence Heifer, for the adoption of the principle of the "margin of appreciation" in WTO practice and jurisprudence, especially in relation to the TRIPS.[75] This aims to restore a better balance between the local/national and global/international levels of governance. It is notable that although some of the WTO's trade-remedy rules articulate a standard of review which does provide leeway for national state judgements, this is not present in the TRIPS.

Indeed, neither Panels nor the AB have explicitly addressed the development of a standard of review against which to evaluate regulations adopted by states, except those of the trade regime itself (notably, the 'least trade restrictive' standard). This is an important reason why trade considerations tend to dominate their decisions, so that they act virtually as a court of appeal in adjudicating the public interest limits on IPRs enacted at national level. This can be seen in the restrictive approach they have adopted to the TRIPS provisions on exceptions to IPRs in both *Canada-Pharmaceuticals* and *US-Copyright*,[76] although in practice, they did offer a pragmatic compromise, in permitting some and invalidating other exceptions.

The main problem with the TRIPS is its strong emphasis on IPRs as private rights, subject only to some limited exceptions to protect the public interest. This obscures the reality that IPRs entail an artificial creation of scarcity (and monopoly rights) by the state, so that the initial definition of the scope of the rights should be determined by public interest criteria. This is particularly important for patents, where the basic provisions on patentability in Article 27 largely derive from WIPO's Draft Patent Harmonization Treaty. However, the TRIPS drafters essentially selected those provisions favouring patent-owners, many of which were actually strengthened compared to the 1991 WIPO draft (the 20-year minimum term, the requirement of product patents, and the reversal of the burden of proof for process patents). In contrast, the power for states to limit patentability was drawn more narrowly, in particular by specifying that it does not extend to micro-organisms or to non-biological or microbiological processes.

On the other hand, although TRIPS specifies the three basic conditions of patentability (novelty, inventive step, and industrial applicability/utility), neither these nor the all important distinction between a discovery and an invention are defined. It is this laxity that has allowed patent offices in some countries, notably the USA, to grant "patents on life," and to encourage bio-piracy and the privatization and commodification of community knowledge and techniques. In this respect, there is a need for greater specificity and less flexibility in the TRIPS. As presently worded, the TRIPS would permit a complaint against failure by a state to allow patenting of micro-organisms and micro-biological processes, but not against over-broad protection due to lax interpretation of patentability requirements. Here again, the structure of the TRIPS agreement favours private rights over public interests.

Nevertheless, developing countries could and should take advantage of the lack of specificity as to patentability standards in the TRIPS.[77] There are strong arguments that they should adopt more stringent standards for novelty, inventive step and utility, limit the scope of patentability (e.g. to exclude therapeutic techniques), and use various other means for ensuring IPR monopolies do not unreasonably restrict competition.

Indeed, a cogent argument can be made, which is not limited to developing countries, for more competition-friendly IPRs, based on a principle of fair remuneration for innovation and creativity, rather than the exclusive rights which derive from the private property model. This recognises that IPRs are not inherent private rights, but created and protected by the state, and hence that their scope and form should be defined in the public interest. We may hope that the debate over the relationship of IPRs and public health will help open up this broader set of issues, rather than remaining confined to the narrower perspective which simply counterposes strong protections of private rights against generally weak limitations and exceptions to safeguard public interests.

COPYRIGHT UNDER LAW OF TORT

Broadly speaking, a tort is a civil wrong, other than a breach of contract, for which the court will provide a remedy in the form of an action for damages.

Prosser and Keeton then criticize as "inaccurate" what they just said, by noting that other remedies, such as injunctions, restitution, and self-help are available. In desperation, Prosser and Keeton try again to define tort:

> "It might be possible to define a tort by enumerating the things that it is not. It is not a crime, it is not a breach of contract, it is not necessarily concerned with property rights or problems of government, but is the occupant of a large residuary field remaining if these are taken out of the law."

Part of the problem in making a precise definition of *torts* is that this area of law has expanded in an *ad hoc* fashion by judges (i.e., common law) and legislatures.

Torts is a large subject area in litigation, in which a victim (e.g., plaintiff) generally seeks money from some person, or some corporation, who harmed the victim.

The easiest way to get a sense of *torts* is to list the major areas of tort litigation:

- personal injury (e.g., automobile accident, slip and fall, dog bite),
- medical malpractice,
- products liability (e.g., defect in either manufacturing or design of product, failure to warn),
- wrongful death: survivor recovers economic value of remainder of decedent's life,
- patent infringement; copyright infringement,[78]
- defamation (i.e., libel or slander),
- intentional wrongs against a person: assault, battery, false imprisonment, intentional infliction of emotional distress. (N.B., assault and battery can also be crimes, see my essay that compares civil and criminal law),
- wrongs involving tangible property: conversion, "trespass to chattels" (N.B., same occurrence could also result in criminal prosecution for theft),
- wrongs involving real property: nuisance against nearby landowner, trespass on land,

- wrongs against a business, such as "unfair competition" or trademark infringement,
- dignitary harms against a person, such as:
  - invasion of privacy: intrusion on seclusion, unreasonable publicity given to private life, publicity placing person in false light; and
  - civil rights violations, e.g., 42 USC § 1983.

Four Elements

There are four elements to a tort, *all* of which must be present before the court can order a remedy:

1. **Duty.** The defendant must owe a legal duty to the victim. A duty is a legally enforceable obligation to conform to a particular standard of conduct. Except in malpractice and strict liability cases, the duty is set by what a "reasonable man of ordinary prudence" would have done. There is a general duty to prevent foreseeable injury to a victim.
2. **Breach of the duty.** The defendant breached that duty.
3. **Causation.** The breach was the cause of an injury to the victim. The causation does not need to be direct: defendant's act (or failure to act) could begin a continuous sequence of events that ended in plaintiffs injury, a so-called "proximate cause."
4. **Injury.** There must be an injury. In most cases, there must be a physical or financial injury to the victim, but sometimes emotional distress, embarrassment, or dignitary harms are adequate for recovery.

COPYRIGHT AND LAW OF TORTS COMPARED

"Copyright as Torts" uses personal injury law to introduce students to copyright, making a link between the doctrines through the notion of "externalities". Just as tort law discourages wastefully harmful behaviour by making perpetrators bear some of the costs inflicted, copyright law encourages beneficial behaviour by enabling authors to capture some of the benefits generated. For persons trained in common law doctrines, therefore, it may be useful to approach copyright law initially as if copyright were tort law upside-down.

While a full economic account of copyright needs to go far beyond the tort analogy (to consider factors such as industry structures, the "public goods" character of authorial work, and so on), the analogy to torts has many applications. Notably, it can help us to understand some of the reasons why the law puts limitations on copyright. For example, consider the motto, "It takes two to tort", and its lesson that both plaintiffs and defendant may need incentives.

In tort, the defence of comparative negligence serves to encourage potential victims to take care; in copyright, rules such as non-ownership of ideas encourage potential follow-on innovators to build on their predecessors. "Copyright as Torts also emphasizes the imperfection of the torts-copyright analogy. Among other things, I suggest, gratitude is often an easier emotion to achieve than forgiveness: The exchange of non-compensated benefits may therefore breed community in a way that the exchange of non-compensated harms might not. Now we have a primary query: Why is copyright law more willing to internalize positive externalities than is the common law of restitution? Part of the answer lies in the difference in structure between the paradigmatic cases in restitution and copyright. The transaction-cost structure and autonomy implications are significantly different in the two contexts. The choice of "carrots" *versus* "sticks" as sanctions (in restitution, copyright, and personal injury torts), and offers observations on the packaging of rights, and the impact of institutional form (primarily legislature *versus* judiciary) on substantive rules.[79]

A better analogy for understanding the liability of individuals is their potential liability in cases of auto accidents if the accidents happen when they are driving on company business. While the company and its insurance carrier may "defend and indemnify" the employee from such a claim, if litigation ensues the individual employee will almost certainly be named as a defendant in the case. In other words, an employee who is driving a car while on the job will likely be named as a defendant, even if the collision were just an accident, without any intent or malice on the part of the employee.

The Copyright Act basically imposes a form of tort liability on the individuals who commit copyright infringement, even if committed in the course of their employment.

Some months ago the federal court for the Southern District of New York articulated this in the case *of Logicom Inclusive, Inc.* Vs. *W.P. Stewart & Co.* In the *Logicom* case the court considered whether four people who worked for the corporate defendant could be held individually liable for copyright infringement of the plaintiffs software. On a 12(b)(6) motion to dismiss, the court found that all four individuals were properly included as defendants, because each was properly alleged to be a "moving, active [and] conscious force behind [the] infringement."

The cases in this field distinguish among "direct" liability, "contributory" liability and "vicarious" copyright liability. While articulated in different ways under these different theories, the two overriding factors in determining individual liability are the degree of wilfulness of the individuals involved in the infringement and the extent to which an individual benefits financially from the infringing activity.

Consider the case of an employee who has no ownership stake in his or her employer, but who intentionally copies bootleg software for use by company personnel. The employee will be individually liable for this conduct, no less than if while driving his car on company business he intentionally ran someone over. Since "statutory damages" under the Copyright Act can be as high as $150,000 per infringement, the liability can be real and very substantial.

There are also cases in which company officers and even shareholders have been held liable for copyright infringement committed by company employees. Consider the situation above, in which a lower-level employee copies software for use by company personnel. As illustrated by the *Logicom* case, individuals who approve such activity can be held personally liable.

Cases based on "vicarious" copyright liability go even further and don't require approval by the supervising employee. They have held that where a corporate officer has the right and ability to supervise infringing activity and has a direct financial interest in such activities, the corporate officer can be liable for the copyright infringement of the corporation. Thus, a company owner-officer cannot claim that he or she is immune from liability on a "see no evil, hear no evil" theory. If he or she has the authority to supervise those who infringe and benefits financially from the infringement, then the plaintiff does not need to prove that he or she had actual knowledge of the infringement in order to prevail against the company owner-officer.

Thus, under the Copyright Act, liability does not stop at the corporate door, as it generally does for a corporate debt. In light of the widespread but mistaken assumption that liability stops at the corporate door, the more effective training approach for companies and their employees is to think of liability as being governed more by the standards of general tort liability.

There is also a very practical reason that companies and employees are best advised to think about the risk in this way: differences in insurance coverage. Most companies carry insurance that will defend and indemnify the company and employee for the consequences of an auto accident. Far fewer companies carry insurance that covers copyright infringement in any circumstance, let alone in every circumstance. The most common situation is therefore that the company and its employees are relying on company resources to defend and indemnify them for copyright infringement.[80]

NOTES AND REFERENCES

1. GATT Uruguay Round, Annex 1C (Agreement on Trade Related Aspects of Intellectual Property Rights), Article 9, 33 I.L.M. at 1197 [hereinafter referred as TRIPS].
2. Berne Convention for the Protection of Literary and Artistic Works opened for signature, Sept. 9, 1886, S. Treaty Doc. No. 27, 99th Cong., 2nd Session I (1986), Article 6 bis, 7 Copyright 137 [hereinafter referred as Berne Convention].
3. TRIPS *supra* note 1.
4. Berne Convention *supra* note 2, Article 5.
5. Under Section 57 of the Indian Copyright Act, 1957, some additional rights are conferred on the author of a literary work as compared to the owner of a general copyright. These rights are also known as "moral rights."
6. David Vaver, *The National Treatment Requirements of the Berne and Universal Copyright Conventions*, Part Two, 17 Infl. Rev. Indus. Prop. and Copyright L. 715, 731 (1986).
7. Raymond Sarraute, *Current Theory on the Moral Right of Authors and Artists Under French Law*, 16 Am. J. Comp. L. 465 (1968); John Henry Merryman, *The Refrigerator of Bernard Buffet*, 27 Hastings LJ. 1023 (1976); Carl H. Settlemyer III, Note, *Between Thought and Possession: Artists' "Moral Rights" and Public Access to Creative Works*, 81 Geo. LJ. 2291 (1993).

8. Roberta Rosenthal Kwall, *Copyright and the Moral Right: Is an American Marriage Possible?*, 38 Vand. L. Rev. I (1985).
9. Merryman, *supra* note 6.
10. Martin A. Roeder, *The Doctrine of Moral Right: A Study in the Law of Artists, Authors and Creators*, 53 Harv. L. Rev. 554 (1940); Sarraute, *supra* note 6.
11. *Ibid.*
12. WIPO Glossary of Terms of the Law of Copyright and Neighbouring Rights 161, WIPO Publ. No. 827 (EFR) (Jan. 1981) as cited from Jeffrey M. Dine, *Infra* note 16.
13. *Id.* note 11, at 161.
14. Merryman, *supra* note 6, at 1023.
15. Frank Emmert, *Intellectual Property in the Uruguay Round-Negotiating Strategies of the Western Industrialized Countries*, 11 Mich J. Int'l L. 1317 (1990).
16. Cindy A. Carson, *Raiders of the Lost Scrolls: The Right of Scholarly Access to the Content of Historic Documents*, 16 Mich. J. Int'l L. 299, 301-7 (1995).
17. Jeffrey M. Dine, *Author's Moral Rights in Non-European Nationa: International Agreements, Economics, Mannu Bhandari and the Dead Sea Scrolls*, 16 Mich. J. Int'l L. 545 (1995).
18. The Berne Convention generally prescribes a copyright term of at least 50 years after the death of the author; special rules apply to motion pictures, anonymous or pseudonymous works, and photographs. Berne Convention, *supra* note 2, Article 7, 7 Copyright at 137
19. Sarraute, *supra* note 6.
20. *Id.*
21. Glossary, *supra* note 11, at 161.
22. England adopted moral rights provisions in 1988. See Copyright, Designs and Patents Act, 1988.
23.. The Copyright Act, 1957: Section 57. Author's special rights:—(1) Independently of the author's copyright, and even after the assignment either wholly or partially of the said copyright, the author of a work shall have the right to claim the authorship of the work as well as the right to restrain, or claim damages in respect of—
    (a) any distortion, mutilation or other modification of the said work; or
    (b) any other action in relation to the said work which would be prejudicial to his honour or reputation. (2) The right conferred upon an author of a work by sub-section (1), other than the right to claim authorship of the work, may be exercised by the legal representatives of the author.

    See also Krishnaswami Ponnuswami, *Intellectual Property*, 23 Ann. Survey of Indian Law 371, 372-74 (1987).
24. Mayer Gabay, *Israel Adopts Moral Rights Law*, 29 J. Copyright Soc'y

U.S.A. 462 (1982); Anita Ramasastry, *Recent Development, Cinematic Sex and Censorship in Indian Film*, 33 Harv. Int'l L.J. 205 (1992) Copyright Ordinance (Amendment No. 4) Law, 5741-1981, S. 3, 35 Laws of the State of Israel 368 (May 20, 1981) (Isr.) (authorized translation from the Hebrew prepared at the Ministry of Justice): Section 4A:

(1) The author shall have the right to have his name applied to the work in the accepted manner and to the accepted extent.

(2) The author has the right to object to any distortion, mutilation or other modification of the work or to any other derogatory action in relation thereto which may be prejudicial to his honour or reputation.

(3) The violation of a right under this section is a civil wrong, and the provisions of the Civil Wrongs Ordinance (New Version) shall apply thereto.

(4) The right of the author under this section shall be independent of his economic right in the work and shall be available to him even after such right has been transferred to another, wholly or in part.

(5) In an action under this section, the author shall be entitled to compensation in an amount determined by the court in accordance with the circumstances of the case, even if no pecuniary damage has been proved. This provision shall not derogate from any other power of the court under Chapter Five of the Civil Wrongs Ordinance (New Version).

25. Visual Artists Rights Act, Pub. L. No. 101-650, ss. 601-610, 104 Stat. 5128 (1990) (codified at 17 U.S.C. ss. 101, 106A, and other sections) [hereinafter VARA]; see Peter H. Karlen, *What's Wrong with VARA: A Critique of Federal Moral Rights*, 15 Hastings Comm. Ent. L.J. 905 (1993).
26. David Vaver, *The National Treatment Requirements of the Berne and Universal Copyright Conventions*, Part Two, 17 Int'l Rev. Indus. Prop. & Copyright L. 715, 731 (1986).
27. Ralph S. Brown, *Adherence to the Berne Copyright Convention: The Moral Rights Issue*, 35 J. Copyright Soc'y U.S.A. 196 (1988); Orrin G. Hatch, *Better Late than Never: Implementation of the 1886 Berne Convention*, 22 Cornell Int'l L.J. 171 (1989).
28. James M. Treece, *American Law Analogues of the Author's "Moral Right,"* 16 Am. J. Comp. L. 487 (1968).
29. Joshua H. Brown, *Creators Caught in the Middle: Visual Artist's Rights Act Preemption of State Moral Rights Laws*, 15 Hastings Comm. & Ent'l. L.J. 1003. 1004 (1993).
30. Martin A. Roeder, *Supra* note 9.
31. *Ibid.*
32. Patricia Rivera MacMurray, *Moral Rights in Puerto Rico: Spanish Tradition and the Federal System*, 57 Rev. Jur. U.P.R. 297, 300-304 (1988).
33. The text of Article 6 bis reads:

(1) Independently of the author's economic rights, and even after the transfer of the said rights, the author shall have the right to claim authorship of the work and to object to any distortion, mutilation or other modification of, or other derogatory action in relation to, the said work, which would be prejudicial to his honour or reputation.

(2) The rights granted to the author in accordance with the preceding paragraph shall, after his death, be maintained, at least until the expiry of the economic rights, and shall be exercisable by the persons or institutions authorized by the legislation of the country where protection is claimed. However, those countries whose legislation, at the moment of their ratification of or accession to this Act, does not provide for the protection after the death of the author of all the rights set out in the preceding paragraph may provide that some of these rights may, after his death, cease to be maintained.

(3) The means of redress for safeguarding the rights granted by this Article shall be governed by the legislation of the country where protection is claimed.

34. Susan Wagner, WIPO Committee of Experts Tackles Model Copyright Law, 4 World Intell. Prop. Rep. 215(1990).
35. Berne Convention, *supra* note 2, Art. 6 bis, para. 2.
36. Berne Convention, *supra* note 2, Art. 6 bis, para. 3.
37. The major agreements of the Uruguay Round are: the Agreement on Trade in Goods, the General Agreement on Trade in Services, TRIPS, the Understanding on Rules and Procedures Governing the Settlement of Disputes, and the Trade Policy Review Mechanism; see also Ralph Oman, *Intellectual Property after the Uruguay Round,* 42 J. Copyright Soc'y U.S.A. 18 (1994); J.H. Reichman, *The TRIPS Component of the GATT's Uruguay Round: Competitive Prospects for Intellectual Property Owners in an Integrated World Market,* 4 Fordham Intell. Prop. Media & Ent. L.J. 171 (1993).
38. TRIPS, *supra* note 1, Article 9,
39. Paris Convention for the Protection of Industrial Property, opened for signature, Mar. 20, 1883, 21 U.S.T. 1583, 828 U.N.T.S. 305.
40. International Convention for the Protection of Performers, Producers of Phonograms and Broadcasting Organizations, done Oct. 26, 1961, 496 U.N.T.S. 43.
41. Treaty on the Protection of Intellectual Property in Respect of Integrated Circuits, Feb. 12, 1987, 28 I.L.M. 1477(1989).
42. TRIPS, *supra* note 1, Art. 4.
43. *Id.*, Article 22.
44. *Id.*, Article 9.
45. Terence P. Stewart, The GATT Uruguay Round: A Negotiating History (1986-92) 2288-89 (1993).

46. TRIPS, *supra* note 1, Article 9, para I.
47. *Id.*, Article 42.
48. *Id.*, Article 61.
49. See *id.*, Art. 64; GATT Uruguay Round, Annex 2 (Understanding on Rules and Procedures Governing the Settlement of Disputes), 33 I.L.M. 1226 (1994); see also Thomas J. Dillon, Jr., *The World Trade Organization: A New Legal Order for World Trade?*, 16 Mich J. Int'l L. 349 (1995).
50. Berne Convention, *supra* note 2, Article 33.
51. Paul E. Geller, *Can the GATT Incorporate Berne Whole?*, 4 World Intell. Prop. Rep. 193, 194 (1990).
52. *Ibid.*
53. Richard T. Rapp and Richard P. Rozek, *Benefits and Costs of Intellectual Property Protection in Developing Countries.*
54. *Ibid.*
55. *Ibid.*
56. *Ibid.*
57. *Ibid.*
58. The Visual Artists Rights Act, 1990 (American Act).
59. *Mannu Bhandari* Vs. *Kala Vikas Pictures Pvt. Ltd.*, 1987 AIR (Del) 13, 21.
60. 1987 AIR (Del.) at 15.
61. *Ibid.*
62. *Id.*, at 19-20.
63. *Id.*, *at* 17-18.
64. *Id.*, at 14.
65. The movie was titled "Samay Ki Dhara" (The Flow of Time).
66. *Id.*, at 20.
67. *Id.*, at 14.
68. Copyright Act of 1957, Sec. 57(a), 15 AIR Manual 234.
69. 1987 A.I.R. (Del.) at 16.
70. *Id.* at 18.
71. AIR 1983 Del 461.
72. http://www.iprcommission.org/text/Views%20Articles%20Text%20 Versions/British_Music_Rights_text. htm
73. *Pharmaceutical Manufacturers' Association a.o.* Vs. *Pres. of the Rep. of S. Africa*, Case No. 4183/98, High Court of South Africa (Transvaal Provincial Division) (2001); for an account and analysis of the case in its political context see Mark Heywood, *Debunking Conglomo-Talk': A Case Study of the Amicus Curiae as an Instrument for Advocacy, Investigation and Mobilization*, available at http://www.tac.za/' last visited Aug. 6, 2003.
74. See F.M. Scherer and Sandy Weisburst, *Economic Effects of Strengthening Pharmaceutical Patents Protection in Italy*, 26 I.I.C. 1009 (1995).
75. Lawrence R. Heifer, *Adjudicating Copyright Claims under the TRIPS Agreement, The Case for a European Human Rights Analogy*, 39 Harvard International Law Journal, 357 (1998).

76. United States—Section 110(5) of the U.S. Copyright Act, Report of the Panel, WTO Doc. WT/DS160/R (June 15, 2000) available at http://www.wto.org.
77. Sol Picciotto and David Campbell, *Whose Molecule Is It Anyway? Private and Social Perspectives on Intellectual Property,* in New Perspectives on Property Law, Obligations and Restitution. (Alistair Hudson ed. 2003).
78. http://www.rbs2.com/torts.htm.
79. http://papers.ssrn.com/sol3/papers.cfm?abstract_id=433660.
80. Forget 'Grokster'—Copyright Infringement Remains an 'At Your Own Risk' Activity Alan J. Haus, http://www.law.com/jsp/article.jsp?id=1119431119062.

Creative Activities in Power Sector (A Comparative Study of U.S.A. and India)

Devesh Darshan Pant

The enactment of the United States Tennessee Valley Authority Act under President Franklin Delano Roosevelt in 1933 unleashed a "New Dimension of Human Creative Activities" when the newly created Government-owned Tennessee Valley Authority applied "a Human Approach" in improving "the economic and social well-being of the people living in said river basin" that included in its all encompassing scope the creation of a string of hydro power stations, all under government-ownership in Capitalist America to supply cheap power to the valley residents.

And this paper thus, seeks the replication in Uttaranchal of the creation of a similar body with the same mandate for the total integrated development of the Ganga River Basin to help provide not only cheap power to the residents of this River Basin but also the same if not more of the type of integrated development that transformed the poorest part of the United States into the economic power house it is today,

But, the question arises, why has such a body not been created so far in India? Shall its replication be an infringement of a copyright to say

or,

are not the people of the Ganga Basin poor enough to deserve the success in poverty alleviation that could be achieved by a TVA-type body for the Ganga Basin in Uttaranchal?

An answer straightaway of this question would be that any law that is inspired by the simple practice of human virtues to alleviate poverty has a universal application.

Any answers to the remaining shall be sought in the spirit and substance of this paper.

HISTORICAL

The enactment of the TVA Act in the U.S. came during the financial crash in modern day America known as the "Great Depression."

*[1]"The Stock Market crash of 1929 marked the beginning of a period of economic and social distress in the United States known as the Great Depression. It was characterized by widespread poverty, unemployment, hunger, and economic despair. Farmers lost their land, workers lost their jobs, and millions of Americans lost their savings as thousands of banks closed."

"Campaigning on the promise of reforms that would alleviate suffering and bring a "New Deal for the American people," Franklin D. Roosevelt won the presidential election of 1932."

The beginning of the TVA—with the Muscle Shoals Hydro Power Station

During the First World War the US Government needed nitrogen-based explosives for its War effort. To do this it had built a $ 145,000,000 hydropower station and dam and two munitions factories at Muscle Shoals, on the Tennessee River to generate cheap hydroelectricity and use it to produce Nitrogen from the air.

After the War, Senator George Norris of the State of Nebraska drafted a bill that the hydro power be generated and distributed by the government and the factories be converted to manufacture fertilizers.

But this was opposed, as government-owned means of production was a *socialist* concept. Controversy had thus been a feature of the TVA since its inception.

Arthur E. Morgan*[2] the first Chairman of the US Government agency the Tennessee Valley Authority (TVA) best describes this debate in his article "Strength in the Hills" as:

> "Let me go back to the time the Wilson Dam or Muscle Shoals, as it was then called, was undertaken as a war measure. Its completion after the War was opposed by those who insisted that the generation and distribution of power should be solely a private industry. Finally the Dam was finished, and then it lay all but idle for six years while a contest was fought out in Congress between the advocates of public and those of private generation and distribution of power. Twice Congress under Senator Norris' lead passed bills for the public operation of the Wilson Dam power plant, but each time the bill was vetoed by the president in office."

Finally, Franklin D. Roosevelt because President of the United States he agreed with Sen. Norris and believing it would stimulate the economy of one of the poorest regions of the United States and the hardest hit by the Depression, gave it his full support.

President Roosevelt won the argument for Government-owned Power Generation and Distribution by the Tennessee Valley Authority

Franklin D. Roosevelt (FOR) was elected President on the strength of his New Economic Deal to uplift the economy during the great depression and Arthur Morgan describes this, (see "Strength in the Hills")

> "Finally President Roosevelt proposed and Congress passed a general program of public generation and transmission of power as part of the Tennessee Valley Authority program."

TVA was not just a Power Company . . .

When President Roosevelt created the TVA he had in mind a totally different kind of agency. He asked Congress to create:

> "... a corporation clothed with the power of government but possessed of the flexibility and initiative of a private enterprise ... charged with the broadest duty of planning for the proper use, conservation, and development of the natural resources of the Tennessee River." (See "The History of TVA" at www.tva.com/about tva)

On 10th April 1933 President Roosevelt asked Congress to set-up the Tennessee Valley Authority (TVA). The munitions factory was to become a chemical plant manufacturing fertilizers and the hydro-electric plant was to generate power for parts of seven US States all under TVA.

> "*3On May 18, 1933 FDR signed the *Tennessee Valley Authority Act*. TVA was to improve navigability on the Tennessee River, provide for flood control, plan reforestation and the improvement of marginal farm lands, assist in industrial and agricultural development, and aid the national defense in the creation of government nitrate and phosphorus manufacturing facilities at Muscle Shoals.
> The Tennessee River ran through seven states, through some of the most disadvantaged areas of the South." (Ref. "The Origins of TVA—TVA: Electricity for all, p. 10)

Boldest Authority given to the TVA under *3 Section 23 of the TVA Act

This is best described from the TVA Archives "The Origins of TVA" as: "Perhaps the boldest authority given to TVA can be found in Section 23 of the Tennessee Valley Authority Act, where TVA was given a mandate to improve the economic and social well-being of the people living in said river basin."(The Origins of TVA—Tennessee Valley Authority Act)

> "Sec. 23. The President shall, from time to time, as the work provided for in the preceding section progresses, recommend to Congress such legislation as he deems proper to carry out the general purposes stated in said section, and for the especial purpose of bringing about in said Tennessee drainage basin and adjoining territory in conformity with said general purposes: (1) the maximum amount of flood control; (2) the maximum development of said Tennessee

River for navigation purposes; (3) the maximum generation of electric power consistent with flood control and navigation; (4) the proper use of marginal lands; (5) the proper method of reforestation of all lands in said drainage basin suitable for reforestation; and (6) the economic and social well-being of the people living in said river basin."

The development of the TVA upset many people in the United States. They complained that a government agency should not compete with private power companies in the generation and distribution of power. This opposition became vehement when it became clear that the unit cost of TVA power was much lower than the rates the private power companies were charging.

President Roosevelt aimed at creating a "Yardstick" to compare costs of power offered by the Government-owned TVA with that of the Private Power Companies

One of the most successful presidents in US history President Franklin Delano Roosevelt ardently believed in and acted upon creating a vast capacity of publicly-owned power and affordable power for all.

Arthur Morgan says further:

"One of his aims was to prepare a "yardstick" of public ownership with which to compare the costs of private ownership. The law provides that power from Muscle Shoals or from other developments must be sold primarily for domestic use in cities and rural areas. Sales can be made to private power companies or for manufacturing purposes, but household and farm use shall come first." (Reference, Strength in the Hills, Arthur E. Morgan)

The President wanted this "Yardstick" to prevent extortion of the poor Valley householders by Private Power Companies!

President Franklin Roosevelt wanted public power institutions like TVA to be:

". . . forever a yardstick to prevent extortion against the public and to encourage the wider use of the servant of the people—electric power." (See Yardstick—ABC's of TVA)

He, the President of a Capitalist Democratic country was distrustful of private power companies. The next Chairman of the TVA David Lilienthal, who had been a lawyer fighting these power companies in New York didn't trust the private power companies either. He felt that public-owned power should be distributed publicly, through a network of local municipal power boards and rural co-ops.

Opposition to the TVA in providing cheap power came from Private Power Companies

*[4]The New Deal Archives—"TVA: Electricity for All", page 3, describe the "Opposition to TVA" as follows:

> "The strongest opposition to TVA came from power companies, who resented the cheaper energy available through TVA and saw it as a threat to private development. They charged that the federal government's involvement in the power business was unconstitutional. . . The fight against TVA was led by *Wendell Willkie,* President of the Commonwealth and Southern Company, a large power utility company."

> "During the 1930s there were many court cases brought against TVA. The Alabama Power Company brought a suit against TVA that was argued before the Supreme Court. They claimed that in entering into the electric utility business, the government had exceeded its Constitutional powers. In February 1936 the Supreme Court ruled that TVA had the authority to generate power at Wilson Dam, to sell the electricity, and to distribute that electricity. . . . In 1939 the Court upheld the constitutionality of the TVA Act."

TVA was thus finally accepted to be a government-owned corporation in capitalist America, which not just competes with private power companies but in providing its core product—wholesale electric power—competitively, efficiently (read cheaply) and reliably it has aimed at and succeeded in setting a standard for public responsibility in providing such power against which private power companies performance can be measured.

No doubt this generates controversy surrounding the TVA,

as government-owned means of production is a 'socialist' concept in the U.S. but the controversy fuels an impetus to maintain its leadership in the industry by setting a better and more viable standard. This has thus been a feature of the TVA since its inception.

This role-model thus holds the lesson for India not only for uplifting the poor not only in Uttaranchal but also in the rest of India as well.

More about the role of the TVA in the "Great Depression" in Poverty Mitigation when the public Distrusted Private Power Companies

*5" . . . Under the Tennessee Valley Authority Act of 1933 the Federal Government provided electric power to States, counties, municipalities and non-profit cooperatives."

"It was a part of the Federal initiatives (under the TVA) to provide navigation, flood control, strategic materials for national defense, electric power, relief of unemployment and improvement of living conditions in rural areas. The TVA was more than just a power supplier."

"Norris Dam was the first TVA constructed dam, completed in 1936." That is significant as it was done in just three years!

"Even by Depression standards, the Tennessee Valley was in sad shape in 1933. Much of the land had been farmed too hard for too long, eroding and depleting the soil. Crop yields had fallen along with farm incomes. The best timber had been cut.

TVA developed *fertilizers*, taught farmers how to improve crop yields, and helped replant forests, control forest fires, and improve habitat for wildlife and fish.

The most dramatic change in Valley life came from the electricity generated by TVA dams. Electric lights and modern appliances made life easier and farms more productive. Electricity also drew industries into the region, providing desperately needed jobs."

"A Human Approach" for Development had to be adopted by TVA for success

However it was the dedication of the TVA officials that helped them to overcome suspicion.

So suspicious and die-hard were the farmers that they would

not listen to TVA officials coming to them in city clothes!

*5 "..."None of this was easy. The TVA officials had to overcome a deep suspicion of government agencies and inculcate what were revolutionary practices into traditional farming communities. They did this by blending in and finding champions.

A Tennessee farmer would not take advice from an official in a suit and tie. The TVA people also had to find the leaders in the communities and convince them that crop rotation and the judicious application of fertilizers were the ways to restore the soil's fertility. Once they had convinced the leaders the rest would follow." (Ref. Wikipedia article on TVA)

In 1940 during World War II TVA supplied cheap power to armament industries

*5"During *World War II*, the United States needed aluminum to build bombs and airplanes, and aluminum plants required electricity. To provide power for such critical war industries, TVA engaged in one of the largest hydropower construction programs ever undertaken in the United States. Early in 1942, when the effort reached its peak, 12 hydroelectric projects and a steam plant were under construction at the same time, and design and construction employment reached a total of 28,000. By the end of World War II the TVA had added 16 more dams!"

By 1960 there was unprecedented growth of TVA in all sectors of its mandate of poverty mitigation

"5*The 1960s were years of unprecedented economic growth in the Tennessee Valley. Farms and forests were in better shape than they had been in generations. Electric rates were among the nation's lowest and stayed low as TVA brought larger, more efficient generating units into service. Expecting the Valley's electric power needs to continue to grow, TVA began building nuclear reactors as a new source of economical power."

By Year 2000 and beyond TVA has given record power output

TVA's power system remained secure and un-interrupted during the massive system (Grid) failures that crippled New York and the entire North-East America in mid-August 2004.

5"TVA's power mix as of 2004 was 11 fossil-powered plants,

29 hydroelectric dams, three nuclear power plants (with five reactors and one restarting), and six combustion turbine plants. Fossil fuel plants produced about 61 percent of TVA's total generation in fiscal year 2004—Nuclear power produced about 29 percent of TVA's generation, and hydropower produced 9 percent

On 25 July, 2005, with temperatures approaching 100°F (38°C) over much of its operating area, the TVA was reported to have generated over 31,703 Megawatts, breaking a one-day record. The following day, TVA reported that it had broken that record by generating 31,935 Megawatts."

The TVA Act upheld by the US Supreme Court is a pro-poor law made in the world's wealthiest nation

The message that TVA power holds for Uttaranchal and also India is given by Arthur Morgan who said:

> "... The law provides that power from Muscle Shoals or from other developments must be sold primarily for domestic use in cities and rural areas. Sales can be made to private power companies or for manufacturing purposes, but household and farm use shall come first"... (Ref. Arthur Morgan)

The Faculty of Law, Kumaon University has drawn eminent legal luminaries to come from near and far to participate in this seminar so a verbatim quotation from the Sections 10 and 11 of the *[3]TVA Act even at the expense of brevity would not be out of place to present the vision of the law-makers of those times and to support Morgan's quotation.

> *Sec. 10.* The board is hereby empowered and authorized to sell the surplus power not used in its operations, and for operation of locks and other works generated by it, to States, counties, municipalities, corporations, partnerships, or individuals, according to the policies hereinafter set forth and to carry out said authority, the board is authorized to enter into contracts for such sale for a term not exceeding twenty years, and in the sale of such current by the board it shall give preference to States, counties, municipalities, and cooperative organizations of citizens or farmers, *not organized or doing business for profit, but primarily for the purpose of*

> *supplying electricity to its own citizens or members:* (Italics and underlines have been added). . . .
>
> . . . Provided further That the board is hereby authorized and directed to make studies, experiments, and determinations to promote the wider and better use of electric power for agricultural and domestic use, or for small or local industries, and it may cooperate with State governments, or their subdivisions or agencies with educational or research institutions, and with cooperatives or other organizations, in the application of electric power to the fuller and better balanced development of the resources of the region.
>
> *Sec. 11.* It is hereby declared to be the policy of the Government so far as practical to distribute and sell the surplus power generated at Muscle Shoals equitably among the States, counties, and municipalities within transmission distance. *This policy is further declared to be that the projects herein provided for shall be considered primarily as for the benefit of the people of the section as a whole and particularly the domestic and rural consumers to whom the power can economically be made available, and accordingly that sale to and use by industry shall be a secondary purpose, to be utilized principally to secure a sufficiently high load factor and revenue returns which will permit domestic and rural use at the lowest possible rates and in such manner as to encourage increased domestic and rural use of electricity. . . .*

What must stir the assembled eminent legal experts and luminaries is that the law-makers in Capitalist America saw that justice lay in distributing the fruits of cheap power generated from public-money invested in TVA power stations to go first of all for to the domestic consumers, i.e., the lay householder whether in the towns or the rural areas of the Tennessee Valley and that sales could be made to private power companies or for manufacturing purposes but only after meeting the needs of the households and farm use first.

A careful reading of the above relevant sections of this Act reveals that the whole emphasis is on public-distribution of this power rather than giving it for profit-making. It is highly significant that the TVA Act is a pro-poor Law upheld by the US Supreme Court, which has been made in the world's wealthiest nation. This Law makes sound economic sense. When the poorest are given the means of production such as cheap energy it alleviates poverty and generates wealth. No wonder, America is the wealthiest nation.

Lesson from TVA for Uttaranchal

What the TVA Act has achieved for the people of the Tennessee Valley is that the spilled waters energy of the streams and rivers constitutes energy that was previously going waste; this has been used for generating cheap hydropower and supplying it cheaply to the residents of this region.

The wealth of this region thus lay in the water power falling from the heights and the purpose of the Act has been to distribute it to the residents of this region.

How the TVA has set about distributing the wealth of this hydropower has already been described. The lesson to be learnt is: is the same logic being implemented in Uttaranchal, especially in its Hill Regions? Seemingly yes but not so fully and therein lies the appeal to this august body to help enact suitable legislation if that is necessary to ensure that this wealth of this region goes to benefit the residents of the Valleys and Highlands of Uttaranchal first and foremost.

That shall need to be done as follows:

1. By eliminating the so-called "losses in Distribution", which is more a euphemism for power theft or it is due to uncollected power bills, or both that is putting the burden on the Hill-men. Stolen power costs nothing and the maximum beneficiaries appear to be in the region of the Tarais and Bhabhars and outlying parts of Dehra Dun where these "loses" are minimum. In this way the Hill-men end up paying by far the highest cost.
2. By eliminating the power cuts that are imposed in the Hills also severely affect the availability of drinking water?
3. By decreasing the cost of power that is available to the residents of the actual Hills, which face the adversity of altitude that is evident the moment a man from the Plains of India sets foot in the hills say in Jeolikote.
4. By restricting the use of Hydropower of profit-making industries as in the case of Electric Arc Furnace factories

that consume the highest quantum of power per each factory unit and give the least employment to the Hill-men.

5. By increasing the pro-rata electricity consumption in the actual Hill Region, whether it is in Domestic, Commercial, Agricultural or Industrial use.

Distribution Loss in the Uttaranchal Power Corporation in First Quarter FY 2004-05

Circle	*Distribution loss as % of Total Distribution Loss of the State*	*Distribution Loss in %*	*Sales as % of total Sales in the State*
Electricity Distribution Circle (EDC), Rudrapur	33.53%	52.95%	17.6%
EDC Roorkee	25.46%	43.70%	19.4%
EDC Haldwani	10.73%	41.38%	09.0%
EDC Srinagar	10.29%	24.13%	19.1%
E Urban DC Dehra Dun	09.78%	27.45%	15.3%
EDC (Rural) Dehra Dun	08.46%	30.06%	11.6%
EDC Ranikhet	1.75%	11.57%	07.9%
Uttaranchal	100.0%	37.16%	100.0%

In the year 2004 the Supreme Court demanded to know of the Delhi Government, which was attributing black outs to rising demand due to theft of power if it had launched prosecution against power theft in Delhi. Nothing more was heard of this though power theft is still very much in the news in Delhi, the Capital of India.

It is not known if any case have been put up in the Special Courts set-up in Uttaranchal even two years after the Act 2003 stipulated this. So this again points to the need for Judicial Activism to give justice to the ordinary man.

In short, what is needed is a replication of the role that has been played by the TVA in the transformation of the Tennessee Valley, which is not just a power company but "had developed fertilizers, taught farmers how to improve crop yields, and helped replant forests, control forest fires, and improve habitat for wildlife and fish. . . . Electric lights and modern appliances made life easier and farms more productive. Electricity also drew industries into the region, providing desperately needed jobs."

The main beneficiaries of the cheap hydropower generated in Uttaranchal have not been the residents in the Hills but the regions with the "High Line Losses".

Selling off half-complete Government-owned Hydro-Power Projects in Uttaranchal to private parties negates the spirit of cheap power for ordinary consumers as was founded in the TVA Act

To put it very bluntly if in Capitalist America the law-makers thought it fit to entrust Hydro Power Generation to a Government Agency, why was it so necessary to sell off half-complete hydro-power stations in Uttaranchal to private parties that too under U.P.?

The entire genesis of the TVA Act stems from the fact that U.S. Government money had been spent on creating the Muscle Shoals Dam and factories, so these were not sold to private parties despite America being a Capitalist country and despite a clamour from private interests. Instead American law-makers created a new Government-organization the TVA because they decided that Hydropower, by its very nature could not be a source of private profit! This is a lesson enough for India and Uttaranchal, which the assembled legal luminaries must now seek to, decide in favour of the public, firstly of Uttaranchal and thereafter for the rest of the country.

The 330 Mega Watt Srinagar Hydro Electric Project was already more than half complete in the year 1989. From 1989 till the year 1994 it was kept in limbo to await some "suitable" private buyer. An MoU was signed with a private party in 1994. Yet the stunning fact is that the Srinagar Project is still incomplete from around 1989 till now the third quarter of the year 2005. It is probably not even started in the year 2005 that is 11 years from the time it was privatized. It was half complete even then so it is still awaiting the sweet will of its present private-owners to complete the remaining half. For all this period the energy from spilled water belonging to the people of Uttaranchal first of all has been allowed to be wasted.

This project should have started producing power by end of

1997 giving three years for a half-complete project. So 1289 M.U. × 8 = 10312 M.U. has been snatched from Uttaranchal people just to serve the interests of a private power company. This energy can be valued @ Rs. 2 PU), involving a loss of Rs. 206240 lacs or Rs. 2062 crores.

Public money had similarly been spent on the Vishnuprayag Hydel Project, which had made substantial progress when again it was put in a state of suspended animation awaiting a "suitable buyer." An MoU was entered into with the present private owner in the year 1992, but the project has not yet been completed even after 13 years!

What was the compulsion to hand over these Projects to U.P.?

The land in use, the energy and the environment belongs to the public of Uttaranchal, and Public money was spent on them probably out of Hill Development Funds earmarked for the development of the Hills so how come the projects were handed over to some Private Power companies that too to U.P.?

Their Power Purchase Agreements also have very extortionate clauses that must appall any public-minded individual who has become acquainted with the spirit and substance of poverty alleviating jurisprudence as was enacted under the TVA Act in America

As per the American Law such a public-funded project had to remain publicly owned to serve to produce electricity cheaply for use by the common people of small towns and cities as well as the rural areas. And the U.S. Law has safeguards that such hydropower must be cheaper than the power from any private power company.

It is a bitter irony that such a Law is to protect the interests of the poor sections of society in Capitalist America not in Uttaranchal perhaps one of the poorest States in India in one of the poorest IIIrd World Countries?

Prima facie it is the then U.P. Government/UPSEB that are to blame for abandoning more than half complete projects and then putting them in limbo to suit the wheeling-dealing with the private companies for the next 8-10 years? But the State Government of U. P. was specifically directed by the Union Power Ministry to rescind such MoUs where work had not started even after a considerable period, as per the Union Power Secretary D.O. letter No. A-32/95-IPC dated 18-01-1995. Considering the fact that a delay in completing the project meant direct loss of wealth in the form of energy of spilled water this letter was necessarily to be implemented.

It only makes it worse that the Uttaranchal Government has been a party to hand over these projects to the private parties under U.P.

This is a fit subject for an enquiry

The fact that such projects well on the path to completion were first stalled for funds and then handed over on a platter to a private Power Company, without even competitive bidding after spending such a huge outlay on its conception, design and execution is a fit subject for an enquiry. It is even doubtful if the Union Power Ministry ever required half-complete Projects to be 'sold' to private power companies.

This enquiry was called for much earlier on the part of Uttaranchal as to why were the delays allowed to occur leading to spilled waters going waste. And secondly, why were the interests of Uttaranchal sold out to U.P. when the erstwhile administration of the undivided U.P. did so much to keep the incomplete projects in limbo?

Extortionate prior conditions in Private Power Producers' Power—Sale Agreements cover up risks for incomplete studies and avoid conservation measures

For example, when government agencies (UPSEB & UP ID) were putting up their proposal of 360 MW of installed capacity for their hydropower plant in Vishnuprayag it was rejected by the Central Electricity Agency on objections citing "inadequate hydrological data" and told to put up river flow data for the next five years. But it was approved for 400 MW no sooner its new private owner put it up for this increased capacity! It is apparent the need for this five year period of discharge measurement was waived-off for the private party!

The Power Purchase Agreement, which this firm signed up with the U.P. Government, stipulates that even if there is insufficient water the private Company, must still get paid on the basis of "Design Energy," which has been "worked out" for a higher generation based on the inadequate studies. The controversial clause 3.11 of the P.P.A. executed with a private power producer runs as follows:

> "If the station has achieved the normative availability level in a contract year, but actual generation falls short of design energy for reasons solely attributable to hydrology, the energy charges for generation up to design energy shall be payable (by the Board) to the Generating company during the first seven years of operation.
> In case of reduced generation due to reasons beyond the control of Generating Company, . . . the energy loss on account of such spillage shall be considered as deemed generation limited to the design energy."

The same project has a Force Majeure Clause, which says if the plant gets affected by an Act of God and it cannot generate power "for reasons beyond its control" it must still get paid on the basis of "Design Energy" as if it were generating that much power in the affected period! A Force Majeure clause absolves both parties to the contract of their obligations for an unforeseen Act of God but here the private party is actually getting "rewarded" for such an event.

This controversial clause is the Clause 14.4 of the PPA, which says:

> "Notwithstanding anything contained in this Agreement:
>
> During any Force Majeure Event, if the Company cannot operate the station at all, or cannot operate the station at full capacity, the Board shall pay the Company the Capacity and Design Energy Charges on the basis that the Unit or Station shall be deemed during such period to be operating at 90% plant availability and Energy Charges up to Design Energy for the period as per Annexure-1 from the date of commencement of Force Majeure Event till the effect of Force Majeure Event is completely over."

Every one knows how fragile the Himalayan Hills are which cause landslides that can block the flow so why have authorities accepted this one-sided clause? This is a very damaging cause and likely to be a recurring loss not just on the State-owned Power Co. but also on the State Government.

It is common knowledge here in the Hills that these huge landslides often block the flow of a river by creating a temporary dam on it. It then gets breached. In either case power generation can't be done so why the private owners must be paid for such periods when they can't generate power and for such expected risks. Even otherwise during monsoon months when the silt and debris content goes up beyond the designed limits the power generation has to stop. So again the firm requires to get paid for not generating the power!

With such lucrative conditions around are the Private Power Producers going to do anything to prevent such occurrences or to mitigate their adverse effects?

These conditions are extortionate to say the least.

A government-owned agency will not inflict such extortionate tactics. Here lies the difference between a TVA-type "yardstick" or a standard organization and an extortionate profit driven private power producer.

Despite the fact that these one-sided Agreements were pointed out and being widely known the Uttaranchal Government has ignored the interests of the Uttaranchal people.

These concerns also take away the chances of cheap Hydro Power that has probably been expected by the Uttaranchal Government. This bears out President Roosevelt's fears about the Private Power Companies' propensity for extortion, which is a lesson for Uttaranchal.

Lure of a promise of "Free Power" by U.P. and the Private Parties have led Uttaranchal to allow U.P. to take over these Projects

But the Government of India holds out that 12% of the power that is generated shall be given free to the state where it is located it is not at all "Free Power" as is in the knowledge of all authorities since the Private Companies have "loaded" the Tariff with the cost of this 12% free energy in their PPAs!

The GoI Gazette Notification of March 30, 1992 sets out that "the per-unit cost of primary energy (meaning the total expenses including *inter alia* the operation and maintenance expenses) shall be calculated by dividing the Total Energy Charges by the Design Energy of the Project. . . ."

However in clause 3.7 of the Vishnuprayag Project the tariff has been worked out by dividing the total energy charges by the Design Energy minus the losses and minus the 12% free energy. In that case the Companies have already 'loaded' the costs of this so-called free energy on to their tariff, i.e. the rate at which they shall sell power to the Distribution Companies. The Srinagar PPA is also a ditto copy of the Vishnuprayag Project.

There is thus no likelihood of 12% "Free Power" to Uttaranchal due to "escape" clauses in the Enron-era P.P.As of these Projects!

If the Force Majeure Clause or the "Deemed Generation" Clause or both get invoked then the question of getting 12% power just does not arise.

So unlike America these private hydropower projects are meant to secure private profit.

Economies of Scale can only be achieved by a single authority developing an entire river basin as done by the TVA and also by the Bonneville Power Administration

Recalling the Presidential task given to the TVA by President Roosevelt, Arthur Morgan the founding Chairman of the TVA had said (Ref. "Strength in the Hills"—Article 6):

> "And in the field of power generation our "framework of reference" has become the unified development of an entire watershed under a single ownership and control."

It was his view shared with President Roosevelt that the unified ownership and control basis of hydropower development of the entire river basin would result in the cost per unit of power coming to at least one-third of what it would cost if there were separate ownerships and operation.

In the words of Arthur Morgan (Ref. Article 7):

> "Such unified control and operation implies government ownership and operation. The control of this great electric-power system by a private corporation would give economic power over the people of the region, which no self-appointed private business men ought to hold. . . ."

The TVA and the Bonneville Power Administration both Federal Agencies (read US Army Corps of Engineers for the latter here) have created economies of scale, i.e. cheap power, by undertaking the total development of an entire river basin under a single authority.

Yet another example on the TVA model in capitalist America of Hydropower Production is that of the U.S. Army Corps of Engineers generating also one of the cheapest Power as in the Colombia River Basin

The Grand Coulee Dam and its Franklin Delano Roosevelt Lake on the Colombia River is the biggest in the US. Its single hydro station produces 14,400 MW.

> "It is the centerpiece of a 29-dam federal hydropower system in the Colombia Basin that has enabled the Bonneville Power Administration to provide electricity to North Westerners at half the average cost nationally."(National Geographic April 2001).
>
> "Built during the Depression, the dam's benefits were manifold. It put 7,000 people to work, created a reservoir for the biggest irrigation project the country had ever seen, provided flood control, and produced electricity that would power America's war effort. . . . As for irrigation the benefits are evident the minute you leave the parched sagebrush country and enter the Colombia Basin Project. Mile after mile is covered in fields of potatoes, onions, carrots, corn, and grain. In innumerable orchards plump apples dangle from the branches. . . . All this is made possible by the dam's power, which pumps water 280 feet up into a 27-mile-long Banks Lake, a huge natural coulee. . . . From there the water flows through 6,000 miles of canals, pipes and ditches to more than 2,000 farms. The result is 640,000 acres under cultivation." (The National Geographic, April 2001.)

The power rates here are again one of the cheapest in the U.S.

Invoke the findings of a Research Paper on "The Economics of Scale and Scope in River Basin Management", by Gary Wolff, P.E., Ph.D., Principal Economist and Engineer, the Pacific Institute, California for Uttaranchal

A research paper on "the economics of scale and scope in river basin management", by Gary Wolff, P.E., Ph.D., Principal

Economist and Engineer, the Pacific Institute, California says,

> "In contrast, many view River Basin Management (RBM) and its close cousins, Integrated Water Resources Management (IWRM) and Watershed Management (WM), as the emerging and better paradigm for water management. . . ." And again he says, The Tennessee Valley Authority (http://www.tva.gov/), created in 1933 by the U.S. Congress as a public corporation governing this hydrologically defined area, has a mandate—regional development—that is far broader than water management.". . . the Authority has been very successful in numerous ways. . ." (Refer Gary Wolff gwolff@pacinst.org)

So this concept of integrating mutually supportive development under one agency has a mathematical model as well, which as pointed out has been successfully implemented in the TVA.

The success of the TVA is more remarkable as it was for the first time anywhere given the mandate to develop an entire river basin—an entire region comprising of seven U.S. States in which development of hydropower was to be just one aspect to be achieved as part of the overall "Basic Harmony"— (Ref. "ABC's of TVA)

> "Gifford Pinchot, Chief Forester of the United States under President Theodore Roosevelt and one of America's early pioneers in conservation, recognized that the basic harmony in nature involves a balance between human beings and natural resources. This view is at the heart of TVA's mission and method: treating nature, including the river, the land, the wildlife, and human beings, as a harmonious whole, and developing each part of this "seamless web" for the common good."

Why must the Ganga River Basin Hydro Power Development be given to a plethora of separate agencies many of them private to negate a Strategic necessity to develop the cheapest hydropower?

Hydropower is part of America's strategic energy reserve and it stands enacted law by the US Supreme Court to utilize this cheap power for household and farm use first and for meeting out defense needs. In war time the cheap hydropower helped the U.S. produce the vast array of armaments and explosives needed to defend the country. The famed Oak Ridge, Tennessee plant produced the World War II atom bombs using enormous amounts of cheap TVA power. This priority for Defense still exists. Do Defense Works get free power in Uttaranchal? They do not.

Doesn't the American example hold out any lessons for the present day Indian political leaders? Self-sufficiency in an internal and cheap perpetual energy resource is a strategic necessity. President Roosevelt of America, who put the entire hydropower and water resources in the hands of the United States Army Corps of Engineers in a major river basin, recognized this long ago and this continues till this day. America has enormous capital and expertise in the hands of its private companies but still it is the U.S.A.C.E., which is generating this cheap hydropower and is the owner of this renewable power. Besides TVA and the USACE the U.U. Bureau of Reclamation is the other Federal Hydropower producer.

The other great strategic interest of the U.S. Government is served by the fact that this cheap power stops the private power companies of charging extortionate power rates. Has India thought about this given the amount of private company frauds in America itself?

Can an Indian Private Power Company secure a previously U.S. Government-owned Hydropower project in the U.S., like the way an American Company secured the Srinagar Hydropower Project? Can American legislators allow such a sell-out of their strategic interests?

We mustn't forget Uttaranchal is getting relatively cheap power thanks to the Government-owned Hydropower Stations set-up in Nehruji's time

It is hardly ever mentioned that Uttaranchal is getting relatively cheap Hydro Power these days as the result of the efforts of the Government-owned Power Sector in the Dr. K.L. Rao the then Union Power and Irrigation Minister and the PM Pt. Jawaharlal Nehru. Incidentally they were in spired from President Roosevelt's TVA idea but it was unfortunately implemented half-heartedly by their successors.

So why is the present Government now parceling out its vast hydro potential piece meal to sundry power producers? Has it ever made public at what rates will these power producers supply power to the public?

Is there any legal binding like in the TVA Act to produce the cheapest hydro power?

Present scenario has it that all this Hydro Power is going to get transmitted to more prosperous regions out of the State

If nothing is done to promote consumption of cheap power in the Hills of Uttaranchal the way TVA does, all this energy is going to get drained away to more prosperous regions. And the government is a party to it. It has picked out that it will construct the transmission lines, which are only the "dead assets", merely the passage providers for the lucrative business of generating energy that is to be privately-owned.

The Transmission Company created post-haste in Uttaranchal is to be just a transport company for privately-owned power.

The Government intends to expand its manpower and Capital assets in the Transmission Company. Its main function is to invest heavily in "dead assets" of the transmission lines and sub-stations, which it will be hard put to maintain in the mountains and in all the vagaries of the weather and at all times.

So the Union Government, or State Governments have money enough for transmission lines but not enough to complete Hydropower stations like Srinagar, Vishnuprayag that are perpetual live assets?

Every aspect of the Uttaranchal Transco thus needs legal scrutiny to examine that an expensive Transmission System doesn't get created if its sole aim is to transport Uttaranchal energy away to distant lands.

The heaviest loss of revenue from power occurs in these distant lands, which have thus nearly free power as testified by the statements of so-called line losses. So Uttaranchal stands to lose even more as it will get its forest wealth cut away, suffer loss of land of its poor owners to provide passage for these transmission lines so that Uttaranchal's energy just literally gets drained away to help gave profit to people in distant lands.

The 800,000 Volt Transmission Line was created to whisk

away the hydro electric power from Tehri Dam to its first stop at Muradnagar near Meerut, which had around 60% to 70% of "line losses," and thence to Delhi that again tops in them. Incidentally, this writer had repeatedly pointed out the wastage of this double transmission—engineers would have gleefully put up another transmission line or lines to bring back some of this power to Uttaranchal. Perhaps this may now end as the Uttaranchal Power Dept hopes to tap the Tehri Power at Rishikesh.

Earlier the Tanakpur Power was first proposed to be transmitted to Almora but no, it went all the way to Bareilly from which some of it finds its way back to Uttaranchal. Likewise Dhauliganga power in Pithoragarh goes to Bareilly not directly to Pithoragarh and to Uttaranchal. The point remains how much of this hydropower going to reach the residents of these Hills from where these waters emerge on their journey to the Plains, if it is to be whisked away in Super High Voltage Lines to outside regions? And when it comes back of it does what shall it cost?

Present priority in power consumption goes to Steel Melting Furnaces importing dangerous scrap!

Recently the Uttaranchal Power Corporation imposed power cuts on its "ordinary" consumers because of cuts in hydropower production due to heavy silt and debris in Uttaranchal's rivers, as well as shortage in such power being imported. But it was not imposed on the Electric Arc Furnace Factories (CEAFs) which makes them VIP consumers.

These classes of industrial consumers have such unusual clout that they can freely transport bomb-laden steel scrap all the way from Western India seaports to their factories mostly in Tarais and Roorkee in Uttaranchal. The first question is: is this economical? These factories consume huge quantities of electricity in melting steel scraps. Can anyone in this august audience think it economical to do household cooking using electricity? So you sirs can well imagine how much electric power must be getting consumed melting steel scrap in these factories!

Steel melting factories were initially allowed power only during times the domestic power consumers' load dropped, which was in the night time and only through independent lines that could be switched off when the domestic demand again picked up.

Now all that has been done away with and these are the VIP consumers to get first pick of the Uttaranchal's power.

The security aspect of live rockets and bombs originating probably from West Asia being freely brought in to Uttaranchal's E.A.F. Factories must bother the Government but does it?

This doesn't seem to bother the governments as is evident from the repeated nature of such news reports in the well known papers starting from the Bhushan Steel Mill case of Delhi and a number of such cases reported from U.P. as well with a case reported in Kashipur of a live missile taking off with a labourer and dashing him to a wall killing him.

It appears likely that checking *per se* is lax all along from the seaports to Uttaranchal. In September 2003 scrap laden trucks were caught by the Police evading trade-tax. More such reports have come in 2005.

If trucks can succeed in evading Police chaukis and checking they can well bring in armaments concealed in the scrap as well. This must worry all well wishers of Uttaranchal, which has a porous border with Nepal.

Economics of Cheap Power demands that steel scrap melting furnaces are located near the sea ports

Is it not more economical to process this scrap where it is unloaded at the sea ports in West India from the war torn countries of its origin instead of its being transported all the way say to Uttaranchal using costly road-transport and guzzling the power that is best promoted to be used much more than at present in the Hills?

Had this locally guaranteed cheaps power not been given to these units the power for domestic use would be more than double of what it is at present. The economics can be worked out in more detail when all facts are available. This is another example of how the benefits are being denied to Uttaranchalis.

So the point remains that our popular governments have not really applied their own minds to seeking solutions to poverty alleviation that the founders of the TVA did when America was desperately poor.

CONCLUSION

These tasks that appears before this distinguished audience is to study the implications of the TVA Act and if its members are united in finding merit in it as has been described at some length in this paper, it shall be a challenge to their moral sense of duty to do their utmost to see that such a body as that of the TVA is founded in Uttaranchal, which can thus the made to ensure finding ways of taxing human ingenuity and dedication to generate and distribute the cheapest power especially in the Hills of Uttaranchal. As facts stand out such a concept has been successfully implemented in America by Franklin D. Roosevelt their President a sincere friend of India, to create just such an organization that is,

> "... forever a yardstick to prevent extortion against the public and to encourage the wider use of the servant of the people—electric power."

N.B.: *Refers to References under quotes. They are as under. Most of the quotations are from the TVA Archives from their Web Site.

NOTES AND REFERENCES

1. ABC's of TVA—www.tva.com/abouttva/abc/index.htm.
2. Arthur E. Morgan—I strength in the Hills under "Portrait of America Survey Graphic in the thirties—http:/ixroads.virginia.edn/NMAOI/Davis/survey/articles/government/gov-jan 34_5.html.
3. The origins of TVA-http;/newdeed.teri.org/tva/tva 01 htm—500 under TVA Article.
4. The new Deal Article—"TVA Electricity for All" --http:/new deal.teri.org/tva/tral 17 htm.
5. 'Teenessee Valley Authority"—http:/www.campus program.com/reference/en/wikipedialt/tel/tenuessee valley authority.html. —The above is a ulikipedia article.

The Nature of Rights and Remedies under the Copyrights Law in India

BHAVANI PRASAD PANDA

The Copyright Law in India (CR Law, hereinafter) is governed by the Copyright Act, 1957.[1] The CR law as on date has been updated and synchronized to international needs by amending Acts in 1984, 1994 and 1999.[2] The concept of copyright law evolved as an offshoot of inventions in printing and mass production of works.[3] The CR law aimed to strike a balance between the intellectual paradigms of private interest of the author and the interest of larger society in the maximization of the circulation of the works. Berne Convention, 1886, the first international congress on the subject, in order to check the pirate trade sought to provide for uniform international standards for protection of copyright."[4] Pursuits of intellectual production has spelled sea-changes over the years, the mechanisms and devices of copying have become faster and the quantum of circulations expanded to multitudes in almost no-time. Information Technology revolution accelerated the increasing importance of copyright law, the information mechanisms of storing in abundance and retrieving from among multitudes caused a short of knowledge explosion triggering for a well defined interface with copyright law. Professor Kamal K. Puri called this as the age of 'copycat'.[5] The art is to go close to the original but not so close as to mislead or deceive or be guilty of infringement of copyright or any other law relating to intellectual property. Copyright-based industries such as those in profession and trade which depend on copyright protection for commercial exploitation of their products and services lobbied for protection of each of the steps in creating, editing, manufacturing, packaging and publishing materials; as information economy has expanded several folds in the current times. *Interalia* of intellectual property rights, copyright law also have become a significant wealth creating asset and their production and commercialisation have gained increasing economic significance.[6] TRIPS Agreements paved the way for inclusion and protection of copyright within the framework of the multilateral trade arrangement under the impositions of the WTO.

The jurisprudence of copyright[7] protection suggests—first, everyman has a natural right over the results of his labour and so also the author who laboured to produce the work shall have a right to enjoy the fruits his investment and abate any unauthorised alterations or tampering to the chastity of the work; secondly, the development of human personality largely depends on the creative pursuits of one's own chosen indulgence; as such copyright protection provide, the necessary cushion to the stimulating features of creative ventures of mankind and development. Creation of a work consumes time, skill and novel indulgence, and such investment cannot suffer disincentive for any subsequent exploitation of the fruits from the work. The endeavour is to invigorate the creativity of the author via copyrighting the work; thirdly, when 'nothing is free in the world' how can the labour of the author go without a price? There has to be just reward to the author who created his work with his tremendous amount of his skill and labour. It is mutual exchange of author's labour with a price for having in hand for exploitation of ones own advantage. And fourthly, the societal interest calls for that the authors should be encouraged to create more, and publish more as these provide the cultural wealth of the society. Copyright law assures the authors with economic reward so that the society will blossom with more and more creative cultural flowering. Copyright law encourages the creation and dissemination of works of author for the benefit of society as well as to the author. Different jurisdiction emphasise on any of the above juridical reliance in objectifying the copyright legislation suitable for the continent[8].

Copyright law being a part and parcel of the intellectual property regime essentially envisages a legal relationship that arise out of an individual's creative gift and communication to society of the intellectual contribution. The laws purpose is obviously to encourage and reward the useful intangible fruits of creativity and intellectual productivity. The first step in the direction is to legally recognise the intellectual creativity and to grant authors, inventors, artists, designers and the like, the right to claim a tangible property interest inherent in their work and exploit their optimum advantage. Universal Declaration of Human Rights, 1948 conceded the need to protect the creator's right as a fundamental social principle. Article 27 of UDHR explicitly declares that—"Everyone has the right to protection of the moral and material interests resulting from any scientific literary or artistic production of which he is the author."

The essence of the copyright is to confer certain exclusive rights on the author to deal with the work in certain ways. Copyright is a sort of monopoly granted for limited duration and wholly regulated by the Copyright Act. The rights envisaged under CR law by the statute are also two pronged in consonance with the above outlined juridical vistas, viz., the economic and moral rights. Economic rights are available to every owner of copyright, whereas the moral rights are available to the author alone. The basic economic argument is that the grant of economic rights pays for the author's labour and skill as well as the investment which the entrepreneur has invested in producing and marketing the copyright work. The apprehension is real and it is perceived as—unless the author-creator is granted an exclusive right in his work, a copyist can reproduce and copy it at low cost.[9]

The Berne Convention for the Protection of Literary and Artistic Works, 1886 (as revised) provided the author two moral rights *(droit moral)* independently of the economic rights (Article 6 *bis)*. Copyrights in common law countries, is primarily concerned with economic rights, protection of moral rights does not exist in these jurisdictions. Moral rights are very significant for preventing debasement, mutilation or destruction of integrity in the creativity of the work. Moral rights include the rights which protect the author's reputation and honour. The underlying fact being is that the author creates a work for earning his livelihood but he juxtaposes the work within the limits of value. Authors take the risk of being ridiculed and face embarrassment when the values in the work do not reflect his view. Author's name and reputation contributes to the publication of a work, and the goodwill emanates from a consistent endeavour. The relationship between the author and the work is inherently intertwined and morally remains eternally tagged and are thus different from the economic rights. Moral rights can not be transferred whereas the economic rights can be bequeathed. Moral rights are perpetual in duration, and are protected when passed into public domain by the author's successors and in their absence by the followers of the authors.

The Copyright Act, 1957, as amended in 1994 provides for the meaning of "Copyright" in terms of economic significance, viz., it is a exclusive right to do or authorise the doing of any of the listed acts in respect of a work or any substantial part thereof, namely:

(a) *in case of a literary,*[10] *dramatic,*[11] *or musical work,*[12] not being a computer programme,
  - (i) to reproduce the work in any material form including the storing of it in any medium by electronic means;
  - (ii) to issue copies of the work to the public not being copies already in circulation;
  - (iii) to perform the work in public, or communicate it to the public:[13]
  - (iv) to make any cinematography film or sound recording in respect of the work;
  - (v) to make any translation of the work;
  - (vi) to make any adaptation[14] of the work; and
  - (vii) to do, in relation to a translation or an adaptation of the work, any of the acts specified in relation to the work in sub-clauses (i) to (vi).

(b) *in the case of computer programme,*[15]
  - (i) to do any of the acts specified in clause (a); and

(ii) to sell or give on hire, or offer for sale or hire any copy of the computer programme, regardless of whether such copy has been sold or given on hire on earlier occasions.

(c) *in the case of an artistic work,*[16]

(i) to reproduce the work in any material form including depiction in three dimensions of a two dimensional work or in two dimension of a three dimensional work;

(ii) to communicate the work to the public;

(iii) to issue copies of the work to the public not being copies already in circulation;

(iv) to include the work in any cinematograph film;

(v) to make any adaptation of the work; and

(vi) to do in relation to an adaptation of the work any of the acts specified in relation to the work in sub-clauses (i) to (iv):

(d) *in case of cinematograph film,*[17]

(i) to make any copy of the film including a photograph of any image forming part thereof;

(ii) to sell or give on hire or offer for sale or hire, any copy of the film, regardless of whether such copy has been sold or given on hire on earlier occasions; and

(iii) to communicate the film to the public.

(e) *in the case of a sound recording,*[18]

(i) to make any other sound recording embodying it;

(ii) to sell or give on hire, or offer for sale or hire, any copy of the sound recording, regardless of whether such copy has been sold or given on hire on earlier occasions; and

(iii) to communicate the sound recording to the public.

Explanation--For the purposes of this section, a copy which had been sold once shall be deemed to be a copy already in circulation.

The copyrights specifically defined in each of the intellectual category of pursuits as listed in clauses (a) to (c) above. The copyrights broadly speaking include the right to reproduction, distribution, or communication to public. Furthermore, in cases of computer programmes, film and sound records a rental right has also been conferred.

The definition of adaptation leaves scope for interpretation as rearrangement, alteration or conversion of a work into another form constitutes adaptation, yet the precise amount of rearrangement or alteration needed to constitute adaptation is to be inferred from each of the contentious case.

The Copyright Act, 1957 avails the author with moral right under Sec. 57—Author's special right,[19] whereby it is envisaged that the author shall have a right to claim authorship of his work and to restrain or claim damages in respect of any distortion, mutilations, modification or other act with respect to his work if such act would be prejudicial to his honour or reputation. It is inalienable from the author and is available even after the assignment of economic rights. However, there is a possibility of some 'tension between economic and moral rights, the traditional position of the common law is that moral rights hinder financial exploitation of copyright works, especially where exploitation takes place in a different medium, for example a book is turned into a film.'[20]

Author's right to claim damages in respect of any distortion or mutilations may be compared with the 'right to ascribe' the work and to defend his right in such work against infringement, i.e., he can insist that the work be published in his name and not be wrongly-ascribed to another person. This right ensures author's recognition, one of the reasons why people contribute to popular chronicles. As regard to the 'modification rights', the author alone has right to amend the work or delete any portion of the work. The right is important to the author's integrity since he may change his mind about some aspects of his work, however in assignment of copyright cases, the author may with the consent of the person to whom the right has been transferred make the alteration, deletion or addition therein and in the event of disagreement the author shall be obliged to pay such fair and equitable compensation. In certain jurisdictions, the author enjoys the right to withdraw his work from circulation, this is one of the moral rights of the author comes into conflict with the economic rights particularly when the work has been commercially assigned.

The Indian CR Law with regard to moral rights is in consonance with the Berne Convention, 1886, as revised. The Universal Copyright Convention makes no provision for the author's moral rights, whereas the Berne Convention regulates the moral rights by providing independently of their economic rights, and even after their transfer, authors retain the right to claim authorship to their works and to object to any distortions, mutilations or other modifications of or other derogatory actions in relation to their works, which would be prejudicial to their honour and reputation. The stipulation seems to recognize two rights, viz., the right to paternity or recognition and the right to integrity in a work.

In English law, four moral rights have since been recognised: (i) the right to be identified as author or director; (ii) the right to object to derogatory treatment of a work; (iii) the right to object false attribution of authorship; and (iv) the right of privacy of a person who commissioned a work.[21]

France is the country where the concept of *droit moral* has its origin, in its ideal form moral rights are considered perpetual, inalienable and imprescriptible. Countries, which have the Roman law background, have generally incorporated moral rights in their copyright law. Most generous treatment of moral rights are thus traced in the civil law countries, commonly under those laws, moral rights are unassignable and after the death of the author, the author's heirs irrespective of ownership of the economic rights, exercise them.[22] A brief enumeration provided by Jeremy Philip[23] is useful for the purpose as—

(i) the right to be acknowledged as the author of the work;
(ii) the right to determine when a work is complete, and to refuse to complete it if he is not satisfied with it;
(iii) the right to repent of one's work and to have it withdrawn before it is published;
(iv) the right to object to mutilation of one's work;
(v) the right to object to undesirable modes of display or exploitation;
(vi) the right to object to the physical destruction of one's work;
(vii) the right to the loyalty of one's publisher; and
(viii) the right to respond to criticism, especially if it is excessive.

OWNERSHIP OF COPYRIGHT

An author is the first owner of the copyright of the subject work. 'Author' has been defined in Sec. 2(d) of the Copyright Act, 1957 and means,—

- (i) in relation to a literary or dramatic work, the author of the work;
- (ii) in relation to musical work, the composer;
- (iii) in relation to an artistic work other than photograph, the artist;
- (iv) in relation to a photograph, the person taking the photograph;
- (v) in relation to a cinematograph film or sound recording, the producer; and
- (vi) in relation to any literary, dramatic, musical or artistic work which is computer-generated, the person who causes the work to be created.

Sec. 17 of the Copyright Act, 1957 in the Chapter IV, "Ownership of Copyright and the Rights of the Owner," it has been exclusively provided for "First owner of Copyright"—Author of a work shall be the owner of the copyright—

- (a) in the case of a literary, dramatic or artistic work made by the author in the course of his employment by the proprietor of a newspaper, magazine or similar periodical, under a contract of service or apprenticeship, for the purpose of publication in a newspaper, magazine, or similar periodical, the said proprietor, shall, in the absence of any agreement to the contrary, be the first owner of the copyright in the work in so far as the copyright relates to the publication of the work in any newspaper, magazine or similar periodical, or to the reproduction of the work for the purpose of its being so published, but in all other respects the author shall be the first owner of the copyright in the work;
- (b) subject to the provisions of the clause (a), in the case of a photograph taken, or a painting or portrait drawn, or an engraving or a cinematograph film made, for

valuable consideration at the instance of any person, such person shall in the absence of any agreement to the contrary, be the first owner of the copyright therein;

(c) in the case of a work made in the course of the author's employment under a contract of service or apprenticeship, to which clause (a) or (b) does not apply, the employer shall, in the absence of any agreement to the contrary be the first owner of the copyright therein;

[(cc) in case of any address or speech delivered in public, the person who has delivered such address or speech or if such person has delivered such address or speech on behalf of any other person, such other person shall be the first owner of the copyright therein notwithstanding that the person who delivers such address or speech, or, as the case may be, the person on whose behalf such address or speech is delivered, is employed by any other person who arranges such address or speech or on whose behalf or premises such address or speech is delivered];

(d) in case of a government work, Government shall, in the absence of any agreement to the contrary, be the first owner of the copyright indepth;

(dd) in case of a work made or first published by or under the direction of control of any public undertaking, such public undertaking shall, in the absence of any agreement to the contrary, be the first owner of the copyright therein;

Explanation: For the purposes of this clause and Sec. 28A, 'public undertaking' means—

(i) an undertaking owned or controlled by government; or

(ii) a government company as defined in Sec. 617 of the Companies Act, 1956 (1 of 1956); or

(iii) a body corporate established by or under any Central, Provincial or State Act;

(e) in the case of a work to which the provisions of the Sec. 41 apply, the international organisations concerned shall be the first owner of the copyright therein;

Author being the first owner of copyright has the right to

reproduce, publish, adapt, translate his work in different languages and customised forms, perform and communicate his work to the public, he has the right to prevent others to do any of the above acts to his work. The copyright envisages a specially qualified inherent right to the author to assign all or any of his rights either fully or for a tenure of limited period or to one or more persons and also licence to do any specific acts out of the bundle of rights grouped as copyright.

ASSIGNMENT AND LICENSING OF THE COPYRIGHTED WORK

The owner of copyright can transfer his rights in an existing or future work by way of assignment as per the provisions under Sec.18[24] or by way of a license agreement as per Sec. 30 of the Copyright Act, 1957. In the case of an assignment transfer, ownership of copyright is transferred, but in the case of a licence, the licensee is entitled to exploit the rights as per the agreed terms of licence. Both the forms of agreements must be in writing and must be duly signed by the assignor or the licensor as the case may be. The copyright interest of the author is further protected by 1994 Amending Act by insistence of certain essentials to confirm to valid transfer viz., the instrument should identify such work, specify the rights transferred, the duration, territorial jurisdiction, amount of royalty payable, etc.; the assignment shall be in writing signed by the assignor or by his duly authorised agent; in case of then period of assignment is not specifically mentioned the presumption will be "that the contract is only for a period of five years" and in case of territorial application, if not specified, it will be presumed that the agreement is limited to India alone. If the assignee does not exercise the rights assigned to him within a period of one year from such assignment, the rights will automatically revert back to the author unless otherwise expressly provided in the agreement.[25] The CR law provided safeguards to the author from the risks involved in a contract agreement. "Copyright" being a property in itself, can be transferred by document and can be bequeathed by will. The rules of succession also apply in cases of intestate succession.

RIGHT OF AUTHOR TO RELINQUISH COPYRIGHT

The author of a work may relinquish all or any of the rights comprised in the copyright in the work as per the provisions of Sec. 21(1) of Copyright Act, 1957; however the relinquishment of all or any of the rights comprised in the copyright in a work shall not affect any rights subsisting in favour of any person on the date of the stipulated notice.[26] The author of the copyright can renounce only such of the rights he had at the time of relinquishment and not any of the rights which he had earlier assigned or for which he provided any licence. Notice to the Registrar of Copyright is mandatory without such notice; the relinquishment will not be effective.

INFRINGEMENTS OF COPYRIGHT

Copyright Law protects the owner of the copyright by conferring a number of rights viz., publication and/or performance of the work, reproduction of the work and sale thereof and the like.[27] Any transgression of the stipulated rights would tantamount to infringement enabling the owner with a right to legal remedy. Generally, the infringements can occur in one or several of the circumstances enumerated below:

1. Literary Works

Copying the work in full or in part amounts to infringement whether such act is done by copying from the original or form authorized or unauthorized copy, copy *per se* amounts infringement. Adaptation and abridgement without any application of own faculty or judgment is also included in copyright law and will come into the offending folds of copyright holder.

2. Dramatic Works

In dramatic works there are number of elements which bring out the holistic dramatic spell on the audience, they range from various scenes, sequences, and succession of events created in a designed environment of space and time. The language, the dialogue, the modulation, the pronouncement, the phrase together with the music and action, etc. altogether co-ordinated cumulatively contributes to the spell cast in the drama. It would be infringement of the dramatic work where the incidents, scenes or music are reproduced or performed or recorded separately or independently.

3. Musical Work

The musical works are susceptible to types of infringements, viz., (i) by printing and selling the copies of the music written down or scripted by its author; and (ii) by performing the musical work in public for profit. To make out case of copyright violation of musical work one has to harp on the 'melody' in the musical product. Mimicry and the like cannot be treated as performances in infringement.

4. Photographs

A similar photograph can be treated as the infringement of the copyright even though any number of persons can click any number of photos of the same object or model if the infringing photograph reflects the same contour, light and shade and the special effects obtained by the original photograph, creating an impression that it is nothing but a retake of the self same original, mere alterations of technique in reproducing the work will not protect such copy from copyright violation. Any artist who sells copyright in his work to another reproduces his work with slight modifications can be charged with infringement of the rights of the assignee of the copyright of the original.[28] Under Sec. 9(4) of Sudanese Copyright Protection Act, 1974, Akolda M. Tier writes, a photographer may take a new photograph of 'anything photographed' before. It is immaterial that the later photographer repeated the personal choices of the first photographer, i.e., the new photograph is taken from the same place and in the same circumstances in which the first photograph was taken. This provider is little puzzling. The right of a copyright owner must relate to a work, copyright does not protect an idea. Moreover, since anything photographed before is not a subject of copyright, it cannot be said that a photographer has a right to it. His right, if any, is in the photograph he took.

Section 52 of Copyright Act, 1957, provides for counter-protection by expressly declaring that certain acts not to be infringement of Copyright. They includes—

1. Fair dealing:[29]—fair dealings with the copyrighted work for purpose of research, private study and for the purposes of review or criticism of the work. However, extensive use of quotations from a copyrighted work for profitable commercial purpose falls out of 'fair dealing' clause.
2. Reproduction of the copyrighted work for the purpose of judicial scrutiny.[30]
3. Reproduction of the copyrighted work for consideration and use in the Secretariat of a legislature and the similar usage in the legislative houses.[31]
4. Reproduction of the certified copyrighted work for usage in accordance with any law for the time being in force.[32]
5. Reading and recitation in public of extracts from copyrighted work.[33]
6. Publication of extracts from a copyrighted work in digests or collections.[34]
7. Reproduction of the copyrighted work for the purpose of teaching and learning.[35]
8. Use of works by a private audience in common usage such as for the residents of a locality in non-profit-making social halls/gatherings as a part of facility availed by the residents therein. This includes usage by the amateur club or society and/or for the benefit of religious institutions.[36]
9. Making of not more than 3 copies by a librarian for use in the library of a book not available in India.[37]
10. Publication in a newspaper of a report of a speech made in public. But publication of a speech made before a private audience amounts to infringement.[38]
11. Reproduction of matters published in official gazette.[39]
12. Reproduction of Acts of Legislatures gazetted provided they are published with commentary.[40]
13. Reproduction of any report of a Committee appointed by the Government subject to the conditions that may be prescribed.[41]
14. Reproduction of any proceedings of legislature or judgments or orders by a court in accordance with the conditions which may be prescribed.[42]

15. Reproduction of artistic works of sculpture permanently situated in a public place in any cinematograph film or by an author in his own study provided he does repeat or copy the design.[43]

REMEDIES AGAINST COPYRIGHT VIOLATIONS

The Copyright Act, 1957 provides for two independent and conjoint remedies, viz.,

1. Civil remedies under sections 54-62 in Chapter XII; and
2. Criminal actions against the offender under sections 63-70 in Chapter XIII.

Civil remedies are of following types[44]—suit for injunction;[45] suit for damages;[46] suit against destruction and mutilation of the work or for preventing action prejudicial to the reputation of the author alive or dead; suit for declaration of authorship[47] and also against slander of title where a publisher publishes a book in the name of a person other than the author; suits as between the owner of the copyrights and his assignees for breach of agreements; suits between the author and any other person for breach of confidence or passing off. In suit for injunction, the remedy sought is to restrain the impending infringement or continuing infringement. The relief claimed may be in the form of perpetual injunction, i.e. permanently restraining the defendant from infringing the copyright or may be in the form of mandatory injunction, directing the defendant to withdraw, hand-over or destroy the infringing works and articles.[48] Whereas in the suit for damages, that damages can be claimed: (i) as an amount of loss sustained by the holder of copyright by reason of infringement; (ii) as an amount representing the profits made by the infringer; and (iii) as amount representing the value of infringing copies. The first two reliefs are alternatives to one another, i.e. one of the two but not both can be claimed. The third relief however, is in addition to one or the other of the first two. Law presumes that all the infringing copies and plates are the property of the copyright holder and hence they are liable to be surrendered to the copyright holder. In the absence of the return in species their value in terms of cash can be claimed. If a person claims damages as a loss suffered by him he cannot opt for profits made by the infringer. Conversely, if a person claims profits gained by the infringer as damages he cannot claim damages as loss suffered by him.

Section 62 of Copyright Act, 1957 outlines the jurisdiction of Courts over the civil litigations, whereas (i) every suit as above in respect of infringement of copyright in any work or the infringement of any other right conferred by this Act shall be instituted in the district court having jurisdiction. The period of limitation in the suits gets computed for three years from the date on which the cause of action arises.

Criminal Action

The copyright holder can as well initiate criminal proceeding. Section 63 of the Copyright Act, 1957. speaks of 'offence of infringement of copyright or other rights conferred by the Act'—Any person who knowingly infringes or abets the infringement of: (a) copyright in a work, or (b) any other right conferred by the Copyright Act, shall be punished with imprisonment for not less than six months and may extend to three years and also fine which shall not be less than Rs. 50,000 and may extend to Rs. 2,00,000. Farther under Section 63-A enhanced penal liability on second and subsequent convictions has been envisaged by the 1984 amending Act, i.e. for the second and subsequent convictions of offence held under section 63, the penal liability is in mandatory terms shall not be less than one year but may extend three years and a fine of Rs. 1,00,000 to Rs. 2,00,000 for each of every subsequent conviction followed.

Section 63-B introduced the law proscribing infringement in computer programme viz., "knowing use of infringing copy of computer programme to be an offence", the minimum mandatory penal liability in terms of imprisonment is fixed at 7 days however may extend to three years and fine of minimum of from Rs. 50,000 to Rs. 2,00,000.

The police are empowered to seize the infringing copies and related plates without warrant under section 64, and that any person having interest in the seized material may make an application to the Magistrate within 15 days of the seizure and claim his case for disposal. In the case of disputed material, after the case has been tried and verdict, the court shall order that all copies of the work or all plates in possession of the alleged offender, which appear to it as infringing copies, or plates for the purpose of making infringing copies be delivered to the owner of the copyright.

The Copyright Act, makes it an offence prescribing punishment up to one year or fine or with both, for making false entries in register, etc. for producing or tendering false entries under section 67, and also making statements for the purpose of deceiving or influencing any authority or officer under section 68.

Lifting the corporate veil, the Copyright Act makes liable of copyright offences, that even person who at the time the offence was committed was in charge of, and was responsible to the company for conduct of the business of the company, as well as the company shall be deemed to be guilty of such offence, and criminal prosecution shall be proceeded accordingly.

The court of Judicial Magistrate, First Class, shall try any offence for any charge brought under the Act (section 70).

CONCLUSION

The Copyright Law in India is in tune to national and international policy for protection of the author's exclusive rights in his work, while at the same time provides space for public interest in the copyrighted work for social and cultural development. In the current years, the economic interest is pursued vigorously, in view for the value addition to the developments in information technology and huge financial investment on the creative and original works by multinationals. The Copyright Law in India has its genesis in the Anglo-Saxon annals, however appropriate to the national requirement, the Copyright Act, 1957 is enacted, and the same law is up dated time and again, assimilating the changes around the world. The rights conferred to the author by the law are recognised as both moral and legal, the legal rights are guarded by civil, criminal and administrative remedies. The Copyright conferred is a property, and accordingly the law has been designed to protect not only the right of recognition or authorship, it protects the ownership and the asset within the right. With the increasing thrust on knowledge power and property, the Copyright law will find more of its application to contain the 'copycat with its everready and swift paws'. The complexities in law will be accruing mostly from digital world wide web, where the very privacy in work are becoming issues, the dilemma is that the portals of knowledge need be opened, yet they need be protected. The moral line of original work and that the author need be acknowledged in accordance to his choice is inherent expectation in creativity and intellectual indulgence, and infringement, or intervention into the province of the author are counter-productive. The codified law recognised this inherent private right with a long history but with a policy of reward as well sustainable development. With the speedy pursuit for originality and creative work; and enhanced thrust on this intellectual paradigm and enhanced economic potential along with the computer regimes of tools and the techniques, the author will have to exercise awareness and legally remain awaken to the requisites in law. Today the property with in the copyright has become more of an enduring capital, and more susceptible to be stolen. New legal methods and tools of protection as well as skills of resolution of disputes need be considered, in furtherance to the existing law.

Notes and References

1. The Copyright Act, 1957 (14 of 1957) 4th June 1957; with effect from 21st January 1958 vide notification No. SRO 269 dated 21.01.1958 notified in Gazette of India Extraordinary, Part-II, Section 3, page 167.
2. International Copyright Order, 1991; SO 657 (E) dated 30th September 1991—in this order, the schedules are provided to make explicit of 'Berne Convention Country', 'Phonogram Convention Country,' and 'Universal Copyright Convention Country' [as amended by SO 170 (E)] dated 6th March 1997.
3. In 1709 the Statute of Anne provided for the first Copyright law of the world in redeeming the grievance of the printing press by granting them the exclusive license to print and publish, this license later culminated in modern copyright legislation world over. Later engravers got copyright under the copyright in 1734, textile designers in 1787, sculptors in 1789, printers, artists and photographers in 1862.
4. The preamble and Article 1 of the Berne Convention provided that protection of copyright shall operate to the benefit of the authors and successors in title, besides the term of protection was extended to 50 years beyond the life time of the author and the nature and scope of the rights available too were enlarged to cover the advances in technology.
5. The intangible characteristic feature of the Copyrights makes it convenient, that it can be stolen through a window without cutting a

pane of glass and it can be carried off by the eye without being found on the person.

6. Beyond the legal regime of IPR, the intellectual property has been gaining vitality as commercial asset by companies and as potential weapon of political economics by certain government.
7. Copyright is classified as moveable property, it is taxable, it is valued goodwill and hence the word royalty found its acceptance with the proceeds of copyright and it is valued goodwill and inherent with the owner because of his creative faculties and by the intellectual abilities. The claim of the copyright goes with the creativity of the product and encompasses automatically every user of the product.
8. American approach has been to lay emphasis on the economic and social aspects of the juridical reliance, whereas the continental nations emphasize on natural law and protection to the author.
9. Akolda M. Tier, 'Rights conferred by the Sudanese Copyright Protection Act, 1974', 38(3) *JILI*, 1996, pp. 331-47. The difference between the two costs is illustrated as follows: 'in the case of a film, a producer must, through his own and his partners investment finance the script writer and any other literacy author involved, and the musical composer, the actors, the support cast, the cost of location and site facilities, and use of sophisticated visuals and sound recording equipment. Once the tangible record has been made of the film, however, particularly if the record is contained in a videogram recording, further records of the work can be reproduced with considerable case and at little cost'.
10. Sec. 2(o) defines 'literary work' to include computer programs, tables and compilations including computer databases.
11. Sec. 2(h) provides that 'dramatic work' includes any piece of recitation, choreographic work or entertainment in dumb show, the scenic arrangement or acting, form of which is fixed in writing or otherwise but does not include a cinematograph film.
12. Sec. 2(p) defines musical work as a work consisting of music and includes any graphical notation of such work but does not include any words or any action intended to be sung, spoken or performed with the music.
13. Sec. 2(ff) explains, 'communication to the public' to mean making any work available for being seen or heard or otherwise enjoyed by the public directly or by any means if display or diffusion other than by issuing copies of such work regardless of whether any member of the public actually sees, hears or otherwise enjoys the work so made available.
14. Sec. 2(a) defines 'adaptation' to mean—
    (i) in relation to a dramatic work, the conversion of the work into a non-dramatic work;

(ii) in relation to a literary work or any artistic work, the conversion of the work into a dramatic work by performance in public or otherwise;

(iii) in relation to a literary work or dramatic work, any abridgement of the work or any version of the work in which the story or action is conveyed wholly or mainly by means of pictures in a form suitable for reproduction in a book, or in a newspaper, magazine or similar periodical;

(iv) in relation to a musical work, any arrangement or transcription of the work; and

(v) in relation to any work, any use of such work involving its rearrangement or alteration.

15. Sec. 2 (ffc) defined the 'computer programme' as a set of instruction expressed in words, codes, schemes or in any other form, including a machine readable medium, capable of causing a computer to perform a particular task or achieve a particular result.
16. Sec. 2 (c) defines 'artistic work' as —

(i) a painting, a sculpture, a drawing (including a diagram, map, chart or plan), an engraving or a photograph, whether or not any such work possess artistic quality; (ii) an architectural work or art; and (iii) any other work of artistic craftsmanship.

17. Sec. 2(f) explains 'cinematograph film' means any work of visual recording on any medium produced through a process from which a moving image may be produced by any means and includes a sound recording accompanying such visual recording and 'cinematograph' shall include any work produced by any process analogous to cinematography including films.
18. Sec. 2 (xx) defines "sound recording" to mean a recording of sounds from which such sounds may be produced regardless of the medium on which such recording is the method by which the sounds are produced.
19. Independently of the author's copyright and even after the assignment either wholly or partially of the said copyright the author of a work shall have the right to—

(a) to claim authorship of the work; and

(b) to restrain or claim damages in respect of any distortion, mutilation, modification or other act in relation to the said work which is done before the expiration of the term of copyright if such distortion, mutilation, modification, or other act would be prejudicial to his honour or reputation.

20. Akolda M. Tier, *supra* note.
21. W.R. Cornish, Intellectual Property: Patents, Copyrights, Trademarks and Allied Rights, 1988, 309-16
22. Copinger and Skone James, Copyright, 12th Ed., London, 1980.
23. Jeremy Phillips, Introduction to Intellectual Property Law, 1986, 92-3.

24. Sec. 18, Assignment of Copyright—(1) The owner of the copyright in an existing work or the prospective owner of the copyright in a future work may assign to any person the copyright cither wholly or partially or either generally or subject to limitations and either for the whole of the copyright or any part thereof:
    Provided that in the case of the assignment of copyright in any future work, the assignment shall take effect only when the work comes into existence.
    (2) Where the assignee of a copyright becomes entitled to any right comprised in the copy right the assignee as respects the rights so assigned, and the assignor as respects the rights not assigned shall be treated for the purpose of this Act as the owner of the copyright and the provisions of this Act shall have effect accordingly.
    (3) In this section, the expression 'assignee' as respects the assignment of the copyright in any future work includes the legal representatives of the assignee, if the assignee dies before the work comes into existence.
25. Sec. 19: Mode of Assignment —(1) No assignment of the copyright in any work shall be valid unless it is in writing signed by the assignor or by his duly authorized agent.
    (2) The assignment of copyright in any work shall identify such work, and shall specify the rights assigned and the duration and territorial extent of such assignment.
    (3) The assignment of copyright in any work shall also specify the amount of royalty payable, if any, to the author or his legal heirs during the currency of the assignment and the assignment shall be subject to revision, extension or termination on terms mutually agreed upon the parties.
    (4) Where the assignee does not exercise the right assigned to him under any of the other sub-sections of this section within period of one year from the date of assignment, the assignment in respect of such rights shall be deemed to have lapsed after the expiry of the said period unless otherwise specified in the assignment.
    (5) If the period of assignment is not stated, it shall be deemed to be five years from the date of assignment.
    (6) If the territorial extent of assignment of the rights is not specified, it shall be presumed to extent within India.
26. Sec. 21(3).
27. Infringement of Copyright—Section 51 of the Copyright Act, 1957.
    When copyright infringed.—
    Copyright in a work shall be deemed to be infringed—

(a) when any person, without licence granted by the owner of the copyright or the Registrar of Copyrights under this Act or in contravention of the conditions of a licence so granted or any of any conditions of a licence so granted or of any condition imposed by the competent authority under this Act—

(i) does anything, the exclusive right to do which is by this Act conferred upon the owner of the copyright, or

(ii) permits for profit any place to be used for the communication of the work to the public where such communication constitutes an infringement of the copyright in the work, unless he was not aware and had no reasonable ground for believing that such communication to the public would be an infringement of copyright, or

(b) when any person —

(i) makes for sale or hire, or sells or lets for hire, or by way of trade displays or offers for sale or hire, or

(ii) distributes either for the purpose of trade or to such an extent as to affect prejudicially the owner of the copyright, or

(iii) by way of trade exhibits in public, or

(iv) imports into India.

Explanation: For the purpose of this section, the reproduction of literary, dramatic, musical or artistic work in the form of cinematograph film shall be deemed to be an infringing copy.

28. N.K. Acharya, Text Book on Intellectual Property Rights, Asia Law House, 2004, 20.
29. Concept of "Fair Dealing"—Ideas, systems, information, things of practical use are not subject to copyright. Nobody can claim copyright in works which are by themselves not original or lacking any merit. Hence, reproduction or use of any of them do not constitute infringement of any copyright. One of the main objectives of the Copyright Law is the promotion of science and arts by recognizing certain monopoly rights to the creator of original works, this purpose is better served even as the protection to the rights of copyright holder are assured if a right to reproduction and use of such works is also granted in favour of the community without diminishing the financial benefit of the community are termed under the Act as fair uses of copyrighted work. Fair dealing is thus a recognized and valid defence to a charge of infringement.
30. Section 52(c).
31. Section 52(d).
32. Section 52(e).
33. Section 52(f).
34. Section 52(g).
35. Section 52(h & i).
36. Section 52(k & l).
37. Section 52 (o).
38. Section 52 (n).
39. Section 52 q(i).
40. Section 52q (ii).

41. Section 52q (iii).
42. Section 52q (iv).
43. Section 52(s & t).
44. Section 55(1).
45. Section 60(a).
46. Section 69(b).
47. Section 56—Protection of Separate Rights and Section 57—Author's Special Right.
48. Section 58.

Copyright as Human Rights under Universal Declaration of Human Rights

R.K. PATHAK

Copyright is one of the kind of intellectual property. Because, it is also a product of the human intellect though it protects the expressions only and not the ideas, as in Patent etc. Copyright is a right given by the law to creators of literary, dramatic, musical and artistic work and producers of cinematography, films and sound recordings. In fact, it is a bunch of rights including, *inter alia*, rights of reproduction, communication to the public, adaptation and translation of the work. Copyright ensures certain minimum safeguards of the rights of authors over their creations, thereby protecting and rewarding creativity. Copyright are like any other property rights—Rights in rem—they allow the creator or owner of copyright to benefit from his or her own work of investment. The basic idea behind protecting copyright is that the creators, innovators and inventors be given such incentives as may encourage them and others to advance the knowledge and techniques in their respective fields. In fact, there is conflicting or competing interest amongst *Individual* Vs. *Society, Individual* Vs.

State or *Individual* Vs. *Whole World*. Hence, these interest must be hormonised on the tune of saving the interest of the owner of copyright, society also must get the benefits of the innovations. The entire body of copyright jurisprudentially is an attempt to draw a balance between above mentioned competing interests.

Various attempts have been made on national as well as International level by conventions (Berne Convention and the Universal Copyright Convention) and Act (Copyright Act, 1957 as amended in 1994 to suit the GATT resolution to protect the social as well as individual right of innovators/creators/inventors, etc.) These rights though created by conventions/statutes are also recognised as Human Rights by Art. 27(2) of the Universal Declaration of Human Rights, 1948 which runs:

> "Everyone has the right to the protection of the moral and material interests resulting from any scientific, litrary or artistic production of which he is the author."[1]

Universalisation, interdependance, economic liberalisation and advance information technology has universalised the problem with regard to intellectual property. It can't be solved successfully right now on territonal level. Primarily works related to copyright were done for name, fame and personal enjoyment but now it is used commercially as a part of business world. So, its abuse can be checked successfully only if the task is taken at universal level. That's why Universal Declaration of Human Right, 1948, International Covenant on Economic, Social and Cultural Rights as well number of provisions of our Constitution like Arts. 19(1)(a), 19(1)(g), Art. 38, Arts. 301 to 307 and Art. 21 read with Preamble gives the idea that the copyright must be treated as Human Right.

SUBJECT MATTER OF COPYRIGHT

Section 14 of the Copyright Act, 1957 defines Copyright as the exclusive right to do or authorise other(s) to do certain acts in relation to —

- Literary, dramatic or musical works;
- Artistic works;

- Cinematograph film; and
- Sound recording.

"Literary work" includes computer programme tables, compilations including computer databases. "Dramatic work" includes any piece for recitation, choreographic work or entertainment in dumb show, the scenic arrangements or acting form of which is fixed in writing or otherwise but does not include a cinematograph film. "Musical work" means a work consisting of music and includes any graphical notation of such work, but does not include any words or any action intended to be sung, spoken or performed with the music.

An "artistic work" means a painting, a sculpture, a drawing (including a diagram, map, chart or plan), an engraving or a photograph, whether or not any such work possesses artistic quality; a work of architecture and any other work of artistic craftsmanship. A "work of architecture" means any building or structure having an artistic character or design, or any model for such building or structure.

"Engravings" include etchings, lithographs, woodcuts, prints and other similar works, not being photographs. 'Photograph' includes photo lithograph and any work produced by any process analogous to photography but does not include any part of cinematograph film.

A work of sculpture includes casts and models.

"Cinematograph film" means any work of visual recording on any medium produced through a process from which a moving image may be produced by any means and includes a sound recording accompanying such visual recording and "cinematograph" shall be construed as including any work produced by any process analogous to cinematography including video films.

"Sound recording" means a recording of sounds from which such sounds may be produced regardless of the medium on which such recording is made or the method by which the sounds are produced.

From the above list it may be seen that copyright subsists in a wide variety of articles created by man, provided they are original in the copyright sense. In fact, one can have a copyright in almost everything created by man which is original.

NATURE OF COPYRIGHT

Copyright is a negative right meaning thereby that it is prohibitory in nature. It is right to prevent others from copying or reproducing the work. It is monopoly right which restrains others from exercising that right which has been conferred on the owner of copyright under the provisions of the Act. Under present law it is creation of a specific statute. So, no right can exist in any work, except as provided in section 16 of the Act. As well, Copyright is not a single right. It consists of a bundle of different rights in the same work. For instance, in case of a literary work copyright comprises the right of reproduction in hard back and paperback editions, the right of serial publication in news papers and magazines, the right of dramatic and cinematographic versions, the right of translations, adaptation, abridgement and right of public performance. Copyrights consists not merely of the right to reproduction but has some related rights termed 'neighbouring rights', which includes right to works derived from the original works; rights like the right or public performance, the recording right and broadcasting right which are as important or even more important than the right of reproduction.

However, the copyright is natural as well moral rights also.

The copyright besides conferring economic benefits also confers moral rights on the author. Such rights though not statutorily defined are as follows:

(1) The right of publication.
(2) The right to claim authorship of a published or exhibited work.
(3) The right of integrity.

The Berne Convention recognises some of these rights and requires member States to provide the author with the right to claim authorship and to object to alterations. These rights remain with the author even after the transfer of copyright and such rights last throughout the entire term of the copyright.

These moral rights are recognised as "Author's Special Rights" under the provisions of section 57 of the Act (as amended by the Amendment Act of 1994).

These rights are:

(a) To claim authorship of the work.
(b) To restrain or claim damages.

The above rights are conferred on the author even after the assignment of the copyright.

The author's computer programmes are treated differently.

The author of computer programme does not have the right to restrain or claim damages when the making of copies or adaptation is done—

(1) In order to utilise the computer programme for the purpose for which it was supplied.
(2) To make back-up copies purely as temporary protection against loss, destruction or damage in order only to utilise the computer programme for purpose for which it was supplied.

The author's moral or special rights can be enforced under other branches of law: for example, if the author's reputation has suffered, under the law of defamation; if any person publishes the work without the author's consent; under the law of contract for breach of implied term of contract or breach of trust; and if some person has mislead the public into the belief that he is the author of the work, under the law of passing off. Section 57 gives statutory recognition to these moral rights which were recognised under common law.

The author's special rights are substantially the same in all countries.

All systems of copyright protection have as their prime inspiration the cultural value of authorship. The Romantic ideal, so ardently pursued two centuries ago, claimed for the creative artist a unique sensibility and foresight, and every age continues to regard with fascination those aesthetic achievements which it treasures as special contributions to the human condition. Indeed, whatever today's scepticism over objective values and universal truths, the arts receive serious and sustained study and participation on a scale previously unknown.

In countries where this complex social force presses urgently, it finds legal expression in a proprietary right which protects the personality of authors as expressed in their creations alongside their economic interests in exploitation. This separate element — the author's so-called moral right (from the French *droit moral)* — has been progressively enhanced in Continental systems of authors' rights over the past century. In the legislative schemes of French and German law and their many derivatives, moral rights rank as a category at least the equal of economic rights. The two schemes in fact differ in basic assumption, since French law renders moral rights perpetual as well as (in some sense) inalienable,[2] thus creating a necessary duality; while German law gives both moral and economic rights the same duration and treats them monistically as branches of the same tree.

In partial recognition of these developments, Article 6 bis of the Berne Convention requires Member-States to provide, in principle for as long as the economic rights, independent rights to claim authorship and to object to modifications or other derogatory action in relation to a work which would be prejudicial to the author's honour or reputation.

Each law within the fold of authors' rights countries differs over the precise content and scope of moral rights, but they are likely to include: a right to decide upon first publication or other release; a right to be named as author; a right to object to modifications of the work and to its presentation in derogatory circumstances. There may also be provision for an author to insist on completion of the original where that depends on the execution of others, to withdraw works of which he no longer approves and to object to destruction or removal of the original.

One driving inspiration for moral-rights doctrine has been the belief that at least some great artists are unworldly prey to the vultures of copyright industries: the voracious among literary and music publishers, recording, stage and film producers and are dealers. Moral rights seek at least to protect the integrity of a work and the author's connection with it. But once that step is taken, it is natural also to buttress the author's economic interest against unfair deprivation, particularly by the entrepreneurs who undertake to exploit the work. There is no simple dividing line between the purely "moral" and the purely economic. For every individual who insists unflinchingly upon his artistic integrity, there are many whose insistence can be compromised at a price.

Equally, the innocent author abroad may well need help in realising his economic potential than in protecting his essential relationship to his work.

INTERNATIONAL CHARACTER OF COPYRIGHT

The enormous technological development of Transport and Communications has resulted in the globalization of trade and commerce. This has its impact on copyright. Piracy of copyright has become international in character. Piracy of copyright work has become extremely easy and inexpensive owing to the availability of gadgets like tape recorder, video, cassette recorder, magnetic tape, photocopying machine and so on. No foolproof method of preventing this piracy has so far been developed.

Copyright is recognised in various international conventions for its protection. India is a member of both the Berne Convention and the Universal Copyright Conventions. Accordingly Indian Copyright owners can protect their right in almost any country in the world.

As technology in all fields of human activities are developing exponentially the field of intellectual property is also expanding correspondingly. Protection of plant varieties, prevention of various forms of unfair competition or misappropriation of goodwill, reputation or trade values, unfair business practices, slavish copying of the details of products, dilution of reputed trade marks and their commercial value by using them by competitors in fields of activity different from the owners are becoming more and more difficult. Piracy of copyright has become international owing to globalization of trade and commerce. Copyright law is one of the fastest growing branch of law today practically all over the world.

Technological progress has made reproduction of copyright material easy and cheep, but at the same time it has made piracy of copyright work simple and difficult to control. The seriousness of piracy in copyright work was realised only after the development of gadgets, like tape recorder, video cassette recorder, magnetic tapes and reprography. These technological innovations have made copyright infringement international in character.

Today the law of copyright is of interest not only to those who deal with litrary, dramatic or musical works but also artists, dress, designers, architects, publishers, person concerned with cinematograph film and recording and broadcasting authorities, and publishing, printing and entertainment industries.

Apart from the above copyright law affects the manufacturing industry as a whole. Copyright subsists in original industrial drawings used in the manufacture of machines and machine parts. The effect of this is that an unauthorised manufacture of a machine or a machine part based on such drawing (i.e. the three dimensional representation of the drawing) is an infringement of the copyright in the original drawing even if the person making the article has not seen the original drawing but has copied only a machine made in accordance with that drawing. This gives better protection than a patent for the article made according to the drawing. Patent expires after fourteen years, whereas copyright protection extends beyond sixty years. Besides, no formalities are required for copyright acquisition whereas obtaining a patent is a laborious and long drawn out process involving considerable expenditure. Kamil Idris rightly remarks:

> With the dawn of the new millennium new challenges and opportunities are before us, most notably, the expanding frontiers of the global economy that continues to grow, many may even say, explode, beyond the most optimistic expectations and beliefs. Conventional thinking had it that at a certain point the economy would stabilise and cease to grow much further. Consistently evolved and reinvolved itself, providing new opportunities and credible means for the still rapidly growing population to continue to survive, thrive and prosper. The key to this expansion of the economy has been the contribution of new knowledge as a crucial factor in sustained economic growth and development, digital technology, the internet, biotechnology, information and communication technologies, and a host of other such developments play a cardial role in the knowledge economy. In such an economic paradigm, incentives for creation of new knowledge are largely provided through the mechanism of intellectual property rights. A proper balance between the protection of intellectual property rights over such knowledge and its quick dissemination and assimilation in the productive enterprises is fundamental to the continued growth of the economy.[3]

COPYRIGHT AND GATT

Consequent upon India signing the GATT and entering the global market economy, a number of changes have been made in the Copyright Act of 1957 by the Amending Act of 1994, to give effect to the obligations arising from the signing of the GATT and to make Indian law more in line with the present law in many developed countries.

In the rapidly changing technological environment, copyright protection is being extended to many areas of creative work particularly in the computer industry, relating to computer software and databases. This has found recognition in the 1994 Amendment Act. Further certain special rights have been introduced for the first time for the benefit of performers like musicians, actors, acrobats, jugglers, snake charmers and so on. Computer software piracy and video piracy is a world-wide phenomenon. To act as a deterrent against such piracy, the provisions relating to protection of computer software have been tightened by substantially enhancing the punishment for infringement of software and increasing the scope of such infringement.

WHY DOES INTELLECTUAL PROPERTY NEED TO BE PROMOTED AND PROTECTED

Object of copyright law is to encourage authors, composers, artists and designers to create original works by rewarding them with the exclusive right for a limited period to exploit the work for monetary gain. The economic exploitation is done by licensing such exclusive right to entrepreneurs like publishers, film producers and record manufacturers for monetary considerations. People who economically exploit the copyright are the greater beneficiaries of the copyright law than the creators of works of copyright. However, several compellings reasons are there for protection of copyrights:

First, the progress and well-being of humanity rests on its capacity for new creations in the area of technology and culture.

Second, the Legal protection of these new creations encourages the expenditure of additional resources which leads to further innovations.

Third, the promotion and protection of intellectual property spurs economic growth, creates new job and industries and enhances the quality and enjoyment of life.

Protection of copyright benefits average person also. It rewards creativity and human endeavour, which fuel the progress of mankind. For example, the multi-billion dollar film, recording, publishing and software industries which bring pleasure to millions of people in all parts of the world would not survive without copyright protection.

TRIPS AND COPYRIGHT

The starting point of the TRIPS provisions on copyright is that all Members must comply with the substantive Articles (1-21) of the Berne Convention, other than the provision on moral rights. At crucial points, these obligations affecting the works of authors, as defined in Berne, are extended or made more explicit. W.R. Cornish rightly has mentioned[4] three general and two special cases deserve note:

(1) General

For the first time in an international instrument, the basic dichotomy of this branch of the law appears (in American form): "copyright protection shall extend to expressions and not to ideas, procedures, methods of operation or mathematical concepts as such." This vital touchstone for balancing exclusivity against free access thus becomes part of international understanding. For all its difficulty of application, it must accordingly remain within our own law.

TRIPS makes general the Berne principle restricting the extent of exceptions in national legislation to the reproduction right. As to term, there is a new minimum of fifty years from the making of a work, where term is not measured by reference to a natural person's life.

2. Special

Computer programs are required to be protected as literary works "under the Berne Convention"; and so are some compilations of data. A rental right is introduced for computer programs, and tentatively for films.

By contrast, in the sphere of neighbouring rights there is no equivalent incorporation of the Rome Convention or the Phonograms Convention (though Members are allowed to adopt the Rome Convention's conditions, limitations, exceptions and reservations). Instead the TRIPS Agreement has its own code of obligations relating to performers, sound-recording producers and broadcasting organisations:

(1) Performers

They must be provided with an exclusive right covering fixation, reproduction, wireless broadcasting and public communication of actual performances (as distinct from recordings of them). It must last for 50 years from the performance.

(2) Sound-recording Producers

They must have an exclusive right in the direct or indirect reproduction of their phonograms, and likewise (subject to certain limitations) to the rental of copies. It must last for 50 years from fixation.

(3) Broadcasters

Either broadcasting organisations themselves must have an exclusive right over fixation, reproduction and re-broadcasting of their (wireless) broadcasts, and a right of public communication in the case of television broadcasts; or else equivalent rights must be given to copyright owners of material broadcast. The minimum term is 20 years from the broadcast.

These provisions impose considerable changes on many countries undergoing development, far less on the industrialised world. Neither the current E.C. Directives nor TRIPS make significant legal adjustments to cater for digitised information systems serving world networks, for information superhighways are too novel and shifting a phenomenon. The implications for copyright, as the most likely tool for shoring up their economic value, is, of course, under urgent scrutiny. Whatever else, the provision of on-line services for education, information, entertainment, business and government promises very considerable realignments in what may be loosely labelled the information industry. In conditions of such insecurity, it seems highly important at least to ensure, if possible, that creators and other providers can secure returns on the uses of their material which correspond to the sale of copies and the showing of material in cinemas and on television in the world to date. There are considerable hopes and considerable dangers in a digitised world.

To conclude, it can be stated that the interests of the inventor with that of the society *vis-a-vis* wrong doer, must be balanced; second, because of technological innovations copyright infringement has taken the International Character, so, international effort in needed to check the abuse of copyright; third, because it is natural as well as moral rights apart from economic character so, its Human right character must be highlighted in national laws vigourously to reach the expected goal. An idea regime of copyright strikes a balance between private incentives for innovators and the public interests of maximising access to the fruits of innovation. This balance is reflected in Art. 27 of the universal declaration of Human Rights, 1948, which recognises moral and material interest in one hand and sharing the benefits on the other hand.[5]

NOTES AND REFERENCES

1. Art. 27(2) of the Universal Declaration of Human Rights, 1948.
2. See, W.R. Cornish, Intellectual Property, pp. 386-87.
3. P. Ganguli, Intellectual Property Rights Unleashing the Knowledge Economy, Tata McGraw-Hill, 2001 at p. XIII.
4. W.R. Cornish, Intellectual Property, pp. 314-15.
5. Article 27:
   1. Everyone has the right to freely to participate in the cultural life of the community, to enjoy the arts and to share in scientific advancements and its benefits.
   2. Everyone has the right to the protection of the moral and material interests resulting from any scientific, literary or artistic production of which he is the author.

Intellectual Property and Copyrights System

KALA MUNET AND S.P. MEENA

INTRODUCTION

At the outset, it may be stated that the role of intellectual property rights is to confer rights on the person responsible for conceiving ideas and reducing these to some usable format. In some situations, most notably concerned with the patent system, the right is close to the monopoly entitlement associated with the ownership of items of real property. In the case of copyright, however, the right is much more limited in its cope and has been described as a 'specialized and limited form of property.'[1]

The difference between the two regimes might be illustrated by reference to the story of Alexander Graham Bell and Elisha Grey. Both men invented the telephone. Alexander Graham Bell reached the 'US Patent Office slightly ahead of Grey.' The patent system works in large measure on the principle 'first come, first served'. Bell was awarded a patent and the exclusive right to exploit the technology describe therein. Even though Grey had worked totally independently, he was unable to exploit his own work, as this would have conflicted with Bell's patent. In the event that the case should have centered on a copyright claim, Bell's protection would have been limited to preventing the copyright of his work. Grey would not have infringed Bell's copyright and would, indeed, have obtained his own copyright for his own work. Patents, it might be concluded, confer a monopoly whereas copyright can only be invoked to prevent copying or certain other forms of unfair exploitation of the work.[2]

The essence of copyright is that this branch of law grants authors and other creators of works of mind, e.g. literature, music, art, etc. certain rights to authorize or prohibit, for a certain limited time, performance of the performer, the producer of the phonogram, the owner of any right in the performance or phonogram, or information about the terms and conditions of use of the performance or phonogram and any numbers or codes that represents such information, when any of these item of information is attached to a copy of a fixed performance or a phonogram or appears in connection with the communication, or making available of a fixed performance or a phonogram to the public. Copyright broadly speaking, embraces the provisions on the protection of copyright in the strict sense of the word and also the protection of what is usually referred to as "neighbouring rights."[3]

In the sphere of copyright, authors' rights have since 1886 been the subject of the Berne Convention for the Protection of Literary and Artistic Works (Berne), and to a lesser extent to the Universal Copyright Convention of 1952 (UCC); while so-called "neighbouring" or "related" rights are partly covered by the Rome Convention for the Protection of Performers, Phonograms and Broadcasting Organisations of 1961 (Rome).[4]

The major provisions of GATT in the field of Copyright protection include the following: (i) An obligation to comply with the provisions of the Berne Convention; (ii) A requirement to treat computer programs as literary works for copyright protection purposes and to provide protection for databases if their selection or arrangement "constitute intellectual creations"; (iii) A requirement to give to authors of computer programs and cinematographic works and producers of phonograms the rights in certain circumstances to control commercial rental of the originals or copies of their works; (iv) An obligation that in respect of works other than photographs and works of applied art, the normal duration of copyright protection shall be at least fifty years from the death of the author; (v) Fair use provisions and similar limitations on the exercise of copyright shall be limited to "certain special cases which do not conflict with normal exploitation of a work and do not unreasonably prejudice the legitimate interests of the right holder;" and (vi) Obligations to afford certain minimum rights for the protection of performers, producers of phonogram, and broadcasting organizations.[5]

DEVELOPMENT CO-OPERATION IN RELATION TO COPYRIGHT

The relevant program WIPO is the Permanent Program for Development Cooperation, Related to Copyright and Neighbouring Rights. The objectives of the Permanent Program are:

1. The encouragement in developing countries of intellectual creation in the literary, scientific and artistic domain.
2. The dissemination, within the competence of WIPO, as it is defined in itself, in developing countries, under fair and reasonable conditions, of intellectual creations in the literary, scientific and artistic domain, protected by the rights of authors (copyright) and by the rights of performing artists, producers of phonograms and broadcasting organizations (neighbouring rights).
3. The development of legislation and institutions in the fields of copyright and neighbouring rights in developing countries.[6]

A new service called the "Joint International UNESCO-WIPO Service for Access by Developing Countries to Works Protected by Copyright" has been created and is available to publishers in the developing countries. The service comprises:

1. Giving advice, on request, on methods of obtaining the necessary authorization for the reproduction, translation or other use of works protected by copyright, that is,

works that cannot normally be lawfully reproduced, translated or, in certain other ways, used without the previous consent of the owner of the copyright in those works, consent which usually is given in exchange for payment; and

2. Assistance, on request, to obtain such authorization in case of difficulty, for example, because the owner of the copyright cannot be identified with the required certainty, or because the owner of the copyright does not respond to a request for authorizations, or because the payments or other conditions proposed by the owner of the copyright appear to be too onerous.[7]

COPYRIGHTS AND INDIAN PERSPECTIVE

The Indian Copyright Act, 1914 and the Copyright Act, 1911 passed by the British Parliament (as modified in its application to India by the 1914 Act) were in force in India at the time when India became independent. These pre-existing laws continued to be in force by virtue of Article 372 of the Constitution of India till 21-1-1958, when the Copyright Act, 1957 passed by the Indian Parliament came into force.

It would be worthwhile to discuss special provision under the Copyright Act that deals with knowingly making use on a computer of an infringing copy of a computer program, where the punishment of imprisonment may extend to 3 years and a fine of not less than fifty thousand rupees, but which may extend to two lakh rupees. The police have been given the power to seize the infringing copies. There has been, however, substantial strengthening of India's copyright law to bring it on a par with international standards. There is no statutory presumption of copyright ownership and the defendant's actual knowledge of infringement must be proved.[8]

The latest threat to copyright law is in the increasing proliferation of Internet. The Internet development has changed the dissemination of information even to the extent of replacing printed works completely. Today a large number of houses/offices throughout the globe are linked to a computer center via viewer/printer consoles. The result is that the supply of one copy of a new work to a central point would make it or even selections from it, available to all offices and houses which are linked to the central point.

Bearing in mind that the whole concept of copyright in modern times arose from the invention of the printing press, even its partial replacement by computers amounts to a revolutionary change, why should not copyright owners be allowed to exercise their copyright at the input stage and look to the computer disseminator for the royalties in the same way that they have looked towards their publishers in the past.[9]

There is yet another challenge to copyright law, which is posed by cable diffusion, and it also requires institutionalized collective administration of the rights and payment of an equitable remuneration for performances and producers of phonograms whose performances or phonograms are used in cable transmission.[10]

In the case of infringement of copyright, however, by reason of recent amendments in law, the offence, which is committed, is regarded as a congnizable offence. A cognizable offence means for which a police officer may arrest without warrant. A police officer, not below the rank of a sub-inspector, on his being satisfied that an offence of infringement of copyright or other rights conferred by the Act is being or is likely to be committed has also the power to seize without warrant all copies of the infringing work and all plates used for the purpose of making infringing copies of the work.

This seizure can be effected wherever the said infringing material is found. This makes the criminal proceedings under the Copyright Act more effective, as the delay in obtaining warrants from the Magistrate before conducting a raid is eliminated. The effect of this provision is that a threatened infringement of the copyright can be nipped in the bud, possibly even before the commission of an offence. In fact, even at the preparation stage the police officer has the power to take custody of the infringing material.

In the field of copyright, India as a signatory to the *Berne Convention* passed the International Copyright Order, 1958 which is now replaced by the International Copyright Order of 1991. It provides the same protection to nationals of member-States as its own nationals. The States so covered are the Berne Convention signatories, the Universal Copyright Convention countries and the

Phonograms Convention countries. Patents and trade marks registered outside the country are protected against infringement in India if they have acquired international reputation and goodwill. The courts often extend the principles of unfair competition or passing off to stop infringement.

Notes and References

1. Brian Martin, Against Intellectual Property, Freedom Press, London, (1998) at p. 1. Brian Martin further remarks: "The Original rationale for copyrights and patents is to foster creative work by giving a short-term monopoly over certain uses of the work. In copyrights perspective, the ability to protect intellectual property is being undermined by modern technological developments."
2. George Minister, Marketplace of Ideas: An Overview of Problems, Random House Publication, Ottawa (1996) at p. 232.
3. Charles M. Gentile, Competitiveness over Information and Ideas, *GNU's Bulletin*, January 1995.
4. Edwin C. Hettinger, Justifying Intellectual Property, Philosophy and Public Affairs, Vol. 18, No. 1, Winter 1989, at pp. 31-52.
5. David Vaver, Intellectual Property Today: Of Myths and Paradoxes, *Canadian Bar Review*, Vol. 69, No. 1, March 1990, at pp. 98-128.
6. James Boyle, Shamans, Software and Spleens: Law and the Social Construction of the Information Economy (Cambridge, MA: Harward University Press, 1996).
7. David Vaver, Rejuvenating Copyright, *Canadian Bar Review*, Vol. 75, March 1996, at pp. 69-80.
8. Determining copyright and other infringement—The difficult point in determining copyright infringement is the determination of originality. When an accused work has originality, even if it is the same as or similar to another's work it is not an infringement. As for the originality of a work, the courts mainly consider whether the author is involved in intellectual labour, and whether the labour is creative. The standard of 'substantial similarity' is applied in determining copyright infringement in software. Where the portion of the software being used constitutes the necessary part, major part of the accused software and originality is not proved, infringement is established.
9. Rahul Matthan, The Law Relating to Computers and The Internet, Butterworths India (2000).
10. Saleem Akhtar, International Copyrights and Neighbouring Rights, Butterworths India (1999) at p. 146.

Protect Rights with Digital Watermark

Deepak Kumar Pandey

INTRODUCTION

Multimedia objects are valuable creature of human being, which is easy to pirate, therefore, it needs to protect. This can be easily done by digital watermarks. Digital watermark is the paramount skill to protect the digital multimedia objects such as audio, video or film including photograph. It is typically cover-signal in organize to communicate the hidden data. Alternatively, watermarking is the process of entrench the information into the objects (i.e. multimedia). Through watermarking one can identify the multimedia objects, as fingerprinting. The watermarks are set of algorithms designed for insertion and extraction and it has a unique identification number which holds all the information such as license condition, version, right holder person or group, format and enforcement mechanisms.

Digital watermarking assists both copy protection and copyright protection. The copy protection is the technical aspect.

It is designed with the help of software mechanism (algorithms and coding) for protecting the piracy. Beside this, copyright is a cluster of rights governed by law to the owner. The concept of Digital Right Management (DRM) evolved from both copy protection and electronic copyright protection.

OVERVIEW OF DIGITAL RIGHT MANAGEMENT

In terms of electronic copyright protection, it is functional with musicians, artists, photographers, composers, cinematographers and those persons who work with the electronic/digital media. DRM focuses the copyright, i.e. the right of author, which addressed as owner's intellectual assets. It also provides more flexibility for *"original works of authorship"*. In addition, the Copyright Act, 1957 as amended in 1983, 1984 and 1992, 1994, 1999 and Copyright Rules, 1958 generally gives exclusive right to owner/author in the respect of their work. There are several focal points (in digital stuff protection and claim for authorship) discussed below:

- *To reproduce* (or coping) of work in any form and including piling up it in any form (can be electronic media);
- *To public performance* (communicate the work in publicly), within dramatic, musical, film, literary, image (photographs and paintings), and different types of audio and video works;
- *Derivative works* (based on the original mechanism, i.e. make cinematography movie, adaptation, translation, etc.) can be set-up; and
- *Broadcasting* (digital audio or video transmission) in recording and during public performance.

A person or group (joint author) who make the original work (published and unpublished) is the owner of the copyright. In case of digital media, the copyright subsists during the life time of the creator and 60 years thereafter. A copyright contains the symbol © (in case of phonorecords of sound recording it contains the symbol ℗ the letter P in a circle) and followed by the creator name, year of registration and warning, i.e. *'All right reserved, unauthorized copying, public performance and broadcasting of this recording is strictly prohibited'.*

WATERMARKING TECHNIQUES

Watermarks are the robust technique to identify uniquely the multimedia object like fingerprinting. Fingerprints (in generally) are set of character's that enables differentiate the object into another similar objects. Consider another scenario, books and its ISBN No. Every registered book has its own unique ISBN No., which can acts as a pointer in the ISBN database. Watermarks are similar to ISBN No. and fingerprint both and provide immense consistency in DRM.

There are several techniques for watermarking in multimedia/digital objects given below in Figure 1.

Public and blind watermarking are almost same. In this process *'cover'* or original signals (media, i.e. audio, video, image) are not required in detecting or extraction process. Alternatively the non-blind also known as private watermarking is totally depends upon the cover signal by using 'private-key' or 'secret-key'. Let P_s is the original cover signal for the private watermark signal, i.e. $W(P_s)$ or C_s and S_k the secrete-key. So that P_s belongs to C_s. After extraction $C_s = P_s$ if and only if the S_k is authenticated.

Most recent technique of watermarking is recognized as asymmetric or public-key watermarking. It is the marvelous combination of public (blind) watermarking and private (non-blind) watermarking. The public key used for verification and the private key is used for embedding. Consider the following

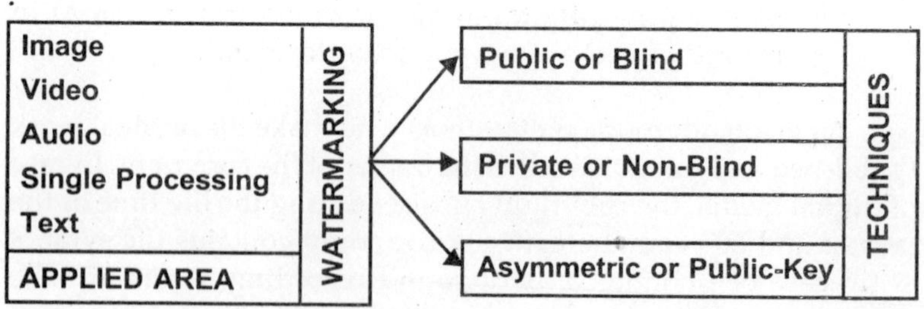

Fig. 1: Types of Digital Watermarking

algebra. Let A_s is the cover signal for the asymmetric watermarking signal $W(AP_s)$. Where $W(AP_s) = W(A_s + P_k)$. Here, P_k denotes the public key. When signals starts for embedding for watermark, the private key required (not related to public key by any means). Again the secrete key (S_k) is also used to remove the watermark from the watermarked digital object. The comprehensive process of embedding and detection process is illustrated in Figure 2.

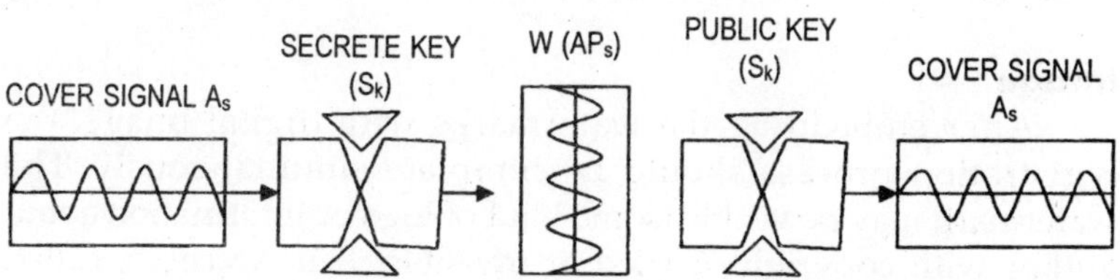

Fig. 2: Embedding and Detection Process

ATTRIBUTES OF WATERMARKING

Watermarking schemes are based on set of algorithms that is used for embedding (information hiding) and extraction (detection). There are three main attributes related to digital watermarking, i.e. *'imperceptibility'*, *'robustness'* and *'security'*.

Imperceptibility

One of the important characteristic of watermarking, i.e. it never changes the quality of the digital media. The embedding and evaluation technique (algorithms) must be transparent in digital object.

Robustness

The watermarking algorithms are written in high-level computing criteria for to accept the digital watermarks application.

Security

The application and its products (watermarked objects)

should contain high-tech security system for hiding the watermarks information about the object(s) and should have the capability to check the unauthorized hacking.

APPLIED AREA OF DIGITAL WATERMARKING

Every digital object can attached with watermark through software. Watermarks acts as copyright protection as well as copy protection (in some cases). It plays a vital role in different areas of digital objects. These are discussed in different heads as follow:

Image

After embedding the watermarks with digital image, the registration process should be complete simultaneously. The watermark may be visible (some kind of logo or information about author with copyright marks) or invisible. If it is visible, called as *'visual image watermarking'*.

Video

Video is combination of frames (set of individual images) that's why, image watermarking is also applied in each frame of video. A Visual logo and information can also be placed in the video frames. Audio/The process of embedding information into digital audio signal is widely used in modern era.

Signal Processing

In this age of information technology the tracing of signal(s) is vital issue for every business company or individual(s). The signal(s) (transmit or broadcast) can also monitor and extract with the help of special hardware and software.

Text

The watermarks can also be embedded into the text in pixels and axis. But it is not widely used because it does not aid (generally) to protect the copyright.

Notice and Remedies on Account of Infringement

Copyright notice is optional for the protection of digital works. However, it is beneficial to incorporate notice. It includes: (i) the symbol of ℗ and © as per the verity of digital object, (ii) the year of first registration, (iii) owner's name and address, and (iv) terms of use with license conditions. The rights of copyright holders (authors/owners) are protected U/S 64 and U/S 66 of the provisions of the Copyright Act.

CONCLUSION

The digital watermarking applications has capability of embedding and extraction of related information of copyright notice etc. Digital watermark is concerned to protect copyright, i.e. audio, video and other works available in digital form. It has a capability to protect, as well as the monitoring an unauthorized use of digital media. 'Watermarking' *(hidden copyright message)* and 'fingerprinting' *(hidden serial numbers or a set of characteristics that tend to distinguish an object from other similar object)* gives better opportunities to improve the business industry and advancement in academics. However, it requires lot of novel advance technique for its betterment.

REFERENCES

Digital Watermarking Frequently Asked Questions viewed at www.watermarkingworld.org

Mahesh, V. (2001), "Digital Watermarks Use them to Protect Your Rights", *Information Technology*, 10(10): 43-44.

Khona Zarana, (2001), "Computer Software: Protection and Copyright", *Express Computer*, 12(25), p. 13.

"New Audio Technology", World of Information Technology, *New Syndicate*, December, 2001, p. 12.

TIFAC:DOC:023 (2004), "Some Questions and Answers on Patents, Copyright, Designs, Trademarks, IC Technology, New Delhi.

Tanenbaum, A.S. (2003), Computer Network, Pearson Education Pte. Ltd., Delhi.

Johnson, Neil F., Zoran Duric and Sushil Jajodia (1999), A Role for Digital Watermarking in Electronic Commerce, ACM Computer Surveys.

Katzenbeisser, Stefan and Fabien A.P. Petitcolas (2000), Information Hiding Techniques for Steganography and Digital Watermarking, Artech House Books.

Petitcolas, Fabien A.P. (2005), The Information Hiding: Digital Watermarking and Steganography viewed at http://www.petitcolas.net/fabien/

Sridhar Madabhushi (2002), The Rigid Regime of Copyright, *The ICFAI Journal of Intellectual Property Rights*, Nov. 2002.

Copyright and Freedom of Speech and Expression under Fundamental Rights

S.R. SHARMA

The copyright law protects the intellectual creations in original literary and artistic works. The Copyright protection commences as soon as the work is created and it does not require any registration. Traditionally the concern of copyright law was limited to books, music, paintings or films, now its protection has taken on new dimensions and today it extends to even computer software and compilations of data. Copyright has some closely related rights that confer similar principles of protection. These are known as 'related rights' or 'neighbouring rights'. These rights protect persons, other than the creators who are involved in the dissemination of copyrighted work. These rights are continued to three specific categories of persons: performers, producers of phonograms and broadcasting organisations.

The Berne Convention for the protection of literary and artistic works, as revised upto 1971, provided the highest level of international legal protection for copyright, prior to TRIPS with the conclusion of TRIPS under the Uruguay Round of multilateral trade negotiations, protection of copyright and related rights became for the first time, a subject covered by the international trade law.

Articles 9 to 13 of TRIPS prescribe the 'minimum standards' for the protection of copyright. Art. 9.1 of TRIPS establishes that WTO members must comply with Arts. 1 to 21 of the Berne Convention, 1971 including the Appendix thereto. The Berne Convention requires that the enjoyment and exercise of copyright cannot be subjected to any formality such as registration. The only exception to adherence to the Berne Convention is Art. 6(b), which obliges the members to protect the moral rights of the authors. Article 9(2) of the Berne Convention contains exception to the exclusive right of reproduction conferred by the copyright law. The pre-requisites for the applicability of this Article are:

(i) These limitations and exceptions should be granted in certain special cases,
(ii) These should not conflict with the normal exploitation of the work, and
(iii) These should not unreasonably prejudice the legitimate interest of the author.

FREEDOM OF SPEECH AND EXPRESSION UNDER FUNDAMENTAL RIGHTS

The right to impart and receive information is a species of the right to freedom of speech and expression guaranteed by Article 19(1)(a) of the constitution of India.

'Freedom of speech' according to encyclopedia is "speech, freedom of liberty to speak and otherwise express oneself and one's opinions." Like freedom of the press which pertains to the publication of speech, freedom of speech itself has been absolute in no time or place.

In politics sense, freedom of speech means 'the right to speak without censorship or restraint by the government.'

By the Legal Dictionary, freedom of speech is "the right to express information ideas and opinions, free of government restrictions based on contents and subject only to reasonable limitations."

Copyright of property beyond all doubt and dispute. As by the provision of sections 18, 20, etc. of Copyright Act, 1957, the right is heritable and transferable and can also be transmitted by bequest and these are all essential attributes of 'Property'. Every possible interest, which a person can acquire, hold and dispose of its property.[1] It is true that the right to "acquire, hold and dispose of property" which was specified as a fundamental right in Article (19)(1)(f) of the constitution has been deleted by the Constitution (44th Amendment) 1978. But in writing a book or performing any other cultural activity, a person if obviously exercising his right to 'Freedom of speech and expression' which is a fundamental right specified in Art. (19)(1)(a).

The categorical dictum in the celebrated seven judge bench decision of the Supreme Court in *Maneka Gandhi*,[2] relying on the earlier decisions in *Kharak Singh*[3] and *Satwant Singh*,[4] is that all 'Liberties' or 'Freedoms' that a person may reasonably require for his growth and development, if not expressly specified in Article 19(1), shall be deemed to be comprised in the expression 'personal liberty' in Art. 21, which takes in and comprises the residue of all Liberties and Freedoms of a person. Four Articles, being Articles 19, 20, 21 and 22 listed under the heading 'Right to Freedom' while Articles 20 and 22 confer protection in respect of trial of and conviction for offences and provide certain safeguards in respect of arrest and detention, including preventive detention, the other two Articles, 19 and 21, cover, in between themselves, all other freedoms and liberties and while 6 of such freedoms or liberties have been distinctly and separately dealt with in Art. 19(1), Article 21 takes in 'Comprises and residue'.

The right or the liberty to write a book, to publish some and sell copies thereof, are also freedom protected as fundamental right under Art. 21. In later decision in *Francis Caralie Mullin*,[5] Justice Bhagwati who delivered the leading judgement in *Maneka Gandhi*, has observed that "reading, writing and expressing oneself in diverse forms" are fully covered by and guaranteed under life/liberty clause in Article 21.

It is also said that 'copyright' is a 'property', then the mandate in Art. 300A to the effect that 'no person shall be deprived of his property save of authority of law'. In case of *R.C. Cooper*,[6] *Shambhunath*[7] and other decisions, the Supreme Court has categorically laid down in *Maneka Gandhi* that "if a law depriving a person of personal liberty (right to speech and expression)" and prescribing a procedure for that purpose with in the meaning of Article 21 is to stand the test of one or more of the fundamental rights conferred under Art. 19, which may be applicable in given situation ex-hypothesis. It must be also liable to be tested with reference to Art. 14 that law must be reasonable, just and fair.

Freedom of press is under right to speech and expression under Art. 19(1)(a). This freedom can only be available in society where there is a right to free speech and expression. Similarly, the freedom of information can be enjoyed only if there are sources from which informations can flow. Freedom of expression and the freedom to receive and impart information are corollary of one another. In fact, there is an overlap between the freedom of expression and the freedom to receive or impart information. The freedom to impart information can be considered as an expression of an opinion, of the informant or of a third person. The seeking of information, on the other hand, precedes the information of an opinion by the person who seeks the information and consequently also its expression. But with regard to the press, freedom of expression and information runs parallel to each other. Press might be the medium of expression, someone else might possess the information. In case of information the only one who has the right of free distribution of that information is the party who is the author, originator or otherwise the intellectual owner of the information in question. Exercising the freedom of expression one must have the freedom of information. In this regard, approval of the freedom of information Bill, 2000 by Indian parliament would be a welcome move. There are various national laws and international conventions providing protection to these rights usually expressly otherwise under the subject 'freedom of speech and expression'. The Universal Declaration of Human Rights (UDHR) under its Art. 19 gives everyone the freedom to hold opinion and to seek, receive and impart information and idea through any media and regard less of frontiers. Art. 10 of the European Convention on Human Rights (ECHR) provides for freedom to receive and impart information. Also Article 19 of the International Convention on Civil and Political Rights (ICCPR), Art. 13 of the American Convention on Human Rights, Art. IV of the American Declaration of Rights and Duties of man, Art. 9 of the African charter of Human and peoples rights, Art. 5 of the

International Convention on Elimination of Racial Discrimination and Arts. 2, 12 and 13 of the Convention on the Rights of the Child, provides for protection of freedom of speech and expression through press. One of the most important components of freedom of speech and expression is free and unhindered use of the appropriate language. A society can not effectively communicate if a restriction of sanction is imposed on it in only mariner whatsoever. A copyright would confer an indirect copyright in the language itself, which cannot be justified in any circumstance. Such a claim would definitely be violative of Art. 19(1)(a) of the Constitution of India.

It must be noted that Art. 21 of the Constitution of India confers a 'right to know' on all person. In *R.P. Limited* Vs. *Indian Express Newspapers,*[8] the Supreme Court read in Art. 21 the right to know Court said that right to know is necessary ingredient of participatory democracy. The ambit and scope of Art. 21 is much wider as compared to Art. 19(1)(a). Thus, any attempt to curb the right to know whether directly or indirectly would be violative of Art. 21 of the Constitution of India.

Notes and References

1. *J.K. Trust* Vs. *Commissioner of I.T.*, 1957 SC 848.
2. AIR 1978 SC 597.
3. AIR 1 963 SC 1295.
4. AIR 1967 SC 1836.
5. AIR 1981 SC 746.
6. 1970 Sec. 248.
7. 1973 Sec. 856.
8. AIR 1989 SC 990.

Intellectual Property and their Protection under Copyright Law

S.K. Pandey

INTRODUCTORY

Human creative activities can be described as creation of the human mind, such as writings, drawings, paintings, sculpture and other art works, inventions, designs and trade-marks. They are known as intellectual property of human being. Every human being wants to protect his property. Therefore, it is necessity to protect the life of human being and his property by the state. Copyright is one category of intellectual property. Intellectual property rights are statutory rights. All intellectual property rights have a common feature. They generally exclude third parties from exploiting the protected subject matter without express authorization of the right-holder for a fixed period of time. The law relating to copyright in India is contained in the Copyright Act, 1957.

Under the Berne Convention and now under the Trade Related Aspects of Intellectual Property Rights (TRIPS) regime, copyright law is intended to provide protection to the rights of intellectual creators with respect to their original literary and artistic work. The subject matter of copyright is the original expression of an idea in literary, artistic and other works. It does not give the right holder any monopoly over ideas, but only protects expression. Copyright protection is now, not confined to books, music, paintings or films, but extends to computer software and compilations of data. It begins automatically from the moment the work comes into existence without the need to comply with any formalities such as registration.

JUSTIFICATIONS

One may question the relevance of seeking justification for a system of legal rules that has existed for at least a couple of centuries in most of the Western World. However, the fact is that intellectual property rights are facing a crisis of legitimacy for a few reasons. The onset of globalisation has had a big role to play in creating this crisis. Intellectual property rights are seen as a very important economic tool for big businesses and often investment into countries will flow only if companies are assured of strong intellectual property protection from the law. Not only is there more pressure to increase the strength of protection (both qualitatively and quantitatively) but also economic interests push for more subject matter to be covered by intellectual property laws.

It is in this context, where the desire for universal notions of rights are asserted as desirable, that a need is felt for understanding the relevance and philosophical significance of these rights, their economic and cultural effects, the possible alternatives serving similar purposes as well as the historical genesis of intellectual property institutions.[1]

In recent years piracy of copyright works has become rampant, particularly with the rapidly advancing technologies that facilitate cheap and easy reproduction and dissemination of these works.

The basic ideas behind protecting intellectual property rights is that the creators, innovators and inventors be given such incentives as may encourage them and other to advance the knowledge and techniques in their respective fields. However, there is a competing interest as well. The benefit of the innovations should be available to the society at large as well consistent with the interest of the owner of intellectual property right. The entire body of intellectual property laws is an attempt to draw a balance between these two competing interests.

COPYRIGHTS AS HUMAN RIGHTS UNDER UNIVERSAL DECLARATION

The object of Universal Declaration of Human Rights (UDHR), 1948 is to provide every kind of right to the human family including right to dignity and worth of human person. Every person wants to keep this property with him and wants to protect this law. This right of human being is universal. This universal right is also provided under UDHR. It declares under Article 17(1) that everyone has the right to own property alone as well as in association with others. Article 17(2) declares that no one shall be arbitrarily deprived of his property. Infringement of intellectual property is under protection in India as human right of a person. This protection is given under Copyright Act, 1957. If any person infringed the intellectual property of another person, he shall be liable for punishment under this Act.[2] The Indian Copyright Act, 1957 has been amended in pursuance of India's obligations under TRIPS by the Copyright Amendment Act, 1994 and the Copyright Amendment Act, 1999.[3] The said amendments introduced a large number of changes in the definitional clauses and substantive provisions of the Parent Act to incorporate, *inter alia*, computer programs and technological developments.

RELEVANCY OF COPYRIGHT UNDER ICESCR

The intellectual property right involves various areas of trade, industry and commerce including production and distribution of books, magazines, newspaper or information and broadcasting industries, media of entertainment including musical works of performances, publication and cinema television. As such the intellectual property right problem, though not in all, but in some respects are international problems. The International Covenant on Economic, Social and Cultural Rights (ICESCR) 1966, recognized the inherent dignity, equality in foundation of freedom, justice and peace in the world. It provides different kind of rights related to economic, social and cultural to the human being. Among these rights the cultural right is directly related to the copyright of a person. Article 15 of the ICESCR provides the cultural rights as copyright of a person in the shape of human right. These provisions of ICESCR is purely related to the copyright of a creative activity of a person. It also provides the obligation on the state parties to take steps for the conservation, development and diffusion of the scientific literary and artistic right of a person. Similarly, the object of copyright law is to encourage authors, composers, artists and designers to create original work by rewarding them with the exclusive right for a limited period to exploit the work for monetary gain.

COPYRIGHTS UNDER TRIPS

Mostly all the intellectual property rights were protected by the Trade Related Intellectual Property Right (TRIPS) agreement. The copyright as an intellectual property was protected for first time in 1886 by the Berne Convention. It was revised in 1971 and again in 1979. Copyright was again recognised by the International Community through Uruguay Agreement, 1994 under TRIPS. Part II of the TRIPS is related to intellectual property rights. Articles 9 to 14 of TRIPS are directly related to copyright.

RELEVANCY OF COPYRIGHT UNDER INDIAN CONSTITUTION

The object of the Indian Constitution is to provide liberty of thought and expression to all it's citizens. Part III of the Constitution deals with fundamental rights and Part IV as Directive Principles of State Policy. In 1976, Part IVA as fundamental duties was inserted in the Constitution. Article 19(1)(a) is relevant as freedom of speech and expression for the purpose of Copyright in India. The freedom of speech and expression means the right to express one's convictions and opinions freely by words of mouth, writing, printing, pictures or any other mode. Therefore, every citizen of India is free to express his views through the literary, dramatic, musical and artistic works. These works are subject matter of Copyright. Article

19(1)(a) covers cinematography films and sound recording as fundamental right of the citizens. It, therefore, includes the right to one's views through the print media or through any other communication channel e.g., the radio and television. Therefore, it can be said that the fundamental rights under Article 19(1)(a) give protect to the Copyright as supreme law of the land.

JUDICIAL RESPONSE TO COPYRIGHT

Copyright subsists in India under the Copyright Act, 1957 and begins automatically from the moment the work comes into existence without the need to comply with any formalities, such as registration. Unfortunately, the courts have not appreciated this basic feature of copyright. Even now we find judicial utterances showing lack of awareness of this fundamental principle.[4] It is true that the Act has established a copyright registry and provided for the maintenance of a register of copyright in which may be entered the names of titles of works, the names and addresses of the authors, publishers and owners of copyright, and such other particulars as may be prescribed.[5] The author or publisher of any work, or the owner of the copyright in it, or any other person interested in the copyright, may make an application for entering particulars of the work in the register. The registrar may thereupon, after holding such enquiry as he may deem fit, enter the particulars in the register. The register is evidence of the particulars entered therein. By virtue of these permissive provisions it has become a common practice to get registered copyright in the artistic features of the get-up of trade mark labels with or without registration of trade mark under the trade marks status.[6] Presumably, this provision for a copyright register has been misunderstood by courts to mean that registration is a pre-requisite for the subsistence of copyright in a work.

CONCLUSIONS AND SUGGESTIONS

The object of copyright law is to protect the author of his work. A review of the legal framework of Indian Copyright law shows that structurally our law is well founded and is flexible enough to respond to changes that advancement of technology may warrant. There are adequate civil and penal provisions envisaged in the legislation to safeguard the interest of the creators. There is a need for trained and well-equipped specialized police force for detection and enforcement of crimes relating to violation of intellectual property rights and there is also a need for change of the judicial mindset in dealing with intellectual property right violations. The authors believes that there are still misconceptions, difficulties of access to the courts, slow growth of copyright bar and delay in disposal of whatever cases reach the courts. It is submitted that redress and access to the adjudicatory machinery must be improved and this can be done in a better manner, if copyright or intellectual property tribunals manned by specialists in the areas are set-up throughout the country.

Hence this is the time proper to think over the matters of protection in totality. It is submitted that there should be International Dispute Redressal Forums. These matters should come under the provision of jurisdiction of International Court of Justice. What our country needs today is nothing more than a set of honest men who will have the interest of the country before them as their prime objective. One can fairly hope that the country will throw up such men in abundance.

Notes and References

1. The TRIPS (Trade Related Aspects of Intellectual Property Rights) Agreement seek to internationalise both substantive and procedural aspects of intellectual property rights law through the mechanism of the World Trade Organisation (WTO).
2. Section 63 of the Copyright Act, 1957.
3. Important changes have been brought about by the Copyright Amendment Acts, 1994 and 1999.
4. *Gulfam Exports & Others* Vs. *Sayed Hamid*, 2000 (20) PTC 496.
5. Sections 44 to 50A of the Copyright Act, 1957.
6. *Camlin Pvt. Ltd.* Vs. *National Pencil Industries*, AIR 1988 Del 393.

Basic Information for Software Copyright

P.C. JOSHI AND DEEPAK KUMAR PANDEY

INTRODUCTION

Software is a set of computer program (arrange instruction or code in recognized manner) to be used to perform for certain task in a computer or other electronic mechanism. The development of software is a time taking process and numbers of software engineers, programmers, analysts, designers are involved to build it. Budget is another sphere of consideration. However, it is easy to pirate and crack and does not give any benefit to the owner/author. The copyright is the spectacular way to protect the software as well as computer program. The Copyright Act, 1957 gives protection to author(s) by prohibiting unauthorized copying. Basically copyright is an assortment of right provided by law which includes literary, dramatic, musical, artistic work, producers of cinematography, film and sound recordings, etc.

Copy Protection Vs. Copyright Protection

The copy protection is the technical aspect, designed with the help of software tools (coding) for protecting the piracy. It is also called *'anti-piracy mechanism'*. Alternatively, the copyright protection is a cluster of rights governed by law to the owner.

Ownership of Software Copyright

In case of computer software, a person or group (joint author) who writes the original computer programs (published and unpublished) is the owner of the copyright. If the work has been done by any contract (service) basis by any employee, the employer is the first owner of the copyright (condition: there is not any agreement ahead). The copyright subsists during the life time of the author and 60 years thereafter. The copyright gives to the owner more flexibility to reproduce or coping of the work, can be made a derivate work based on the original work, communicate it to public, to shell or give on rent, etc. The ideas, logics, algorithms, systems, methods, concepts are not protecting by the Copyright Act.

Software Copyright Registration

In the modern business scenario, it is very crucial to register the software by which, nobody can use the software directly or indirectly without the permission of the author. Dully filled application form *(Form IV—Application for Registration of Copyrights)* with the registration fee should deposit in the copyright office. There are several focal points which must be clear before fill up the application form discussed below:

(i) *Authorship:* The name and address of the owner with the enclosure of computer program (with text code literary) and user's manual.

(ii) *Creation year:* The date is specified in the application form clearly.

(iii) *Derivative work:* Any work which is derived from the original work should also be registered (i.e. revised software etc.).

(iv) *Computer program without trade secret:* Three copies code of Published or unpublished computer program duly enclosed with the application form.

(v) *Computer program with trade secret:* If newly created or revised computer program is registered for trade secret, it is mandatory to mention it in cover letter along with the copyright notice.

Software Copyright Notice

Copyright notice is optional for software program. However, it is beneficial to incorporate notice for informing to public that the work is protected by copyright. It is the responsibility to the owner that it keeps in mind the whole information of license agreement and term of use by which owner can claim for the work without prior concern of copyright office. Copyright notice contains the symbol © or abbreviation "Copr." followed by the author's name and year of registration.

Remedies of Copyright Infringement

The right of copyright holders is protected *U/S 64* & *U/S 66* of the provisions of Copyright Act. The court has empowered to grant temporary and permanent injunction.

CONCLUSION

The anti-piracy code should be written in high level computing criteria and contain high-tech security system for protecting the software application and its product. The copy protection and copyright protection assist digital right management and gives better opportunity to improve the business industry and advancement in academics. However, copy protection requires lot of advance techniques for its betterment.

REFERENCES

Khona Zarana (2001), "Computer Software: Protection and Copyright," *Express Computer,* 12(25), p. 13.

TIFAC:DOC:023 (2004), "Some Questions and Answers on Patents, Copyright, Designs, Trademarks", IC Technology, New Delhi.

Software Copyright Guidelines (2004) viewed at http:/www.rgs.uci.edu/

24

Some Aspects of Copyright Law in India

A.K. Pandey

Copyright is a right which provides protection against misuse or unauthorized use of a work. It is available to the creators of literary, musical, dramatic and artistic works to do or authorise the doing of certain acts regarding to their creations. The rights of authorship, distribution, communication, reproduction broadcasting, adaptation and translation are generally included under this right. The name of this right may vary from a class of work to another class of work and from country to country.

Though the territorial base of copyright is nation yet some international treaties and convention like Universal Copyright Convention, Berne Convention for the Protection of Literary and Artistic Work and the Agreement on Trade Related Aspects of Intellectual Property Rights provides protection of copyright of nationals of member-country in all other member-countries.

Copyright is an intangible property right. It can be transferred to another person. It can be inherited also. Copyright is an intellectual property right and it is for a limited duration. So the copyright is a sum of many exclusive rights.

INDIAN POSITION

The Copyright Act, 1957 as amended in 1999 governs the copyright. The works are classifies into three classes under the Act:

(1) Literary, dramatic, musical and artistic works. Works which express in print or writing are the literary work. Dramatic works includes choreographic work. Musical work includes any graphical notation consisting the music, painting, sculpture, drawing, photograph, architecture work, craft work are included in the artistic work.
(2) Cinematograph films: It includes any work of visual recording in any medium making a moving image produced by any means.
(3) Sound recording which can be produced regardless of the medium.

The rapid changes taking place in the field of computer technology led to the creation of new work and material. The traditional communication media, print, sound, visual, are included in one, i.e. multimedia. So looking into the new technologies the computer programs and computer databases are also included into the classes of work.

Under the Copyright Act some rights are available, which are as follows:

(i) Reproduction Right

The section 14[1] of the Copyright Act recognizes the reproduction right for the authors and producers of phonogram. Under this right the owner has to authorize the making of one or more copies of a work or any part of it in any material form. As far as this right in the digital environment is concerned it is already extended specifically to the authors of literary, musical and dramatic works.

(ii) Right of Distribution

The right of distribution has been recognized by majority of the countries in one or the other form.[2] Different practices exist regarding the territorial application of this right. The purpose of introducing specifically this right was to recognize the concept of national exhaustion of this right. The Indian Copyright Act has not specifically recognized the right of distribution for the authors, performers and phonogram producers. It is generally understood that the right of publication under section 14 includes the right of distribution as well. The Copyright Act has expressly prohibited the importation of infringing copies into india.[3]

(iii) Right of Rental

The right of commercial rental was recognized for the first time in the TRIPS agreement for limited works. Article 14(4) of the TRIPS agreement indicate that the mandatory commercial rental right was confined to computer programs, cinematographic works and works embodied in phonograms. Article 14(4) of TRIPS agreement was not fully incorporated in the Indian copyright amendment in 1994. Later on the Copyright Act extended this right to computer programs, Cinematograph films and sound recordings.

(iv) Translation Right

Translation means the expression of a work in a language other than that of an original version. This right is mentioned in Article 8 of the Berne Convention. The Indian Copyright Act recognizes this right for all literary, dramatic and musical works. For the translation the authorization of copyright is needed.

(v) Right of Adaptation

Under this right the author is authorise to alter his work. The Berne Convention[4] does not define the alteration but says 'adaptation, arrangement and other alterations of the work'. The Indian Copyright Act clearly provides this right to every literary, dramatic, musical and artistic works and computer programs. The Act says that the adaptation means:

(a) in relation to literary work or artistic work the conversion of work into dramatic work by way of performance in public or otherwise,
(b) for dramatic work, the alteration of work into a non-dramatic work,
(c) regarding musical work, any arrangement or transcription of work, and

(d) in relation to any work, any use of such work involving its arrangement or alteration.

(vi) Right of Communication to the Public

The Act says that the communication to the public means 'making any work available for being seen or heard or otherwise enjoyed by public directly or by means of display.'[5] Communication through satellite or cable to more than one household or residence is also covered under this head.

(vii) Right of Sale

The owner of copyright in computer programs, cinematograph films and sound recording have right to sale or offer for sale any of the work, regardless of whether such copy has been sold on earlier occasion. But in computer program the principle of first sale exhaustion applies. The resale share rights are also available under the Act.

(viii) Moral Right

This right is related to the author's dignity. It is reflection of the personality of creator. It is an independent right and even remains with author after transferring all other rights. The right is a safeguard against distortion and misuse of an author's work.

The duration of copyright is limited one. The Berne Convention provides it for lifetime of author plus fifty years thereafter. In USA and Europe the duration is lifetime plus seventy years. In India for the literary, dramatic, musical and artistic works the duration is life time of author plus sixty years if they are published within the lifetime of the author. In case of cinematograph films, sound recording, photography, posthumous publication the duration is sixty years after publication.

Normally the ownership of copyright vests in the creator or author. But some exceptions are there in case of government, public undertaking, public speech on behalf of another person work done in course of author's appointment, etc.

Without the authorization of copyright owner any duplication, adaptation, communication to the public or broadcast, etc. or violation of condition of licence in case of license assigned is an infringement of copyright. But subject to certain conditions criticism, fair deal for research, study, review, news-reporting, work in library, schools and legislatures are allowed to balance the interest of society and the owner.

The Registration of work is not essential under the Act but registration is an evidence of ownership. There is an office for registration in which one Registrar and one or more Deputy Registrars of copyright are appointed. The Registrar is a quasi-judicial body. And have the powers of the civil court.

There is a provision for establishment of copyright board under the Act which consists of one chairman and two or more but not more than fourteen members. The chairman is of the level of a judge of High Court. The board is a quasi-Judicial body and has power to:

(i) hear appeal from the order of registrar,
(ii) hear and decide dispute about publication,
(iii) grant licence to produce and publish a translation of literary work after a period of seven years from the date of publication,
(iv) hear disputes on assignment of copyright,
(v) fix rate of royalties, and
(vi) hear application about entries in the register.

The aggrieved person may appeal within the three months of the final order of the board to the High Court having jurisdiction.

The owner can administer his own right. But the Act also provide for the establishment of copyright societies for collective administration. The owner and registered society having right can institute a suit for infringement, which may be civil or criminal proceedings. Injunctions and damages may be granted against infringers. There is also a provision for fine of fifty thousand to two lakhs and imprisonment of six months to three years in case of infringement of copyright.

With a view to the points discussed above there are some suggestions are to be made which are the following:

(1) There should be cell at District Level to check the copyright infringement.
(2) The police should be sensatised regarding the copyright violation.

(3) It would be better that the owner must prefer to make the society. So that they can know that where and how their copyright is infringed.

(4) After thorough study of the law the functions and powers of the Copyright Board should be increased.

(5) Implementation level of the law should be increased.

(6) Awareness programme must be conducted widely. So the public may know about the copyright law.

Notes and References

1. S. 14(a)(i) reads "... to reproduce the work in any material form including the storing of it in any medium by electronic means."
2. Articles 14(1) and 16(1) of Berne Convention.
3. S. 51(b)(iv) reads, "When any person ... imports into India any infringing copies of the work. ..."
4. Article 12 of the Berne Convention.
5. S. 12 (ff) of Indian Copyright Act.

References

Andrew Christie, Reconceptualising Copyright in Digital Era.

B.N. Pandey, Edited, Intellectual Property Right.

Iyengar, The Copyright Act Edited by R.G. Chaturvedi.

W. Carnish, Intellectual Property, Patents, Copyright Trade Marks and Allied Rights, 2003.

Gopalkrishnan, *The Academy Law Review*.

Online Copyright Violation: With Special Reference to Liability of Internet Service Providers

PALLAVI GUPTA

INTRODUCTION

The arrival of Internet has raised many unexpected issues that do not find solution in the existing legal regime. Internet is that technology which has allowed the content community at large[1] to expend their market at an unprecedented rate, the same technology allowed anonymous and invisible pirate to copy and disseminate instantaneously anything that is available on the Internet.

Among various issues one of the most debatable issue is associated with the internet facilitation of information distribution is the liability of internet service providers for transmitting contents created by others or for online infringement of IPRs or Copyright. Could the service provider be held responsible for illegal activities committed by their users? Should online intermediaries be held responsible for third party material put on the internet by users of their facilities? If yes, what should be the extent of their liability?

MEANING OR DEFINITION OF INTERNET SERVICE PROVIDERS (ISPs)

ISP is an entity that connects people to the internet and provides other related services such as website building and hosting. An ISP has the equipment and the telecommunication line access required to have a point of presence on the internet for the geographic area served.

In India term *Network Service Provider*[2] has been used for Internet Service Providers and "Network Service Provider" means an *intermediary.* Term "Intermediary" defined with respect to any particular electronic message means any person who on behalf of another person receives stores or transmits that massage or provides any service with respect to that message.

ROLE OF INTERNET SERVICE PROVIDERS

According to definition two main services are provided by ISPs as—

(i) Web site building and hosting; done by an entity that provides space and management for individual or business web sites; and

(ii) Access providing; done by an entity that arrange for an individual or an organization to have access to the internet.

It is common for a single legal entity to provide a complete range of these services. ISPs are instrumental in transmitting or disseminating third party content.

Basis of Liability of ISPs

The liability of ISPs for copyright infringement rests on three theories—liability for direct infringement, liability for vicariously infringement and liability for contributory infringement. Direct infringement occurs when a person violates any exclusive right of the copyright owner[3].

The dissemination of copyrighted works online involve two of the internet rights, viz. the right of reproduction and the right of communication to the public. As soon as a work is transmitted on the internet from one point to another, ISPs are involved in the transmission. If such ISPs participate in transmitting etc. materials provided by another which infringe copyright or related rights, they could be liable for copyright infringement and such liability could arise in one of two ways:

(i) If the ISP itself is found to have engaged in unauthorized acts of reproduction or communication to the public; and

(ii) If he is held responsible for contributing to or making possible the act of infringement by another.

WIPO

For the first time, this issue caught attention of the International Community in WIPO.[4] Where two treaties were finalized, i.e. WCT[5] and WPPT[6] to counter the challenges posed by the new phenomenon of the internet. Under these treaties an additional right was granted to the Copyright owner in the context of Internet which is totally new and referred as the right of communication to the public and right to distribution or online dissemination specially spell out.

These treaties incorporate right to make available to the public the work in such a way that the members of public may access the work from a place and time, individually chosen by them. Further it made clear that mere provision of physical facilities for enabling or making a communication doesn't itself amount to communication with the meaning of this treaty[7].

The agreed statement clearly signed that an ISP cannot be held liable for direct infringement, insofar as the 'right of communication to the public' is concerned. However, the statement does not rule out liability for indirect infringement.

LEGAL STATUS FOR ISPs LIABILITY IN DIFFERENT COUNTRIES

ISP Liability under the DMCA—US

US is the first country who legislate on the treaty provisions by incorporating DMCA[8] in 1998 to fix ISP's liability. By codifying US court decision[9], "that passive automatic acts shall not become grounds for a finding of online copyright infringement," this Act adds a new section 512[10] to Chapter 5 of US Copyright Right.

This Act sets own guidelines with respect to copyright infringement online and specifically states only four circumstances where ISPs are exempt from liability for damages.[11]

This Act enables the copyright owner to determine the identity of an online infringer. It permits a copyright owner to act on the owner's behalf to request a clerk of 'any United States district court' to issue a subpoena to an ISP requiring identification of an alleged infringer.[12] Here DMCA goes a step further that it provides for extensive 'notice and take down' procedures.[13]

ISPs Liability under the German Teleservices Act

German Teleservices Act[14] as been enacted to cover any kind of liability for contents online; no doubt including copyright infringement also. Main Characteristic of this Act is its *filtering mechanism*. Under this mechanism the ISPs are made liable according to the general provisions of law related to the conduct of the ISP in question. It means if ISP is guilty of defamation then he shall be guilty under defamatory laws of Germany and if the ISP is accused of copyright violation then his liability will be determined as per the provisions of the German Copyright Act.[15]

Categories of ISPs are another characteristic of this Act. This Act mentions three categories of ISPs[16]—Content providers, Host providers and Access providers.

Content provider includes those entities, which provide own contents and make them available and their liability is to be determined according to the general provision of law and no specific limitation has been created for them.

Host providers[17] include those entities, which provide third party contents and make them available. Usually host service providers are operator of a server; they store third party content within their own or rented facilities and they are responsible for them under Art. 5(2) of German Teleservices Act.

Access Providers[18] includes those entities, which provide third party contents and merely provide access.

Under German law ISPs are entirely liable for damage from the moment it finds out or is modified of the infringing material, if it does not immediately remove it, though it would be technically possible and may reasonably be expected. This liability may arise on mere knowledge. They are required to stop an infringement that has come to their knowledge if it is technically possible to do so and if reasonable be expected.[19]

It is noticeable that a single ISP may fall into more than one category if it performs more than one service or function. With respect to each of these functions or services the ISPs liability may differ. Accordingly same contents may create different types of liability for different ISPs.

ISP Liability under the—European E-Commerce Directives

Like German Teleservices Act these directives[20] seek to harmonize the treatment of liability among its member-states.

Art. 13 distinguish between three types of storage or functions by an intermediary like:

(i) Storage for the purpose of carrying out transmissions (mere conduit);
(ii) Storage for the purpose of making more efficient the information's onward transmission (proxy caching); and
(iii) Storage of information provided by a subscriber (hosting).

A mere-conduit (Access provider) is not liable[21] if it: (a) initiate the transmission; (b) does not select the receiver of the transmission; and (c) does not select or modify the information contained in the transmission.

ISPs[22] (host service provider) may, that store third party content on their servers, be held liable for damages if they fail expeditiously to block access to the information or upon becoming aware facts or circumstances from which illegal activity or information is apparent.

ISP Liability under the—Provider Liability Law of Japan

On the same line of the German Teleservices Act Japan has also introduced an Act *"Provider Liability Law"* for ISPs to hold them liable for online copyright infringement. This Law states that an ISP is liable only if it is technically possible to prevent transmission of the infringement material; and the ISP knows of the existence of the material and; (i) knows that it is infringing, or (ii) reasonable ought to know that it infringes.[23] A person whose rights have been infringed can ask a provider to disclose information about the person transmitting the material if the information is necessary for a legal claim or other legitimate reason.[24]

INDIAN POSITION

ISP Liability under the Copyright Act

The Copyright Act, 1957 does not contain any express provision for determining or limiting ISP liability. But under sec. 51(a)(ii)[25] ISPs could be held liable for Copyright infringement by interpreting this section accordingly. Two term *'permits for profit' and 'any place' used under this section are having crucial meaning.*

ISPs allow their server and other telecommunication facilities for storing user's material and for transmitting that material. The Computer servers and other telecommunication facilities are actually located at their business premises and hence they would verily come under the expression "any place" and could be held liable for the infringing activities of third parties whose material they store or transmit if other requirements are fulfilled.

Further, the expression "permits for profit" means that to be held liable the activities of ISP should be for profit meaning thereby that he should be financially benefiting out of the infringing activities. So the above two requirements are fulfilled by ISPs for most of their activities in case they transmit or store infringing material.

Further, any person who knowingly infringes or abets the infringement of copyright . . . is made criminally liable under the Act.[26] 'Can an ISP be said to have abetted the infringement of copyright' is a question to be decided by the courts in light of actual facts.

ISP Liability under the Information Technology Act, 2000

This Act specifically mentions several provisions for ISPs.[27] It is hereby declared that a *network service provider* shall be liable *under this Act,* for any third party information or data made available by him if the offence or contravention of law was committed *with his knowledge* or he had not exercised any *due diligence* to prevent the commission of such offence or contravention. But ISPs can escape liability[28] if it could be proved that he was unaware of all that was stored and passing through his servers. Thus in certain cases they are exempted from liability; if they prove that they had no knowledge of the occurrence of the alleged act and that they had taken sufficient steps or (due diligence) to prevent a violation. But if he is put under a notice that an infringing material is either stored or passing through his servers, he has to take proper action for removing or disabling that material otherwise he could be said to have knowledge of the infringing material and held liable.

Criticism

It is criticized that 'Knowledge' requirements for proving culpability in India differ from one field of law to another. With regard to s. 79, which applies to any form of liability, the object of knowledge is not evident. Does it mean that the ISP has merely to be aware of the content or he has to be aware of the illegality of the content as well?

No classification of ISP has been attempted under this Act. 'Network service providers' include within it all kinds of internet service providers irrespective of what function they perform in the long chain of intermediaries that transport Internet content to the desired destinations.

Generally asked by the people that—Should ISPs be treated as electronic publishers, and thus made directly liable for all the infringing gigabytes flowing through their servers? Or are they merely the postmen of the Internet, common earners exempt from all liability? Which approach is good?

CONCLUSION AND SUGGESTIONS

After discussing various national and international aspects regarding ISPs liability I come to the conclusion that due to very nature of digital networking the liability of ISP is one of the most legal controversial issues. Different approaches are adopted by different countries. It is relevant to say that compatible approach to this issue be adopted around the world. In the Indian Copyright Act liability of ISPs should define with express provisions for contributing to illegal activities. Although IT Act, 2000 is a welcome step but it is desirable to say that like German Telecommunications Service Act, in the IT Act of India various types of ISPs should be distinguished, depending upon the specific functions they perform and their liability should also be fixed keeping in mind the role they play in the overall transmission.

The categorization attempted by the German Teleservices Act is excellent and helps in pinpointing the liability of ISPs for exactly the role they have played in the overall network communication.

To provide exemptions in IT Act to ISPs from the liability it should adopt approach like approach of DMCA. A narrow limitation on copyright infringement liability should be established for ISPs so that those who are building the Internet will have a clearer sense of how and when they might be held liable for online copyright infringement. A heightened level of certainty about their liability will help speed the growth of the Internet by encouraging more entrepreneurs to enter the ISP industry.

NOTES AND REFERENCES

1. Comprising of researchers, educators, artists, publishers and music and entertainment industry.
2. Sec. 2(w) of Information Technology Act, 2000 of India.
3. These exclusive rights include the rights of authorship, reproduction, distribution, communication to the public, broadcasting adaptation and translation.
4. World intellectual property organisation.
5. WIPO Copyright Treaty; it incorporate TRIPS provisions and updated Burne Convention.
6. WIPO Performances and Phonograms Treaty.
7. Agreed Statement with Article 8 of the WIPO Copyright Treaty.
8. Digital Millennium Copyright Act; Public Law 105-308, Oct. 28, 1998.
9. *Religious Technology Center (RTC)* Vs. *Netcom Online Common Services*, 907 F. Supp. 1361 (N.D. Cal. 1995).

10. Chapter 5 of the US Copyright Act deals with the enforcement of rights.
11. S. 512(a)—(c), the US Copyright Act; Circumstances: (i) Transitory digital network communications; (ii) System catching; (iii) Storing information on systems or networks at direction of users; and (iv) Information location tools.
12. Sec. 512 (h) of the US Copyright Act.
13. Notice and take down procedure provides that when a copyright owner becomes aware of Infringing material or infringing activity residing or taking place on an ISP's system or network, that copyright owner may notify the ISP of the infringement and require the ISP to remove or disable access to the infringing material or activity. The ISP in this case will be exempt from liability to its subscribers for its good faith removal of or disabling access to allegedly infringing content residing on its server at the direction of the subscriber. Sec. 512(g)(1) of the US Copyright Act. Specifically, the Act immunizes service providers from liability "to any person for any claim based on the service provider's good faith disabling of access to, or removal of, material or activity claimed to be infringing or based on facts and circumstances from which infringing activity is apparent regardless of whether the material or activity is ultimately determined to be infringing."
14. Teleservices Act was enacted as Art. 1 of the information and Communication Service Act in 1997 (informations—und Kommunikationsdienstegestz), Bundesgestzblatt 1997 1 1870.
15. Art. 5(1) of German Teleservices Act states: "services providers are responsible according to the general provisions of law their own contents which they make available for use.
16. Arts. 5(1)-(3) of German Teleservices Act.
17. Art. 5(2) providers are only responsible for third party contents which they make available for use, if they have knowledge of those contents and are technically able and may responsible by expected to prevent their use.
18. Art. 5(3)—providers are not responsible for third party contents to which they merely provide access for use. Automatic and temporary storing of third party contents upon a user's request is deemed providing access.
19. Art. 5(4) of German Teleservices Act mainly functions as an exception for access providers. It states: "duties to bar access to illegal contents under the general provisions of law remain unaffected, if the service provider gains knowledge of those contents in compliance with the telecommunication privacy requirement under sec. 85 of the Telecommunication Act and is technically able and may reasonable be expected to bar access.

20. Directives 2000/31/EC of the European Parliament and the Council of June 8, 2000 on certain legal Aspects of Information Society Services, in Particular Electronic Commerce in the Internal Market.
21. Art. 12 reads: 1. Where an information society services is provided that consists of the transmission in a communication network of information provided by a recipient of the service, or the provision of access to a communication network, member-States shall ensure that the services provider is not liable for the information transmitted on condition that the provider; (a) does not initiate the transmission; (b) does not select the receiver of the transmission; and (c) does not select or modify the information contained in the transmission. 2. The acts of transmission and of provision of access—include the automatic, intermediate and transient, storage of the information transmitted in so far as this takes place for the sole purpose of carrying out the transmission in the communication network, and provided that the information is not stored for any period longer than is reasonably necessary for the transmission. 3. This Article shall not affect the possibility for a court or administrative authority in accordance with Member-States' legal systems, of requiring the service provider to terminate or prevent an Infringement.
22. Article 14 reads—1. Where an information society service is provided that consists of the storage of information provided by a recipient of the service. Member-States shall ensure that the service provider is not liable for the information stored at the request of a recipient of the service, on condition that: (a) the provider does not have actual knowledge of illegal activity or information and, as regards claims for damages, is not aware of facts or circumstances from which the illegal activity or information is apparent; or (b) the provider, upon obtaining such knowledge or awareness, acts expeditiously to remove or to disable access to the information. 2. Paragraph 1 shall not apply when the recipient of the service is acting under the authority or the control of the provider. 3. This Article shall not affect the possibility for a court or administrative authority, in accordance with member-states 'legal systems' of requiring the services provider to terminate or prevent an infringement, nor does it affect the possibility for member-states of establishing procedures governing the removal or disability of access to information,
23. Art. 3(1), Provider Liability law of Japan, 2001 reads: (i) When circulation of information via specific Telecommunication results in infringement of rights of the other person, specific Telecommunication service Provider using specific Telecommunication facility for the use of such specific Telecommunication is not liable for damage unless it can technically apply measures by which transmission of such information resulting in the infringement of rights is prevented and

where either of the following item apply, provided that the forgoing shall not apply if such Related Services Provider is sender of such information resulting in the infringement of rights:

(i) where such related Services Provider knows that such other person's rights are infringed by circulation of information via circulation of information, or

(ii) where such related Services Provider knows circulation of information via circulation of information and there is an appropriate reason, which is enough to determine that it should have been able to know that such other person's rights are infringed by the circulation of information via such specific telecommunication.

24. Art. 4(1), Provider Liability Law of Japan, 2001 reads; A person alleges that its rights are infringed by circulation of information via specific Telecommunication, has a right to require specific Telecommunication service provider using specific Telecommunication facility for the use of specific Telecommunication to disclose sender information related to such alleged information of rights (name, address or other information useful to specify sender of infringing information to be stipulated in the applicable ministerial ordinance of the ministry of public management, Home affairs, posts and telecommunications) in the possession of such disclosure-related services provider if all of the following items are satisfied:

    (i) it is obvious that rights of such person requesting for disclosure of sender information are infringed by infringing information, and

    (ii) such sender information is necessary for such person requesting for disclosure of sender to claim damages, or such person has otherwise justifiable reason to require the disclosure of sender information.

25. When any person, without a licence grantee by the owner of the Copyright or the Registrar of copyright under this Act or in contravention of the conditions of a licence so granted or of any condition imposed by a competent authority under this Act . . . *permits for profit any place* to be used for the communication of the work to the public where such communication constitutes an infringement of the copyright in the work, unless he was not aware and had no reasonable ground for believing that such communication to the public would be an infringement of Copyright.

26. Section 63 of Copyright Act: Offence of infringement of Copyright or other rights conferred by this Act—Any person who knowingly infringes or abets the infringement of: (a) the copyright in a work or (b) any other right conferred by this Act, except the right conferred by sec. 53A shall not be less than six months but which may extend to three years and with fine which shall not be less than fifty thousand rupees but which may extend to two lakh rupees.

27. Sec. 79 IT Act, 2000.
28. Sec. 79 of IT Act, 2000: For the removal of doubts, it is hereby declared that no person providing any service as a network service provider shall be liable under this Act, rules or regulations made thereunder for any third party information or data made available by him if he proves that the offence or contravention was committed without his knowledge or that he had exercised all due diligence to prevent the commission of such offence or contravention.

Copyright Law—A Humane Approach

SYED SADIQ H. ABIDI AND O.N. MISHRA

In the contemporary informative society human rights means rights of human, that is to say, "Rights essential for human beings to live a humane life." Every individual is born with such rights and entitled to the inherent and inalienable rights, and most nations around the world have guaranteed the human rights to their particular subjects, fundamental freedoms and rights desirable in the National Constitution in the form of Fundamental Rights, basic rights, Bill of rights, etc. There have been numerous controversies and debates which history reveals throughout the world what human dignity is and what is needed to uphold the human dignity. The term dignity is also included in Article 1 of the Universal Declaration of Human Rights. "All human beings are born free and equal in dignity and rights. They are endowed with reason and consciences and should act towards one another in a spirit of brotherhood." Before declaration of Universal Declaration of Human Rights freedom, dignity and equality, etc. was considered necessary for a human being as the Indian history discloses but stepping towards the modern times people started to realize all the human beings deserve inherent dignity regardless of their social status determined by their birth. A lot of endeavours were made to turn this concept into action and reality as emancipating and feminist movements, unconcerned happenings of the world indirectly affected the rights. The tragedy of two world wars and fascism made people aware of the necessity that value of human rights should be universally accepted, and internationally protected, the United Nations created in 1945, concluded that protection of fundamental freedoms and rights are essential in achieving world peace, and adopted and proclaimed the Universal Declaration of Human Rights in its 1948 General Assembly. The world has undergone a great transformation in recent years. The knowledge-based society has replaced the national-based society. Today, the world is living in the midst of information revolution therefore intellectual property is the commercially exploitable potential. The property in the form of intellectual property, which is a result of the human intelligence, has come to play a vital role in the lives of human beings of world at large. The Universal Declaration of Human Rights showed that everyone has the right to access to the benefit of science and technology.

Article 27,[1] reads every one has the right, freely to participate in the cultural life of the community, to enjoy the arts and to share in scientific advancement and its benefit and has the right to the protection of the moral and material interests resulting from any scientific, literary or the dignity of the human person. So the word 'human dignity' appears to be phrases that have come to be used as an expression of a basic value accepted in broad sense by all people of the world.

The word 'Human dignity' appeared in the second paragraph of Preamble of the Charter of the United Nations as an ideal that we the people of the "United Nations" are "determined" "to reaffirm faith in fundamental human rights, in the dignity and worth of the human person, in the equal rights of men and women and of nations large and small." The Declaration established a common standard for the human rights that all people and all nations on the globe should accept and have without any kind of distinction such as political, economic, cultural and religious differences. The Human Rights was realized in the form of an effective international law after 1966, when the

UN adopted two International Covenants on Human Rights, one is International Covenant on Economic, Social and Cultural Rights and the second the International Covenant on Civil and Political Rights. Afterwards the UN continued to come out with the additional international standards and laws to protect the human rights of the underprivileged class including women and children, etc.

COPYRIGHT IN INDIA

In India copyright is recognized, granted and enforced by the Indian Copyright Act, 1957. It recognizes and protects copyright in original literary, chamatic, artistic and musical works, cinematograph films and sound recordings. The Act further classifies that under the present setup there is no uniformity in law of copyright[2] in India. The Act also does not require registration of copyright as a pre-condition to claim its protection.

INFRINGEMENT OF COPYRIGHT

Copyright is an exclusive right and its infringement consist the violation of exclusive right. Thus, a copyright is said to be infringed only when someone else does any of the various things, the right to do infringement is deemed to have taken place when a person use another's copyright work without permission; the other way of encroachment over the right where in knowingly facilitates the unauthorized use of another's copyrighted work; draws commercial benefit from an activity involving the use of another's copyrighted work; and exercises any of the rights which only the owner of copyright is allowed to use. The means, ways and methods of infringement may be different but only common element in all situations that is the knowledge or permission must be absent to invite legal action against the user of copyright of the legitimate owner.

Thus, the Copyright Act, aims of punishing the primary infringer and secondary infringer both, because primary infringer actually infringes the right of copyright and the secondary infringer facilities the primary infringement in consonance of penal permission, whoever, either prior to or at the time of commission of an act does any thing in order to facilitate the commission of the act, and thereby facilitates the commission thereof, is said to aid the doing of the act.[3]

The copyright in any work or other subject matter is infringed when any act which the copyright owner has the exclusive right to do, is done by a person who is not owner or the authority, for instance when a work prohibited or reproduced without copyright owner's permission. It is not necessary the whole work or subject matter be reproduced or more than one copy made for infringement of copyright, as photocopying a work or part of a work shall be infringement of copyright. Further copying into the CD or DVD that contains copyright material and downloading copyright material from the Internet and printing it, copying it into a CD or saving it in to own computer may also be a form of copyright infringement. The copyright may also be infringed by authorizing or facilitating someone else to do any above referred infringings act. It is also an infringement of copyright to import infringing material for commercial gain. However, the law does provide exceptions to the definition of infringement by introducing the concept of fair use.

THE LOOK AND FEEL TEST

To determine the infringement of copyright is look and if the reader spectator after having read or seem both the works get an impression that the infringement work or film is an imitation of the other.[4] It shall be infringement of copyright.

For initiating legal action, the burden of framing infringement rests on the plaintiff I to establish that the defendants had reproduced the infringing copy from the plaintiff's copyright work. Furthermore, for the plaintiff to maintain his suit for infringement must also establish that his own work was original as copyright protects only the original work.

The element of *mens-rea* is also required for the offence under section 63 of the Copyright Act, 1957. Every person who knowingly infringes or abets the infringement of the copyright in any work or any other right conferred by the Copyright Act, committing the offence of infringement under the Act. However, these acts are protected by the exception provided under section 52 of the Act, and the court while interpreting section 63 held that the words used are "knowingly infringes"[5] which implies that there has to be knowledge on the part of the accused that the other has copyright over the work to constitute the offence which is indicative of *mens-rea*.

RELATION OF COPYRIGHT AND HUMAN RIGHTS UNDER TRIPS

World of today is world of change, fast moving, scientific and of technological advancements. It is dominated by "Intellectual Capital" that holds the key of socio-economic, technological advancement of the society. The human society can be broadly divided into people who have knowledge and those who have nots.

Trade Related Aspects of Intellectual Property Rights (TRIPS) is outcome of the Uruguay Agreements, 1994. Almost all the Intellectual Property Rights were protected by the TRIPS agreement which is inclusive of several forms of intellectual property, i.e. Copyright, Trademarks, Geographical Indication, Industrial Designs, Patents, Integral Circuits and undisclosed information. Articles 9 to 14 TRIPS of the agreement are directly related to copyright which could not have unanimity from all quarters. This agreement was opposed by developing countries notably India, Brazil, Egypt, Argentina and Yugoslavia which were in favour of framing rules on trade in counterfeit goods but were against those on TRIPS in general. These countries feared that greater protection under the TRIPS would strengthen the monopoly power of multinational companies and adversely affect the poors by increasing the price of food and medicine.[6]

Most of the people on the developing or under-developed countries do not have access to cure for HIV/AIDS in a situation where the spread of AIDS is virtually threatening of significant part of the world. The reason, people affected by HIV/AIDS cannot be taken cure for the disease, is the high priced drugs for which companies are charging in the name of exercising their patent right. In 1944 under TRIPS agreement patent, copyright, computer programming, performer's right (Prohibition on Unauthorised "broadcasting" and prohibition on production of unauthorized phonograms) Trade Marks, Plant Breeder Rights, protection to designs and protection of undisclosed information were taken in the consideration. It was the first time that undisclosed information had been specially protected in an intellectual property by the member-countries. India being a member of W.T.O. has to implement the TRIPS Agreement in totality irrespective of the distinct local conditions. The Indian intellectual property laws inclusive of trade mark, copyrights, design are almost in conformity with the provision of TRIPS Agreement.

The TRIPS Agreement, which came into force w.e.f. 1 January, 1996 till date is the most comprehensive multinational agreement entered into, as one of the new areas under the GATT and TRIPS Agreement have far reaching provision on intellectual property. TRIPS Agreement affecting patent laws which would certainly over-burden the Indian economy and endanger the indigenous economic structure.

After the TRIPS Agreement every country, developing or developed would be put under the same umbrella of equal application and protection but not equitable because every country categorized as developing or developed, have its own distinct reservation, connection and varying conditions that alike with certain concession in terms of time of embarrassing the TRIPS agreement.

In the present changed conditions it is notable that a tendency to possess copyright is getting strong change throughout the world copyright is becoming an investment protection law. Loosing its original intention, The World Trade Organization agreement on Intellectual property is outcome of demands of advanced countries, which have competitively in the information and culture industry. The agreement was set in favour of developed countries and forced other countries to follow the same copyright system failing to setup policies of knowledge and culture that are fit for each country.

CONCLUDING REMARKS

Since human beings are rational beings all human beings by virtue of their being human possess certain inalienable rights which are commonly referred as human rights and extremely necessary for the existence, survival, growth and development of a human being. All such rights, a human being enjoy only due to the reason that he/she is born as human being.

Similarly, copyright can also supposed to be the fundamental right which provides the protection to the owners of creative work. Intellectual property rights are as important as human rights because these rights not merely help in growth and development of an individual but these rights play a vital role in the scientific and technological progress of the whole society. The Universal Declaration of Human Rights itself safeguards the copyright through its various provisions. Article 19 of Universal Declaration of Human Rights provides that everyone has the right to freedom of opinion and expression, this right also includes freedom to hold opinion without interference and to seek, receive and impared information and ideas through any media and regardless of any frontiers.

The given right is capable enough to include performers' right. Similarly, Article 12 of Universal Declaration of Human Rights ensures privacy and gives a right to a copyright holder to prohibit any other person from transmitting his creation.

Since intellectuals of the country constitute a distinct class and they cannot be equated with general people. Therefore, the rights enjoyed by the general human beings in the form of human rights must be different in nature than that of intellectual class.

Hence the submission is that the people who are entitled to enjoy copyright over their original creation their rights must be given in the name of "special human rights", so that the very rights of copyright holders could be protected with the same intensity as human rights.

Notes and References

1. Universal Declaration of Human Rights.
2. *Manojah Cine Production* Vs. *Sundaresan*, AIR 1976 Mad 22.
3. Sec Explanation 2 of Section 107 of IPC.
4. *Anand* Vs. *Deluxe Films*, AIR 1978 SC 1613.
5. *Sheoratan* Vs. *V.G.C. Nepali*, AIR 1965 All 274.
6. Jayanta Bageli, WTO, 2000, p. 47.

Natural Law Theory of Property and Copyright: An Analysis

S.C. Roy

I. INTRODUCTION

Economic life of the individual in society involves claims. First, the control of certain things on which human existence depends. Second, there is a claim to freedom of industry and contract as an Individual asset. Third, is a claim to promised advantages, to promised performances of pecuniary value by others, and the final is a claim to be secured against interference by outsiders with economically advantageous relations.[1] Legal recognition of these individual claims are the foundation of our economic organisation of society. Men must be able to assume that they may control their property for the purposes beneficial to themselves, what they have created through their labour under the existing social and economic order.

II. CONCEPT OF PROPERTY

The term property poses different meaning to different

people. To a scientist, property means 'elements of matter', to an economists, 'a means of production', but to a lawyer, it is 'bundle of rights' flowing from the concept of ownership and possession. This sense had developed from the paleolithic age when it was understood that it can protect them from enemies. Hence, they started collecting stones. Perhaps with this urge for 'belonging' heralded the birth of the concept of property which afterwards, different types of people have defined if in different ways. Whatever may be the sense, it is not the matter as such which is the property, it is knowledge about its use and intense mental security in it that human being attach in the 'possessiveness' that makes the matter a property. This possessiveness creates bundle of rights: i.e. Right to possession, ownership, application, enjoyment and alienation. These are the bundle of rights that the owner possess or enjoys as a matter of his claim to the exclusion of others of course subject to the laws of social behaviour.

III. NATURE OF INTELLECTUAL PROPERTY AND COPYRIGHT

One of the most valuable and intangible resources is knowledge. It emanates from the exercise of human brain.[2] It is a product emerging out of the intellectual labour of a human being. It involves the visible expression of a mental conception, the work of both brain and hand.[3] The two chief items are the writings of authors and inventions made by inventors. In its broadest sense, the term 'Intellectual property' includes, on one the level, ideas, concepts, know-how, and other creative abstractions, and on a second level, the literary, artistic or mechanical expression that embody such abstractions.[4] The basic difference between this form of property and other forms is that, the product itself. For example, in Literary property (copyright), it is not the book which is termed property, but the intellectual creation which comprises ideas, conceptions, sentiments, thoughts, etc. Fixed in a particular form that is considered property for protection.[5] His incorporeal, invisible and intangible in nature. Law relating to copyright deals with protection of rights beings. Though it originated as a right to protect the intellectual labour of a man in his books. In modern times, it is extended to protect the intellectual labour of a man in literary, dramatic, musical and artistic works.[6]

IV. ISSUES RELATED TO COPYRIGHT

Infringement of copyright is the main issue. According to Copyright Act, infringement to copyright means reproduction or import of a copy in contravention of the Act or any of the follows:

1. Reproduction of Literary, dramatic, musical or artistic work other than cine-film.
2. Copy of cine-film by any means.
3. Copy of sound recordings by any means
4. Sound recording or video recording of any programme or performance where "broadcast reproduction rights" or "performers" subsists.[7]

When the exclusive right of the copyright owner is violated, it amounts to infringement. It involves the infringement of moral and economic rights of a copyright owner. These rights emanate from the investment of time, mind, energy and capital. By the mixing of these inputs in mind, there is a creation of literary, artistic, dramatic, cinematographic products. Hence the violation of these rights either by individual or by press discourages the copyright owner.

V. PHILOSOPHY OF COPYRIGHT PROTECTION

From the nature of copyright, it is obvious that copyright is "the exclusive right" to do or authorise others to do certain acts in relation to:

(1) Literary, dramatic or musical works,
(2) Artistic work, and
(3) Cinematograph film and sound recording.[8]

But copyright protects:

(1) Only the form, not the idea, and
(2) Only the labour, skill, judgement and capital of the author not the wisdom, literature, merit or equality of the author's work.

Article 27(2) of the Universal declaration of Human Rights provides "Every one has the right to the protection of the moral and material interests resulting from any scientific, literary or artistic production which he is the author."

This human rights stems from two ways in intellectual thought:[9]

(1) Copyright protection is the only way of rewarding the author for his skill judgement, labour and capitals. The initiative in an individual that peoples him/her to generate literary, artistic, musical or other work must relieve recognition and protection. If the desire to create is quelled because of rampant copying without consequential benefits to the author, the world would suffer immensely.
(2) The evolution of copyright law, especially in the U.K. was at the instance of the printing and publishing community which desired protection of its investments. This historical fact indicates more than the inherent right of the author. It is the investment of the entrepreneur which is sought to be protected so that the exploitation of copyrighted works may be carried out in full faith and due regard to the needs of the general public.

In 1709, the Act of Anne was passed as a response to the demands of the publishers. Though its object as reflected in the preamble was encourage learning, in spirit, it embodied the interests of commercial exploitation. But the development of copyright law in America was different from that of United Kingdom. American copyright law was rooted to both 'utilitarian and natural rights' unlike British law where the motivations were purely economic. The copyright law enacted in 1709 provides as follows:

(1) Protection of the author or his assigns of any book, map or chart upon publication, for 14 years.
(2) Privilege of renewal of another 14 years if author was alive.

The framers of American Constitution also provided in Article 1, Section 8 that the congress were "to promote the progress of science and useful arts by securing for limited time to authors and inventors the exclusive right to their respective writings and discoveries.

The foremost proponent of the 'natural right' basis of copyright protection was France. By its 1795 enactment, it accorded exclusive performing rights to authors of dramatic and musical works. It recognised the rights as inherent in the very nature of things."[10]

Though there are several differences in the copyright laws of United Kingdom, America and Continental countries, but they have some general features in common:

(1) They protected all intellectual productions whether literary, artistic or intended for performance.
(2) They recognised the basic rights of performance and reproduction.
(3) These rights were restricted in public interest.
(4) The rights were to be enjoyed during the life time of the author and for a short period thereafter.

But Indian copyright law which was first enacted in 1847 (Act XX of 1847) on the lines of the U.K. Copyright Act of 1842. It still protects the economic rights but, far away from the American and continental concept of copyright philosophy, i.e. "concept of utility and natural rights".

VI. NATURAL LAW THEORY OF PROPERTY AND COPYRIGHT

Grotius, the older natural law theorist propounded that "all things were originally *res nulliua.*" A person who occupies finest the 'res nulliua' becomes the owner of the same. But Pufendrof propounded the principle of "res communis" One was owner of those things. They were subject to use by all but in the course of time, men came to abolish the negative community through mutual agreement and thus established private ownership. And what was subject to acquisition by discovery and occupation.[11]

But in recent years, revival of natural law brought a new phase of justification of property upon the basis of human nature. The economists suggested like this, deduced property from the economic nature of man as a necessity of the economic life of the individual in society.[12] Generally, this view is associated with a 'psychological theory' on the one hand and a 'Social utilitarian theory' on the other.

Since copyright is an intangible property which is the creation of human mind has three factors:

1. Economic and labour,
2. Psychological, and
3. Social utilitarian.

Therefore, when the rights of the copyright owner is infringed the above factors are affected which has ultimate effect on the author/creator/producer. Because, the person who labours to create something must be protected as per labour theory. The creator is attached with his/her creation is psychological factor and unauthorised use mars the social utilitarian principles. What the American copyright law has introduced in her constitution.

VII. CONCLUSION

Since property is a domain, therefore, the philosophy of law has had most to say. Among various theories of properties, natural law theory proceeds on the philosophy of 'reason' derived from the nature of thing. Copyright is a right conferred to the creator of art which must be protected not only due to their labour or capital investment, but for social utilitarian principles also as mentioned by American and continental copyright law.

Hence, the copyright law needs further amendment—with the introduction of 'natural rights' as well as 'Social utilitarian principles' of American copyright law and French copyright law. Secondly, universal declaration of human rights should be inserted in the copyright so that state and national human rights commission can take action on the violation of the copyright as human right.

Notes and References

1. Roscal Pound, An introduction to the Philosophy of Law, Chap. 5, p. 107.
2. Jeremy Phillips, Introduction to Intellectual Property Law (London: Butterworths, 1986), p. 3.

3. Simonds, "Natural Right of Property on Intellectual Protection" 1 Yall L.J. (1891-92) published in IP and Criminal Law HLSIU, Bangalore by NS.
4. Gopal Krishnan, p. 143.
5. I.P. and Criminal Law, N.S. Gopal Krishnan, p. 145, Baton S. Drone, p. 6.
6. *Recording Industry Association of America* Vs. *Hapstar*, 2001 http/ www.eff. org./pp, P&P: 239 F-59.
7. S. 13 of Copyright Act, 1957.
8. Introduction of Intellectual Property, HLSIU Publication, p. 35.
9. Article 1, Section 8 of American Constitution.
10. Introduction to Intellectual Property, HLSIU Publication.
11. Res nullius—ownerless object.
12. Roscoe Pound, p. 117.

Whether Infringement of Copyright is Violation of Human Rights: An Assessment

KIRAN SAKSENA

I. INTRODUCTION

Intellectual property, in its literal sense, means the things which emanate from the exercise of the human brain. It is the product emerging out of the intellectual labour of a human being, involves the visible expression of a mental conception, the work of both brain and hand. The two chief items are the writing of authors, and inventions made by inventors. In its broadest sense, the term 'intellectual property' includes, on one level, ideas, concepts, know-how, and other creative abstractions, and on a second level, the literary, artistic or mechanical expressions that embody such abstractions.

Law relating to copyright deals with protection of rights on certain types of works resulting from the intellectual labour of human beings. Though it originated as a right to protect the intellectual labour of a man in his books, in modern times it is extended to protect the intellectual labour of a man in literary, dramatic, musical and artistic works.

The purpose of recognising and protections the copyright of the author is to protect his work and inspire him to exercise his creative faculty further. The essence of the copyright is to protect the labour, skill and capital of the author. The Copyright Act confers on the owner of the copyright to enable him to reap monetary benefits. If any of the above acts are carried out by the person other than the author the copyright without a license from the owner, it constitutes infringement of the copyright. Copyright is granted for a specific period of time. Hence, infringement of copyright depends on the fact whether copyright is subsisting in the work or not. At the expiry of the copyright (Life time plus sixty years), the work falls in the 'public domain'. Hence, copying or reproduction of such work does not amount to infringement.

II. WHAT CONSTITUTES INFRINGEMENT

Copyright subsists in literary, dramatic, musical, artistic, cinematograph film and sound recording, etc. The act which constitutes infringement depends upon the nature of the work.

Section 51 of the Copyright Act, 1957, defines infringement in general terms. According to Section 51 of the Act copyright in work shall be deemed to be infringed.

(a) When any person without a license from the owner or the Registrar of copyrights does anything, the exclusive right to do which is by this Act conferred upon the owner of copyright or permits for profit, any place to be used for the communication of the work to the public, unless he was not aware and had no reasonable ground for believing that such communication would be an infringement of copyright, or

(b) When any person:

  (i) Makes for sale or hires or sells or lets for hire or by way of trade displays or offers for sale or hire any infringing copies of the work covered by copyright, or

  (ii) Distributes, either the purpose of trade or to such on

extent as to affect prejudicially the owner of the copyright, any infringing copies of the work, or

(iii) Exhibits in public by way of trade any infringing copies of the work, or

(iv) Imports into India any infringing copies of the work except the copy of any work for the private and domestic use of the importer.

As per this section, the reproduction of a literary, dramatic, musical or artistic work in the form of a cinematograph film shall be deemed to an infringing copy i.e., (a) the unauthorised video films in circulation in the market of popular Hindi movies is infringement of copyright in cinematograph film, (b) A book is published in U.K. by a publisher there. An Indian visitor to that country gets a copy of the book, makes further copies of the said books and floods the Indian market. He is guilty of infringement under provisions of Section 51 of the Act.

III. ELEMENTS OF INFRINGEMENT

Thus, the elements needs to be present to make an action to be present to make an act on infringement; within the meaning of an act are:

(i) Substantial copying, and

(ii) Direct evidence of copying from the source in which copyright subsists.

In order to decide substantial copying, following factors are taken into consideration:

(i) The volume of the material borrowed by the defendants. In *Ladbrokes Ltd.* Vs. *William Hill*, (1964) I WLR 273, it was held that substantiality is a question of fact and degree determined on the basis of importance of the parts reproduced.

(ii) Whether the substantial copying has been intended for the purpose of saving himself of the labour?

(iii) The extent to which the plaintiffs and defendant's work are competing with each other.

In the case of *D. Narayan Rao* Vs. *V. Prasad*, (1979) 2 APLJ 231, the defendant had borrowed a part of the speech which was only of $2^1/_2$ minutes duration in a 3 hour film. Yet it was held that substantial part of the speech had been copied.

IV. DIRECT EVIDENCE OF COPYING

In copyright infringement cases, the direct evidence of copying, is generally difficult to furnish. Hence, copying the copyrighted work even with minor additions, omissions, or alterations would still amount to infringement of the copyright because such minor additions, omission or alterations in the copied work would not make it original work.

In *Shyam Shah* Vs. *Gaya Prasad Gupta*, AIR 1973, Allahabad 192, the Court held that a person is at Liberty to draw upon Common source of information. But if he saves himself from the trouble and labour requisite for collecting that information by adopting another's work with colourable violations, he is guilty of infringement of copyright even though the original work is based on material which are common property.

Indirect Copying

There can be infringement by indirect copying also. A work may be copied by making a copy from pre-existing copy of the same work.

It has been approved in the case of *Manf Staengal* Vs. *Empire Palace* (1984) Ch. 109.

In the case of *Schlesinger* Vs. *Turner* (1890) 63, LT. 764, it was held that plays based upon novels which in turn were based upon original plays amounted to infringement of the original plays.

Even sub-conscious copying is sufficient to constitute infringement of copyright.

Retrography, making of copes of a work by photo-copying or similar means is also a infringement of copyright.

V. ACT WHICH DO NOT CONSTITUTE INFRINGEMENT

Section 52 of the Copyright Act provides the act which do not constitute infringement, these are:

(i) A fair dealing with a literary, dramatic, musical or artistic work not being a computer programme for the purpose of private use including research criticism or review, making copies of the computer programme for certain purposes, reporting current events in newspapers and magazines or by broadcasting or in a Cinematograph film or by means of photographs.

(ii) Reproduction of judicial proceedings and reports thereof, reproduction exclusively for the use of members of the legislatures in a certified copy supplied in accordance with law.

(iii) Reading or reciting in public of extracts of literary or dramatic work.

(iv) Publication in a collection for the use in educational institutions in certain circumstances.

(v) Reproduction by teacher or pupil in the course of instruction or in question papers or answers.

(vi) Performance in the course of the activities of educational institutions in certain circumstances.

(vii) Making a maximum of 3 copies for the use of a public library.

(viii) Publication in newspapers or magazines a report of a lecture delivered in public, etc.

(ix) Reproduction or publication of a translation of acts of legislature or rules.

(x) Reproduction of unpublished work kept in a museum or library for the purpose of study or research.

(xi) Reproduction in newspaper and magazine of an article on current economic, political, social or religious topics in certain circumstances.

VI. CONCLUSION

Hence, Section 51 of the Copyright Act ascertain and protects the rights of the copyright owner. This right is related to moral and economic rights. Moral rights emanates from labour and capital invested by the author. Berne Convention of the copyright declares that moral right of the copyright owner is more vital because it is the reflection of personality. Whereas economic rights of the author is the return of labour and capital invested by the author. Thus, the personality of the author contains both rights—moral and economic. And human rights includes these rights. Therefore, the infringement of copyright is violation of human rights enshrined under Articles 14, 19(1)(a) and 21 of the constitution. And it must be protected in order to encourage creative work and improve economic status of the creator.

Copyright under Indian Constitution as Human Right with Reference to Directive Principles of State Policy and Fundamental Duties: An Overview

S.M. SHUKLA

I. INTRODUCTION

The very foundation of copyright law is, "thou shall not steal."[1] Copyright law protects the author's labour, skill and capital from appropriation by others without permission. An artistic, literary and musical or computer programming is the brain child of the creator. The creator has to invest his time, mind and energy and the work is a product which is socially useful. Since there is a creation of incorporeal product, therefore, it is called property. Without this intellectual creation, no country can develop.

The Oxford Dictionary defines 'copyright' as the exclusive

legal right granted for a specified period to an author, designer, etc. or another appointed person to print, publish, perform, film or record original literary artistic or musical material.

Copyright is a statutory right. It is applicable to all types of work. Whether published or unpublished. The rights prevents unlawful copying, reproduction and exploitation, of any material like literary, dramatic, cinematographic work translation, etc.

Section 13 of the Copyright Act, 1957 provides that the copyright subsists in the following classes of work:[2]

(i) Original literary, dramatic, musical and artistic works;
(ii) Cinematographic films; and
(iii) Records.

II. ART. 19(1)(a) AND ART. 300-A

Article 19(1)(a) of Indian constitution is correlated to Section 13 of Copyright Act, 1957. As Art. 19(1)(a) protects the freedom of expression. The same is with copyright. In copyright, idea is not protected. It is expression which is protected from any type of copying. The copyright not only protects the fundamental right enshrined under Art. 19(1)(a) but also protects under Article 300A[3]. Although Art. 300A is meant for immovable property but copyright is intellectual property which incorporeal. It cannot be exploited by any person without prior permission of the creator. Incorporeal property is still not mentioned clearly under Article 300A, therefore, the copyright owner has to face problems inspite of different civil as well as criminal remedies available.

III. DIRECTIVE PRINCIPLE OF STATE POLICY (DPSP)

In Part IV of the Indian Constitution, the Directive Principles of State Policy (DPSP) has been introduced. This part has vision to being economic and social justice. From Arts. 37 to 51, the State shall secure a social order in which social, economic and political justice shall inform all the institutions of national life.[4] Wealth and its source of production shall to sub-serve the common good, and there shall be adequate means of livelihood for all.[5] Baba Saheb Dr. B.R. Ambedkar has explained the underlying object in laying down the DPSP as "In my judgement, directive principles have a great value, for they lay down that our ideal is economic democracy."[6]

It is observed from the DPSP that any person who does some creative work has economic value also in order to maintain his own livelihood as well as serve the society. The copyright owner has 'right to copy' under the Act[7] for life time plus sixty years. After that period, it falls under public domain. But before, it falls under public domain, the creative owner has all the rights to exploit his/her creation in order improve his economic means which is also protected by Art. 23 of the Constitution. The DPSP also protects moral rights. In *Keshavananda Bharti* Vs. *State of Kerala*,[8] Justice Mathew explained the importance of the directive principles—

"I think there are rights which are inherent in human being because they are human beings—whether you call them natural rights or by some appellation is immaterial. As preamble indicates, it was to secure the basic human rights like liberty and equality that the people gave up to themselves the constitution was also enacted by the people to secure justice, political, social and economic, therefore, the moral rights embodied in Part IV of the constitution are equally an essential feature of it, the only difference being that the moral rights embodied in Part IV are not specifically enforceable as against the state by a citizen in a Court of law in case the state fails to implement its duty but, never the less, they are fundamental in the governance of the country and all the organs of the state including the judiciary, are bound to enforce those directives. By examining the aforesaid statement it is quite clear that Directive Principles of State Policy protects moral and economic rights of the copyright owner which is inherent rights of a human being, which is called as human rights. More so, there is a balance between Fundamental Rights and Directive Principles of State policy as declared in *Minerva Mills Ltd.* Vs. *Union of India*[9] that harmony and balance between Fundamental Rights and Directive Principles is basic feature of the Constitution.

IV. FUNDAMENTAL DUTIES (FD)

Under Article 51A Chapter IV-A of the Constitution,[10] fundamental duties has been inserted. Art. 51A(h) reads as "to develop the scientific temper, humanism and the spirit of inquiry and reform," and Art. 51A(j) reads as to strive towards excellence in all spheres of individual and collective activity so that the nation constantly rises to higher levels of endeavour and achievement."[11&12]

Although, FD has been imposes duty on citizen and not upon the state, yet it seem to protect the human rights of those who strive towards excellence, i.e. creative, author.

V. CONCLUSION AND SUGGESTIONS

The analysis of Copyright Act, Berne Convention, DPSP and FD, inference can be drawn that the DPSP and fundamental rights both protect the moral and economic rights of the copyright owner. Berne convention also declares the moral rights of the copyright owner to be protected as it is the reflection of personality. Art. 51A imposes duties upon citizens and commands that no citizen shall be barrier in 'individual excellence'.

Inspite of all these Constitutional provisions, copyright has not been recognised their human rights.

SUGGESTIONS

1. The period of copyright should be decreased and it should be brought to life time plus twenty years so that the 'creative work' may fall into public domain very soon.
2. The copyright/intellectual property rights should be included under Art. 300A of a Constitution.
3. Writ of 'Mandamas' may be sought to implement by suitable amendment against the citizen individual in order to enforce the fundamental duties under Art. 51 A(i) and (j) in order to protect the human rights of copyright owner.

NOTES AND REFERENCES

1. Copyright Law by P. Narayana.
2. Section 13 of the Copyright Act, 1957.
3. Article 300A provides that no person shall be deprived of his property save by authority of law.

4. V.N. Shukla, the Constitution of India, p. 297.
5. *Ibid.*
6. Constituent Assembly Debates, Vol. III, pp. 494-95 quoted in V.N. Shukla, 'the Constitution of India'.
7. The Copyright Act, 1957.
8. AIR 1973 SC 1461.
9. AIR 1980 SC 1789.
10. Inserted by Constitution (42nd Amendment) Act, 1976.
11. Arts. 51A(h) and 51A(j), DPSP.
12. *Ibid.*

Freedom of Speech and Expression and Copyright in the Light of Human Rights—An Analysis

V.K. SINGH

Nature has made human beings intellectually the most developed species of the animal kingdom. Keeping pace with the time, as life becomes more and more complex for variety of reasons, his intellect plays a crucial role.

The subject is basically based on creation and inventions, as outcome of human efforts is being recognized by law and exploited in global economy. The creations, inventions, works or originality and novelty in the form of patents, trademarks, copyright, designs, etc. has been encircled by the respective legislation so as to give safety from abuse.

Copyright is well-recognized form of property rights, which has its roots in the common law system and subsequently came to be governed by the national laws in each country. It is an exclusive right of the author produced by him in the literary, dramatic, musical and artistic works. It is now extending its field to sound recording, films, broadcast, cable program, and typographical arrangements of publications and also includes computer programs. If any person makes copy of the created works that is expression not ideas like piracy, it amounts to infringement of copyright property. Provisions have been included in the national law and also International agreements, which restricts others from exploitation, reproduction of the work or from piracy of work.

The concept of individual's mental creative properties, i.e. the copyright had been protected by U.N.O. by accepting Universal Declaration of Human Rights, 1948 at the International level. By the mental capacity, a person creates intellectual property which needs to be protected by law. Article 17(1) of U.D.H.R. accepts the concept of owing intellectual property by human beings and provides protective measures.

Article 17(2) prevents arbitrary deprivation of such property. Article 27(2) of U.D.H.R. clearly declares the protection of everyone's moral and material interests resulting from any scientific, literary or artistic activities of which he is the author.

At national level, this intellectual property rights was brought in cognizance by Indian parliament in the year 1957 as Copyright Act, 1957. This Act provided the meaning, its assignment procedures, registration and also the punishments in case of its infringements. This Act was amended several times in the years of 1983, 1994 and 1999 to cope with developing changes and complications to save the copyright property. The idea of human creative activities was again accepted by the General Assembly of United Nations through its one of the important instrument like the International Covenant on Economic, Social and Cultural Rights, 1996. It reflects the ideas of Copyright Act, 1957 under sections 13 and 14. I.C.E.S.C.R. provides the obligation on the state parties to take steps for the conservation, development and diffusion of the Scientific, literary, and artistic right of a person. It also asks the state to respect the individual's creative activity and to protect their benefits.

Trade Related Intellectual Property Rights (TRIPS) Agreement, 1994 also protected the Copyright in the form of intellectual property rights under its Articles 9 to 14. These provisions support the ideas Burne Convention extending Copyrights to expression not to ideas, Computer Programming in compilation of computer data's were also accepted for their protection.

Copyright includes many rights like moral rights, economic rights and bundle of different rights such as right to translate, to adopt, to convert in music, to abridge, to dramatize, etc. Even though law does not recognize moral right as a legal right but no body has a moral right to steal the expression or creative work of another and make profits there from by its reproduction or published work. The author has also right to prevent from making any damage to the owner—the right of integrity. The moral rights of the author are recognized u/s 57 of the Act. The economic rights emanating from labour, skill and capital invested by the author have been provided in monetary terms.

This right of the owners of the copyright has been protected by different provisions in the Act and any person infringing such provisions are liable for punishment. By infringement of the copyright, it takes away the skill, labour and capital investment in the copyrighted work. Hence, it takes away the moral economic and other multiple rights emanating from this property. It is essential to note that Intellectual property of the creator is essential for nurturing, living and prosperity of the author. Hence, violation of such right is the violation of Article 19(1)(a) of the fundamental right and in other words is violation of human rights.

Our Constitution provides a number of provisions to protect the interests of individuals. It imposes duty upon the state to protect and promote welfare of the people. In Part 3 (Articles 12 to 35) of the Constitution, a number of fundamental rights are guaranteed to the individuals. Part IV (Articles 36 to 51) lays down Directive Principles of State Policy, which are not enforceable in law but are fundamental in the governance of the county. Article 39 imposes duty on the state to ensure adequate means of livelihood and fair distribution of state. This lays down the idea of economic democracy and concept of a welfare state.

Article 19(1)(a) secures to every citizen the freedom of speech and expression. These are the rights to express one's convictions and opinions freely by word of mouth, writing, printing, pictures or any other mode. These freedoms include the freedom of propagation of ideas.

The object of copyright law is to project the freedom of speech and expression subject to Article 19(2) of the Constitution. It also creates legal rights of the authors, composers, artists and designers and also encourages them for original works by way of granting exclusive rights to them to exploit the work for some monetary gains. They give licenses to entrepreneurs, publishers, film producers, record manufacturers for consideration in money.

Copyright is now extending to many new fields of technology, computer industry, and photographers. But piracy of copyrighted works has become simple and it infringes the rights of copyright owner and violates the right enshrined under Article 19(1)(a) of the Constitution and ultimately negates the Human Rights.

Many legal protections to safeguard the customers from the exploitation by the creators have also been provided in the Act. A limitation has been given to the rights of the owners. The inventor can earn profits for a fixed period such as for a maximum period of 60 years or the life of creator. After the expiration of such period every producer will be free for use of any inventions.

• Certain kinds of inventions, which have been listed in the Act, are not allowed to be patented. This is a kind of safeguard to protect the interests of consumers and public at large. Such inventions are:

(1) Inventions contrary to law or morality or injurious to public health cannot be patented.
(2) Any method of agriculture and horticulture cannot be patented.
(3) Any process of medicinal, surgical, curative, prophylactic or treatment of human beings is not patentable.
(4) Any invention related to atomic energy is not patentable etc.
(5) Any invention that in effect is of traditional knowledge or duplication of known properties of traditional knowledge cannot be patented etc.

Some infringements are permitted after a serious study of the problems found by consumers and are known as permissible infringements. These safeguards assist customers and society to use patented or registered inventions without affecting the rights of the producers. For example:

(a) Restricted use of patented invention is permissible for research or experimental purpose or even for imparting knowledge or for instructing students. For example, a Professor of an engineering college can depict or explain to show the functioning of a patented invention to his students. This is not a violation of any provision of law.

(b) The Government is entitled to use any invention even without the payment of royalty to the Creator. According to the Patent Amendment Act, 1999, the Government of India may use a patented drug for the purpose of distribution through any dispensary maintained by the government. The government is entitled to grant Exclusive Marketing Right. The government may cancel the exclusive marketing rights if it deems necessary in public interest. Further in Copyright Act, 1999 a number of infringements are allowed. For example:

   (1) A fair dealing with literary dramatic, musical or artistic work for the purpose of a private use including research autism or review would not constitute infringement.
   (2) Reproduction of judicial proceedings and reports in a certified copy.
   (3) Reading and recitation in Public extracts of literary or dramatic works.
   (4) Publication in a collection to be used in educational institutions.
   (5) Reproduction by teacher or pupil in the course of instructions or in question paper and answer.

In conclusion, we find that Intellectual property rights and human rights are to the maximum extent same things. The natural law, UDHR, ICESCR, TRIPS and the national instruments prescribe fundamental duties to protect both the copyright and human rights. The intangible rights have also taken cognizance as these are closely related with the safety of individual's property rights as also the moral rights. No doubt, many restrictions have been imposed on the creator's rights to prevent its misuse and the welfare of the society and also the exploitation of the consumers. These restrictions are also for the free flow of the ideas and inventions to the general mass.

In India, we find that there are a number of scientists, scholars and philosophers who invented new art or skill, used it and died. In the field of medicine and engineering many inventions have been made since time immemorial? There are certain scholars and scientists who did not patent or register their materials because they devote it for self-defense. Some inventions are not patented due to lack of money, lack of knowledge, and certain other factors. Governments, Non-Governmental Organizations; Voluntary Organizations should come forwards to patent and register such inventions.

In India nearly 40% of the people live below the poverty line. Nearly 24 crore people live in absolute poverty. The interests of such people should be safeguarded against new regime of Intellectual Property Rights. The Government of India should take effective measures to protect the interests of weaker sections of the society.

Copyright Law Furthers Free Speech Value in Constitutional Frame

SYED NASEER H. RIZVI AND O.N. MISHRA

Copyright is an exclusive right. Copyright is a right given to the owner or to the licensee against the copying of original work of cultural information and entertainment production. Thus, it protects the expression not the idea itself but in a tangible form. Copyright means the exclusive right to copy or reproduce a work in which the copyright subsist; wholly or in part in any material form. In India copyright is recognized, granted and enforced by the Indian Copyright Act, 1957, under the present frame of laws there is no uniform law of copyright. The Act does not require registration as a precondition to claim protection under the law, originality as the primary requirement for any copyright protection but yet originality and creativity are a matter difference no concurring base has been found. U.S. courts always insisted on originality in the copyright meant only that the work owes its origin to the author, i.e. is independently created and not copied from other works, this creativity need not use an inventive leap only a spark or modicum of creativity is enough.[1] The reason for this is that no fact can originate from the author, so mere discovery of a fact is not rewarded and what is rewarded is a creation. The question whether copyright subsists in the deciphered text, the Israeli Supreme Court observed and laid-down Qimron applied his knowledge, skill, imagination, in which he applied discreation and choose among various options. He applied his discreation and creativity since there was no way to reach a single reconstruction did have a copyright in the work[2] the Indian position on the entire issue is not quite clear. There has been no clear pronunciation by courts on the issue of the contents of originality requirements in the Indian Law.

NATURAL THEORY OF PROPERTY ON THE COPYRIGHT

Copyright is a property, but the property is an intangible one. It is the right of the author in the creation of his intellectual copyright being a property right, can be transferred or assigned to another person.

It can also be inherited during the time it exists. Copyrights are governed and regulated by the municipal laws of the country. The protection of copyrights is possible, and limited within the territorial limits of the country, however, international treaties like the Berne Convention for the Protection of Literary and Artistic Works (1886), the Universal Copyright Convention (1952) and the Agreement on Trade Related Aspects of IPR (1994) are to ensure protection of copyrights to nationals of member-countries. Copyright is a bundle of exclusive right but is not a monopoly right as others are not prevented from making a similar work independently like other properties. Where two writers write on the same theme both are likely to be different from each other and both have exclusive right on their intellectual work.

COPYRIGHT VIS-A-VIS HUMAN RIGHTS UNDER INDIAN CONSTITUTION

Everyone has right to freely participate in the cultural life of the community, to enjoy the arts and to share the scientific advancement and its benefits. Similarly, everyone has right to protection of the moral and material interests resulting from any scientific, literary or artistic production of which the author has. Thus, at the fundamental level of human rights law, a balance is expected between the interests of the community and the interests of the individual on important exceptions related to fair use. At the end of the legislated period of protection the copyright works moved to the public domain in which it may be freely exploited by all. The purpose of the limited right conferred for a limited time was to allow author to benefit materially for a time in order to encourage production. Moral rights on the other hand are enduring and designed to protect the rights of the authors beyond the period of any economic reward particularly right of attribution and the right of integrity. These rights enable the author to assert and be recognized for her or his authorship and aim to ensure that the work is not modified or distorted.

U.S. and U.K. laws defines copyright as a property right and author's rights as human rights. The key difference is that a property as defined means something which can be freely traded. In this context "free trade of copyright" is therefore the rights to be governed by economic power.

FREEDOM OF THOUGHTS AND FREEDOM OF EXPRESSION

Freedom of thought and expression is the World Human Rights Declaration which the U.N. adopted on December 10, 1948 the best prescribed freedom as human rights so for. Under the provision of Article 18 Universal Declaration of Human Rights of all human beings have a right to have freedom of thoughts, conscience and religion. This right includes freedom of change to his or her own religion or faith and freedom to express his or her own religion or faith in the form of discussion event, worship or ceremony, alone or in group, publicly or secretly.

Article 19 of Universal Declaration of Human Rights express that all human beings have right to enjoy freedom of opinion and expression. This right includes right to have an opinion without interference and to pursue, to obtain, to convey information and thoughts regardless of a border.

Freedom of thoughts may be expressed as freedom to choose own views on the world, life and politics and when this thought is expressed outwardly, it becomes freedom of press, publication, assembly and association. Further in regard to faith it becomes freedom of religion, in regard to truth seeking, it becomes freedom of learning and as such freedom of thoughts is theoretical foundation of all the spiritual and political freedom and basic of basics. Therefore, freedom of thoughts means freedom of expression, and includes inner thoughts of which nobody is aware of, but can be protected. Freedom of thoughts and expression has always been considered to be superior to other human rights and that is because the expression of an individual is the most fundamental activity for self-fulfilment. Therefore, the media of expression, the press is an essential condition of democracy through which people participate in forming a political decision. Constitution of India adopted the same resolution of the U.N. and put freedom of expression under Article 19.

The Preamble of our Constitution envisages the liberty of thought and expression. Every citizen of India enjoys full liberty to express himself or their self. The Preamble of Indian Constitution plays a vital role in determining the purview of fundamental rights guaranteed to the people which is enshrined in Part III of the Indian Constitution. The conceptual dimension of fundamental rights or human rights are contained in the Preamble of Constitution itself.

The Constitution of India is not to be construed as a mere law, but as the very source by which all the laws of the land are derived. It is a living and organic thing and therefore must be construed liberally.

The importance and utility of the Preamble has been pointed in several decisions of the Apex Court. Though by itself is not enforceable in a Court of Law.[3] The Preamble of a written Constitution states and abides which the Constitution seeks to establish and promote and also aids the legal interpretation of the Constitution where the language found to be ambiguous.[4] Therefore, aims and objects settled down in Preamble should be considered the very aims of the Constitution because it is the part of the Constitution.

Universal Declaration of Human Rights also declares that all human beings are born free and equal in dignity and rights. They are endowed with reason and conscience and should act towards one another in a spirit of brotherhood.[5]

There are several rights and freedoms recognized in the form of Human Rights under Universal Declaration of Human Rights and these rights have also incorporated in the Constitution of India in toto. The Universal Declaration of Human Rights stoutly prohibits any sort of discrimination on the ground of sex, colour, race, sex, religion, birth, etc. Freedom of speech and expression guaranteed under Article 19 of the Indian Constitution is also directly emanated from the Human Rights Values which are expounded through Universal Declaration of Human Rights.

Furthermore, no distinction shall be made on the basis of the political jurisdiction or international status of the country territory to which a person belongs, whether it is independent, trust, and non-self governing or under any other limitation of sovereignty.[6]

The expanding horizons of Human Rights and Fundamental Rights also covers the very concept of 'Copyright'. The thirst of this paper is to study the effect a copyright recognition over the freedom of speech and expression[7] which is guaranteed in the term of fundamental right in the Constitution. The basis of copyright protection is the originality and creativity of a human being. Originality is the primary requirement for any copyright protection, is largely uncontested in most legal discourses.

Prior to 1911 in England, there was no requirement of originality by the statute.[8] Thus, in Walter and Lane[9] copyright protection was granted. The decision of Delhi High Court in *Eastern Company* Vs. *Navin*[10] created confusion as regards the current position of the Indian law. In the case the plaintiff had claimed copyright in the head notes, in the section, manner of arrangement and in the manner of presentation of the judgment in both printing and electronic form in law journal as the process of compilation required some amount of skill, labour and expertise. The court first observed that in the case of compilations another person can also make a similar compilation but can not infringe upon the copyright of the previous compiler by using the fruit of her labour. She has to go around compiling the work herself. Therefore, here the court seemed to be affirming its faith in the sweat of brow theory. But the court soon made a turn around. It is said that the orders and judgment of the court are in the public domain and any one can publish as they are in the nature of facts, the protection of copyright must be in a creativity them, original and selection of facts and not in the creative means used to discover the facts. Here the court itself is not affirmed about the recognition and enforcement of right to express of an individual as a fundamental right but in later opinion the right has been recognized as a fundamental right by the court. The whole debates is centralized around what is the purpose of copyright protection, which in turn has a bearing upon how much protection should be afforded. The Advocates of 'Sweat and Brow' obviously come from a Lockean need to reward labour to promote intellectual property. Those requiring an element of creativity are narrowing the scope of copyright protection, since the communities interest in accessing these compilations is greater than the individual interest in monopoly over them.[11] Followers of Locke also support their rationale in the ultimate community goods only, i.e. only if one provides incentive by reward with newer ideas in the form of property accrue to human kind.

On the other hand, those requiring a modicum of creativity in the work may have been inspired by the Hegelian theory of personality of the author as reflected in the work to be the basis of copyright protection.[12]

The copyright is a sort of 'economic right' which has to be recognized and protected in the form of human rights. The Constitutional context of Human Right discussed by Chief Justice 'Leela Simon' in the following terms.

"Human rights granted in the Constitution of India through its admission of "Fundamental Rights". Since the Indian Constitution was written after the U.N. Declaration of Human Rights in 1948. The makers of the Constitution inserted Part III, that discusses "Fundamental Rights" that every citizen of India has, and these rights as "inviolable in the sense that no law ordinance, custom, usage or administrative order can abridge or take away these rights. Copyright law restrict speech. It restricts what writers may write, what painters may paint, what composers may create. It does not limit itself to slavish copying but prohibits people from creating entirely new works, so long as those work use even if only in part another's expression."[13]

In India Part III of the Constitution provides Article 19(1)(a), i.e. freedom of speech and expression which has close concern with the protection of copyright in India. This is a basic right which is recognized and it imply for individual's (citizen) right to express his/her opinions freely by writing, by uttering words, by pictures and painting, etc. The citizen of India is free to express his opinion through the dramatic, musical, literary and artistic works, which is the subject matter of copyright,[14] and all such rights have been guaranteed in the term of fundamental rights are subject to the restriction imposed by clause (2) of Article 19. The Allahabad High Court in a case[15] held that the right of a citizen to exhibit films in picture theatre or T.V. screen is a part of the fundamental right enshrined in Article 19(1)(a) of the Indian Constitution which can be abridged or taken away only by invoking the provisions of the Constitution. The same opinion has reaffirmed by the Supreme Court of India.[16] Section 13(b) of the Copyright Act, 1957 covers the cinematography, films and sound recording in the very subject matter of copyright,[17] and therefore these copyrights has been treated as a fundamental right of a citizen.

In India Article 19(1)(a) of Constitution should be construed liberally, so that a citizen can express his views through any media e.g. newspaper, advertisement, magazines, radio, television, etc., but such freedoms are being checked by the reasonable restrictions imposed by the Constitution. As no right can be absolute in its nature and it always subject to respective duty. Therefore, it would be incumbent over all the citizens to develop the scientific temper, humanism and the spirit of inquiry and reaffirm,[18] and to value and preserve the rich heritage of Indian Composite culture.

CONCLUSION

Protection of Intellectual Property Right in India continues to be strengthened further. The year 1999 witnessed the consideration and passage of major legislation with regard to protection of Intellectual Property Right in harmony with international practices and in compliance with India's obligations under TRIPS for instance the Patents (Amendments) Act, 1999, that provides or establishment of a mail box system to file patents and accords exclusive marketing rights for certain time period.

The Trade Marks Bill, 1999 which repealed and replaced the Trade and Merchandize Marks Act, 1958, The Copyright (Amendment) Act, 1999. A Sui-generis legislation for protection of geographical indication called the geographical indications of Goods (Registration and Protection) Act, 1999 by second amendment of Patents Act confirming TRIPS. In addition to the above legislature changes, the Government of India has taken several measures to streamline and strengthen the Intellectual Property Rights administration system in the country.

The restrictions imposed on the freedom of speech provided under Indian Constitution do not contain any specific provision related to copyright. Neither copyright can supposed to be an antithesis of the very concept of freedom of speech in the light of Constitutional provisions. Since copyright explicitly protects the forms of expression and does not provide any protection to the ideas expressed. Therefore, copyright laws are not restrictive in nature over freedom of speech.

The ultimate aim of copyright protection is to protect the "intellectual endeavours" made by the real authors of the work and to limit the fruits and benefits of that original work only to the owner of that creation.

Hence, such protection can never come in the form of an impediment, so far as question of realization of right to freedom of speech and expression is concerned.

Hence, it is submitted that as the copyright does not restrict the right to speech and expression guaranteed under Article 19 of the Constitution therefore it may be treated as right to speech and expression. Therefore, it acquires the status of human rights.

Notes and References

1. Melville and David Nimmer on Copyright, 2000 at pp. 2-9.
2. *Hershel Shanks* Vs. *Elisha Qimron*.
3. *A.K. Gopalan* Vs. *State of Madras* (1950) SCR 88 (198); *Union of India* Vs. *Madan Gopal*, (1954) SCR 541 (555).
4. Re Berubari Union, A., 1960 SC 845 (846).
5. Article 1 of Universal Declaration of Human Rights.
6. Article 2 of Universal Declaration of Human Rights.
7. Article 19(1) of Constitution of India.
8. E.P. Stroke James *et. al.*, Copinger and Skore James an Copyright (London; Swet & Maxwell 1911) at 58.
9. (1900) AC 539.
10. 92 (2001) DLT 403.
11. Ironically, this communitarian view has been taken by and of the most individuals of societies.
12. For detailed discussion of the justifications of intellectual property in Locke and Hegel, see Justin Hughes, "the Philosophy of Intellectual Property," Dec. 1988 77 Geo. LJ 287.

13. Note: that we speak here of copyright claims brought based on material that's express for free speech purposes books, marks, songs, painting, etc.
14. *State of W.B.* Vs. *Subodh Gopal*, AIR 1954 SC 92, 95.
15. *Anirudh P.S. Yadav* Vs. *Union of India*, AIR 2000 All. 123.
16. *Ramesh* Vs. *Union of India*, (1988) SC 668.
17. *State of Bihar* Vs. *Shailabala Devi*, 1952 SCR.
18. Article 51, A(h) and (f).

Infringement of Copyright

R.K. CHAUBEY

I. INTRODUCTION

Copyright is a form of Intellectual Property and is the result of man's intellectual labour and the aim of Copyright is to protect the fruits of man's work, labour, skill or test from annexation by other people. Under the Berne Convention[1] and now under the TRIPS[2] regime Copyright is intended to provide protection to the rights of intellectual creators with respect to their original literary and artistic works. The subject matter of Copyright is the original expression[3] of an idea in literary, artistic and other works. Copyright does not give the right holder any monopoly over ideas but only protects the expression. Copyright protection begins automatically from the date of *creation of the protected* work—it does not need any formality like registration.[4] Copyright protection lasts for the life of the author plus fifty years after the death of the author.[5] Copyright protection is not confined to books, music, painting or films only but it now extends *interalia* to computer, software and compilation of data.[6]

It must be clearly understood that Copyright law is not

concerned with the idea but with the expressions of ideas as expressed in *Donoghue* Vs. *Allied Newspapers Ltd.*[7] Since there is no copyright in ideas or in information, it is no infringement of Copyright to adopt the ideas of another or to publish information derived from another, provided there is no copying of the language. Copyright prevents the copying of the original work and not the ideas contained therein. This is natural as the protection of ideas will give a deathblow to all the avenues of the research, scholarly activity and all the frontiers of human knowledge and hence its protection is out of question. In other words, unlike Patent and trade secret, Copyright law protects the expression of an idea rather than the underlying idea itself.

Copyright does not extend to any procedure, process, system, method of operation or concepts—Copyright is said to protect the expression in the programme which may include such programme elements as source code, object code, screen displays, etc.[8]

The TRIPS agreement envisaged that the member-states should revise and amend the Copyright Act in their respective states according to the provisions and obligations incorporated therein. Hence the Indian Copyright Act, 1957 was amended accordingly. This introduced great many changes regarding the definition and provisions of the Parent Act. The new Act (The Copyright Amendment Act, 1994 and the Copyright Amendment Act, 1999) provided for the inclusion of computer programme and technological development in the present Act.

II. OBJECT OF THE COPYRIGHT

The quality of creative genius of artists and authors determines the maturity and vitality of any culture. The Copyright law protects not only interest of the artist or the author but it also enriches culture and thus it also protects social interest. The Copyright law aims to check piracy[9] so that deserving authors or artists may enjoy the fruits of the labour and the pirates may not be able to indulge in theft of Intellectual Property.

The main object of Copyright law is to protect the Copyright in works from infringement and piracy. The owner of Copyright is granted exclusive right to do certain acts in respect of the work. If any other person does any of these acts without proper authority, he may be guilty of infringement of Copyright in the work. In other words, if a copyrighted work is exploited by any person for profits,[10] he is guilty of infringing the Copyright.

III. ESSENTIAL CONDITIONS OF COPYRIGHT EXISTENCE AND PROTECTION

(i) The work must be original. The work may not be expression of original or invented thoughts but it must not be copied from other works.
(ii) Copyright protects expression of ideas and not the ideas themselves.
(iii) Copyright does not require registration as a pre-condition to claim protection under the act.
(iv) Use of original skill or labour or mental faculty is essential to acquire Copyright in a work.

The Copyright subsists throughout India in original, literary,[11] dramatic, musical[12] or artistic works, cinematograph, films, sound recording, etc. vide section 13 of the Copyright Act, 1957. The meaning of the word Original is that the work must not be copied from the another work but must originate from the author.[13]

IV. WHAT CONSTITUTES INFRINGEMENT OF COPYRIGHT

There is no infringement of Copyright if a defendant has borrowed an idea and uses his mental faculty and labour and skill and has revised and altered it in such a way as to produce an original work.

The general principle in determining the infringement is that "has there been reproduction of plaintiff's work in substantial forms?" In this regard the Supreme Court of India in *R.G. Anand* Vs. *Delux Films,*[14] has adopted the Doctrine of "Dominant Impact". It means if the viewer, after seeing the film gets a total impression that the film is by and large a copy of the original play, violation of Copyright may be said to have been proved. While dealing with the law relating to Copyright and its infringement in this case, the Supreme Court has laid down the criteria of "Substantial Taking". It means that in order to be actionable, the copy must be substantial and material one, which at once leads to the conclusion that the defendant is guilty of the act of piracy. In other words, infringement occurs only when the defendants work closely resembles the plaintiff's work and the features of the plaintiff's work have been substantially used in defendant's work.

In order to constitute infringement of Copyright two elements are essential:

(i) There must be sufficient objective similarity between the infringing work and the copyrighted work.
(ii) The copyrighted work must be the source from which infringing work is derived but it need not be the direct source.

Copyright is said to be infringed when—

(A) Copyrighted work is used by another person without permission.
(B) A commercial benefit accrues to the violator of the Copyright.
(C) When any one exercises any of the rights, which only the owner of Copyright is permitted to do.

However, concept of fair use[15] has been provided in the law whereby the use of Copyrighted works for research, making of backup copies of computer programme, etc. is not considered to be violative of Copyright. Infringement of Copyright in a literary, dramatic or musical work, occurs only when there has been a reproduction of the whole or substantial part of the protected work. If a work has been produced independently and is identical with Copyrighted work but nothing has been reproduced therefrom, it does not constitute any infringement of Copyright.[16]

It is worthwhile to point out that the burden of proof regarding infringement lies on the plaintiff. It is he who has to prove that the defendant is guilty of violating the Copyright. Moreover, in order to maintain his suit for infringement the plaintiff has to establish that his own work was original and that he had not copied from another source as a Copyright protects only the original work.

In *Barbara Taylor Bradford* Vs. *Sahara Media Entertainment,*[17] the Calcutta High Court examined various aspects of the Copyright

Act. The plaintiff filed a suit for infringement restraining the defendants from telecasting the serial "Karishma—The Miracle of Destiny". According to her the serial was based on her book, "A Woman of Substance". To establish this she relied on a published interview of a journalist with the director of the serial where he told that the story was influenced and based on the book. But it was contended by the defendant that the story was not based on the book though the theme and some of the characters resemble to that in the plaintiffs book. There was substantial difference between the book and the serial and the serial was more than 200 episodes and first episode was schedule to be telecast on 12.05.2003. The single judge issued an *ex parte* order on 07.05.2003 but the same was vacated by the division bench on 12.05.2003 on the ground of suppression of facts. It was contented that a similar suit was filed before the Bombay High Court and was withdrawn by the plaintiff and the same was not brought to the notice of the court. Against the judgment of the division bench the plaintiff filed an appeal before the vacation judge of the Supreme Court in the evening of 12.5.2003 and the court granted an injunction preventing the telecast of first episode. But before this could be communicated the first episode was telecast. The Supreme Court then vacated the stay on 30.06.2003 and ordered the deposit of Rs. 25 lakhs to pay the damages, if any, at the end.

One of the questions examined by the court was the concept of originality and the idea/expression dichotomy. Following the ratio in R.G. Anand[18] the court summarized the policy of copyright law in this regard thus:[19]

> "The law protects originality of expression but not originality of the central idea, not merely because of the balancing of two conflicting polices. The two policies are as follows: The first is that the law must protect originality of artistic work, thereby allowing artists to reap the fruits of their labour and stopping unscrupulous pirates from enjoying those fruits. The second policy is that the protection must not become an over protection, thus, curbing down future artistic activity. If mere plots and characters were to be protected by copyrights, no original artist could write anything "original" at all, on a similar plot or on simual characters."

Another important issue contended before the court was that the serial is an adaptation of the book. It was argued that since the words "rearrangement and alteration" included in the definition of adaptation in section 2 is similar to that of English law it shall be interpreted to prohibit any kind of rearrangement or alteration following the precedents from England. Rejecting this, the court asserted:[20]

> "This type of statutory construction is not permissible. One is not permitted to impute to our Parliament both the fact of copying and the charge of copying badly. If Parliament has said something, may be following some Act somewhere else, may be unwisely, yet it is law made by Parliament and the plain words have to be given plain, fair and reasonable meaning."

The court interpreted the word "alter" thus:[21]

> "In our opinion, the large change meaning cannot be ascribed to the word "alter" in Section 2(a)(v) of the Copyright Act, 1957 because it renders the interpretation absurd. Minor changes, slight changes, not making the original something beyond recognizable possibilities, changes in some of the details, this would be the meaning that would fit the word alter in sub-section (v). In our opinion this sub-section might have a very good bearing when applied to copyright in computer programme and databases, but in relation to literary works, the sub-section does not bring in any very great change in law; one can at best say that the sub-section would make it slightly, we repeat only slightly, easier for an author or authors to establish infringement, after its introduction, that it would have been before the introduction."

On the question of infringement of copyright in the book of the plaintiff the court following the ratio in R.G. Anand explained thus:[22]

> "The details are everything in copyright action. It is the easiest thing in the world to take a fat book running to

hundreds of pages and to take a serial which will go into about 300 episodes and to say in the three or four lines that these are common to both. If what is common to both, both of which are large, can be said in a few words, then the similarity so described, must be so central and so essential as so extraordinary, that like the magic quality of a very small looking nuclear bomb, it can more than match the power of masses of details i.e., masses of mundane or ordinary weapons of destruction. We are of the opinion that the admissions obtained by Pammi from Sabir are no where near this type of extraordinariness. They do not make act even a *prima facie* case that the actions, the scenes, the events, the details and the portrayed conceptions, serials by serial, would match either substantially or at all, the situation and incidents in the book."

The court also lamented on the sorry state of affairs of copyright awareness and litigation in India thus:[23]

"Be that as it may, we say confidently that even eminent and highly prized counsel did not bother to read the book, the copyright of which was the subject matter of this appeal, because and simply because, there are hardly any copyright action in India, and the copyright law is very imperfectly understood, if at all, and because it is not realized commonly that infringement of copyright can be demonstrated by and only by, the attention to details, and analysis of the similarities of the details, which are the expression, and the only copyright.

V. REMEDIES AGAINST INFRINGEMENT OF COPYRIGHT

As the famous saying goes, "Ubi Jus, ibi remedium" which means where there is right there is a remedy. No body is at liberty to take away the result of another man's labour or his property. Therefore, violation of Copyright has different remedies. The Copyright Act of 1957 provides three types of remedies for violation of Copyright namely—

(i) Civil remedies,
(ii) Criminal remedies, and
(iii) Administrative remedies.

All the three remedies are independent and can be pursued independently or separately.

VI. CIVIL REMEDIES

The main remedies which are available to a Copyright owner, are "an injunction to restrain the continuation of the infringement and damages to compensate the Copyright owner for the depreciation caused by the infringement to the values of his Copyright". Innocent infringement is not a defence against infringement as such. But if the defendant proves that at the time of infringement, he was not aware and has no reasonable ground for believing that Copyright subsisted in the work, the plaintiff will be entitled to only an injunction and a decree of the whole or part of the infringing copies. Plaintiff will not be entitled to any remedy in respect of conversion of infringing copies.

A. Interlocutory Injunction

There is also a provision of Interlocutory injunction[24] in civil remedies. A plaintiff may apply for an Interlocutory injunction pending the trial of action or further orders, to secure immediate protection from a threatened infringement or from continuity of infringement. Very often an *ex parte* injunction is also sought, i.e. a temporary injunction granted for a short period, for a week or so before the defendant has notice of the suit or is heard for obtaining an Interlocutory injunction. Plaintiff has to establish a *prima facie* case and that the balance of convenience is in his favour and that if the interim order is not granted, it will cause irreparable injury to him. The defendant is entitled to compensation if the case is not proved against him. And hence the plaintiff is required to furnish an undertaking in this respect and only then Interlocutory injunction may be granted by the court. In granting the Interlocutory injunction the court must weigh the pros and cons of the whole matter and has to examine the strength of the claim and the strength of the defence and then decide what is best to be done. The remedy by way of Interlocutory injunction must not be made the subject of the strict rules.[25]

B. Damages or Account of Profits

Two types of damages are available to a successful plaintiff:

"Under section 55 of the Copyright Act, 1957, under infringement and the other under section 58 of the Copyright Act, 1957, for conversion."

The Copyright owner is entitled to treat all infringing copies of his work as if they were his own property so he will have to take civil proceeding for the recovery of possession thereof or in respect of conversion thereof. As an alternative to damages, a successful plaintiff may claim account of profit.

In the case of piracy, these remedies are not effective. As it is done in an organised manner and the large number of sales outlets of an impermanent nature are used for the illegal transaction, it is not possible to lay hands on all the outlets of sales simultaneously. Thus, the linkage between the various outlets is difficult to prove. Moreover, the service of the writ commencing an action for infringement by giving notice to the defendant, may precipitate the destruction of vital evidence regarding source of supply and extent of sales. Finally, there is a possibility that the financial resources and other assets of a pirate, may be removed from the jurisdiction in which legal proceedings are commenced against him and thus the Copyright owner may be deprived of the possibility of recovering the damages.

Hence in response to this need, a number of developments took place and the foremost development in preliminary remedies is Anton Piller Order.[26] It is an order granted by the court permitting the inspection of premises on which it is believed, some action is carried on which infringes the right of the plaintiff. The main features of this order are:

1. The order is to be granted *ex parte*, i.e. on the application and in the presence of Copyright owner without prior warning being given to the defendant. Thus, it takes the defendant by surprise and precludes the defendant from destroying or removing vital evidence.
2. The term on which the order is granted, enables the Copyright owner to inspect the premises of the defendant and all the documents (bills, invoices, sources of supplies and customer list) relating to the alleged infringement.

   Thus the Copyright owner is given the means whereby

he may be able to establish the source of supply of the goods and the extent of sales and this will assist in establishing the amount of damages.

3. The order for inspection will often be accompanied by an injunction restraining the defendant from altering or removing in any way articles or documents referred to in the order for inspection. Thus, Anton Piller Order is an important weapon in the armory against piracy. However, in order to protect the rights of the persons against whom it is granted, two safeguards have been provided—
   (i) Anton Piller Order will only be granted where it is essential that the plaintiff should have inspection so that justice can be done between the parties. The Copyright owner will have to prove that there is a clear evidence that the defendants have in their possession incriminating documents and there is a grave danger that these documents will be destroyed or hidden if the defendant is forewarned.
   (ii) The second safeguards is that there should be proper respect for the defendant's right in the execution of the order. Copyright owner must be accompanied by a lawyer and he must give the defendant adequate opportunity of considering the order and not force his entry into the premises without the permission of the defendant. However, in relation to Anton Piller Order, it may be noted that the effectiveness of the order was brought into question in one case[27] where a defendant pleading the privilege against self-incrimination successfully applied to discharge orders on the grounds that they would expose him to real risk of prosecution for a criminal offence. The privilege against self-incrimination was accepted by the Supreme Court Act of 1981 in the U.K. as a basis for refusing to comply with the Anton Piller Order.

It must be noted that Anton Piller Order is not a search order. It has been clarified many a times by Lord Denning that Anton Piller order is not a search warrant. The order only authorises the inspection by permission of the defendant. The plaintiff is not entitled to enter the premises without permission. The courts in England have emphasized that Anton Piller Order should be made only in the most extreme circumstances, as the form of order is very drastic and its aftereffects are far-reaching. It involves serious inroads on the principles of personal freedom. Hence in order to safeguard the defendant, the order provides that it is to be served and carried out in the presence of a supervisory solicitor who is wholly independent of the plaintiff and his solicitor and who has to ensure that it is carried out with meticulous care, and who has to give the defendant an opportunity to consult his solicitor.

VII. CRIMINAL REMEDIES

In addition to Civil Remedies the Copyright Owner can initiate Criminal Proceeding against the infringer. These two remedies are distinct and independent and can be availed of simultaneously. The offence of infringement is punishable with imprisonment which may extend from a minimum period of six months to a maximum of three years and with a fine of Rs. 50,000 to 2,00,000. Under the Copyright Act, 1957, a Presidency Magistrate or a Magistrate of First Class can try this offence. The court trying the offence, may order that all infringing copies and instruments for making such copies in possession of the defendant, may be delivered to the Copyright Owner without any further proceeding. The court may also order a police officer not below the rank of Sub-Inspector to seize all the infringing copies and all other instruments and produce them in the court.

It is worthwhile to note that there have been very few prosecutions under the Act. The High Courts do not view Criminal Prosecution for infringement of Copyright with due seriousness. Two examples may be cited to show that the attitude of the court still is to treat Copyright infringement a Civil Right rather than a serious offence.

The Delhi High Court in *Sita Ram Silk Mill* Vs. *State,*[28] quashed the F.I.R. and Criminal Proceeding subject to the payment of Rs. 10,000 as costs to the legal aid and advised Board Patiala House, on a petition filed U/s 482 of Criminal Procedure Court for Compromise of the Criminal Case. In *Gulfam ExDorts and others* Vs. *Saved Hamid,*[29] Bombay High Court was reluctant to invoke Criminal Jurisdiction when a civil suit was pending. The complaint was quashed on the plea that the Copyright was not registered and the Civil Suit was pending. It may be noted that the registration of Copyright is not mandatory for claiming Copyright Protection Under the Act and existence of Civil remedies is not a bar for prosecution. Even the Supreme Court in *State of Andhra Pradesh* Vs. *Negoti Venkataraman,*[30] changed the punishment from minimum imprisonment of six months and fines to only enhanced fines, even though it upheld the findings of the trial court that the accused was guilty U/S 52(a) of the Copyright Act, 1957 read with section 63 of the Copyright Act, 1957.

In *M/s Vissa Television Network Ltd.* Vs. *The Gemini Television P. Ltd.,*[31] the Andhra Pradesh High Court examined the scope of corporate criminal responsibility in case of copyright infringement. In this case the respondent filed a private complaint alleging copyright infringement of their telugu film "Badi" telecast by the appellant without permission. The Magistrate took cognizance and issued summons to all including the corporation and the directors. This was challenged by accused nos. 3 to 7 directors of the corporation before the High Court on the ground that they had no knowledge of the violation since they did not get involved into the day-to-day affairs of the corporation. The High Court accepted this and discharged the directors from the case though retained the case against the corporation.

VIII. ADMINISTRATIVE REMEDIES

The Copyright Act of 1957, provides U/S 53, effective and speedy administrative remedy to the Copyright Owner to prevent importation into India of copies of a work, made out of India which if made in India, would infringe the Copyright in the work. Sec. 53(i) of the Act empowers the Registrar of Copyright to make an order prohibiting the importation into India of such copies in the application of the owner of the Copyright in any work, after making such enquiries as deemed fit.

The remedy available U/S 53 of the Copyright Act is quasi-judicial in nature and an appeal can be made to the Copyright Board U/S 22 of the Act. The Supreme Court[32] has held that the powers conferred by the section can be exercised by the registrar even when goods are at the Indian Port in the Course of transit enroute to a destination outside India.

IX. CONCLUSION

Copyright laws in India have been brought at par with the modern world laws. It is well founded and is flexible to meet all the exigencies of the situation. It is competent to safeguard the interest of the Copyright holders who play important role in the social and economic development of the nation. But there is a glaring lack of enforcement. The result is that piracy of Copyright materials, viz. popular friction films, computer software programmes, audio and video labs and CDS is increasing day-by-day. Only the passing of law is not enough. It has to be enforced in a proper way, forcefully and vigorously and only then desired results can be achieved. Hence the following suggestions in this connection can be considered relevant:

1. The police staff must be imparted proper training on the subject matter. They should be familiarized with all the pros and cons of the problem of piracy and the complexity of the matter. The technological aspect associated with the piracy should be fully explained to them so that they may be well versed in tackling the problems skillfully and successfully. Police staff should also be made aware of the immense loss caused to the country by way of piracy and the urgent need to stop such activities in National interest.
2. Sec. 64 of the Copyright Act, 1957 may be amended. At present police officers of the rank of the Sub-Inspector of Police have been empowered to make search and seizures. This should be amended. A senior officer not below the rank of Deputy Superintendent of Police should be empowered to make searches and seizures as it will prevent chances of misuse of the powers.
3. Specialized courts, presided over by the Judicial Officer well versed in the laws pertaining to the infringement of Copyright and piracy, should be set-up in the country. There is also a need for the change of the mind set of the judiciary. Up till now the judges have been taking a lenient view of the infringement of Copyright laws but in view of the gravity of situation and increasing piracy

leading to enormous loss to the nation, stringent punishment and heavy penalties must be imposed so that a wrong signal may not go to the wrong doers and infringers may not dare to commit the crime again.

4. In addition to Copyright Board, Intellectual Property Rights Court may be established in India.
5. Regular seminars and campaign should be held extensively throughout the country to impart Copyright awareness education, so that people may imbibe Copyright culture in the country.
6. Back up copies are frequently made throughout the world for personal study, research and record, etc. by various individuals. Laws should be made so that successor of a copied work may legally dispose of such work.

It is well to remember that India is a leader in software and we also need Copyright protection throughout the world. The people of India are pioneers in software programming, production of creative and artistic work and therefore we must try to safeguard our creative interest and adopt Copyright culture.

Notes and References

1. See, Section 57 of the Copyright Act, 1957 and Article 6 bis of the Berne Convention for the protection of Literary and Artistic Works (Paris Act of 1971) (Hereafter Berne Convention).
2. The successful conclusion in 1974 of the controversal negotiations on the Agreement of the Trade Related Aspects of Intellectual Property Rights (TRIPs) as a part of the Uruguay Round of Multilateral Trade Negotiations has been held as a major landmark in the international trade relations. TRIPS now forms part of the legal obligations of the newly founded successor organization to the General Agreement of Tariff and Trade (GATT), the World Trade Organization (WTO). TRIPS has been described as the most wide-ranging and far-reaching international treaty on the subject of the intellectual property to date and marks most important milestone in the development of international law in this area. TRIPS, when fully implemented, will strengthen protection of IPRs almost worldwide. It will bring the standards of protection of major developing country members of the WTO closer to those that exist in developed countries. Thus TRIPS has

necessitated change in IPR laws of all WTO countries, including India, which is a member thereof, without exception. This obligation has led to various amendments in the IPR legislations in obligers in a single undertaking, new standards on as many as seven types of IPRs (namely, copyright and related rights, trademarks, geographical indications, industrial designs, patents, layout designs of integrated circuits, and undisclosed information).

3. Jayashree Watal, Intellectual Property Rights in the WTO and Developing Countries (Oxford, 2001) at 207.
4. Part-UU, Section 1 in Article 9 of the Agreement on Trade Related Aspects of Intellectual Property Rights envisages that members shall comply with Articles 1-21 of the Berne Convention (1971) and the appendix thereto. However, it makes it clear that members shall not have rights or obligations under this agreement in respect of the rights conferred under Article 6 bis of that convention or the rights derived therefrom.
5. See, Article 12 of the TRIPS.
6. See, Article 10 of the TRIPS.
7. 1937, 3 All ER 503.
8. The acts, which come under the ambit of Copyright, are specified in Section 14 of the Copyright Act, 1957. While they vary from one of work to another, generally comprise reproduction including storing in any medium by electronic means, issuing copies, communication to the public, public performance, translation and adaptation. In the case computer programmes, cinematograph films and sound recordings sale and commercial renting are also part of Copyright.
9. *Supra* Note 3, Watal at 209. The International Convention for the protection of performers, producers of phonograms and Broadcasting organizations. 19C—Subsequently, two new international agreements, the Convention for the protection of producers of phonograms against unauthorised Duplication of their Phonograms, 1971 (commonly known as the Phonograms Convention) and Convention Relating to the Distribution of Programmes Carrying Signals Transmitted by Satellite, 1974 (Commonly known as the Satellite Convention) were concluded under the auspices of the WIPO.
10. Section 51, *inter alia*, states that when any person, permits for profit any place to be used for the Communication of the work to the public where such communication constitutes an infringement of the Copyright in the work, unless he was not aware and had no reasonable ground for believing that such communication to the public would be an infringement of copyright.
11. Before the amendment in 1984 the provisions read: "literary work" includes tables and compilations. After the 1984 amendment and

before the 1994 amendment it read: "Literary work" includes tables, compilations and computer programmes, that is to say, programmes recorded on any disc, tape, perforated media or other information storage device, which, if fed into or located in a computer or computer-based equipment, is capable of reproducing any information.

12. See, Section 2(p) of the Copyright Act, 1957 as amended in 1994 which reads as "Musical work" means a work consisting of music and includes any graphical notation of such work but does not include any works or any action intended to be sung, spoken or performed with the music. Before the amendment it read, "musical work" means any combination of melody and harmony or either of them, printed, reduced to writing or otherwise graphically produced or reproduced.
13. See, *Camlin Pvt. Ltd.* Vs. *National Pencil Industries,* 2002 (2) Raj 464 (Del.) RFA (05) No. 6/1986.
14. AIR 1978, Supreme Court, 1613.
15. The Copyright Act, 1957 puts such uses under Section 52 with the heading 'Certain acts not to be infringement of Copyright' and uses the expression 'fair dealing' in sub-section (1)(a) therein.
16. The WIPO (World Intellectual Property Organisation), Copyright Treaty (WCT) (1996) makes it an obligation of the contracting parties "to provide adequate legal protection and effective legal remedies against circumvention of effective technological measures that are used by authors in connection with exercise of their (copy) rights . . . and that restrict acts, in respect of their works, which are not authorised by the author's concerned or permitted by law" (see Article 11 therein).
17. 2004 (28) PTC 474 (Cal).
18. *Supra* note 14 at 1620.
19. *Supra* note 17 at 507.
20. *Id.*, at 500.
21. *Id.*, at 502.
22. *Id.*, at 504.
23. *Id.*, at 505.
24. The Law governing interlocutory injunctions is contained in the Civil Procedure Code, 1908, Order 29, Rules 1 and 2.
25. See, Halsbury's Law's of England, 4th Edition, Vol. 9, Para 944 and *American Cyanamid* Vs. *Ethicon* (1975) RPC 513 at pp. 539-42 (H.L.) (Lord Dipplock)
26. *Anton Pillor K.G.* Vs. *Manufacturing Processes and others* (1976) Ch. 55 (In Short Anton Pillor).
27. *Rank Film Distributors Limited* Vs. *Video Information Centre* (1981) 2 Aug. ER 76.
28. (2001) PTC (21) 600 (Del.)

29. Recently, the Bombay High Court quashed the Criminal Complaint on the ground that the Copyright was not registered and the Civil Suit against the accused was pending.
30. (1996) 6 SCC 409.
31. 2004, Company Law Cases 677 (AP).
32. *Grammophone Co. of India Limited* Vs. *Birendra Bahadur Pande* (1984) 2 SCC 534.

Protection of Copyright under Copyright Law

SUBHASH CHANDRA GUPTA

Copyright now is established as human right property created by the wisdom, reason and knowledge by human being is protected by the positive or written law. Therefore, wisdom-based created property as a form of intellectual property is the human right of human being. Copyright are recognized as human right under universal declaration. The international covenant on economic, social and cultural rights (ICESCR) under trips and Indian Constitution.[1]

The regime of Intellectual Property Rights is not new and has been in existence in major trading and Industrial countries of the world in some form or the other for many centuries. The knowledge of IP has been key to success in this modern world and IP has been responsible for wealth generation for all in the forthcoming centuries. An intellectual property regime has been necessary to create order in industrial activity. The absence of IPRs would result in chaos, as every body would presume the freedom to duplicate the product invented or made. The Trade Related Intellectual Property Rights (TRIPS) agreement laying down minimum standards to be followed by member-states deals with 7 items. These items constitute IP for practical purposes and are open to dispute settlement process of World Trade Organisation (WTO). These are:

- Copyright,
- Trade Marks,
- Patents,
- Designs,
- Geographical Indications,
- Integrated Circuits, and
- Confidential Information.

There is no mechanism for simultaneous international protection of IPRs. Each of the IPRs may be protected in each nation separately by fulfilling national legal requirements. IPRs are also been dealt with international treaties which inform us as to minimum level of protection which must be provided by each nation. However, copyright is somewhat international as it extents in the territories of all TRIPS members and members of berne union[2] without any formality. A work is vested with copyright as soon as it is created. With the onward march of civilisation and scientific innovations in technology, the scope of copyright has broadened from the literary and artistic works to dramatic, musical works, cinematographies films and sound recordings. In the present years the law of copyright has seen further advancement as the computer, audio-video recording, reprography, cable television, satellite broadcasting and internet have unfolded not only a *clamour* for having copyright but also posed challenges to copyright law as these scientific invention have made the scope of piracy much more wider and easier.

The most basic right conferred by copyright law is the right to exclude unauthorised reproduction of the copyright work. In addition, certain acts, such as performing the work in public, making a sound or audio visual recording of the work, making a motion picture of the work, broadcasting or publicly communicating the work, and translation or adaptations of the work, have also come within the ambit of copyright protection. In addition to these bundle of economic rights, moral rights, which normally include the right to claim authorship and to prevent the work from mutilation or distortion, have come to be recognised.[3]

The first piece of legislation in England was Copyright Act of 1709 (8 Annex. 21). This statute of Anne for the first time gave the legal protection to the consumers of copyrighted works. The copyright as an intellectual property was protected in 1886 by the Berne Convention. The major change in the Copyright Act (of England) came in the year 1842, which extended the period of copyright to the life of the author and 7 years after his death or for 42 years which happened to be longer. The succession of arts threw the law into confusion which the Act of 1911 sought to end. It was the Copyright Act of 1911, which was the basis of the Indian Copyright Act, 1914. The Copyright Act, 1914 was amended and consolidated by the amending Act of 1957, as the U.K. Act does not fit in with the constitutional status of India. It was necessary to enact an independent self-contained law. The present Act was amended in the years 1983, 1984, 1994 and 1999 to accommodate the international Convention on copyright and to meet the challenge of piracy.[4]

INFRINGEMENT

The breach of right conferred on the owner of the copyright is infringement. It is the unauthorised use of the protected work without the consent or license of the right holder or the competent authority under the Act. The question of the infringement depends upon the degree of resemblance between the two works. One of the more efficient ways of finding violation is to compare both the works as a whole. The exclusive rights comprised in the copyright in the different classes of protected works are spelt out by section 14 and the general limitation in respect of them are set out by section 52 (commonly known as 'fair-dealing' provisions). Section 51 deals with infringement.

Section 51 of the Copyright Act, 1957 defines "Infringement" as:

(a) doing anything without license for which the owner of the copyright has exclusive rights;

(b) permitting for profit without license any place to be used for the communication of the work to the public where such communication constitute an infringement of the copyright in the work; and

(c) making for sale or hire, selling or offering for sale or hire, distributing, exhibiting in public or importing into India infringing copy of the work.

However, bringing one copy in India for private and domestic use of the importer is permitted.

Section 2(m) of the Act defines "infringing copy" to mean reproduction of copy or import in contravention of provisions of the Copyright Act of any of the following:

(a) Reproduction of literary, dramatic, musical or artistic work otherwise than inform of cinematographic films;
(b) Copy of cinematographic film by any means;
(c) Recording embodying "sound recording" by any means; and
(d) Sound recording or visual recording of a program or performance where "broadcast reproduction rights" or "performer's rights" subsists.

Further, for the purpose of section 51, even reproduction of literary, dramatic, musical or artistic work in the form of cinematograph film is also deemed to be an "infringement".

The copyright has comprehensively been defined under section 14 of the Copyright Act of 1957 as exclusive right to do or authorised other(s) to do certain acts in relation to (a) original literary, dramatic, musical or artistic works, (b) cinematograph film; and (c) sound recording.

Copyright subsists only in expression of an idea. There is no copyright in idea or a concept, theme or plot. What is protected is not the original thought or information, but the original expression or thought or information in some concrete form.[5] Violation of copyright is confined to the form, manner, arrangement and expression of the idea by the author.[6] Copyright is a beneficial interest in movable property.[7]

For a possibility of the work to be infringed the foremost requirement is that work should enjoy copyright. If yes, then section 14 read with section 51 has been infringed aim who is the right holder as author or assignee or licensee. The next thing is that the duration of copyright has expired or not and whether the author/owner has abandoned the copyright in the concerned work.

The use of a copyrighted work by any person other than an owner of copyright is an infringement. However, the Copyright Act recognizes certain act which if done by a person other than the owner do not amount to infringement such as:

1. fair scholarly uses;
2. educational uses;
3. media reporting uses;
4. uses of state produced materials;
5. making of records of literary, dramatic or musical work;
6. performance of such works;
7. use by public libraries;
8. use of engraving, etc;
9. cinematograph film-use by makers and exhibitors; and
10. uses relating to artistic works.

In *State of Andhra Pradesh* Vs. *Nagoti Venkataraman*, (1996) 6 SCC 409 the Supreme Court held that keeping in view the object underlying sections 52A and 68A of the Act, it would be infringement of copyright, if the particulars on video films, etc. as mandated under section 52A are missing. The absence of the evidence of the owner of the copyright does not constitute lack of essential elements of copyright. However, in the instant case, the Supreme Court after holding the accused guilty changed the sentence of six months imprisonment and fine of rupees three thousand imposed by the trial court as upheld by the session court to only fine of rupees ten thousand, as it felt that the punishment by way of fine only would meet the ends of justice.

REMEDIES

"Ubi jus ibi remedium," i.e. mere is no right without a remedy. The owner of the Copyright under the Act has three types of remedies available to him in case of infringement. There are:

(A) Civil remedies;
(B) Criminal remedies; and
(C) Administrative remedies.

(A) Civil Remedies

This type of remedy provides for a right to the creator to seek injunction damages and accounts. The law requires that owner of the copyright must be a party to the proceeding.[8] When the infringer had no knowledge of infringement of Copyright or had sufficient grounds that no copyright existed in the work only injunction and profits are the remedies. In such cases court does not award any damages[9] and permits seizure of the equipments used to make infringing copies. Therefore, damages in case of infringement usually depends upon the fact of *mens-rea* being present while duplication in being done.

(a) Injunction

To secure immediate protection from a threatened or continued infringement the court may pass an injunction pending further orders or final trial. For obtaining an injunction the plaintiff has to establish a *prima facie* case and prove that the balance of convince is in his favour and that if the interim injunction is not granted it will cause irreparable injury to him. Plaintiff also undertakes to pay compensation to the defendant if he is injured as a result of default.

Section 36 of the Specific Relief Act provides that preventive relief is granted by the court by exercising its discretion by temporary or perpetual injunction. The need for an injunction arises not only where rights have already been invaded but also in cases where invasion of such rights is imminent as shown by the conduct of the invader. This injunction may be:

(i) temporay, or
(ii) permanent.

(i) Temporary Injunction

To secure immediate protection from a threatened or continued infringement, the court may pass a temporary injunction pending further orders or final trial and the *status quo* is maintained. The nature of this injunction being provisional, does not conclude the rights of the disputing parties. The temporary injunction shall not be granted where the defendant might suffer irreparable injury, or where the plaintiffs interest can be protected by passing an order against defendant to keep an account. The courts are duty-bound to weigh the amount of substantial mischief done or threatened and compare it with injury it can inflict upon the defendant.[10]

(ii) Permanent Injunction

Permanent injunction is usually granted in those cases where at the trial, infringement of copyright has been established. The idea is to stop the violator from future violation of rights conferred by copyright law if monetary damages can not be treated as adequate relief.

(b) Damages

The next civil remedy available to a person is award of damages. The objective behind award of damages is to compensate the sufferer in some measure and make good the loss he may have suffered because of infringement of his copyright, since damages are dependent upon loss suffered by the copyright owner.

(c) Accounts

A plaintiff can claim account of profits from the defendant. Two types of damages may be claimed by the plaintiff, one for infringement of copyright and other as ownership of all infringed copies of his work. The plaintiff will have to take proceeding for the recovery of possession thereof or in respect of conversion thereof. As an alternative to damages, a claim may be made for account of profits. The idea is to arrive at a fair conclusion while determining the damages since an order on accounts can not be passed if there is no profit. A copyright owner has to choose between damages and accounts. He is not entitled to both the remedies, since both are alternative and incompatible.

(B) Criminal Remedies

The infringement of copyright has been declared as an offence,[11] punishable with imprisonment which may extend from a minimum period of six months to a maximum of three years and with a fine for Rs. 50,000 to Rs. 2 lakh.

The purpose of criminal proceeding is to punish the persons who have infringed copyright *mens-rea* is an essential part of any criminal offence, which is manifested here in the form of "knowledge" under the copyright law. Criminal remedy can be availed simultaneously with the civil remedy. Imprisonment of the accused or imposition of fine or both, seizure and delivery up of all infringing copies to the owner of copyright are the criminal remedies. Copyright infringement has been made a cognizable offence. The law gives powers to the police to seize all copies of the infringing work without any warrant once congnizance of the case has been taken by the Magistrate.[12] Even a person who makes or has in his possession plates used for infringement is made liable under the penal provisions[13] and has to hand over the plates to the owner of such copyright.[14]

(C) Administrative Remedies

Administrative remedies consist of moving the Registrar of Copyright, who is competent to safeguard the rights of the Copyright owner, by passing appropriate orders.[15] Ban on the import of infringing copies into India and the delivery of confiscated infringing copies to the owner of the Copyright falls under administrative remedies.

Indian Copyright laws are most progressive and developed. Problem, however, in India not with the law but with its enforcement. The efficacy of the law depends much upon its enforcement. The advent of new technology of copying audio cassettes, video cassettes and digital media and piracy has become a global problem. The problem of piracy and necessity for taking sufficient anti-piracy measures required amendment to copyright law in the year 1984 and onwards. The Copyright Act under section 64 gives wide powers to the police officer to check the piracy. The success and failure of any regulating statute depends much upon the proper enforcement of the statute. Therefore, the issue of its enforcement would attract the prime importance by putting life into the copyright law, unless strict enforcement is ensured violation of copyright can not be contained. The mantle of enforcement generally falls upon the enforcement agency, i.e. police. In India, the police is over-burdened with the law and order problem and investigation of crimes and they are neither sensitized to the copyright problem nor have time to tackle the same. Therefore, in the present scenario, there is very need to make independent effective machinery. Aims of legislation and enforcement machinery on copyright should be to protect right of copyright aggrieved.

Notes and References

1. Human right is a natural right of human being, it can not be taken away from him till his death. Therefore, it is the duty of the civilized state to recognize this right as supreme and inalienable right of human being. For detail, see "Human Skill Creation under Copyright as an Exclusive Human Right"—Dr. S.D. Sharma, Reader and Dean, Faculty of Law, Kumaun University Campus, Almora, AIR Jan. 2005, page Journal 11.
2. Prior to the TRIPS, the Berne Convention for the Protection of Literary and Artistic works, as revised in 1971, provided for international copyright protection, under the Berne Convention and now under the TRIPS (1994) regime, copyright law is intended to provide protection to the rights of intellectual creators.
3. Art. 6 bis of the Berne Convention. Also see. Art. 9(1) of the TRIPS.
4. Dr. Bharai B. Das, Reader, Berhampur University, AIR Feb. 2005, p. 74.
5. *R.G. Anand* Vs. *Delux Films*, AIR 1978 SC 1613. Followed in *Manju Bhardwaj* Vs. *Zee Telefilms Ltd*. (1966) 22 CLA 72 (MRTPC).
6. *Chic Chandran* Vs. *Ammini Amma*, 1996 (1) KLT 608 (Ker HC).
7. *Gramophone Co. of India Ltd*. Vs. *Shati Films Corpn*., AIR 1997 Cal. 63.
8. Sec. 61, Copyright Act, 1957
9. *Id*., Sec. 58
10. *American Cyanamid Company* Vs. *Ethion Ltd*., 1975 AC 396
11. Sec. 63, Copyright Act, 1957.
12. Sec. 64, Copyright Act, 1957.
13. *Id*., Sec. 65.
14. *Id*., Sec. 66
15. *Id*., Sec. 53.

Copyright Infringement: A Perspective View of Software Piracy

RAKESH CHANDRA AND TAPAN CHANDOLA

Copyright is the right given by law to the creators of literary, dramatic, and musical and a variety of other works of mind. It ordinarily means the creator alone has the right to make copies of his works or in other words excludes all others from making such copies. The basic idea behind such protection is the principle that innovations require incentives. The Copyright laws recognize this need and give it a legal sanction. Moreover, commercial exploitation of copyright yields income to the creators and thus making pecuniary rewards to individual's creativity.

BACKGROUND AND DEVELOPMENT OF COPYRIGHT LAWS

The origin of copyright had a link with the invention of printing press by Gutenberg in the fifteenth century. With the easy multiplying facility made possible by the printing press, there was voluminous increase in the printing and distribution of books, which in turn, led to adoption of unfair practices such as unauthorized printing by competing printers.

Though piracy was born by the end of the fifteenth century, it was only in 1710 the first law on copyright in the modern sense of the term came into existence in England. The law, which was known as 'Queen Anne's Statute', provided authors with the right to reprint their books for a certain number of years. The 1710 law was confined to the rights of authors of books only, and more particularly the right to reprint. It did not include other creative works such as paintings, drawings, etc. which also by that time became targets of piracy, in addition to other aspects relating to books (e.g. translation, dramatization, etc.) To overcome this problem a new enactment namely, 'Engravers Act' came into existence in 1735. There followed a few more enactments in the subsequent periods and ultimately Copyright Act, 1911 saw the light of the day.

Developments in this regard also took place in many other advanced countries, notably among them being France, Germany and the USA. In France a Copyright Decree was adopted in 1791 which sanctioned the performing right and another decree of 1793 established author's exclusive right of reproduction. In Germany, a Saxon Order dated Feb. 27, 1786 recognized author's rights. In America the first federal law on copyright, the Copyright Law, 1790 provided protection to books, maps and charts.

The copyright in India has traveled a long way since it was introduced during the British rule. The first law on copyright was enacted in the year 1847 by the then Governor-General of India. When Copyright Act, 1911 came into existence in England, it became automatically applicable to India, as India being an integral part of British Rule. This Act was in force in the country until after independence when a new Copyright Act (the Act of 1957) came into effect in 1958. The Act has undergone many amendments to suit the changing requirements. The latest in the series is the 1999 Amendment, which came into force in January 13, 2000. By these amendments some new sub-sections to Section 2, namely the interpretation clause were add and Section 2(o) of Copyright Act was amended so as to include the computer programs and computer database in the definition of 'literary work'. These amendments were in consonance of recommendations of WIPO in late 1970 that computer software should be protected under Copyright Acts.

The Indian Copyright Act confers copyright on (i) original literary, dramatic, musical and artistic works, (ii) cinematographic films, and (iii) sound recordings. The Copyright Act of India provides right holders dual legal machinery for enforcing their rights. The enforcement is possible through: (1) the Copyright Board, and (2) the courts. Legal remedies include imprisonment and/or monetary fines—depending upon the gravity of the crime. Sometimes remedies also include seizure, forfeiture and destruction of infringing copies and the plates used for making such copies. The 1984 amendment has made copyright infringement a cognizable and non-bailable offence. Under the provisions of the Act any person who knowingly infringes or abets the infringement of copyright is considered as an offender and is punishable with a minimum of six months imprisonment, which may extend to three years and a fine between fifty thousand and two lakh rupees. The 1994 Amendment has incorporated a special penal provision for knowingly using infringing computer software. The punishment provided for this Act is imprisonment for a term of seven days to a maximum of three years and a fine between fifty thousand and two lakh rupees. In case the infringing copy of the computer software is used not for pecuniary gain or in the course of trade or business, the imprisonment can be relaxed and fine can be maximum of fifty thousand rupees. Besides amending the Copyright Act the Indian Government has taken few more steps in strengthening the enforcement in the country, a Copyright Enforcement Advisory Council has been set-up for advising the Government on measures for improving the copyright enforcement. Training programmes and seminars are arranged for police personnel. Necessary legislation was made for bringing video shops, cable operators under regulation. State governments are encouraged to set-up IPR cells for exclusively dealing with copyright and other IPR violations. In spite of all these, enforcement of IPR violations, particularly copyright violations has not been strong enough in the country and piracy prevails exits in all types of copyright works notably musical works, video films and software.

Since we have entered into the digital era where the computer-aided technologies like E-mail and Internet have made communication more speedy and economical. While all these have made communication among people more effective and efficient both in terms of time and cost, they pose the greatest threat to the copyright world. Modern communication channels, being intensively relying on a variety of copyrighted products (esp. software), are liable to be pirated in large scale, if adequate precautions are not exercised.

COPYRIGHT INFRINGEMENT OF SOFTWARE

According to "Wikipedia, the Free Encyclopedia" the copyright infringement of software, also called software piracy, refers to several practices when done without the permission of the copyright holder:

Creating a Copy and Selling it

This is the act most people refer to as *software piracy*. This is copyright infringement in most countries and is unlikely to be fair use or fair dealing if the work remains commercially available. In some countries the laws may allow the selling of a version modified for use by blind people, students (for non-educational product) or similar. Differences in legislation may also make the copyright invalid in some jurisdictions, but not the others.

Creating a Copy and giving it to Someone Else

Copyright infringement in most jurisdictions. Not infringing under specific circumstances such as fair use and fair dealing.

Creating a Copy to Serve as a Backup

Seen as a fundamental right of the software-buyer in some countries, e.g., Germany. It can be infringement, depending on the laws and the case law interpretations of those laws, currently undergoing changes in many countries. In the US, legal action was taken against companies which made backup copies while repairing computers [*MAI Systems Corp.* Vs. *Peak Computer, Inc.* (1993)] and as a result, US law was changed to make it clear that this is not copyright infringement.

Renting the Original Software

Software licenses often try to restrict the usual right of a purchaser of a copyrighted work to let others borrow the work. In some jurisdictions such as the validity restrictions are disputed, but some require permission from the copyright holder to allow renting the software.

Reselling the Original Software

Licenses often say that the buyer does not buy the software but instead pays for the right to use the software. In the US, the first-sale doctrine, *Softman* Vs. *Adobe and Novell, Inc.* Vs. *CPU Distrib., Inc.* ruled that software sales are purchases, not licenses, and resale, including unbundling, is lawful regardless of a contractual prohibition. The reasoning in *Softman* Vs. *Adobe* suggests that resale of student licensed versions, provided they are accurately described as such, is also not infringing. But it is important to note that in India the Copyright (Amendment) Act, 1994 effectively eliminates the 'First Sale' doctrine, under which a legitimate owner of a copyrighted work could further sell, transfer, lease or rent the work to another. Taking advantage of the First Sale doctrine, many rental companies used to purchase software programs (packages) and offer them for short-term rentals—a practice which resulted in widespread reproduction of copyrighted works. The 1994 Amendments brings Indian law in conformity with the TRIPS Agreement. However, the TRIPS Agreement is less stringent than the amended Indian law in that it allows a purchaser of a copyrighted work to sell his copy and adds the caveat that, in respect of computer programs, this obligation does not apply to rentals where the program itself is not the essential object of the rental.

Virtually all software programs today carry an end user license agreement, or EULA. Upon installing the software, the end user must agree to the EULA, or *click-through-license,* before the software will install. The EULA lays out conditions under which the software may and may not be used in keeping with copyright protections. Software piracy involves breaking the EULA agreement on one or more conditions.

Some other common examples of software piracy are:

Making Counterfeit Copies for Sale

Counterfeiters try to fool the consumers by selling duplicate software. The purchasers feel that they have bought a legitimate product in the sense that the packaging and manuals look like original products. These may actually be fakes and carry the common risk of operational defects and viruses.

Hard-disk Loading

Another form of software piracy is selling a computer system with illegal software already installed. Generally, the buyer does not receive manuals, license agreements, or even the CDs or diskettes containing the original program.

Internet Sharing

Software that is neither freeware nor shareware cannot be legally disseminated online. However, many software programs are readily available over P2P (peer to peer) networks, via binary newsgroups or in chat rooms. This type of software piracy is referred to as *warez* and has commonly been cracked to make it usable by anyone without restrictive copyright securities in place.

Unrestricted Client Access

Installing software on a server without a network license and allowing clients to access that software is considered software piracy.

OEM/Unbundling

Selling OEM (original equipment manufacturer) software separate from the hardware if it comes bundled with is another form of software piracy.

Using Personal Software for Commercial Purposes

Many software programs are free for personal use, but require a license for commercial use.

Using Shareware Beyond the Trial Period without Paying for it

According to most shareware EULAs, a user must either pay for shareware or uninstall it after the trial period to avoid software piracy.

Tampering with the Copyright of any Software, including Freeware

Even freeware can be the subject of software piracy, when the copyright is illegally changed or the program is illegally modified then redistributed. The redistributed product does not require an original price tag to qualify as pirated software.

Arguably, the most controversial form of software piracy relates to what many people consider simple 'personal use'—buying a software program, and then installing it on more than one personal machine. Some software licenses prohibit this, a restriction that many consumers see as corporate greed, especially where 'non-optional' programs such as operating systems are concerned. In many cases this has aligned otherwise law-abiding citizens with hackers and crackers when they seek ways around the specific copyright security provisions that they see as unfairly restrictive.

The following Table 1 shows the ranking countries with the highest piracy rates and the lowest piracy rates as per the Global Software Piracy Study, 2005 conducted by Business Software Alliance (BSA) and International Data Corporation (IDC).

The following chart (on p. 352) shows the trend of software piracy rate region-wise during 2003 and 2004.

Different countries show vastly different piracy rates and losses. The more developed nations in general have lower rates of piracy as compared to the developing nations. But absolute level of piracy in software in the developed countries will be higher because of the larger size of the computer market. The largest information technology markets—the United States, Japan, United Kingdom and Germany have higher losses due to software piracy even though their piracy rates are relatively low.

According to the Second Annual BSA and IDC Global Software Piracy Study, 2005 in India the piracy rate was 73% in 2003 and 74% in 2004. And the losses due to software piracy were $ 367 m and $ 519 m respectively in 2003 and 2004.

FACTORS DRIVING PIRACY IN INDIA

The main reason of software piracy is the large difference in price of the original software *vis-a-vis* the pirated software. With technological development copying the packaged software into a

TABLE 1

Software Piracy Rankings

20 Countries with the Highest Piracy Rates			*20 Countries with the Lowest Piracy Rates*		
	2004	*2003*		*2004*	*2003*
Vietnam	92%	92%	United States	21%	22%
Ukraine	91%	91%	New Zealand	23%	23%
China	30%	92%	Austria	25%	21%
Zimbabwe	90%	87%	Sweden	26%	27%
Indonesia	37%	88%	United Kingdom	27%	29%
Russia	87%	87%	Denmark	27%	26%
Nigeria	34%	84%	Switzerland	28%	31%
Tunisia	84%	82%	Japan	28%	29%
Algeria	83%	84%	Inland	29%	31%
Kenya	33%	80%	Germany	29%	30%
Paraguay	83%	83%	Belgium	29%	29%
Pakistan	32%	83%	Netherlands	30%	33%
Bolivia	30%	78%	Norway	31%	32%
El Salvador	80%	79%	Australia	32%	31%
Nicaragua	30%	79%	Israel	35%	35%
Thailand	79%	80%	UAE	34%	34%
Venezuela	79%	72%	Canada	36%	35%
Guatemala	78%	77%	South Africa	37%	36%
Dominican Republic	77%	76%	Ireland	38%	41%
Lebanon	75%	74%	Portugal	40%	41%

CD-ROM has been an easy and inexpensive proposition. Sangeeta Gupta, Vice-President, NASSCOM, also supports this notion that the high cost of commercial software encourages piracy.

The multinational companies generally dictate the price and they are not flexible with respect to licensing policies. Multinational companies charge the same rate for software in developing countries like India as would be prevailing in their own country. Since they do not have any differential price rate policy based on average purchasing power of a country. Besides, these companies also do not generally give corporate license for

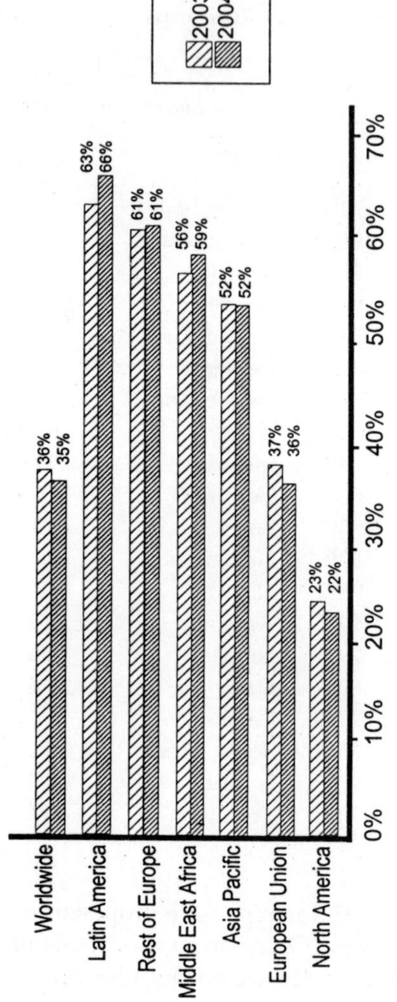

Piracy Rate Region-wise

using particular packaged software and as such each PC has to have a legal copy of software.

Another reason for piracy of software is that identifying pirated software is not an easy task. There are two reasons. First, there is hardly any difference between original software and pirated software, once it is copied onto hardware. Second, detection of piracy requires access to software or hardware or both, which may not be feasible in many cases.

Some of the other reasons are lack of stringent enforcement laws, lack of awareness of IPR laws by users, easy availability of pirated software in the grey market/high usage of assembled PCs in India, wherein unauthorized bundling of pirated software with hardware takes place, growing availability of illegal software on the Internet, and improper software asset management by organizations.

IMPACTS OF SOFTWARE PIRACY

Considering the role of the software sector in driving the country's growth, the impact of piracy on the Indian economy is substantial. As India is on the path of becoming a knowledge-based economy, the protection of knowledge capital becomes essential for future growth. And with the software industry growing more rapidly than traditional industries, it will become a prominent driver of economic growth.

According to Harish Krishnan, Director of Information Technology at CII, parties affected by the piracy scourge include:

- *Individual software vendors*: Increase in financial loss, loss of reputation, loss of quality manpower, loss of market share.
- *IT industry in general*: Reduction of growth, lower manpower growth, lower economic growth, loss of motivation.
- *Government*: Loss of tax revenue, wrath of the industry.

Waning revenues for vendors on account of piracy might make India an unattractive Foreign Direct Investment (FDI) destination for existing affected as well as prospective software vendors. Punit Vanvaria, Microsoft India's manager for business development points out that Indian and foreign software companies, which invest in local employees, research and business partners, cannot compete with those selling illegal software at a fraction of the original cost. "The cost of software products is reflective of the R&D that is required to develop the product for sale—not reflective of the CD that it is burnt onto. Prices also incorporate a component for intellectual property," Vanvaria explains.

Piracy's Ripple Effect

For end users, apart from obvious security issues like viruses and backdoors, using the pirated software can mean unwanted legal and financial complications. A lesser-known consequence is eroding of new products coming into market. Piracy leads to brain drain as skilled workers move to environments where their intellectual property will be respected. Losing skilled workers has a negative impact on the country's economy and intellectual reputation.

According to the President NASSCOM, Kiran Karnik, "A proportion of every rupee spent on purchasing original software is channeled back into research and development so that better, more advanced products can be produced. When one purchases pirated software that money goes directly into the pockets of software pirates. The developer cannot recoup his R&D costs. At the same time, their intellectual property rights are being infringed, thus stifling innovation."

The effect of copyright infringement is not confined merely to the arena of creativity and its economic exploitation in the country of its origin. It has emerged as a major factor in international relations. In the recent past, the trade relations between the US and China deteriorated considerably over the issue of protection of Intellectual Property Rights (IPRs).

It was observed in a study on copyright piracy in India by BSA/IDC that the copyright violations with respect to Indian software are negligible. This is because Indian companies are mostly involved in customized software rather than packaged software. Though few companies are releasing packaged software in the field of accounting, anti-virus, etc., but their sales in the domestic market is negligible as compared to other imported packaged software in the field of Word Processing, Data Base

Management Systems, Statistics, Graphics, etc. They are also of the view that copyright violation with respect to imported package software is relatively much higher. It therefore follows from the facts that the copyright violation (piracy; estimated for software in the case of India mainly relates to the packaged software sold by the SPA companies). The Indian software companies are not losing much on account of software piracy. However, Government of India has lost import duty worth of about Rs. 54 crores (10% duty) which would have been collected if Rs. 545 crores had spent on importing the packaged software.

TABLE 2

Ranking by 2004 Software Piracy Losses

Piracy of $ 100 Million or More			
	$M		*$M*
United States	16.645	Sweden	304
China	3.565	Denmark	226
France	2.92a	South Africa	196
Germany	2.266	Norway	184
United Kingdom	1.963	Indonesia	183
Japan	1.737	Thailand	183
Italy	1.500	Turkey	182
Russia	1.362	Finland	177
Canada	889	Taiwan	161
Brazil	659	Malaysia	134
Spain	634	Czech Republic	132
Netherlands	626	Austria	128
India	519	Hungary	126
Korea	506	Saudi Arabia	125
Australia	409	Hong Kong	116
Mexico	407	Argentina	108
Poland	379	Ukraine	107
Belgium	309	Greece	106
Switzerland	309		

The Figure 2 shows the Dollar losses by region due to piracy of software during 2003 and 2004:

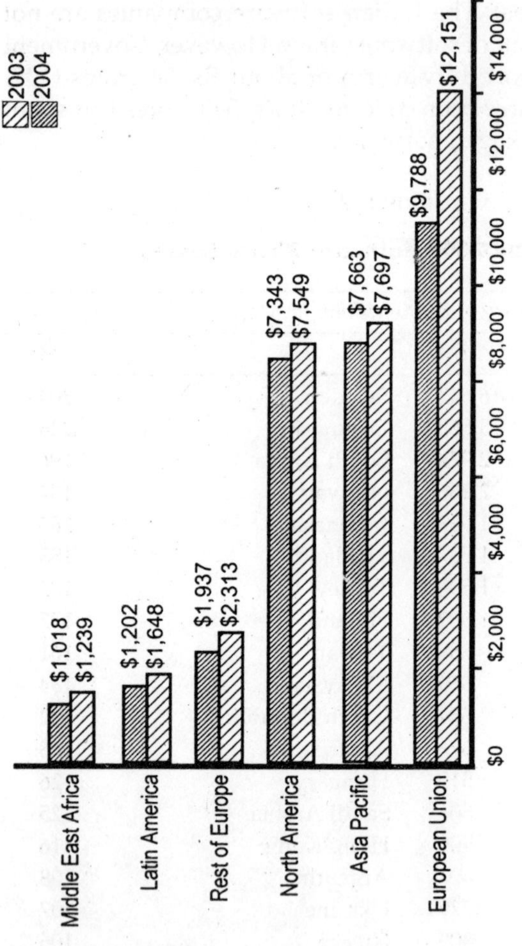
2003
2004
Middle East Africa
Latin America
Rest of Europe
North America
Asia Pacific
European Union
$1,018
$1,239
$1,202
$1,648
$1,937
$2,313
$7,343
$7,549
$7,663
$7,697
$9,788
$12,151
$0
$2,000
$4,000
$6,000
$8,000
$10,000
$12,000
$14,000
Dollar Losses by Region (SM)

THE HURDLES IN COMBATING SOFTWARE PIRACY

The problem of copyright piracy in India should be viewed in the background of the socio-economic dimension of the country. India is a large country with underdeveloped infrastructure and markets. Most of the copyrighted products are being used in a large number of places and violations may occur in numerous forms, though all of them may not lead to large-scale loss of commercial interest to the right holders.

Though we have a full-fledged copyright law in India in the form of the Copyright Act, 1957, which contains elaborate provisions protecting copyrights in computer programs (software). Though the law is in place but the implementation of the same gives out a very dismal picture. Another snag is the slow process of the judicial system.

The police department is so over-burdened that IT crimes are at the bottom of their priority. Most of the time they hesitate to file FIRs and even if they do, the case is assigned to junior level officers, who are not well equipped to handle such cases.

CONCLUSION AND SUGGESTIONS

Given the complexity of the problem for a country of India's size, it is not feasible to control copyright piracy in its every manifestation through legal means alone. Large-scale improvements in the general level of awareness among the public will be the first and foremost deterrent to the malady. Copyright law enforcement machinery must succeed in securing exemplary punishment to the king pins that are guilty of serious violations, rather than attempting to cope with a large number of petty violations.

The following suggestions may have the scope to deal with the present situation effectively:

I. To curb the software piracy in India there is a need of combination of raids, litigation and an active education campaign/the campaign is imperative to educate users about the advantages of using legal software, the problems associated with copied software, legal penalties, etc.

II. The awareness campaigns should be organized regularly so the users could differentiate between legal and counterfeit software.

III. There is a need of designated Software Courts adequately equipped to handle these cases.

IV. There is a lack of adequate number of police personnel who can fully devote to copyright crimes alone so a separate cell for IT crimes should be created in each state, with a separate anti-piracy squad.

V. The MNCs supplying software should adopt a differential pricing rate based upon the purchasing power of the importing country, it will definitely lower the piracy rate in developing countries like India.

VI. The agency like NASSCOM should design a refresher course to tackle the software piracy and it should be offered to the Judicial Officers, Lawyers and the Police officials so they can deal with such cases properly.

ABBREVIATIONS USED

(In the order as they appear in the paper)

1. WIPO—World Intellectual Property Right Organization
2. IPR—Intellectual Property Right
3. TRIPS—Trade Related Intellectual Property Rights
4. EULA—End User License Agreement
5. CDs — Compact Disks
6. P2P—Peer to peer
7. OEM—Original Equipment Manufacturer
8. BSA—Business Software Alliance
9. IDC—International Data Corporation
10. NASSCOM—National Association of Software and Service Companies
11. PCs—Personal Computers
12. CII—Council of Indian Industries
13. SPA—Software Publisher Association
14. IT—Information Technology
15. FIR—First Information Report

REFERENCES

Indian Copyright Act, 1957.

A Handbook of Copyright Law issued by Government of India, Ministry of Human Resource Development.

NASSCOM: Annual Report, 2004-05.

Second Annual BSA and IDC Global Software Piracy Study, 2005.

A Study on Copyright Piracy in India conducted by National Development Council assigned by Ministry of Human Resource Development.

www.bsa.org

http://www.idc.com

www. nassco m. org

http://infotech.indiatimes.com/articleshow/1 063722.cms

http://infotech.indiatimes.com/articleshow/msid-10637 22,curpg-2.cms

http://www.expresscomputeronline.com/20030721/indtrend1.shtml

www.wisegeek.com

www.wikipedia.org

http://eijwarwick.ac.uk

Copyright or Author's Authority is the Protector of Human Right Generation to Generation

JAY PRAKASH YADAV

In India the concept of right has been well recognized since the ancient time the Mahabharata preached, "Sarve Bhavantu Sukhinah, Sarve Santu Niramayah, Sarve Bhadrani Pashyantu Maa Kashachit Dukhbhag Bhaivet."

Human is the wisest animal of this planet and hence it is his duty to protect not only his rights but also the rights of the others.

So far as copyrights or author's authority is concerned they protect the bundle of human rights such as:

1. Economic rights.
2. Moral rights.
3. Right to claim share in resale price of a work.
4. Right to resort to administrative remedies.
5. Right to claim the possession of the infringing material.
6. Right to take civil and penal action, and so on.

The Author is more powerful than any great soldier because of the potential of his pen can influence an individual, society, state and the world at large. That's why "pen is mightier than sword" quotation is used for the authors.

The Copyright Act, 1957 protects Indian author's right, which is amended from time to time. The most recent being done in 1999, which came in effect from May 2000. The Act provides a comprehensive meaning of the term 'author' which includes a writer, a composer of music, an artist, etc. This gives an idea about the subject matter of the copyright protection.

Section 2(y) and Section 13 of the Copyright Act classifies the rights of author in to following categories:

1. Literary, Dramatic and Musical work;
2. Artistic work;
3. Cinematograph film;
4. Sound recording; and
5. Computer programs.

The rights regarding these works can be classified into:

1. ***Economic Rights:*** Includes the rights of reproduction, broadcasting, public performance, adaptations, translation, public recitation, public display, distribution, etc.
2. ***Moral Rights:*** The author's right to raise objections in case of any distortions, mutilation and any other modification in his work by others apprehending to injure his reputation or honour, to claim author authorship, to restrain or claim damages.
3. ***Right to Claim share*** in resale price of a work.
4. ***Right to resort*** to administrative remedies.
5. ***Right to claim the possession*** of the infringing material.
6. ***Right to take civil and penal action.***

COPYRIGHT INFRINGEMENTS

The following are some examples of infringement of copyrights:

1. Making infringing copies for sale or hire or selling or letting them for hire.

2. Permitting any place for performance of work in public where such performance constitutes infringement of copyrights.
3. Distributing infringing copies for the purpose of trade or to such an extent so as to affect prejudicially the interest of the owner of copyright.
4. Importation of infringing copies in to India.

Copyright infringement and its abetment is a criminal offence under section 63 of the Copyright Act. It is a cognizable and non-bailable offence. Infringement is punishable with minimum six months' imprisonment with the minimum fine of fifty thousand rupees. Any subsequent conviction is punishable with one-year imprisonment and one lakh rupees fine.

LIMIT OF COPYRIGHTS

Copyright is the right of creator or author to exclude others from making copies of their work exploiting it commercially and doing any modification, which hurt the reputation of author or creator.

One of the most important limits of copyrights is "fair use doctrine" which permit some use of other's work even without their approval. Though the 'fair' or 'reasonable' cannot be precisely defined but here are a few benchmarks.

Uses that advance public interests such as criticism education or scholarly uses are favoured, particularly if a little of another's work is copied.

Important to note that uses that generate income or interfere with the copyright owner's income are not accepted as fair use. Commercial uses of author's work are also disfavoured.

Fairness also means crediting original authors or creators.

Section 52 of Copyright Act provides for certain examples of fair uses, these are as follows:

1. Fair scholarly use (for research or private studies);
2. Educational uses;
3. Use for media reporting;
4. Use for judicial proceedings;
5. Reconstruction of 'heritage buildings'; and
6. For criticism or review.

The copyright laws basically protect the human rights of authors or creators from generation to generation though it is not perpetual. But the protection provided by copyright laws enables the author and his next few generations to gain monetarily from the original work. Here I want to refer Munshi Premchand, who was a great writer lived in financially poor conditions throughout his life but successors travel by air but for the copyright as a human right.

This protection is in case of an individual's work till the lifetime of the author and till sixty years after his death.

In case of a joint work of individuals it is till the lifetime of the authors and till sixty years after the death of the last survivor.

In case of an institution's work till sixty years after publication of the work.

But at the same time it is also important that copyright laws enable the developed countries to exploit the underdeveloped and the developing countries. The developed nations deny developing nations free access to their research and educational resources giving the argument that having to pay for knowledge would encourage developing countries to come up with their innovations. The recently held Creative Commons Conference in Johannesberg in May 2005 it stressed to pay more attention to link between improving quality of life and the quest for making knowledge more accessible.

The father of Creative Commons Lawrence Lessig says that, "the idea of putting a price on ideas is attractive to the few who can afford to pay the cost. Costly protects the powerful."

The copyright laws up to some extent giving a tool to exploit the poorer countries in the hands of richer countries like USA, France, Germany, UK, etc. This is the reason wants IPRs be strengthened under the banner of "TRIPS plus."

Hence the more humanistic approach would be flexible approach of the developed nations regarding access of their research and educational resources, and then only the quality of life could be improved globally. Otherwise we would be creating base another divide between the developed and the developing nations.

REFERENCES

"Intellectual Property" by W.R. Cornish, Universal Law Publishing Co. Pvt. Ltd., Delhi, India, 3rd ed., 1st Indian Reprint, 2001.

The Copyright Act, 1957 amended upto 2002.

A Handbook of Copyright Law by Government of India, Ministry of Human Resources Development.

Prof. Prabuddha Ganguli in "Relevance of Copyright and Related Rights for SMEs," an article published on internet.

www.nic.in

http://www.mayin.org/ajayshah/MEDIA/2000/digital_ipr.html

www.mofa.go.jp.com

www.grequebercrcmp.com

Protection of Actors' Rights as Copyright: Need to Accord Actors with 'Moral Rights'

SUBHASH CHANDRA SINGH

As you know, the Indian film stars have a global fan following which translates into considerable commercial value. As of today, the copyright law does not confer any rights on actors in films. Keeping in mind this view this paper argues that the Indian Copyright Act, 1957 be amended to confer 'moral rights' actors in films.

A copyright is a largely negative right that, simply put, prevents the copying of the material form of author's intellectual expression. For example, without the idea portrayed in a film (boy meets girls, they get married amidst parental apposition) is an idea that is not protected its expression in material form is protected as a copyright. The Copyright Act is the residuary of all copyright provisions under Indian law. The Copyright Act grants certain rights to all 'works' under the relevant Section 2(Y). These rights are known as copyright and consist largely of economic rights such as the right to reproduce and to prevent unauthorized reproduction (as mentioned in Section 14). Such rights can be transferred (for example, such rights in a film can be sold by the producer). The Copyright Act also provides for certain 'performers' rights under Section 38. These rights are also economic rights, but they pertain to performers whereas copyright pertains only to 'works'.

A unique feature of copyrights worldwide is the provision for 'Moral Rights', which are inalienable and always remain with the creator of the work, legally known as the 'author'. 'Moral Rights' are broadly divided into the right to integrity and the right to paternity. The right to integrity is the right to prevent mutilation/distortion of an author's work and the right to paternity is the right to be acknowledged as the author of the work. These rights cannot be transferred. For example, the artist Amar Nath Sehgal could prevent mutilation of his painting even after selling the same to the Government. 'Moral Rights' have been defined in the Berne Convention to which India is a signatory (Article 6 bis of the Berne Convention) for Protection of Literary and Artistic Works (Paris Revision, 1971). It has accordingly been incorporated into Indian law in the form of Section 57 of the Copyright Act, which confers these rights on authors.

As of today, the Copyright Act does not confer any rights on actors in films. There are only three conceivable ways in which rights can be granted by the Copyright Act:

1. If acting in a film qualifies as a 'work' as defined in Section 2(Y) of the Copyright Act, it would be entitled to a copyright by virtue of Section 13(1). However, a division Bench of the Bombay High Court has held in *Fortune Films* Vs. *Dev Anand* (AIR 1979 Bom. 17) that acting in cinematograph films does not fall under any of the enumerated types of 'works' and is therefore not entitled to a separate copyright.
2. An actor as a performer right be entitled to certain right under Section 38 of the Copyright Act, as the section even grants certain 'performer's rights' to 'performers'. However, actors in cinematograph films cannot avail of the same unlike musicians and the theatre actors. This is because Section 38(4) expressly bars actors who have 'consented to their performance' in films from being accorded any rights as performers.

3. The Copyright Act confers special rights or 'Moral Rights' on 'authors' by Section 57. If an actor can be termed as the 'author', he would be entitled to certain 'special rights' popularly known as 'Moral Rights'. However, actors are not listed in the definition of 'authors' as defined in Section 2(d). It is thus clear that the framers of the act did not confer authorship on actors.

Further India intends to be a signatory to the WIPO Performances and Phonograms Treaty (henceforth WPPT) as can be evidenced from the committee set-up by the government to change Indian laws in this regard. However, the WPPT has expressly denied 'moral rights' to audio-visual performers such as actors, partly due to the powerful producer's lobby, which seeks to deny actors any rights. It is thus clear that even today, the legislature is against conferring 'authorship rights' to actors.

Thus, actors can neither avail of copyright, nor author's special rights (moral rights), nor indeed performer's rights. It is thus amply clear that actors are conferred no rights by virtue of the Copyright Act, and that the position of Indian law in this regard is unambiguously explicit.

Conferring an entire 'copyright' or 'performer's rights' to actors is impracticable. The copyright in the film vests in the producer. 'Copyright' and 'performer's rights' being essentially economic, accordingly these rights to actors would create an overlapping of rights and a conceptual as well as practical aberration. However, conferring 'moral rights' to actors would merely give them basic rights (the right of paternity and integrity) and would not in any way inhibit the economic rights vested in the producer.

As stated above, actors are not accorded any rights under the Copyright Act. But such a position clearly conflicts with a jurisprudential rationale, namely, the protection of creativity. In addition with enormous commercial value being attached to actors and such value being a creation of the actor's 'on-screen image', the principle of equity demands especially in the absence of other protective laws, the conferring of copyright to actors.

There are two broad reasons why actors must be accorded with 'moral rights'. The first is embedded in the very rational behind copyright itself to protect the creativity of individuals and to provide economic incentive for further such creativity. It is obvious that actors are creators who creatively contribute to the development of their characters. There are some creative components in each film and that is, shaped by the actors, so they must be accorded separate rights. In fact, Section 13(4) of the Copyright Act recognizes such a possibility by envisaging an independent copyrightable existence in "any work in respect of which . . . the film . . . is made." The Supreme Court has reiterated this conceptual possibility in *Indian Performing Rights Society* Vs. *Eastern India Motion Pictures Association* (AIR 1977 SC 1443). But while accepting that a copyright can be vested in creative components of films, the Copyright Act curiously denies actors such right. English common law on the other hand expressly grants copyright to acting in cinematograph films. In the celebrated case of *Horowzian* Vs. *Arks* (1998 FSR 394) the English Court recognized that acting in an advertisement film is a dramatic work that is capable of an independent copyrightable existence.

The second reason for according copyright to actors is one of need. It is to be noted that the US law conferred copyright to computer programmers and the US court in *Apple Computers* Vs. *Franklin Computer Corp.* [714 F2d 1240 (1983)] reiterated the definition of 'literary work' and read the literal computer code into the definition. In doing so, copyright was conferred on computer programmers.

It is noted, no other law in India accords protection to the image of an actor. The 'right to publicity' is not a copyright, but a US case law evolved equitable remedy. Within the ambit of the right to privacy the court protects the unauthorized commercial use of a public figure's image.

Trends in the international opinion favour the conferring of moral rights on actors. It is unfortunate that the WPPT has not conferred 'moral rights' on actors. It is thus urged that Section 57 of the Copyright Act be amended and actors be conferred 'moral rights'.

Patent Paranoia

JYOTI PRIYADARSHINI SHRIVASTAV

The pace of man's intellectual growth outstrips the law's ability to cope. This is surely true, if not of others, at least of intellectual Property laws.

Very recently Intellectual Property laws have been bothering a large section of intellectuals of the world. Although it may seem just a decade since we have attuned ourselves to heaving about it, the concept of Intellectual Property is age old.

The most important difference between intellectual property and other forms of property is that it is intangible, that it cannot be defined or identified by its own physical parameters. The defining of Intellectual Property started in Italian city-states. It has been reported that the first patent was granter to Fillippo in 1421 in the Republic of Florence.

Laws as we understand, on Intellectual Property like patents, trademarks, and designs existed in England, America, Germany, Japan, even in as early as 15th Century.[1] The Indian legal system modeled on the British enacted a law on inventions in as early as 1856. Intellectual Property became a subject of International legal system in 1883 when the Paris Convention was adopted.

Thereafter there have been milestones in the international legislations. GAIT, World Trade Organisation (WTO), World Intellectual Property Organisation (WIPO) and now TRIPS (Trade Related Intellectual Property). They have all tried to establish an international policy on Intellectual Property. But there are still grey areas.

Simply put Intellectual Property means a creation of the human mind that is of value to the society. The laws aim at safeguarding creators and other producers of intellectual goods and services.

Intellectual Property in TRIPS agreement refers to copyrights, neighbouring, rights, trademarks, geographical indications, industrial designs, layout of integrated circuits, undisclosed information (trade secrets) and patents.

In the Indian context we have legislations governing Patents, Designs, Trademarks and Copyrights. TRIPS has led to legislations like "The protection of plant varieties and farmer's right".

Industrial Designs

It means the features of shape, configuration, pattern of ornament applied to any article by any industrial process or means.[2]

Trade Marks

It is a visual symbol in the form of word, device or a label applied to article of commerce with a view to indicate to the purchasing public that they are goods manufactured or otherwise dealt in by particular persons as distinguished from similar goods dealt in by others.[3]

Copyrights

It means the exclusive right to do or authorise others to do certain acts in relation to:

(a) literary, dramatic, musical, and artistic works,
(b) cinematography films, and
(c) sound recordings.
(Includes software)

Neighbouring rights refer to rights neighbouring on copyrights like the rights of:

(a) performing artists in their performance,
(b) producers of phonograms in their phonograms, and
(c) broadcasting organisation in their radio and television broadcast.[4]

TRIPS defines geographical indication as a goods originating in the territory of a member or a region or locality in that territory where a given quality, reputation, or other characteristic of the goods is essentially attributable to its geographical origin.

Patent rights are created by statute. It consists of a bundle of rights in relation to certain material object created by the owner. It can be a right to sell, use or grant licence by the owner. It may relate to a product or process of manufacturing existing or new. After the expiry of term of patent it becomes public property and anybody can use the patented invention.

A patent is a monopoly granted to a person who has invented a new an article or the process. It is to be noted that—

"novelty or inventiveness,"
"usefulness," and
"non-obviousness" are the essential ingredients on which patentability rests.

Although concept of patent is universal, subject of patent has become the sore point in the international legal system. Despite all efforts TRIPS has not been able to bring the nations of the world to a common understanding on the issue. The patent law varies diversely and even among countries that are signatory to international conventions on patents. Every convention necessarily has to be implemented through municipal legislation and this gives the scope for the ambiguities in the law on patents. The 1970 Act of India differed greatly from the international standards. It did not include product patents in areas of food, medicines, drugs and chemical substances. It gave only process patents. It had excluded agricultural seeds, plants, animals and all life forms. The government can *suo motu* apply for license to any patent after 3 years on grounds of "Public Interest." The onus of proof lies on the patentee to prove that there is infringement of the patent when he alleges so. Whereas under TRIPS the accused is presumed guilty and has the onus of proving his innocence.

Besides legislative differences, the patent has great socio-culture, political, economic, technological and ethical implications. The rich will grow richer and the economic divide wider, which initially called for greater economic reforms and resulted in GATT, WTO and global economy. The developed countries, needless to say, succumb to the MNCs, may that be in arms or agriculture. Patent is one such measure by which MNC's seek to make great edge in the global business.

India backed by other developing and under-developed nations has emerged as a strong voice against the monopolistic policies on patents being imposed by the developer countries through WTO and TRIPS. India had reasons well founded for opposing TRIPS although for some time it had only succeeded in buying time at the Doha ministerial conference.

The most sensitive issues to India are—

1. Issues relating to bio-diversity.
2. Product patient in case of agricultural plants, seeds, medicines and drugs.

The most likely to be affected by it are the farmers. The timer's right to protections bill is in fact only a "breeder's right protection" and its disastrous end could be shortage of food supplies.

The Haldi, Neem and Basmati Patent had created some controversies in the recent past. In the Haldi case the U.S. Patent office cancelled the patent when India could successfully allege lack of inventiveness in the medical use of Haldi and claim prior knowledge supported by documents in Sanskrit and an article published in journal of Indian Medical Association.

The neem case was slightly misunderstood. It was only a process patent of extracting and treating reactive substances from neem seeds to use for storage and pesticide. The neem will still be available to Indians for traditional purposes.

The Basmati ease rested on the issue whether the word "Basmati" was a generic term or a geographical indication. The Supreme Court reprimanded the Indian government for its failure in quick action in the matter.

The field of patents has become interesting due to the recent application, which is now seeking patenting of human cloning process in the US, especially as it involves ethical issues. Similarly the medicines and drug patent can cause a great hardship in implementing health policies to the government besides depriving the masses of life saving drugs at affordable prices.[5]

The common heritage of mankind principle adopted by India in the past went against its own interest and the breeders' right came in. But it would be relevant now to redefine common heritage rather than discard it altogether. India has vast amount genetic resources and if it is not checked, corporations from advanced countries will access them without paying for them and make patentable product out of them and sell them back to us without compensating the farmers of India.

It calls for interpretation of TRIPS not in isolation but in harmony with other conventions including the WTO, Convention on Bio-diversity, Universal Declaration of Human Rights (right to health and medical care) and the supreme laws of the home country.

NOTES AND REFERENCES

1. Narayan, P., "Intellectual Property Law", Eastern Law House, 1997.
2. Section 2, The Copyright Act, 1957.
3. Section 2, The Trade Marks Act, 1999.
4. Sections 2 and 13, The Copyright Act, 1957.
5. Narayan, P., "Intellectual Property Law", Eastern Law House, 1997.

The Intellectual Copyright Regime, should India Copy the Global Trend: An Overview

SAMARIKA SINGH AND APOORVA BHUMESH

INTRODUCTION

The evolution of the human society has also led to the evolution of new laws and rights. Man's quest to reach the epoch of civilization was contributed significantly by the development of new rights and liabilities. Human rights have also evolved in the similar way. These rights have been recognized as the minimal rights, which every individual must have against the State or other public authorities by virtue of his being a member of the human family, irrespective of any other consideration. The paper therefore looks at the copyright in the frame of reference of Human rights whether it would be feasible to call it a Human Rights under the prevalent Indian laws.

The word 'copyright'[1] is derived from the expression 'copier of words' first used in the Oxford Dictionary in 1586. It is only a monopoly right, restraining the others from exercising that right which has been conferred on the owner of copyright under the provisions of the Act. The basic object of the copyright law is to encourage authors, composers and artists to create original works by rewarding them with the exclusive right for a specified period to reproduce the works for publishing and selling them to public.[2] The law therefore attempts to stop one from appropriating to himself what has been produced by the labour, skill and capital of another. The copyright law, in essence, is concerned with the negative right of preventing copying of physical material existing in the field of literature and art. The moral basis for protection under copyright law exists in the Eight Commandment *"Thou Shall Not Steal."* The law does not permit one to appropriate to himself what has been produced by the labour, skill and capital of another.

The paper draws a comparison between the notion of copyright[3] under the American system where the utilitarian theory dominates in the construction of copyright as an economic right and under the European system where it is still thought as a sacred bond between the author and his artistic work. It further investigates why a need is being felt for recognizing protection of copyright as one of the basic human right even under the American law and the growing trend towards its realization. Part I of the paper essentially deals with the prevailing trend at the International arena. Under Part II, we have tried to explain the status of copyright under Indian laws. The large ambit of statutory benefits enjoyed by the author keeps it at no shorter a pedestal than a fundamental right. The paper also highlights the scope and significance of the copyright under The Copyright Act, 1957 the nature of the rights and the remedies available in cases of infringement.

COPYRIGHT IN THE INTERNATIONAL ARENA

Copyright protections are ubiquitous to contemporary European and Western societies, but the rationales behind them are widely divergent. The two basic schools of thought for copyright are the European system construing copyright as Moral Right and the American system maintaining copyright as a Economic Right. Copyright as Economic Right means that copyright protections are intended to encourage innovation by protecting what is rightfully the property of the creator because of his labour and *"creative spark"* and is thus concerned more with balancing the rights of creators with market access. On the other hand, Copyright as Moral Right view the work as being in some way an extension of the creator's self, and therefore sees a need for more expansive protections. This difference generally represents the difference between the American (economic) justification and the European (moral) justification, and is well illustrated by the differing approaches of the United States and the European Union to the question of protecting rights of the authors.

The European System

Under the European system the copyright is essentially taken as a natural right of the author. European author's rights are based primarily on notions of Natural justice: *'author's rights are not created by law but always existed in the legal consciousness of man*[4]. In the pure *droit d'auteur* philosophy, copyright is an essential unrestricted natural right reflecting the sacred bond between the authors and his personal creation.[5]

The doctrine of Moral Right (frequently seen in French as *droit* morale), which is underlying basis of European school, is a significantly broader construction of copyright. While economic rights can be bought and sold, and are connected to the "work" as a commodity, moral rights are viewed as something intrinsically possessed by the "author" of the "works" because of his "genius." As one textbook phrases it, the moral rights of authors with respect to their works are construed as "inalienable, natural rights, arising from a conception of the work as an extension of the author's personality."[6]

As a 'natural' right based on a mix of personality and property interests, copyright in continental Europe has its constitutional basis, either in provisions protecting rights of personality or in those protecting property. The ECHR[7] does not expressly recognize copyright or intellectual property as a human right. Although neither the European Court nor the European Commission has ever been called upon to consider copyright as such, arguably, a fundamental rights basis for copyright may be construed both from the 'property clause' of Article 1 of the First Protocol to the ECHR[8] and from the 'privacy clause' of Article 8 ECHR.[9]

The American System

Copyright in America is basically taken as Economic Right arguably developed from the philosophies of Adam Smith and John Stuart Mill, which find the primary purpose of copyright in its status as a tool for maintaining a duly competitive market.

To illustrate, market economics recognizes intellectual property as a public good which is: (1) non-excludable; and (2) non-rivalrous, meaning that more than one person can enjoy the property without excluding one another from its benefits. Copyrights, though monopolies for a period of time, are therefore tolerated because authors and inventors would, arguably, have no market incentive to create absent the right to exclude others from their works. There has long been a debate in the United States over whether one should hold more closely to John Locke's view of property as a perpetual right in personhood, which is borne of one's mixing his/her labour with nature. Indeed, many amendments to copyright laws have been made that bring the United States closer to European standards.

THE GROWING TREND

In Europe, the protection of copyright as a human right is thought to be implicit in constitutional provisions that guarantee private property, rights of privacy and personality, artistic freedoms, and so forth. In addition, protection for copyright follows directly from Article 27(2) of the Universal Declaration on Human Rights or Article 15(1)(c) of the United Nations Covenant on Economic, Social and Cultural Rights.[10]

It is also to be observed that according John Locke's labour theory of property anything earned from the sweat of the brow rightfully belongs to the person. To bring the Copyright law in conformity with this theory there have been many amendments which have brought the United States' laws to the European standards, thereby recognizing author's right as his legitimate human right.

To study an illustration; under the German Constitution the moral rights element, is considered an indivisible Part of copyright, which is therefore protected under Articles 1(1)[11] and 2(1)[12] of the Federal Constitution *(Grundgesetz)*. The copyright owner's economic rights are protected by Article 14(1)[13] which secures private property, subject to the limits set by the law. Article 14(2)[14] expressly recognizes that property rights serve a social function, thus providing a constitutional basis for limiting overbroad copyright protection.

Even in the cases where the copyright has come with the direct conflict with the free speech, the courts have observed that a balance be struck between protecting copyright and the public interest.[15]

In recent years, however, this concern for social welfare has gradually given way to a more protectionist approach. As Leinemann observes, this development seems to run against the tide of history. Whereas the scope of other property rights increasingly is limited by the realities of the modern social welfare state, copyright just keeps expanding. Thus, it is very clear that the growing trend in the International arena is tilted towards identifying copyright as a human right of the author.

To identify author's labour, to give more sanctity to the relationship between author and his work, it is felt that the association should be stronger. The law protecting copyright cannot be complete unless it confers right which recognizes and preserves his or her personality. With the advancement of technology, realization of this right as human right has become vital as the reproduction of creator's work has increased.

POSITION UNDER INDIAN CONSTITUTION VIS-A-VIS COPYRIGHT

Copyright as Property Right

Laski, one of the political philosophers has pointed out that our rights are not independent of the society. We have them because we are the members of the state. We have them by reason of an organization through which in the world as it is, the contribution of that uniqueness can alone be made. Our rights are not independent of the society, but inherent in it. When we a part of the society, the rights given by the state. Property is a form of regulated control and cannot be claimed against the well-being of society.

The rights according to Honore[16] were the rights to use and to manage, the right to an income, the right to the capital, the right to possession and the right to security. The further incidents were:

transmissibility, absence of term, prohibition of harmful use, residuary character and the liability to execution.

Thus the purpose of rights is two-fold. In the first place, they aim at the enrichment of Human personality. Secondly, they promote social cohesion and collective progress by enabling each individual to shoulder his responsibility in the communal effort.

Similarly, Intellectual property law protects the property rights in creative and inventive endeavors and gives creators and inventors certain exclusive economic rights, generally for a limited time, to deal with their creative works or inventions. This legal protection is designed as a reward to creators to encourage further intellectual creativity and innovation, as well as enabling access by the community to the products of intellectual property. Because intellectual property protects rights, rather than physical property, intellectual property is an intangible form of property. It is property which cannot be seen or touched.

Copyright, being a part of intellectual property, is a type of property that is founded on a person's creative skill and labour. It is personal property. It may be bought, sold or passed on by the owner by way of a will. It is designed to prevent the unauthorized use by others of a work, that is, the original form in which an idea or information has been expressed by the creator. Copyright is not a tangible thing. It is made up of a bundle of exclusive economic rights and moral rights. These rights include the right to copy, publish, communicate (e.g., broadcast, make available online) and publicly perform the copyright material

Property Right as Constitutional Right

In India copyright is a statutory right under the Copyright Act of 1957. It is certainly not recognized as a Human right or a fundamental right guaranteed to the author. The Indian Constitution guarantees freedom of speech and expression under Article 191(a) as a basic right, which are recognized as the natural rights inherent in the status of a citizen. Assuming that every copyrighted work consists at least in part of information and ideas a potential conflict between copyright and freedom of expression is apparent.

The very constitutional basis of property, i.e. the right to property has been deliberately omitted from the constitution. The (Forty-fourth Amendment) Act, 1978 inserted Article 300-A and simultaneously deleted the fundamental right to property included in Article 19(1)(f) and Article 31. Considering the different aspects of judicial views on the Right to Property and in view of constant problems in the working of the right to property, it had been removed from the category of fundamental right. The first challenge was made in respect of Bihar Land Reforms Act, 1950 before the Patna High Court in the case of *Rameshwar Singh* Vs. *State of Bihar*,[17] wherein the court held in the favour of the plaintiff. Considering the effect of this case the Parliament amended the Constitution under the title of the Constitution (First Amendment) Act, 1951, thereby inserting Article 31-A and Article 31-B together with the Ninth Schedule. However, the validity of the amendment was challenged in the case of *Shankari Prasad* Vs. *Union of India*, which upheld the validity of the amendment.

Later in the decisions given by the Apex Court in three landmark cases led to a further amendment of Article 31. First was the case of *State of West Bengal* Vs. *Bela Banerjee*, which questioned the principle for measuring compensation under Article 31(2). The court held that just and equivalent compensation should be awarded while the acquisition of property is done. Second, came the celebrated case of *Dwarkadas Shrinivas* Vs. *Sholapur Spinning & Weaving Co. Ltd.*,[20] wherein the court held that the provisions of Sholapur Spinning and Weaving Company (Emergency Provision) Act, 1950 offends Article 31(2) and hence was declared to be void. Third, was the case of *State of West Bengal* Vs. *Subodh Gopal*[21] which laid down the principle that the amendment did not deprive the right of a purchaser at a revenue sale substantially as to amount to deprivation of its property within the meaning of Article 31(1) and (2) of the Constitution.

In view of this the Constitution (Fourth Amendment) Act, 1955 was passed. Through this amendment Article 31(2) was substituted so as to keep the law regarding compensation for acquisition of property outside the scope of judicial review. Further Article 31(2A) was added so that the law should satisfy the test of reasonableness as laid down under Article 19(1)(f).

Under the Constitution (Seventeenth Amendment) Act, 1964 proviso to Article 31(A)(1) and forty-four statutes under Ninth Schedule were added. Later in the case of *Vajravelu* Vs. *Special Deputy Collector*[22] and *R.C. Cooper* Vs. *Union of India*[23] question of compensation *vis-a-vis* jurisdiction of courts came up. This was followed by the Constitution (Twenty-fifth Amendment) Act, 1971, which inserted Clause (2B) and Clause (C) to Article 31.

With *Keshwananda Bharati*[24] acting as the last straw, led the Parliament to pass the Constitution (Forty-fourth Amendment) Act, 1978 which shifted the provisions relating to Right to Property from Part III of the Constitution.

Hence it can reasonably concluded, that copyright in a sense a property right conferring economic and moral benefits on an author. However, the Indian Constitution does not recognize property as a fundamental right; it has been given a statutory recognition with extensive protection in cases of infringment. Although not being a Fundamental Right it enjoys status of a right much closer to what is guaranteed in Part III of the Constitution on account of the privileges and benefits enjoyed and the remedies available against copyright infringement. The position is well in place and in conformity with prevailing socio-economic conditions of the country.

Copyright Regime in Indian Perspective

This part deals with the question why copyright under Indian laws can not be construed as a Human right. What are the statutory benefits enjoyed by the copyright holder and what are the remedies available to them against infringement. The arguments conclude on the reasoning that when the Indian Legislators have given such a wide ambit to the copyright, there exists no apparent need to include copyright as Human right in India.

Copyright: Its Scope and Purpose

It is fundamental to note that copyright protects the original expression of the author of the literary work. It is thus a right given to or derived from works and it is not a right in novelty only of ideas. It subsists only in material form to which ideas are translated. It is thus the form in which a particular idea, which is translated, that is protected.[25] Since there is no copyright in ideas or information, it is no infringement on copyright to adopt the ideas of another, provided there is no copying of the language in which those ideas have or that information has been previously embodied.[26]

The applicable definition of originality is thus of pivotal

importance in assessing whether the work may gain protection.[27] The Indian Copyright Act, 1957, which, protects original literary, dramatic, musical and artistic works and cinematograph films and sound recordings from unauthorized uses[28] does not require that the thought or the intellectual investment input into the work must necessarily be original or novel. For subsistence of copyright the requirement is that it has to be a work within the meaning of Section 2(y) of the Act. A work comes into existence only with labour, effort and expenditure of skill, etc. the expression work excludes "ideas" from its ambit. Copyright protects the expression of idea in material form. The principle is that the concepts and ideas are available for all to use and that one is free to create his own expression of any concept or idea including introducing deviations and perversions as long as he does not copy another author's form or expression. However, where an idea or expression is inseparable, copying of the expression appears permitted, since protecting of the expression would confer a monopoly upon the idea. What is important is that the manner of expression must be original and not be copied from another work.[29]

This system of not protecting ideas and requirement of originality of expression disallows copying or exploitation of the same work but allows production of similar work, copyright does not restrict competition in the same product but promotes others to produce similar works or improved works even drawing upon the knowledge and experience from the perusal of previously protected works. What is relevant is the sweat and labour. One may produce anything with one's own labour and effort.

Being a bundle of rights, copyright, which can be exploited independently, the nature of these rights depends upon the category of work. Copyright law grants the holder of the copyright a number of exclusive rights. Like the upcoming European Copyright Directive,[30] the Indian Copyright Act contains three broad rights. First of all, hence the name copyrights, a reproduction right.[31] This right also encompasses the right to prepare derivative works; for instance, the adaptation of a book into a motion picture. Secondly, the right of communication to the public.[32] This is indeed a very broad right: it entails all the various ways in which a work is made available to the public, varying from the performance or display of a work to making it available on-line. Thirdly, copyright holders are granted an exclusive right of distribution to the public by sale or otherwise.[33] But one right, which is common to all works, is the right to reproduce or make copies of the work. The owner of the copyright may exploit the work himself or license others to exploit any one or more of the rights for a consideration in the form of royalty or a lump sum payment.[34]

Copyright is a right given by the law to creators of literary, dramatic, musical and artistic works and producers of cinematograph films and sound recordings. In fact, it is a bundle of rights including, *inter alia,* rights of reproduction, communication to the public, adaptation and translation of the work. There could be slight variations in the composition of the rights depending on the work. The Copyright Act, 1957 protects original literary, dramatic, musical and artistic works and cinematograph films and sound recordings from unauthorized uses. Unlike the case with patents, copyright protects the expressions and not the ideas. There is no copyright in an idea.

Rights Conferred on the Copyright Holder

Copyright establishes the economic and moral rights of creators and other rights holders to control the publication and commercial exploitation of their works, protect the integrity of their endeavors, and ensure that they are properly remunerated. The law provides creators and other rights holders with a number of legal rights to authorize the use of works.[35]

The economic philosophy behind copyright is the conviction and encouragement of individual effort by personal gain is the best way to advance public welfare through the talents of authors. Although creative works are encouraged and rewarded, the ultimate goal is to promote broad public availability of literature, music and the other arts.[36] Thus while immediate effect of copyright is to grant valuable rights to the authors, thereby enabling them to secure a fair return for their creative efforts the ultimate aim of this incentive is *"to stimulate artistic creativity for the general good."*

The fundamental components of copyright based upon the doctrine of Economic Right are that it provides rights for a limited time[37] and that it protects the exclusive right to copy, distribute, sell the work during that time[38] and also provides for the exclusive rights to create derivative works, to perform a work publicly, and to display it publicly were added.[39] The limited scope, and originally the limited time, allowed for the author and publisher to enjoy the profits for the early run of the work while preventing copyright regulations from obstructing the free use of new ideas and thereby inhibiting the market process, which was the most important factor for the Utilitarian mindset.

The Copyright Act, 1957 also provides creators with certain non-economic rights known as moral rights. They are the right to decide whether or not to publish the work (the right of publication), the right against false attribution of authorship and the right of integrity of authorship (the right of paternity) and the right against alteration and other actions that may damage the author's honour or reputation (the right of integrity). It is, however, possible for an author to provide a written consent in relation to certain treatment of his or her work that might otherwise constitute an infringement of moral rights.[40] These rights remain with the author even after the transfer of copyright and the protection lasts during the whole of the copyright term.

Remedies Available Against Infringement

Intellectual property rights are enforced by an action for infringement of those rights before the District Court or High Court. There are three kinds of remedies against infringement of copyright, namely:

(i) *Civil Remedies:*[41] this includes injunction, damages, and an account of profits.
A suit or other civil proceedings relating to infringement of Copyright can be filed in the District court having jurisdiction.[42] The period of limitation for filing of a suit for damages for infringement of Copyright is three years from the date of infringement[43] Section 5 read with Section 54 provides that an exclusive licensee can also file a suit for infringement. But where the suit is instituted by the exclusive licensee, unless the court otherwise directs, the owner of the copyright must be made as a defendant and when such owner is made a defendant, he will have a right to dispute the claim of the exclusive licensee.[44]

(a) *Injunction*: The primary remedy sought in most copyright suits is an injunction to restrain the defendant from continuing to do acts which constitute infringement. The law relating to infringements is contained in Specific Relief Act, 1963.

(b) *Damages for infringement*:[45] The owner of the copyright in a work is in title to recover the damages for the loss or damage is costing him by the infringement of the copyright. Get it is no provision in the act for the award of additional damages in a special circumstances such as the flagrancy of the infringement.

The Act also declares that all infringing copies of any work in which copyright subsists and all plates used or intended to be used for the production of such copies shall be deemed to be the property of the owner of the copyright. It then entitles him to take proceedings for the recovery of possession of the infringing copies and plates or in respect of the conversion thereof.

(c) *Remedy by way of accounts*: The plaintiff is also entitled to require the defendant to account for the profits made by him by his piracy instead of claiming damages for infringement or for conversion.

(ii) *Criminal Remedies*:[46] This includes imprisonment and heavy fine and seizure of infringing copies of the work, which will be delivered to the copyright owner.

(iii) *Administrative Remedies*:[47] This consist of moving the Registrar of Copyrights to ban the import of infringing copies into India when the infringement is by way of such importation and delivery of the confiscated infringing copies of the owner of the copyright and seeking the delivery. An effective and quick remedy is made available by the Act to prevent importation in to India the copies of a copywriter work made outside India, which is made in India, would infringe on copyright in the work. Section 53 of the Copyright Act empowers the Registrar of Copyrights to made an order prohibiting the importation into India of such copies of the application of the owner of the copyright in any work, party his duty authorised agent after making such inquiry as he deems fit.

INDIAN COPYRIGHT LAW: A BALANCED APPROACH

The main objective of any law on copyright is to protect the commercial value of the productive effort of the individual's mind. Since the intention is also to protect all intellectual property capable of reproduction the concept of copyright has to be harmoniously construed by adopting a rational approach, not only to the protection of the intellectual work in this age of technological advancement, but also the aim of the copyright law which is to secure a fair return to the author for his creative labour.[48]

From the above discussion it is very clear that copyright enjoys extensive protection under Indian laws. The rights conferred on the copyright holder and the remedies available in cases on infringement are extensive enough to give it the same sanctity as that of fundamental rights. Further the Berne Convention India also recognizes copyright of the people living outside India and would give protection to their artistic work in the country.

Analyzing Copyright under the Locke's theory of labour social order is as important for the peaceful production and disposal of property as labour itself. *Most labour is social labour.* Socialist advocates assume that labour alone is the standard of distributive justice. Further, private gain need not be the only incentive to labour. Lord Haldane remarks that the desire to distinguish in the service of the state is as potent a motive with the brainworkers as the desire to amass a fortune. Plato was neither a fool nor a visionary when he claimed that the satisfaction derived from performing a congenial task or from rendering public service was a reward in itself.

The underlying basis of property i.e., the right to property is no longer a fundamental right; hence the very premise falls apart. Moreover, once recognized it cannot be retraced back and will only result in complicating the situation.

NOTES AND REFERENCES

1. The first piece of legislation to explicitly deal with copyright was the Statute of Anne of 1709. This statute came into being to protect authors, creators, composers and makers of copyright works in the face of the first major threat of multiple copying that was posed by the printing press.
2. U.S.A. Copyright Act: object of the Act is to promote the progress of science and useful arts, by securing for limited times to authors and inventors, the exclusive right to their respective writings and discoveries.
3. Quite lately a new dimension has been added in the concept of property rights, where innovations have been recognized as an exclusive *commercial asset* to the inventor. Though, a negative right, it has classically been given against the copying of defined types of expression of ideas as in writing, music and pictures.
4. E.W. Plomann and L. Clark Hamilton, Copyright: Intellectual Property in the Information Age, 39 (1980a).
5. Grosheide (note 8), at 207. Admittedly, other rationales underlying the copyright equation (economic efficiency, protection of culture, dissemination of ideas) are recognized as well in Europe; see Grosheide (note 10), 129-43.
6. (Joyce, 608).
7. European Commission on Human Rights.
8. First Protocol to the ECHR, Paris, 2 March 1952, Article 1 reads: "Every natural or legal person is entitled to the peaceful enjoyment of his possessions. No one shall be deprived of his possessions except in the public interest and subject to the conditions provided for by law and by the general principles of international law. The preceding provisions shall not, however, in any way impair the right of a State to enforce such laws as it deems necessary to control the use of property in accordance with the general interest or to secure the payment of taxes or other contributions or penalties."
9. Article 8 ECHR reads: "1. Everyone has the right to respect for his private and family life, his home and his correspondence. 2. There shall be no interference by a public authority with the exercise of this right except such as is in accordance with the law and is necessary in a democratic society in the interests of national security, public safety or the economic well-being of the country, for the prevention of disorder or crime, for the protection of health or morals, or for the protection of the rights and freedoms of others."
10. Article 27(2) of the Universal Declaration on Human Rights reads: "Everyone has the right to protection of the moral and material interests resulting from any scientific, literary or artistic production of

which he is the author." Article 15(1)(c) of the United Nations Covenant on Economic, Social and Cultural Rights reads: "The States Parties to the present Covenant recognize the right of everyone: [...] (c) To benefit from the protection of the moral and material interests resulting from any scientific, literary or artistic production of which he is the author." See F. Dessemontet, 'Copyright and Human Rights', in: Jan J.C. Kabel and Gerard J.H.M. Mom (eds.), *Intellectual Property and Information Law—Essays in Honour of Herman Cohen Jehoram*, The Hague, London, Boston: Kluwer Law International 1998, p. 113; M. Vivant, 'Le droit d'auteur, un droit de Phomme', [1997] 174 RIDA 60; A. Kerever, 'Author's rights are human rights', [1999] 32 Copyright Bulletin 18.

11. Article 1(1) of the German Constitution reads: "The dignity of man is inviolable. To respect and protect it shall be the duty of all public authority."
12. Article 2(1) of the German Constitution reads: "Everybody has the right to self-fulfilment in so far as they do not violate the rights of others or offend against the constitutional order or morality."
13. Article 14(1) of the German Constitution reads: "Property and the right of inheritance shall be guaranteed. Their substance and limits shall be determined by law."
14. Article 14(2) of the German Constitution reads: "Property entails obligations. Its use should also serve the public interest."
15. Leinemann (note 20) at 58.
16. Honore, A.M., *'Ownership'*, Oxford Essays in Jurisprudence, ed. A.G. Guest (Oxford: Oxford University Press, 1961), pp. 107-47
17. AIR 1951 Pat. 91.
18. AIR 1951 SC 458.
19. AIR 1954 SC 170.
20. AIR 1954 SC 119.
21. AIR 1954 SC 92.
22. AIR 1965 SC 1080.
23. AIR 1970 SC 564.
24. *Keshwananda Bharati* Vs. *State of Kerela*, AIR 1973 SC 1461.
25. *Jefferys* Vs. *Boosey*, (1854) 4 HCL 815.
26. *Donoghue* Vs. *Allied Newspapers Ltd.*, (1937) 3 All ER 503.
27. *R.G. Anand* Vs. *Delux Films*, AIR 1978 SC 1613.
28. Section 13 of the Copyright Act, 1957.
29. *C. Cunnian Co.* Vs. *Balraj & Co.*, AIR 1961 Mad. 111. See also *Jagdish Prasad* Vs. *Parmeshwar Prasad*, AIR 1966 Pat 33; *Govindan* Vs. *Gopalakrishnan*, AIR 1955 Mad 391; *University of London Press* Vs. *University Tutorial Press*, (1916) 2 CH 609.

30. Christiaan Alberdingk Thijm, Institute for Information Law, University of Amsterdam.
31. Section 14 of the Indian Copyright Act provides for exclusive right to reproduce the work in any material form including the storing of it in any medium by electronic means.
32. Section 14 of the Indian Copyright Act further provides for issue copies of the work to the public not being copies already in circulation. In cases of dramatic or musical work it provides for the exclusive right to perform the work in public, or communicate it to the public.
33. Section 14 also provides for selling or giving on commercial rental or offering for sale or for commercial rental any copy of the computer program. In cases of cinematograph film to sell or give on hire or offer for sale or hire, any copy of the film, regardless of whether such copy has been sold or given on hire on earlier occasions and in cases of sound recording to sell or give on hire, or offer for sale or hire, any copy of the sound recording regardless of whether such copy has been sold or given on hire on earlier occasions.
34. Intellectual Property Rights: An Overview of Intellectual Property by the JISC Legal Information Service.
35. Section 18 of the Copyright Act, 1957 provides for Assignment of copyright.
36. *Twentieth Century Music Corp.* Vs. *Aiken*, 422 U.S. 151, 156 (1975).
37. Chapter V of the Copyright Act, 1957 provides for term of copyright.
38. Section 14 of the Copyright Act, 1957.
39. *Ibid.*
40. These "moral rights" are recognized as the 'Author's Special Rights' under the provisions of Section 57 of the Act.
41. Chapter XII of the Copyright Act, 1957.
42. Section 62(1), it has been held that the expression 'District Court' would include the High Court having original jurisdiction, Penguin Books, AIR 1985 Del. 29 at p. 38.
43. Article 88 of the Limitation Act,1963.
44. Section-61(1) of the Copyright Act, 1957.
45. Section 55(4) of the Copyright Act, 1957.
46. Section 63 of the Copyright Act, 1957.
47. Section 53 of the Copyright Act, 1957.
48. *Lal's Commentaries on the Copyright Act*, 3rd ed., Delhi Law House, 1998.

Articles

Cornish, W.R., *Intellectual Property*, Universal Law Publishing Co. Pvt. Ltd., 3rd Edn., Delhi, 2003.

Shukla, V.N., *Constitution of India*, Eastern Book Company, 10th Edn., Allahabad, 2003.

Wadehra, B.L., *Law Relating to Copyright*, Universal Law Publishing Co. Pvt. Ltd., 2nd Edn., Delhi, 2000.

A Companion to Contemorary Political Philosophy, Blackwell Publishers, Cambridge, USA, 1996.

Heywood Andrew, *Political Ideologies*, Palgrave MacMillan, New York, 2003.

Asirvatham, Eddy, Mishra, K.K., *Political Theory*, S. Chand & Co., 13th Edn., New Delhi.

Roscoe Pound, *Introduction to Philosophy of Law*, Universal Law Pub. Co. Pvt. Ltd., 2nd Edn., New Delhi, 1998.

Statutory Compilations

1. Copyright Act, 1957.
2. Constitution of India.

Websites

1. Economic Right, Moral Right, and Databases, http://cwru.edu
2. Intellectual Property Rights, http://www.jisclegal.ac.uk/ipr
3. Property Rights are a Fundamental Human Right by Walter Williams, http://www.capmag.com/index.asp
4. A Hand Book of Copyright Law, http://www.education.nic.in/htmlweb/main.htm
5. Copyright and Freedom of Expression in Europe, hugenholtz@jur.uva.nl

Norms of Creative Activities

S.D. SHARMA

1. There should be clear provisions in domestic laws to protect the copyright as human rights on the line of International Convention, Declaration and Covenant, etc.

2. Invention in primary stage as unclosed information shall also be protected under copyright law, for this purpose Copyright Act, 1957 should be amended on the line of TRIPS agreement.

3. Provisions Article 27[1] and [2] of Universal Declaration of Human Rights, 1948 should be inserted to Copyright law, so that the State and National Human Rights Commissions can take action on the violation of the Copyright as human right.

4. Although Copyright Act, 1957 in India enacted before the Burne Convention, 1971 and TRIPS agreement 1994 and amended thereafter accordingly. However, it is germane to suggest that the object should be inserted in the beginning of the Act on the basis of Burne Convention and TRIPS agreement.

5. Copyright Board should be established in all levels like District, State, and National level and for this purpose section 11 of the Copyright Act, 1957 should amended.

6. Copyright Office should also be established on all levels

like—District, State and National Level and for this purpose section 9 of the Copyright Act, 1957 should be amended.

7. Beside the Court, a separate civil remedy system should be diffused under the Copyright Act, 1957.

8. Copyright should be treated as fundamental right under Article 19 (1)(a) of the Indian Constitution, because the source of Copyright is speech and expression.

9. Copyright recognized by some countries in the world as constitutional guarantee such as America, Britain, Argentina, France and Sweden. On the same track the Copyright should be recognized by each country of the world as Constitutional right.

10. Through the Copyright law more and more freedom should be given to the authors on the books, which will result in the foundation of brotherhood of mankind.

11. On the basis of the famous quotation that *"New Challenges demand new solution"*, the Copyright Act in India should be amended to avoid the piracy in Internet.

12. Due to the lack of Consciousness in public, the law relating to copyright is not efficiently enforcing by the agencies, thus the awareness programme should be organized by grass-root level. Awareness programme cell should be established.

13. Enforcement mechanism in copyright law is weak in India, it should be strengthened by the amendment of Copyright Act.

14. According to the development of new areas, there should be new paradigm in IPR laws.

15. Traditional knowledge is a part of Copyright, therefore this knowledge should be protected by this law. The Educational institutions should come forward to protect traditional knowledge.

16. Anti-piracy cell should be established in each district.

17. Right to publicity be included as copyright under the Copyright Act in India.

18. Training should be given to the police force for the awareness of the copyright law.

19. There should be an amendment in Sec. 64 of the Copyright Act, 1957 that power to seize infringing copies should be given to the Dy. S.P. instead of S.I. Police.

20. Sec. 52 of the Copyright Act, 1957 is wide, it is an

exception in nature, it should be amended and restrictions should be imposed on the ground of fair use of the literary, dramatic, musical and artistic work, etc.

21. There should be a empirical investigation and evaluation of the functioning of the office of the registrar and Copyright Board. So that Copyright infringement must be assessed out of court settlements.

22. It is an urgent need of the hour that penal provisions be made more stringent to prevent the infringement and unauthorized exploitation of the precious economic and moral rights of the authors. To fulfil this recommendation "Proviso" of Sec. 63 of the Copyright Act, 1957 should be repealed.

23. The role of Judiciary is much expedient to interpret the Copyright in such manner as it should be exclusively beneficial to the owner of the property.

24. Section 5 of the Copyright Act, 1957 should be amended and film actors be conferred "moral rights."

Table of Cases

Index